TOM WAITS
ON TOM WAITS
INTERVIEWS
AND ENCOUNTERS

EDITED BY PAUL MAHER JR.

CHICAGO
REVIEW
PRESS

Library of Congress Cataloging-in-Publication Data

Tom Waits on Tom Waits : interviews and encounters / edited by Paul Maher, Jr.

    p. cm.

  Includes bibliographical references and index.

  ISBN 978-1-56976-312-4 (pbk.)

  1. Waits, Tom, 1949- —Interviews. 2. Singers—United States—Interviews. I.

Waits, Tom, 1949- II. Maher, Paul, 1963–

  ML420.W13A5 2011

   782.42164092—dc22

                                           2011013874

Cover and interior design: Jonathan Hahn

Cover photograph: Rob Verhorst/Redferns/Getty Images

© 2011 by Paul Maher Jr.

All rights reserved

Published by Chicago Review Press, Incorporated

814 North Franklin Street

Chicago, Illinois 60610

ISBN 978-1-56976-312-4

Printed in the United States of America

Vanity Fair: On what occasions do you lie?
Tom Waits: Who needs an occasion?

from "Proust Questionnaire," *Vanity Fair* (November 2004)

CONTENTS

PART III

INTRODUCTION

Tom Waits, even with his barnyard growl and urban hipster yawp (there are dozens of such descriptions of his voice in these pages—dozens!), may just be what the *Daily Telegraph* claims him to be: "the greatest entertainer on Planet Earth." He mystifies, startles, and tames his rowdy audiences with his wit. Waits is a practitioner of the fine art of conversation, spinning yarns like a carny or a Depression-era hobo ridin' the rails toward some unforsaken promised land.

Over a span of almost four decades, Waits has transformed both his music and his persona. He is not one to suit the ever-changing morphology of our times, nor is he ever yanked by the puppet strings of his record company's whims. While many of his singer-songwriter contemporaries, like Bob Dylan and Neil Young, lost themselves in the 1980s, Waits ripped out his demons, claw by claw, from his soul and filled the cavity with a seething broth of musical brilliance. Waits has forged an aural universe album by album.

Waits's spoken rap is as compelling as his diamond-precision lyrics. He becomes, at times, a synthesis of inflections that reflect a Who's Who of verbal influences: Allen Ginsberg, Jack Kerouac, Louis Armstrong, some anonymous vaudevillian huckster, a pool-hall attendant, hobo, folkie, Mark Twain, Charles Bukowski, Dean Moriarty, or the anonymous singers of the Library of Congress folk songs recorded by Alan Lomax. At his darkest he becomes a seedy slathering of organic word ooze reminiscent of his one-time collaborator, William S. Burroughs. This synthesis allows his world to be both grounded and "out there." He is, in his own words, "real gone." However, appearing that way becomes another defense mechanism; in truth Waits is well read and informed with a heightened awareness of contemporary pop culture. He never comes across as a bitter old fogie living in the past, even when his music avidly borrows from it. Waits openly acknowledges his indebtedness to music forms new and old. He is everything but conventional, and that is just the way his fans like him.

Tom Waits's carnival house-of-mirrors persona exudes humility more than celebrity entitlement. He seems to be "one of the guys," the bullshitter we all know, who always tells the jokes the best and can spin a story out of anecdote. Rather than succumbing to an obligatory rock-and-roll tar pit of substance abuse, he obtained his personal nirvana by building a family—one that, to this day, he relentlessly shields from adoring fans and those prying interviewers intent on being the first to crack themselves a journalistic coup. He is accessible without accessibility.

Waits is the teacher we wished we had. Imagine that voice, a shard of tin scraping his throat as he reads from *Moby-Dick*, *The Adventures of Huckleberry Finn*, John Steinbeck. Or maybe even warning against the inherent perils of authoring run-on sentences. Wouldn't he make it interesting? I'm waiting for him to put out an audio book reading the Holy Bible—wouldn't he make stoic converts out of doubting atheists? He nails your attention span to the wall and keeps it there. Though many have tried to grease the same wheel as Waits, most fail, coming across as pale pretenders, more arrogant and clueless than wizened and dignified.

Waits is also a formidable stage presence; his rare concert appearances, whether in New York, Denver, or El Paso, more often than not guarantee a sold-out show. His words (which he may or may not regard as poetry) are underscored by baritone-heavy horns, or the dissonant rhythms of garbage-can lids on the fender of a Chevy, or the tinkling of broken ivory keys on a stand-up piano gathering dust in the corner of a Larimer Street bar. In his many bootlegged recordings, one hears a man confidently interacting with an appreciative audience. He engages a bold synergistic dynamic, effortlessly achieved either by being himself, or by putting on one of the biggest con acts in the history of rock and roll.

A phenomenal character actor, Waits has to his credit a spectrum of worthy film roles enviable of any Oscar-nominated thespian. He is a doomed homeless man (*Ironweed*), a sun-baked desert prophet on the lunatic fringe (*Domino*), a fly-eating straitjacketed lackey of Count Dracula (*Bram Stoker's Dracula*), a born-loser alcoholic limo driver (*Short Cuts*), a pool-table soda man spouting philosophy to members of a street gang (*Rumble Fish*), or Satan himself (*The Imaginarium of Doctor Parnassus*). For me, the only reason to sit through some of these films is to savor the precious screen time taken up by Waits's charismatic performances (he makes it clear to one interviewer that he does more "acting" than he is an "actor").

Waits by most accounts is either a splendid or a frustrating interview, depending on the objective of the journalist. If one enters this formidable task intent on cracking the code, then one is more likely to leave the interview with useless anecdotal wisdom than a story. Waits's strategy of deflection becomes an art form. Often armed with a notebook filled with *Farmer's Almanac* folk wisdom, Waits will plow through an interview with one foot stuck in anecdote, another in honoring the press junkets he may be contractually bound to. He creates a labyrinth even when interviewing himself. In many cases, Waits, like Dylan, will shift the premise of an interview to suit his mood. Says *Newsweek*, Waits is "more Dylan than Dylan." His command of knowledge, quantified by an endless well of experience that he draws up by the bucketful, offers many quotables, perhaps only surpassed by the Bible and Benjamin Franklin.

The pages within do not attempt to cover every aspect of Waits's career. Instead they will illustrate his creative progression through the years. There were many interviews I wished to have included but could not obtain the necessary permissions to reprint. For the most part, the interviews collected here are plucked from obscure music rags that were as popular in the 1970s as Internet blogs are in the 21st century. Though Waits often gave interviews to major publications like *Playboy, Rolling Stone,* and the *New York Times*, their hefty permission fees make it economically unfeasible to include them, and for the most part they are readily found in other books or via the great Internet resource, the Tom Waits Library. I have tried to include those instances in which Waits may have shared something truly unique with an interviewer. Waits does not put on more airs for a magazine like *Vanity Fair* than he would for a skateboarding magazine. Read this tome like you would a *Farmer's Almanac*, for it imparts a similar function, bringing to the world some dispensable wisdom, that same brand of knowledge dearest to Waits's heart. Flipping through the pages, one detects that Waits's rapid-fire talk is more closely derivative of ancient folk wisdom than rock star ego, and for that we fare all the better. Waits continues to spawn new keepers to his flame, inspiring an awestruck admiration for the integrity, immensity, and range of his music. He opens a door of uncompromising art stripped of any commercial sensibility.

This book serves to preserve some of these precious relics of Waits's history. In one interview Waits said, "Music paper interviews, I hate to tell ya but two days after they're printed they're lining the trash can. They're not binding, they're not locked away in a vault somewhere tying you to your word." This book does not try to tie Waits to his word but instead serves as a file cabinet to his impressive past, when rock journalism reigned as an art form and Waits became one of its most worthy subjects.

Much thanks to the exemplary and thorough Yuval Taylor for his editorial excellence and for taking this project on and helming it through thick and thin and to Chicago Review Press and my tireless literary agent Michael K. Dorr of LitPub Ink. My deepest gratitude goes to the many journalists who were both selfless and generous in their wish to be included in this collection. Also to Ken Langford, who has researched most thoroughly every detail, significant or not, of Waits's early career. Without his research, mine would have been doubly more complicated and time-consuming. Also to all of those who have contributed to the Tom Waits Library, a repository for all things Waits of which the subject himself should be highly proud.

PART I

PART I

CLOSING TIME (1973)

Tom Waits's earliest years as a performer were the mid- to late sixties—not as a folkie, but as a rock musician. He kept rhythm on a Saint George electric guitar for a band called The Systems, though that didn't last very long.

Later, in Southern California, Waits participated in Hoot Nights at places like the YMCA, the Bonita Inn, the Back Door, and the Manhattan Club ("hooting" is folk/country parlance for the stage being opened up for performers to play impromptu). At Mission Beach, California, as scores of long-legged, tanned teenaged girls and bands of roaming hippies burned bonfires on the sand, Waits fell into his own circle, intent on finding his way as a performing *and* earning musician. He never got caught up in Beatlemania in his early teenaged years, nor did he hike to Haight-Ashbury to be among the flower children. Working as a bouncer and doorman at the Heritage on Mission Boulevard, Waits waited his turn to step up to the stage. Having a girlfriend working as a waitress didn't hurt either, for she often put in a good word for him with Heritage management. More important, Waits's small-time job gave him a fringe benefit: he got to listen, and by listening he absorbed a slew of musical styles and inflections that he would continue to draw from for the length of his music career.

By November 1970, the humble doorman and probably the world's politest bouncer was advertised in the *San Diego Tribune*: "Singers Marko and David plus Tom Waits at 8:30 and 10:30 P.M., Friday and Saturday." According to Bob Webb, who owned the Heritage, "Thomas Waits," as he signed his name, warmed the stage for the folk/pop duet Michael Claire, featuring Michael Milner and Claire Hart.

In 1971 Waits tried his luck in Los Angeles at the renowned Troubadour on Santa Monica Boulevard, where scores of musicians tried to sell themselves. If Waits was lucky, he was able to sing four songs on Monday nights once a month. Slipping under the radar, for nobody knew his name or his face, Waits sometimes got away with doing it twice. This continued through 1972—until Waits caught the attention of David Geffen one night at the Troubador.

According to Jay S. Jacobs's 2000 biography of Waits, *Wild Years*,

> Geffen wasn't planning on staying long when he dropped by the Troubadour that night in 1972, but he quickly changed his mind. Commanding the

stage was a guy who looked more like a vagabond than a rock musician. But Geffen had barely taken his seat before Waits's seductive aura had encompassed him. "He was singing a song called 'Grapefruit Moon' when I heard him," Geffen recalled recently. "I thought it was a terrific song, so I listened to the set." He watched, he listened, and the wheels started turning. Here was an artist who could make some intriguing records. "After [the show], I said that I was interested in him. He said, 'Well, I'll have my manager, Herb Cohen, call you.'" Geffen left the Troubadour thinking that since Cohen had his own record company, this would be "the end of it." But, to his surprise, Cohen did finally call: "He was interested in making a deal with me for Tom. . . . Herb had said that he didn't really think that it was right for him to make the record. My making the record would help him with the publishing. So I made a deal for [Tom]. And he made a great first record."

Tom Waits's band for his first *Closing Time* tour, which ran from April to June 1973, consisted of Waits on acoustic guitar, piano, and vocals, Webb on stand-up bass, Rich Phelps on trumpet, and John "Funky Fingers" Forsha on guitar. The tour occasioned Waits to explore his diverse interests, absorbing the immensity of the country with the avidity of his hero, Jack Kerouac. The first stop was Washington, DC's Cellar Door, playing for six nights as the warm-up band for Tom Rush. They went north to Cambridge, Massachusetts, and played another five dates at Passim Coffeeshop in Harvard Square. While there, Waits and Webb took a side trip to Lowell, Massachusetts, in an effort to locate the unmarked grave of Kerouac, who had died less than four years before. At Max's Kansas City in Manhattan, the band opened for Charlie Rich, with other dates in Bryn Mawr, Pennsylvania, and Atlanta (warming up for Buffalo Bob Smith). By the time they reached the West Coast, Waits headlined for the first time in Redlands, California, playing for a general audience that had offered a one-dollar donation to attend (Arthur Lee Harper and the Buffalo Nickel Jug Band warmed up for Waits).

Waits's enthusiasm bled from a desire to reach beyond his San Diego confines, where he had been working side jobs as he pursued his musical inclinations. He explained to *Music World*'s Jeff Walker in 1973: "San Diego musicians stay there and hope something is going to happen, but it never does. Nothing happens down there. You play in a rock band in high school and when you get out you end up playing in some swank club behind a girl singer or you stay in the rock band, play GI dances and get paid peanuts." Waits tried to up the ante by driving north to Los Angeles. "I came up as often as I could, but I didn't want to move here until something was happening. I just didn't want to wind up in a gas station." Barney Hoskyns interviewed Walker for his biography of Waits, *Lowside of the Road* (2009):

> "He was so open." Walker recalls, "We talked about music and jazz and Beat poetry. He picked up a trumpet and played a little riff on that. We loved him." Waits, says Walker, was smarting from a tattoo he'd just had done in a downtown parlor. "Thursday afternoon, sober as a judge," he said of the heart and flowers design. "And yes, it hurts."
>
> As Jeff and his photographer girlfriend Kim Gottlieb drove home to Laurel Canyon, they decided to make Waits the cover star of the June issue. "Because we were a free magazine, we didn't have to put somebody well known on the cover," says Gottlieb. "We could afford to take somebody that not too many people knew and put them on the cover." Adds Walker, "We went away and said to ourselves, 'This is going to be an important record and this guy's going to be an important artist.' You felt really privileged to be meeting him." Walker saw Waits' boho-beatnik act as a conscious assertion of identity. "It seemed to me this was all *very* deliberate, pushing the boundaries and genres that he had come out of," he says. "But he was fairly forthcoming. He wasn't holding back or mysterious."

In its forty-plus years of radio broadcasting, KPFK's *FolkScene* has been vital to the dwindling audiences of contemporary folk music. The show was well received by folk music fans and musicians, who appreciated hosts Howard and Roz Larman's purist devotion to the genre. Waits's appearances on the radio show bracketed him into the folk genre, which he ultimately placed behind him in favor of a more eclectic approach to his music. Roz Larman recollected those early years in 2010:

> I don't really know why Waits was drawn to *FolkScene*. We invited him to come on the program, and he agreed. It might have been because he could perform live on the radio. I think we were the only live music program in L.A. at that time. One thing I can remember was that I gave Tom a dollar

to buy a *Rolling Stone* magazine to see the review of his first LP. A few years ago we got this idea to use one of Tom's performances from the San Diego Folk Festival back in the 1970s as a thank-you gift for one of our fundraisers at our local station. Tom called me, and asked me not to use it. At that time we joked about that dollar, that with interest, he now owes me a small fortune. All I can remember about Tom and Howard was that they got along well. He must have enjoyed doing the program, as he came back again. He said things on the program at that time that we are no longer allowed to say, something about his "monkey-shit-brown car."

Interview with Tom Waits
FolkScene, KPFK
September 21, 1973
Howard Larman

Tom Waits: I'm from San Diego, really. I was born in Whittier, California; that's where President Nixon was from. In fact he used to go to our church on occasion, I think. That was a long time ago; he's come a long way since Whittier. Then I moved to San Diego and I guess I kind of grew up around San Diego; I moved there when I was about ten.

Howard Larman: I heard that you tried to write country songs—is that true?

TW: I used to write a lot of them down there at KSON, which is the big country station. I listened to that a lot and wrote a lot of country songs. They don't get me off anymore. I still got a whole closet full of them, but I've been trying to go in other directions with my songwriting.

HL: Were you playing more guitar then?

TW: Yeah, I was playing quite a bit of guitar and I've been playing the piano for a couple of years. Writing on the piano is different than writing on guitar: you get different feels; in fact a lot of times you write a tune with some other artist in mind. I got one right here where I kind of had Ray Charles in mind—it's called "San Diego Serenade."

HL: You wrote that with Ray Charles in mind?

TW: Yeah, I kind of thought he'd like to do it—I don't know. I don't know him; I don't talk to him.

HL: I guess you performed in San Diego?

TW: I played around San Diego quite a bit for a couple of years while there were clubs still open down there—it's very difficult to find a place to play now. Like Folk Arts—Lou Curtiss still has that outfit going on weekends. I used to play at The Heritage—it's closed now—and they turned it into a spiritual bookstore or something. Bob Webb owned it and I used to sit on the door. I used to hoot down there and then I gave that up and I said I'll sit on the door, made five dollars a night, and then I started doing a weekend occasionally. Jack Tempchin was playing around the area at the time. I haven't been doing too many gigs here in L.A. but I was out for two months on the road with a group on the East Coast—did that—and I've been back about a month now. I did a thing out in Redlands, not too many clubs around town though right now. I still hoot at the Troubadour occasionally; I haven't been booked there yet. There's supposed to be a club opening up called Roxy that I'll probably play at on the Strip—but for now I've been staying home, getting a lot of sleep, trying to write tunes.
[*Plays "Ol' 55" on piano*] That tried to be a single but didn't. It was on my record, *Closing Time*, kind of an old song about my car, a "car" song.

HL: How did you get out of San Diego and into other bookings?

TW: I was coming up on the bus and doing four or five songs on Monday nights. I guess I kind of made the big jump into showbiz there, met Herb Cohen, and got a songwriting contract and wrote for a couple of years before I got a recording contract with Asylum Records. After the record came a tour and it went real well. I'd never done anything like that. I'd never even been to most of the places that we played, real exciting tour. I went with stand-up bass, Bob Webb, and Rich Phelps on trumpet and a guitar player, John "Funky Fingers" Forsha.

HL: How long were you out for?

TW: Two months, covered most of the East Coast and played Detroit, Philadelphia, Atlanta, Georgia, Denver, Boston, New York, all over.

HL: Were you writing songs for other people during your songwriting contract?

TW: That's the general idea—I was writing and then the songs were run around to other artists that don't write but put out that they want a song about a frog or something. A lot of people just write, they're staff writers that just write for various groups. I was just writing for anybody who would record it, and nobody did, but maybe that'll change.

HL: Who do you listen to?

TW: I listen to AM radio a lot cause I don't have an FM. I listen to Ray Charles; I got a lot of old Ray Charles records. Let's see, Diana Ross, I like her a lot. I got some old Billie Holiday records; I listen to her. Mose Allison, I'm real fond of Mose Allison, Dale Evans, Miles Davis, a little bit of everything. I try to integrate different styles in my writing, it's important to do that. With a piano it's easier for me to write, I can find a lot more things that I could never find on guitar, so it helps with writing on the piano. I played guitar before I played piano. I'm no technician, no big "fancy" fingers. Writing on an instrument is different than being a real master of an instrument. It's more of a process of investigation than anything else, so you may be lacking in technique but high on the investigation scale. Right now I'm looking forward, sometime this month, to going into the studio and work on another album with Asylum. I'm trying to keep the group together in order to do that. I guess writing is the most difficult thing and the one thing I'm trying to do the most of.

HL: While writing for Herb Cohen, did you drop out of performing?

TW: I just hooted at the Troubadour a lot; that was about it, not too many L.A. appearances. I used to be at the Heritage a lot, but that's in the past.

HL: Did you always want to be a musician?

TW: Yeah, I guess so, I couldn't think of anything else I really wanted to be. It seems to be today that nobody wants to be anything, but nobody wants to be a baseball player anymore or anything. Everybody wants to be a rock 'n' roll star. I was always real interested in music; it never really struck me to write until I guess about the late sixties, about '68 or '69. I started writing. Up until then I just listened to a lot of music, played in school orchestras, played trumpet in elementary school, junior high, high school, went through all that and hung around with some friends of mine that played classical piano and picked up a few little licks here and there. Played guitar and stumbled on the Heritage, and actually the first real songwriter I really saw and really got enthused about was Jack Tempchin, and that was in about 1968 at the Candy Company on El Cajon Boulevard. He was playing on the bill with Lightnin' Hopkins, and he was real casual and everything. It was just something I wanted to try my hand at, so I tried my hand at it. I don't know. I guess you get better as you go along. The more music you listen to, the more perceptive you become toward melody and lyric and all. The only places really to play in San Diego were folk clubs. I used to go to a lot of dances. I played in a band in junior high called The Systems.

HL: Was that trumpet?

TW: I played rhythm guitar and sang. I listened to a lot of black artists, quite a few black artists. I had a real interest in that. James Brown and the Flames were real big. I went to O'Farrell Junior High School, an all-black junior high school, and I went out to Balboa Park and saw James Brown. He knocked me out, man, when I was in seventh grade. So I've kept up on that scene too and I listen to as many different kinds of music as I can.

[*Starts playing "Depot, Depot"*] A little bluesy thing about the Greyhound bus depot downtown. It's funny, not many people go to downtown L.A. *Los Angeles Free Press* did a big article called "Downtown L.A., Who Needs It?" I've been going there since I moved here—I've been here a year—I go to hang out down there. I live in Silver Lake, so I'm about ten minutes from downtown. I go down there just to hang out. Not too many people live down there really, people work down there and hang out, that's all.

[*Starts playing "I Hope That I Don't Fall in Love with You"*] You take all the bar songs in the world and put 'em together, they'd stretch all the way to Kansas City I guess, millions of 'em. This is just another one.

[*Starts playing "Closing Time"*] It's an instrumental done with stand-up bass, trumpet, and piano. It was real effective in concert. We closed the show with it.

[*Plays a portion of "The Heart of Saturday Night"*] It's a new song, I'm anxious to play it. It's kind of about driving down Hollywood Boulevard on Saturday night. Bob Webb and I were kicking this around one afternoon, Saturday afternoon it was, the idea of looking for the heart of Saturday night, hadn't really worked on any tune about it yet, we're both real Jack Kerouac fans and this is kind of a tribute to Kerouacians I guess.

HL: Do you feel under the gun going into the studio, to write more songs?

TW: I'm not really pressured about it. I wrote a lot before I went on tour, but it's best to go in with more than you need in order to select the twelve or fourteen or however many you can squeeze on both sides.

HL: Do you do that selection yourself?

TW: It'll be in conjunction with a producer as far as which tunes for a record. If I had my druthers I'd call it *Looking for the Heart of Saturday Night*, I think, but that's all up in the air right now until I get down to going in. So I've just been trying to write, beat your head against the wall for tunes. Sometimes they come out easy; sometimes they don't come out at all.

[*Plays "The Heart of Saturday Night"*] I spit it out in five minutes. It's a problem with writing songs, for me it's just conceiving the idea for a song, visualizing it in your head and then putting it down is nothing, it comes out real easy. Trying to come up with something, that's challenging for me, I guess, to deal with as the raw material for a song, something to take and develop rather than just, say, well, a love song, well, "I love you and. . . ," it's usually the idea. Like that "Semi Suite" song, that came out real quick too. I don't know, the ones that come out hard are usually the ones that aren't any good, I guess. You can usually tell if a tune was hard to write or if you were having trouble deciding whether to use "love" or "dove" or "above," you know?

[*Starts playing "Big Joe and Phantom 309"*] I don't know who wrote this, I don't know anybody who'd know who wrote this, in fact if somebody does know, maybe you could call and tell me. I first heard Ray Bierl do it, another San Diego musician. This is the first real folk song that just knocked me out. I heard Ray do it and it gave me chills up and down my back.

Waits began his second tour in November 1973. Though it was a financial loss for Waits, it expanded his name to the East Coast. Bob Webb (who by now had been sharing motel rooms with Waits to save money) recalled one show in late November 1973 to Waits historian Ken Langford:

> At some point we were hustled into the limousines again and driven to an undisclosed location in midtown Manhattan. Speculation was rampant, but no one seemed to know where we were going. We went deep into an underground garage in midtown, maybe six floors down, to a giant set of doors like a hotel entrance, which led to big elevators, and we were swept up to a floor that included a giant room full of grand pianos and the most swank dressing rooms I ever saw—showers and fresh fruit and flowers. We were told then that we were in Avery Fisher Hall, in Lincoln Center, and there's where we performed that day, to an audience of nearly four thousand of the rowdiest, most stoned New Yorkers I ever saw. It was the first gig I ever played with an electric bass, and I think it must have been Tom's first time on an electronic keyboard (he was strictly a piano-man in those days). It was also the largest stage we had ever been on, and we faced the most unruly crowd either of us had ever performed for. I'm sure neither of us will ever forget it!

The following day, the band left New York City to play two shows with Frank Zappa in Ontario, Canada. They returned to the states for some shows in Ohio. In Lowell, Massachusetts, Waits performed at Costello Gymnasium at Lowell Tech. Local writer Bob Baumann, who was in the audience, wrote for the *Text*: "Tom Waits is a decent group with a 'misty' blues sound. The man himself has a voice perfectly suited to that sound, and the group is well balanced (which is easy for one as small as theirs to be) and mellow. They are a fine intro group, and that is all that need be said about them." Another show in Massachusetts prompted a reviewer to set the tone for all journalists to follow: "Tom Waits opened Sunday night's concert with beret and bass player. With or without a cigarette in his mouth his lyrics were unclear, his voice raspy and disintegrating amid the gym's echoes. I saw nothing special in his music but felt that he suffered somewhat from playing on a high stage to a large audience. In a close, small concert with clear acoustics he probably shows as a fine entertainer, being easy and intimate with the audience." Whether listeners "got" him or not, Waits persevered, comfortable in his skin regardless of critical contempt, wearing it as confidently as Jim Morrison's lizard-skin jacket.

On December 3, Waits and Webb returned to Los Angeles, their relationship as bandmates ended. The two tours in support of *Closing Time* did not earn Waits any money. He vented his frustration to Lou Curtiss in January in the following interview.

Curtiss's San Diego institution, Folk Arts Rare Records, made it a likely attraction for Waits. Curtiss shared his firsthand experiences with the Tom Waits Library:

> You know I think it was Tom's storytelling ability that attracted me to him first. We'd stand out in front of The Heritage—Tom and fellow musicians Ray [Bierl], Wayne Stromberg, Tom Presley, sometimes Bob La Beau—or we'd go down to Saska's Steakhouse for a burger and beer after The Heritage closed and sit and talk, swap stories, bullshit about people, politics, etc., till the early morning hours or until they chased us out. That boy could talk with the best of them and that's probably what I miss the most. . . . I've still got the tape of that "Dirty Joke Workshop" he took part in with his buddy and fellow musician Ray Bierl.

"From Bouncing to Hooting to Playing the Road"
San Diego Reader
January 13, 1974 (issue date: July 18–24, 1974)
Lou Curtiss and Stephen Swain

Tom Waits evokes a nostalgic feeling for the good old days without sacrificing originality. He has a keen interest in the music, events, and Beat culture of the late 1950s yet his songs and performance stand up in today's music market.

Tom is a collector and researcher of bawdy stories and songs and participated in a workshop dealing with these topics at the Eighth annual San Diego State Folk Festival, where he also appeared as a concert performer.

His songs speak of hot cars with flames on the side, subterraneans in dim-lit coffeehouses (nothing like the ones he started out playing in) and all of those things mourned for in nostalgia films, books, etc. Yet if you never lived in those days or don't want to remember, they still give you a kick of being new, exciting, and different. Tom's an original. A nice guy who's getting somewhere without forgetting where he and his listeners have been.

THE HERITAGE (a folk club in Mission Beach begun in the early 1960s and closed in 1972):

Lou Curtiss: I know you're from Chula Vista, Hilltop High School. I remember the first hoots at the Heritage. [Hoot is an amateur night where prospective singers perform for free.]

Tom Waits: Right before Bob La Beau took over and I was coming down and hootin'. I started with Bobby Dylan songs. Was singing a lot like that, but I wasn't writing anything. I was trying to learn some more tunes, more traditional vein, to be able to sit in at the Heritage a little better because it didn't seem as though songwriting was in vogue at the time. I was doing Mississippi John Hurt and that sort of thing.

LC: And you got your first weekend at the Heritage somewhere along that time.

TW: The first weekend I had at the Heritage it was Bob La Beau and Tom Waits and we split the bill a couple of times after that. It was Bob Webb, at first, who gave me a weekend there. I'd been hootin' for quite a while and I had a girlfriend who got a job waiting tables too. So she was kind of putting a good word in for me with Bob and finally he came around and said, "We'll risk it." And I was the doorman and that was one of the important steps for me because I got to listen every weekend. It was one place you could run into someone you haven't seen in three or four years and that was usually the place you went when you got back in town to see who was in town.

All those people that used to hang out there. When the Heritage closed it was hard for a long time to even make contact with them and now you can make contact with them at Folk Arts. Some of those nights at the Heritage were just as entertaining as what was going on inside. There was like two shows. There was the people that would come down at night, wouldn't even go inside sometimes.

LC: The joke-telling session. Did you ever think of maybe becoming a comedian, a humorist? A humorist is better than a comedian.

TW: It's a better word. It's hard sometimes to get up and just introduce a song as "This one is called. . . ." I feel real shaky about not trying to get a chuckle or two out of an audience. I guess it's important to make an audience feel at ease. At the same time I think it has to be a spectacle and entertaining as well. You can't get too loose. It's just kind of like sitting around your living room, but people don't have to pay in their living room and they want a spectacle. I like to pull off some off-color jokes whenever I can. I think the audience feels a lot more at ease if you do.

LC: Now earlier, were you involved in music back in the South Bay?

TW: Various groups, mainly junior high, doing Surfaris, and Ventures, and Beach Boys, and that sort of thing. Nothing like what I'm trying to do now. Actually, the first songwriters on record, I guess, were James Brown and Ray Charles. The first album I ever bought was *Papa's Got a Brand New Bag*. I was going to Farrell Jr. High and James Brown was my idol at the time. But the first real songwriters I came into firsthand contact with were around San Diego. All local people at the Heritage and the Candy Company and the Back Door and eventually Jack Tempchin, Ray Bierl, and Ted Staak [credited by LC as being San Diego's first folk songwriter, now living as a recluse in Oregon]. There weren't that many, but the ones that were playing here were all worth listening to.

LC: You were just playing guitar then, what got you to switch over to piano?

TW: I had a couple of friends that played piano and we had one at home but I wouldn't go near it because it scared me to death. I just didn't know how to approach it. I finally broke down and invested a couple of hundred dollars in a piano. Started sitting down, fooling around with it and after about a year or so I started writing on it. Now I write primarily on piano. It provides a lot more freedom for me.

LC: I hear some familiar licks in your piano playing, a little Floyd Cramer involved in there.

TW: Yeah, a little bit of that.

LC: Maybe some ragtime?

TW: I'm real ragged. To use the word ragtime would be about right. I'm just real pedestrian in how I approach it. It's mainly from a writing standpoint, so when it comes to performing I try to do my best. I am by no means a pianist, but I can pull it off.

THE FIRST ALBUM: *Closing Time*

LC: Now, what do you think about the whole deal of making an album and all that stuff? How did it work out?

TW: I'd been living here in San Diego and taking the bus up to the hoots at the Troubadour, sitting out in front and waiting, going up and doing four songs on Monday night as often as I could. They allow you one night a month. At first nobody really knew my face or my name so I could do it twice sometimes. The Troubadour is kind of like a marketplace, like a slave auction. Everybody's trying to sell what they do.

LC: How did you get in with Asylum Records?

TW: At first I met Herb Cohen and he signed me to a songwriting contract. I met him at the Troubadour and then in turn, and myself, took the tape to Asylum Records and I was signed for recording. So that's where I am now. I'm under contract for an album a year.

LC: What does it feel like to go into a studio with all this super equipment that you've never seen before?

TW: It was kind of frightening. You just realize how much you have at your disposal. I was fortunate enough to have pretty much my own rein in the studio. I had a good group and we got along fine. We had like a week and a half, two weeks, of rehearsal and then went right into the studio.

LC: How long did it take to do the album?

TW: About four weeks. One thing I realized right away was the matter of being explicit enough in the studio to tell a musician exactly what you want rather than just say: "Let's see how it sounds," and give *him* full rein. Because any fine competent musician in L.A., a studio musician, can play any number of different styles, so you have to know exactly what you want and I guess that's the hardest thing. Because you realize that you have all this equipment, you're open for twenty-four tracks, you can just shoot your rocks. The hardest thing is to be discrete. Definitely a learning experience. I was pleased with it.

TOURING

LC: You've been on the road a lot. How many tours have you done?

TW: I've done two. First one, I went out with a [four-piece] group. We rehearsed a week and split to the East Coast. I'd played in various groups but it was the first time I was really faced with having a backup band and that was real exciting for me. We did mainly small clubs. We'd gotten the opportunity to open for a number of people I'd admired for a number of years. Opened for John Hammond in San Francisco, at the Boarding House. That was a great week. We opened for Charlie Rich in New York City, and he at the time was on a comeback road, before his hits now. He was just cool as ice. Did a lot of rhythm and blues, very little country-western as a matter of fact. Opened for Tom Rush in Georgetown, DC, Danny O'Keefe in Boston, and Tim Weisberg in Denver. So I felt real good about opening for people that I had followed for quite some time. It was good to travel as a group.

LC: The second tour was with Frank Zappa?

TW: That was the most recent one, it lasted about three weeks. That was me and Bob Webb. We were opening the show for Frank (and the Mothers of Invention) doing about thirty minutes in mostly college concerts, a few civic theaters. I was just really impressed. And oddly enough he was really satisfied with what I was doing too. He'd had somebody else opening the show for him and apparently she was undergoing a lot of stress and strain with some of the audiences so she would rather do clubs. So he needed an opening act, and we have the same manager, Herb Cohen, and he said go out and rendezvous with Frank. I rendezvoused with Frank in Toronto and we finished up the last leg of the tour.

LC: What are your plans for the future?

TW: I'm going to the East Coast for about two weeks by myself. I can't afford to go with any group. I lost some money on the first tour with the four pieces. I'm going to go back and be playing the same clubs by myself and trying to pull that off. It will be the same situation, just opening the show for whoever's top. Be gone for about six weeks.

LC: And then a second album is in the works?

TW: The second album will be called *Looking for the Heart of Saturday Night*, if I have my druthers. I'd like to record some old things that I was writing when I was working at the Heritage. I wrote a lot after the second album, which was really surprising to me. It seemed like I had all these songs stacked up, that I was ready to get out and get [illegible] and I came down to being just dry as a bone and being faced with letting a record and a certain amount of popularity stifle me as a writer.

LC: When you go on the road now, do you do material mostly off your album?

TW: I do half and half. I've been doing more new material than album material. Most of the clubs that we play at it's a matter of promoting the record because a lot of people don't know me from Adam. Now I think, looking forward to a second tour, there'll be some people remember me from a year ago. So, looking forward to going.

Journalist Kenny Weissberg on the first time he interviewed Waits: "There were only scant hints that he would go on to become one of the most influential and

imitated musicians of our time. His debut LP *Closing Time* had recently been released, he was pigeonholed as a mellow Asylum Records singer-songwriter, and there was only a tinge of rasp in a voice that would eventually make Satchmo seem like Nat 'King' Cole in comparison."

Waits was still enduring his opening act stint when he came to Denver, Colorado. At the 230-seat club Ebbets Field (where Waits met Chuck E. Weiss), he first opened for Roger McGuinn, John Stewart, and Gene Clark for two nights, and then for Jerry Jeff Walker for five. Weissberg's memories of the singer-songwriter echoed those of other writers who came into close proximity with Waits: "He looked like a cross between a beatnik and a hobo, played most of his songs seated at a piano a la Randy Newman, and had developed little of the poetic patter that would soon become his trademark."

Sharing coffee at the Oxford Hotel, Waits confided his thoughts on burgeoning fame: "I wonder if it's a blessing or a curse for an artist to get recognition. I've gotten a little exposure, but not enough to make my head spin and I'm glad about that. I did a three-week East Coast tour, opening for Frank Zappa in front of three to four thousand people a night. I got a lot of produce thrown at me, but I did it to challenge myself."

"Tom Waits: Saturday Night Seeker"
Colorado Daily
February 18, 1974
Kenny Weissberg

Four years ago, Tom Waits was a pizza utility man for Napoleone's in National City, California. For five years he served as a cook, janitor, plumber and maintenance man. "We made the best pizza in town, so it was worthwhile, but after awhile it got to be more than just a job. It was a second home which got to be a bit too much."

There was always a guitar and ukelele at Tom's house and he grew up playing a combination of Spanish romantica and surfing music. He transcended his Safaris stage and began playing folk music at the Heritage in San Diego. He's currently at Ebbets Field in Denver (through Sunday), where he's been opening shows for Roger McGuinn and Jerry Jeff Walker.

"At this point, to open a show is ideal for me. I don't feel that much pressure because no one's paid $4 to see me. I do feel a responsibility to make contact with the audience and I'm working hard on that. Being here is a lot easier than it was when I toured with Frank Zappa."

Tom was discovered by Zappa's manager Herb Cohen, while performing at a Monday night hoot at L.A.'s Troubadour. He would take the 6 o'clock bus from San Diego, make a couple of transfers and try and get a good spot in line. Once onstage he'd only have an opportunity to do three or four songs before having to sprint to the station to catch an early morning bus back to San Diego.

"The Troubadour hoot was like a slave market. People sell their souls to get up and play. A lot of times it pays off. People come from Georgia, Texas, New York City . . . if they don't make it. . . ."

Tom only had to risk a three-hundred-mile round-trip and he played nearly every Monday for more than a year. "I'd hear stories like there were all these guys with cigars there to sign you up. You know McGuinn's tune 'So You Want to Be a Rock 'n' Roll Star?' Well the Troubadour is where it all starts."

His first album, out about a year now, is called *Closing Time* and the only description that comes to finger is intuitive barroom nostalgia. "Virginia Avenue" tells of walking the main strip after the clubs have closed for the morning, finally opting for the security of a Greyhound escape. "I Hope That I Don't Fall in Love with You" relates the frustrations of barroom fantasies. "Martha" is about a guy who laments forty years later that the immature teenage lust he had written off has been the ultimate in life for him. He still loves Martha but they're both married with kids, though even that hasn't dulled his vivid memories.

"Ol' 55" is, predictably, about a man's love for his car, especially at 6 A.M. after a warm night with his lover. It was also Tom's first single and even snails beat it up the charts. That seems to be the only snag in the satisfying pace of Tom's career. Because the album did not produce a successful single, Asylum won't let Tom continue his professional association with producer Jerry Yester.

"As far as I'm concerned, Jerry Yester's a great man and a great producer. I was expecting to record my second album with him but Asylum wants to find someone that can take my songs and make hits out of them. I've been ready for about four months but they haven't found anyone yet.

"The album is going to be called *Looking for the Heart of Saturday Night*, and is going to follow a thread all the way through as opposed to a random selection of songs."

In the meantime Tom does club dates, his first album having endeared many club owners like Chuck Morris who are happy to call Tom to open shows. "A first album is like a diploma . . . like a BA. No matter how good you are, you can't play a club like Ebbets unless you have an album. I'd just like to do my second album because the first one's old already."

Tom's songs will never grow old and I'd tell you more about him if I had the space. If you can't get to Ebbets by Sunday, *Closing Time* is worth the inflated price of the vinyl you're paying for. It's a masterpiece.

Prior to the release of his second LP, *The Heart of Saturday Night*, Waits again endured the arduous task of warming up the rowdy fans of Frank Zappa and the Mothers of Invention. By April 24, 1974, he had built up enough clout as a local favorite to be included on the roster for the Eighth annual San Diego Folk Festival held in Montezuma Hall. Three days later he participated in an afternoon "Spicy Stories" workshop. Fresh from four more dates with Zappa in California, Waits returned to *FolkScene* for an interview.

Interview with Tom Waits
FolkScene, KPFK
July 23, 1974
Howard Larman

Howard Larman: A lot of acoustic acts have had trouble opening for rock bands.

Tom Waits: You're looking at one of them right now. I'm getting better I guess, but it takes a certain attitude that you have to develop after a while. You have to just go out there with the intention of trying to entertain when people don't want to be entertained by you. It goes all right most nights. In the South we played some small halls and they were good for me and I thought I did real well in spite of everything.

HL: It seems like such a massive challenge.

TW: It is, but it's good, because I guess you can really get tired of performing for people who just think you're the greatest thing since sliced bread before you open your mouth. I enjoyed the challenge and the travel so it was real good.

[*Starts playing "On a Foggy Night"*] This is the soundtrack for a film, the soundtrack was written quite a bit later than the film. The film came out about 1947 and I wrote it just a couple of weeks ago and it's about a foggy night on one of those "triangle" films that you see on *The Late Show*. This is just about the eternal triangle, like George Raft and Fred MacMurray and Rosalind Russell, and somebody has to go, and it's going to be George Raft in this case and Fred MacMurray's got this old Plymouth and he's on this foggy road with MacMurray in the trunk with a little bit of his lapel sticking out the back of the trunk and this song comes on the radio.

HL: Are you working on your second album now?

TW: I just finished one before I went out with the Mothers; I finished a record with Bones Howe producing, called *Looking for the Heart of Saturday Night*. It's going to come out sometime in mid-September.

HL: Is "Foggy Night" on it?

TW: Yeah, I think it might be, we recorded fifteen songs and he's picking twelve off there, eleven or twelve, 'cause some are kind of long and I did some spoken-word stuff, it's just a veritable . . . just like a fruit salad of all different kinds of songs and I'm real proud of it. I think it's gonna be a blockbuster, I don't know, it's kind of speculation but I listen to it a lot at home so I think it's a good record. I enjoyed very much working with Bones Howe and I had a good group behind me. The songs were strong, I thought, so it'll come out in September; we'll see what happens then, I guess. On a record you're faced with a real collective effort with so many people that have to be happy with it so it's not one man's decision at all. I enjoy working with a group; I very rarely get an opportunity to when I perform so I enjoy it very much. I think they complemented the songs rather than put a Band-Aid on them like a lot of groups do to people's songs. I'm proud of it.

HL: At the San Diego Folk Festival you did "Ghosts of Saturday Night" together with "The Heart of Saturday Night." Was that a spur-of-the-moment thing?

TW: Yeah, it kind of was. They said everybody gets one song, so I figured if I just stretched a song far enough I could really do two. So, I did that poem and very quickly did the song and it seemed like it was part of the song, so I got away with two songs really.

HL: You got called back for an encore.

TW: I enjoyed that whole festival. That's the first time I've been on a roster at the San Diego Folk Festival; I've been there many times but never been asked to play, so I felt really a part of it, so that's good. See, at that songwriting workshop, Jack Tempchin was there and Jim Ringer was there and Bruce Phillips was there and that was the first time I'd been able to see Bruce Phillips perform and he slayed me. He's slick as deer guts on a doorknob. He's the cat's meow and I haven't had so much fun since Granny put her tits in a wringer.

HL: Are you doing a lot of poetry?

TW: A couple of things like that. I don't know if it's really poetry, but it's just like, instead of writing a song, I just wrote a mouthful of words and just talked 'em instead of singin' 'em. I guess you could call them poems. Yeah, there are a lot more. They can be palatable for an audience I think, in a lot of cases, more so than a song when you get hung up on the melody and the mood, and what kind of voice this guy's got and the sound of his instrument. You can lose a lot of the lyric, so I like that piece you're talking about.

[*Starts playing "The Ghosts of Saturday Night"*] It's about National City, which is primarily a sailor town, a suburb of San Diego, where the infamous Mile of Cars is on National Avenue and at the north end is the Burge-Roberts Mortuary, the Golden Barrel, Escalante's Liquor Store, and sandwiched in between a Triumph Motorcycles shop and Burge-Roberts is Napoleone's Pizza House, it's been there for a good twenty-five years, and I worked there when I was real young. I've worked there since I was fifteen. Not until I was away from it for a long time could I really sit down and write something constructive about it.

[*Plays "The Heart of Saturday Night"*] All we did with that song was bass and guitar. We taped a little traffic on Cahuenga, just stuck microphones out there and got about twenty minutes of rush hour, cut it down and put it on there. It really sets it up.

HL: Is *Closing Time* still available?

TW: I don't know, I haven't seen it anywhere recently. In fact, it may even be out of print. It broke even for me and got a little bit of action and did all right but I think they pulled it off now. Friends of mine are looking for it and can't find it. Maybe they'll re-release it when the second record comes out, we'll see what happens. I wanted to have a brand-new song for tonight and I worked on this rascal and I just didn't come up with anything. By the next time I'll have a whole new thing. It's called "Looking for a Romantic Investment with Emotional Dividends." I think it could really skyrocket to the top of the charts. It's not done yet.

HL: Did you write new songs especially for the new album?

TW: I wrote some stuff that, conceptually, I guess, I had in mind for an album storyline with some sort of collection of songs, like chapters, that weren't just a random handful of ballads, but something that tied together. Once I wrote "Saturday Night," I started thinking in terms of other ways of approaching Saturday night and things like that.

[*Starts playing "Depot, Depot"*] This is a bit of local color here. This is about Sixth and Los Angeles in downtown Los Angeles. It's about the Greyhound bus depot, about going down to the depot on a Saturday night with plenty of quarters for the TV chairs, and it's just a great place to take a date.

[*Starts playing "Diamonds on My Windshield"*] This is about driving in the rain. I used to make that track from San Diego to Los Angeles a lot, usually with several pit stops on the way with engine trouble. So this is about driving in the rain, circa 1973. So slip me some crimson, Jimson.

HL: How did you get into doing those kinds of spoken-word pieces?

TW: I don't know—the first time I heard any spoken word that I was really impressed with was an album called *Jack Kerouac/Steve Allen*—and he talked while Steve Allen played some stuff and he just talked over the top of it and it was real, real effective. I never heard anything like it, so I wrote a few little things.

HL: I guess there was kind of a craze for that in the fifties.

TW: Yeah, Lord Buckley and all that, it frees you as a songwriter to be able to just throw down some color and not worry about any sort of meter at all. I enjoy writing stuff like that. Lately I seem to be more concerned with that than writing real songs.

HL: You read a lot of Kerouac, don't you?

TW: Well, I've read all of his work. Actually I've discovered some magazine articles by him that are in some very colorful magazines like *Rogue* and *Cad*. He used to publish stories and there were a lot of articles written about him in those skin magazines. I've read everything I can get my hands on by him.

HL: Any other writers?

TW: Oh, yeah, Charles Bukowski is probably one of the most colorful and most important writers of modern fiction, poetry, and prose in contemporary literature right now. I'd say he's at the vanguard in my book; he just levels me.

HL: What are your plans now?

TW: Right now I guess I'm gonna stay in one place for a while. I think I've got a gig at Redlands and I think I've got one at McCabe's and I got one at Folk Arts in San Diego at the end of August. In September, when the record comes out, I'll go out on the East Coast for probably three months and do the club circuit out there.

HL: Is there a legal commitment to tour when the record comes out?

TW: Well, I guess it's for your own good. Essentially you're going out and playing your record. You're going out and doing the hard sell, pimping for yourself, if you will. That's what everybody does. You talk to magazines and stuff and see if it does any good, so I'll do that in September. Up until then, I'm gonna write a bunch of stuff, and if this record does all right, I'll go into the studio and do another one, I hope.

HL: What is your approach to songwriting—is it a craft or something that just comes to you?

TW: It's a craft by all means, you can tell it's a craft when you hold two songwriters up side by side, one who's good and one who isn't, you can tell who is craftier, I guess.

HL: I know a lot of songwriters who say things just float in?

TW: No, that's not true. It's not some kind of divine inspiration or anything. There are times when you're moved to write something, but I don't think you quake and talk in tongues or anything. I think that's a lot of poppycock and balderdash myself. You work on a concept, on an idea, and you read and you listen to other writers and you listen to the radio and you listen to the *Hit Parade* and you listen to KPFK, and then you get better, hopefully. Of course it's all a matter of opinion. There are songwriters that I like that aren't so well liked. It's still a matter of what your own taste is, but I do think there's a strong difference between someone like Randy Newman, who is certainly a craftsman when it comes to putting a song together, someone who can evoke such a feeling from his listeners, and it comes from him really sweating over a song. Then you take somebody like, I don't want to slander anybody, we're on the air, but take somebody like [*mumbles incoherently*] who really writes ridiculously childish songs that don't have any meat to them or a real vision. I think it's certainly craft.

HL: Are there other songwriters you listen to besides Randy Newman?

TW: Yeah, I listen to him and I like Mose Allison. I think he's a very economical songwriter. He's so damn stylized that you can't help but love him to death. He's like honey poured all over you. I admire him a great deal. I still listen to "These Foolish Things (Remind Me of You)." Now was that George Gershwin or was that Cole Porter? That was Cole Porter [actually, it was written by a pair of British songwriters, Eric Maschwitz (words) and Jack Strachey (music)]. There was a similar song along the same lines by Gershwin. So now I have to pick a real crafty song. "Drunk on the Moon" was kind of crafty. It was a matter of taking a whole bunch of words and trying to hang them in the right place on a melody.

Sometimes you get so many words you don't know what to do and sometimes you don't need 'em at all, and sometimes you do. I think that's a crafty song. "Ghosts of Saturday Night" is kind of crafty, it's stylized.

THE HEART OF SATURDAY NIGHT (1974)

In October 1974, Asylum Records released Waits's sophomore album, *The Heart of Saturday Night*. All the songwriting credits were retained by Waits with Bones Howe credited as engineer, producer, and soundman. Howe and Waits maintained a comfortable working relationship, for Howe's background in jazz was a source of awe for the young troubadour, who yearned to keep one foot in the jazz idiom. Howe recalls: "I told him I thought his music and lyrics had a Kerouac quality to them, and he was blown away that I knew who Jack Kerouac was. I told him I also played jazz drums and he went wild. Then I told him that when I was working for Norman Granz [founder of Verve Records, manager and producer for Ella Fitzgerald, and one of the jazz idiom's most talented entrepreneurs], Norman had found these tapes of Kerouac reading his poetry from the Beat Generation in a hotel room. I told Waits I'd make him a copy. That sealed it." Howe also knew how to best capture the soulful resonance of Waits's baritone, and Howe's knowledge of how to best mic Waits in the studio gave these early recordings a vintage quality.

Jim Hughart was Tom's bassist. In 2000, he told *Bassics* magazine,

> He keeps his show on little scraps of paper in his pocket. We'd go to the session, and sometimes it was just Tom and me to begin with. This is probably my one and only complaint about Tom: we'd go into the studio and he'd rummage through the scraps of paper he had in his pocket and say, "OK, give me something like this," and snap his fingers to give me the tempo. He'd just sort of growl these words over the bass line that I was playing, and that became the tune. My complaint about it is when the record came out, it was "Words and Music by Tom Waits." It would have been nice to give me a credit; it wouldn't have cost him much to give me an opportunity to share the royalties, because nobody else does his material, I don't think, or very few people do. But it was all enjoyable working with him, every bit of it was enjoyable.

The Heart of Saturday Night Press Release
October 1974
Tom Waits

The blur drizzle down the plate glass and a neon swizzle stick stirs up the night air, as a cue ball maverick of a moon rolls across an obsidian sky and the busses groaning and wheezing at the corner of restless blvd. and midnight road, across the trucks from easy street and window shoppers beat the cement stroll and I sit scowling over this week's special Norm's pancakes and eggs $.69 trying to stretch out in the bowels of this metropolitan area. I've tasted Saturday nights in Detroit, St. Louis, Tuscaloosa, New Orleans, Atlanta, N.Y.C., Boston, Memphis. I've done more traveling in the past year than I ever did in my life so far, in terms of my level of popularity, on the night spot circuit, I remain in relative obscurity and now upon the release of a second album, which I believe a comprehensive study of a number of aspects of this search for the center of Saturday night, which Jack Kerouac relentlessly chased from one end of this country to the other, and I've attempted to scoop up a few diamonds of this magic that I see. Musically pulling influence from Mose Allison, Thelonious Monk, Randy Newman, George Gershwin, Irving Berlin, Ray Charles, Stephen Foster, Frank Sinatra. . . .

My favorite writers, Jack Kerouac, Charles Bukowski, Michael C. Ford, Robert Webb, Gregory Corso, Lawrence Ferlinghetti, Larry McMurtry, Harper Lee, Sam Jones, Eugene O'Neill, John Rechy, and more. I drive a 1965 Thunderbird that needs a valve job and at least four quarts of Pennzoil a week and gets four miles to the gallon on a long distance; the trunk is busted. And I have three warrants on traffic violations in the Los Angeles Metropolitan area alone. I am a pedestrian piano player with poor technique but a good sense of melody. I write in coffee shops, bars, and parking lots. My favorite album is *Kerouac/Allen* on Hanover Records.

Born December 7, 1949, in Pomona, California, I drink heavily on occasion and shoot a decent game of pool and my idea of a good time is a Tuesday evening at the Manhattan Club in Tijuana. I reside now in the Silver Lake area of Los Angeles and am a dedicated Angelino and have absolutely no intention of moving to a cabin in Colorado. I like smog, traffic, kinky people, car trouble, noisy neighbors, crowded bars, and spend most of my time in my car going to the movies.

Now, with two diploma albums, *Closing Time* and *The Heart of Saturday Night*, I trust I will secure enough club dates to keep me moving. I've been an opening act for many artists including Frank Zappa and the Mothers, Buffalo Bob and the Howdy Doody Review, Charlie Rich, John Stewart, Billy Preston, John Hammond, Jerry Jeff Walker, Bob La Beau, Danny O'Keefe, and others, and I've met Ed Barbara of Manhattan Furniture.

Your friend and mine,

Tom Waits

Waits's hectic touring schedule gave him ample opportunity to try out new songs on occasion. At Ebbett's Field in Denver, Colorado, as he was seated at the piano, Waits spread a ragged piece of paper, smoothed it with his hands, and performed an early version of "Nighthawk Postcards." This gesture, half for effect, half genuine, nonetheless conveyed a lyrical content that had undergone Waits's rigorous quality control. The songs were unpolished diamonds, meticulously eked out of marathon sessions of midnight coffees in smoky diners, or backstage, or late nights far away from home in a motel room, smoking one cigarette after another, waiting to hit the spotlight.

Waits elicited (and still does) favorable impressions from many musical contemporaries. John Hammond recalled an encounter with Waits in Scottsdale, Arizona, in late 1974. Scheduled to perform later that evening, Hammond decided to arrive early at Balcony Hall to catch the opening act: "When Tom went on, I did that double take: 'What? Who is that?' This is before Tom's voice had gotten rough, and he did the most incredible songs, I didn't want him to stop, and then when the show ended, I didn't want to go on. I wanted him to do another set. But I went on and played, and after the show he was hangin' out and told me he was a big fan of mine. I said I'd never heard anything like him before. . . ."

Onstage and off, Waits was amusing, charismatic, charming, and fun. His song dedications directed to random audience members gave the show a more personable vibe. At one such concert, he dedicated the core of the songs to a drunken patron passed out in the front row. By tour's end, his between-song banter had metamorphosed into humorous monologues. When he performed in Denver, he made constant references to Denver's notorious Larimer Street, the skid row section that his heroes Neal Cassady, Allen Ginsberg, and Jack Kerouac passed through in the late 1940s. Waits was all too aware of the dangers of bringing the realities of hard living into one's art, much like the ill-fated Kerouac. He rode the crest of his passions, staying, in his own words, "as busy as a one-armed bass player."

Interview with Tom Waits
FolkScene, KPFK
January 12, 1975
Howard and Roz Larman

Larmans: You were on the road for three months?

Tom Waits: Uh huh, I got back around Christmas and I started in Denver and just did that club circuit and ended up in Pittsburgh and it was a pretty good tour. I toured for three months.

L: Was it all clubs?

TW: One concert in Philadelphia, the rest was all clubs. Played the Troubadour here—a lot of them. It was OK.

L: Better than opening for Zappa and the Mothers?

TW: Yeah, it just beat the hell out of those.

L: Who were you booked with?

TW: Buffalo Bob and the Howdy Doody Review—I did real well on that bill. I was at a club in East Lansing, Michigan, called the Stables. What they did was take an old horse stable and converted it into a nightclub. If you listen at night after they close, you can hear the thoroughbreds in the back row. It's a huge joint, about as intimate as a bullring. It's hard to pull off. I was on a bill with Martha and the Vandellas. There was a small little postage stamp of a stage and they said they'd provide a piano, so they put it way in the back row. They didn't say anything about putting it onstage. I've been on some strange bills and some good ones. I opened a show for Billy Preston once; that was the pits. I've had some good bills. Occasionally you get involved with an experiment in bad booking, but I get some good ones now and then. I like to go out and open the show for whoever happens to be top bill at the club that I'm at, so I don't tour with a group. I travel alone.

L: Your last album got good reviews; are you starting on another one yet?

TW: Uh, yeah, I haven't been in the studio but I'm writing stuff for one. Maybe called *Easy Street*, I don't know. I'm toying with some ideas for some songs so I'm working on some material right now.

L: Did you get any writing done on the road?

TW: It's difficult to do because it's hard to be able to get the opportunity to sit down at the keyboard, except to perform. I was mostly doing two, sometimes three shows a night, six nights, and then leaving on the seventh night to open, like on a Monday. Some were Monday through Saturday, some were Monday through Sunday, so it's hard to get a chance to sit down and concentrate and think in notes. So, I wrote a lot of verse, but it is a problem, the road. I don't know, everybody has to have a different climate in order to create, so I managed OK. I'll probably go in the studio sometime in May. I've got quite a while to be at home now—plenty of time to write songs—but it's hard to write out there.

L: You keep developing—even "Diamonds on My Windshield" is different now than on the record, right?

TW: Yeah, it is. Everybody that writes has got spare parts and it's just a matter of tearing down and rebuilding. It's like a carburetor. I just blew a head gasket on this '54 Cadillac. I bought it, first car I ever bought on a car lot, 'cause I don't know, they're all con artists, real professional grifters. I was down in Burbank on Victory and I went to this place called Jerry Lee's Used Cars. I saw this black '54 Caddy, big sucker, it's late '54, it's the limo model and I swear it runs like a sewing machine. I had this old Oldsmobile, Chevrolet rattletraps, you take 'em around the block and they just cough up once you get to the lights. I paid $400.00 for this damn Cadillac and I just took it into Nogales and it ran, it just hummed. It's got one of the most musical transmissions.

L: What happened to the Thunderbird you used to talk about?

TW: I just parked it. I'm gonna use it for an office. It doesn't run much. It's kind of monkey-shit brown and in terrible condition. I got in a four-car pileup before I left town in Vermont in the rain. I was responsible, my first accident. I was out doing about twenty-five, the traffic, you know how the lights come down, they say they're all stacked up, but it looks like everybody's moving smoothly because of the lights and the whole rainbow-blur effect on the street and James Brown's "Papa's Got a Brand New Bag" just came on the radio and I was going crazy out of my mind. So it was worth getting in an accident over the first time I heard that song.

L: You'll probably write a song about it?

TW: No, I have to remain nameless for about the next six months. I got lawyers and things. We shouldn't even be talking about this on the air, but it was just one of those things. My T-Bird is temporarily out of service, not in service at this time. I just parked it and I'm going to sell it to this cat up the street for $25.00. Right now I got this Cadillac and it's just wonderful. That was the Hydromatic Dyna-flow transmission and it's just *lalalalaala . . .*—a wonderful automobile. I've never really compromised on comfort for economy, but it loves oil, crazy about Super Shell, can't get enough of it.

L: Do you write with anyone else in mind to do your songs?

TW: Couple of times I did. Not usually. It's very difficult to write when you've got to think about finances and residuals and dividends and appointments and shag carpets and polyester fabrics in the fifteenth floor of the Cahuenga office build-ing, Formica coffee tables, and stuff like that. I usually try to, like I said before, you need a different climate to create something. That thing called "Easy Street," I was kind of in the bowels of the metropolitan region at the time and writing from that point of view rather than, I don't know, you get too much Pekingese shit on your Bazanti boots off those shag carpets. You can't write anything.

L: Do you do anything to force the songs at all?

TW: I have a vice out in the garage, I used to put my head in it, screw it tight. Yeah, I don't force them but if you don't jump on your back a little bit now and then, you won't write jack so I usually try to. . . . I got a chance to write a couple of songs for Barbra Streisand now and it's hard to put yourself in, I mean it's hard to write for somebody else but me. I'm working on a couple that she might do. I'm sure she'd get thousands of 'em but I just at least get to ante in too. I don't know. Coffee and beer usually helps for a writing climate for me. Mrs. Olsen has been on my back for several years. I got a Maxwell House jones and that usually helps to write. You never know when something's gonna hit you.

L: At the Troubadour you looked sort of awkward with all of Little Feat's equipment up there.

TW: They had a lot of furniture up there. I almost had an artificial vasectomy on those little cymbals hanging out there. A lot of electronic accoutrement I had to dodge and duck under, but I pulled it off OK, I think. I just used a spotlight to not light up all that chrome up there. It was OK. On opening night I was pretty inebriated, there was a lot of press there and everything, and it just has the tendency to make you a little neurotic, I guess. Then I went to Minneapolis, and then I went to Pittsburgh, and then I came home. It was a real nervous gig. On top of everything else, I had never played there before. I had hooted there several times, so playing there, and having a formal engagement there was a little difficult somehow, but it went off OK.

[*Starts playing "Drunk on the Moon"*] This is about Denver, Colorado. I always stayed at a place called the Oxford Hotel which is down on Seventeenth and Wazee about a block away from Larimer Street, Larimer being just full of a lot of ghosts, down there on Larimer Street shopping for images in the trash cans. Boy, that's old Kerouac and Cassady's stomping grounds. It's really changed quite a bit. They put up what's called Larimer Square now, which is kind of like a contemporary, little boutique-sort-of shopping center. It looks awful ridiculous 'cause right across the street is some real bona fide serious winos, right out in front of a place called the Gin Mill. Another place is called the Terminal Bar, which is a block away from the Santa Fe train depot. They called it the Terminal Bar but they had no idea that like twenty years later the place'd be filling up with terminal cases. This is called "Drunk on the Moon," there's all different kinds of moons—silver-slipper moons and there's cue-ball moons and there's buttery cue-ball moons and moons that are all melted off to one side, and this is about a muscatel moon.

Sitting with Marco Barla for an interview at the beginning of 1975, Waits vowed to preserve his artistic integrity despite how he was otherwise perceived. He requested that his interviewers remain close to the facts, with no attempts to clean up either his image or the shabby environ he met them in. Barla recalls:

> I did the interview with Tom Waits for the *LA Free Press* in 1975 and I thoroughly enjoyed the assignment. I admit that I was a big fan at the time, as was the then editor of the paper, John Carpenter, and that we had both just seen him perform at the Troubadour club a few nights before in Hollywood, which is right down the street from Duke's Coffee Shop and the Palms Bar, where the interview took place. It was Carpenter's intention to elevate the content of the paper to a West Coast version of the *Village Voice*, particularly with regard to music and film, but sadly he was killed in a hit-and-run accident less than a year later. Regarding the interview, Waits was a bit nervous at first because he held the then features editor of the paper in very high esteem and he knew the piece would be reviewed by him. Tom asked that I be very accurate with the information he provided, beer and humor notwithstanding. I took my notes and we went over them together. Afterward, Tom gave me the go-ahead. This was quite a few years ago, but I appreciate his work now more than ever, eccentricity included, built as it is on a timeless foundation of poignance and nostalgia and truth.

"Tom Waits: Los Angeles Is Poetry"
LA Free Press
January 17, 1975
Marco Barla

"You know there's a blurred drizzle down a plate glass, there's a neon swizzle stick a-stirrin' up a sultry night air, and a traffic jam session on Belmont as a yellow biscuit of a butter cueball moon is rollin' maverick across an obsidian sky . . . and you know the buses are groanin' and they're wheezin' down the corner I'm freezin' on restless boulevard, midnight road cross town from Easy Street, with the tight knots of moviegoers and out-of-towners on the stroll and the buildings tower high above lit like dominoes . . . now you know the used car salesmen with all their Purina checkerboard slacks and Foster Grant wrap-arounds are pacing in front of that rainbow $39.95 Earl Scheib merchandise like barkers in an arcade, all dressed up in jackal-striped jackets with the blue denim dye and color TV test pattern, double-knit polyester slacks throwing out some kind of a Texas Guinan routine.

"They say: 'Hello, sucker, we like your money just as well as anybody else's here,' and luring all the harlequin sailors on the stroll in search of like new; new paint, factory air, and AM-FM dreams . . . but you know the piss yellow gypsy cabs are stacked up in the taxi zones and they're waitin' like pinball machines to take off a joy ride to some magical place or they're waitin' in line like 'Truckers Welcome' diners with dirt-lots full of Peterbilts and Kenworths and Jimmys and the like doing some serious highballin' with bankrupt brakes, and they got the overdriven, underfed, underpaid, a day-late—a dollar-short with their eyes propped open and their eyelids at half mast and I'm on the corner. . . .

"I'm standin' on the corner like a just-got-in-town jasper on a streetcorner with a gasper lookin' for some kind of a Cheshire billboard grin strokin' a goateed chin and using parking meters as walking sticks . . . I'm out here on the inebriated stroll. I am . . . and you know the sun come crawlin' yellow out of a manhole at the foot of Twenty-Third Street and a Dracula moon is making its way back dodgin' shadows to its prepaid room at the St. Moritz Hotel and the El train is tumblin' across the trestles soundin' like the ghost of Gene Krupa with an overhead cam and glass packs and over at Chub's Pool and Snooker it was a nickel after two. . . .

"Yeah, with a nickel after two and the cobalt steel blue dream smoked, the radio groaned out the hit parade and the chalk squeaked and the floorboards creaked and an Olympia sign winked through a torn yellow shade and Jack Chance is leaning up against a Wurlitzer seriously eyeballin' out a three-ball combination shot. . . .

"I'm looking for some kind of an emotional investment with romantic dividends and leaning up against a banister I'm held over . . . held over for another smashed weekend."

Tom Waits slouches on the corner stool in Duke's Coffee Shop, a shamble of newspapers at his feet, his place at the counter cluttered with utensils, ashtray and a package of bound volumes—a kind of spontaneous collage, he is, mirror to three months on the road, then home again on Santa Monica Boulevard, here, underneath the Tropicana Motel—this bright, clattery, bustling, public dining room, his cap and vest and crumpled shirt, his eyes a little weary, bleary, wary—a sly grin rising from an empty coffee cup.

"I love this city," he is saying, "I love Los Angeles, but right now my point of view is a little blurred because I don't have a car.

"I'm lookin' for a car, and I'm under a lot of pressure to get something decent, you know, like I get this 'What are you doing, man, you drop 100 bucks, then you sink $3,500 more and it turns around and scratches your eyes out and you gotta sell it for $12. I mean you can't go on like that forever.'"

I think of the Tom Waits songs and stories, references to Roadmasters and musical Dynaflow transmissions and an older, out-of-phase value system, where comfort was the essential item and, as he says it, "You put a hunk of tape over the gas gauge, knowing you could always make it to Gila Bend."

I suggest a Mercedes-Benz or a Porsche, possibly with skis resined to the roof.

"Uh huh. I gotta think of my image, but what I'd really like to find is a creative chariot, like an old Plymouth. A Plymouth Batmobile, or something with a nice physique." We decide to forego the frenetic disarray of Duke's and amble across the street instead. Once entrenched in the Palm's Bar, quaffing beers, we resume.

"I love to drive," he says, "and it's conducive to writing for me. Everybody needs a different climate in which to create, like for some people it's the sun streaming through the blinds, or the Rocky Mountains, or a room sanitized for your protection.

"There ain't no music out in the country. All the music's in the city. Symphonies on Twenty-Third Street. Traffic jam sessions going on all the time. There were times when I was out on the road where I would have given my left nut to be on the Harbor Freeway at 5:30 in the afternoon, just to listen. I love it."

I think his cacophony a bit overpriced myself, but his sentiments are appreciated, particularly since they are delivered without the facetious posturing of less talented, more ornately advertised performers. Tom Waits has a feel for the continuous roll of vowels and consonants, pieced together to relate experience in an honestly poetic medium which, unfortunately, is not often dealt with in those enlightened terms.

The Gray Fifties

His identification reaches back to the gray alcoholic stupor of the fifties, when degrees of perception and radical artistic whim were greeted with, as he says himself, "the Gilette Blue Blade treatment," and the kinds of critical vitriol indicative of fear. The ghost of Jack Kerouac, the hobo Gregory Corso, and the throngs of disconnected, disillusioned barflies who, only incidentally, had a touch of undiluted genius.

"I'm just coming in right now. I'm just finding that I've got a lifestyle, and as far as how it relates to any popular or fashionable sort of lifestyles that have become before or are going on now or will be arriving, I don't know. I just do what I do."

Experience seems to have been the best teacher, Waits taking his references from "juggling pizzas at Napoleone's Pizza parlor in San Diego till three in the morning, right there on the front lines, swimming around in the bowels of the metropolitan, late-night Naugahyde crowd. I didn't get jack shit out of high school."

At the same time, an interest in literature seemed neither out of context nor out of reach, Waits terming his eclectic readings a "natural progression," something which facilitated the step from pizza parlor to stage, the influence of Kerouac, the Troubadour auditions, and the record contract, somehow falling into place. His most important preoccupation lies not so much with reasons as with extending the process, cutting the distance between himself and the audience, and continuing to grow.

"I try to take myself up on stage and reach some level of spontaneity and just be as colorful and entertaining as I can without having to memorize it all. I want to avoid the unnaturalness of performing."

His audience rapport has at its base a kind of loose, breezy, slurred barroom humor, incorporating awkward instances and clever fumbling, rambling recollections and well-timed punch lines.

"I like comics. I like people who have a sense of humor about their stage pre-sentation. I don't like people who go up with a semi-professional slump and tell you about their internal hurt. There should be some sort of redeeming entertain-ment value to a stage performance. I don't like it when it's a church out there."

Waits performs alone, calling it "an express route to an audience." He has been an opening act on the club circuit for over two years, his experience stretch-ing from "banana daiquiri crowds to fifteen-year-old kids who just polished off a couple of bottles of Mr. Clean."

His next trip on the road will be as a headliner, however, a goal achieved with no small amount of concentrated effort. He has other, loftier aspirations, though: "Someday I'd like to own a garage or a used-car lot. That would really be somethin.'"

For the moment, basking in a Coors afterglow, Tom Waits would be content to pursue his craft, to record his third and most important album, *Easy Street,* and to watch its predecessor, *The Heart of Saturday Night,* do well enough to keep the ball rolling. He has no aspirations for Top 40 heroics, his allegiance to a verbal tradition clear and well defined, the best present example offered as addendum to hops-and-sage philosophy, the Palms Bar a backdrop, an L.A. welcome, a new beginning.

One evening, Tom DeLisle sat in Waits's car following a rousing performance at the Palomino Club in North Hollywood. "Waits drove out to John [Stewart, of the Kingston Trio] and Buffy's house in his '54 Cadillac with John as his passenger. His driving was so erratic, smoking and talking and weaving as he drove, that when they pulled up at the Stewarts' home, John crawled out of Waits's car on his hands and knees and kissed the ground in appreciation." Waits was the veri-table nighthawk he wrote about, enduring the early hours of the morning as he told stories, spouted snatches of poetry, and sang songs. DeLisle left at 4 A.M. but returned to the Stewarts' home by noon and found Waits still awake. "The sun was blazing up from the Pacific down below Malibu Road, and Waits squinted at it and said, 'I'm waiting for it to get dark again. How long does this last?'"

Onstage he fashioned his stage patter show by show, honing an eclectic syn-thesis of polished lyrical delivery with controlled frenzy. His rapid-fire transmu-tation of Beat literature, folk wisdom, and hobo wit sometimes eluded his audi-

ence members, but most critics intuited Waits's genuine art. Jon Landau, a journalist for *Rolling Stone*, reported, "Waits onstage is something to behold. He
bobs, weaves, smokes and snaps his fingers from the moment he enters until the
moment he leaves. He has now advanced to a point where his entire set revolves
around his command of the language. He raps as much as he sings, but these are
no average raps. He has become a master storyteller, and the whole set now
feels like one long story—beautifully told. He functions throughout at one of the
highest levels of energy I've ever seen in a top performer."

Behind Waits's stage presence and the energy of his performance was an
arsenal of musical influences that continued to stir in him new possibilities. One
friend of Waits's from San Diego, Francis Thumm, whom he had met in 1969, was
also a member of the eclectic Harry Partch Ensemble; Partch had created a body
of music that profoundly influenced and inspired Waits. Thumm, who had once
studied conducting with Leonard Bernstein, shared his experiences with Waits
with reporter George Varga of the *San Diego Union Tribune* (October 3, 2004):

> Tom has a background that he doesn't give himself credit for, a very old-
> fashioned music background, where you're making music in the home. He
> got a lot of that from his mom and church songs. When we met, that's what
> we found ourselves doing, singing great tunes by Gershwin. We'd sit down
> at the piano and go through all these Gershwin songs, like a couple of old
> men in the retirement home. Tom is great at leveling the playing field in
> music; there's no distinction for him between classical or any other style.
> He's a slave to sound and to music, and you have him from the instant you
> play anything for him. It's a very childlike response, and also very refined.

"Waits: The Beats Go On . . ."
Melody Maker
June 21, 1975
Jeff Burger

NEW YORK—Looking as if he might have just hopped a freight train into town,
Tom Waits settles into a booth at a cheap, noisy luncheonette.

After stretching his legs across a bench intended for two people, he orders a beer, lights an Old Gold and motions his companion into silence.

Over the sound of clanking glasses and silverware, the instrumental music on the speaker system is barely audible but Tom quickly identifies the tune and fills in its lyric: "Soon it's gonna rain / I can *feel* it / Soon it's gonna rain / I can *tell* / Soon it's gonna rain . . ."

Tom leans back and takes a sip from the beer delivered during his impromptu performance. "This place is really the pits," he says, smacking his lips and glancing contentedly around the dimly lit restaurant, "but I like it."

Tom calls his two albums, *Closing Time* and *The Heart of Saturday Night*, his "diplomas," explaining that "having a record out gets your foot in the door. You can't play these fucking clubs without an album or two or three. And even then, you're faced with a tremendous amount of competition."

Though, as he himself puts it, Tom Waits "ain't no household name," he is doing quite well. His dark-toned ballads, which conjure up a Beat poet's nighttime world of hookers, sailors, waitresses and truckers, have been covered by Iain Matthews, Lee Hazlewood, Tim Buckley, and, most notably, the Eagles (who included his "Ol' 55" in their bestselling album *On the Border*).

As an on-the-rise performer, Tom has encountered his share of instant friends and hangers-on; they apparently suit him no better than do large concerts or record company offices.

"You get a few breaks," he says, guzzling what remains of his Budweiser, "and suddenly, everybody's your pal, everybody's asking you questions and people are shooting you full of self-confidence.

"But songwriting is a very solo effort. You just come to grips with your own creative imagination and work at it and it's *yours*. You know what you're proud of in what you do. You know where you are; you know how far you've come."

He landed his first job in 1965, when he was fifteen. For four years, he cooked, washed dishes, and serviced toilets in a National City, California, pizza house. Then, all of a sudden, he began to switch jobs almost as frequently as he changed his clothes.

"I worked in a jewelry store," he recalls. "Oh, I was a firefighter for a while, and drove an ice cream truck. Deliveryman, bartender, doorman at several clubs. You know, just hanging around, trying to pay the rent."

While playing his version of "What's My Line?," Tom began to write songs on an old Gibson acoustic and to toy with the idea of pursuing a musical career. He performed at small nightspots in the San Diego area and then at L.A.'s Troubadour.

On Monday evenings when that club opened its stage to all comers, Tom would take the 150-mile bus ride up from San Diego; after standing in line for several hours, he would be called onstage in time to do only a few numbers before catching a bus that would deliver him back home as the sun was coming up.

One night in 1972, Frank Zappa/Tim Buckley manager Herb Cohen heard Tom perform at the Troubadour. Impressed, Cohen added the singer to his client roster and helped him get a contract with Asylum. A little more than two years later, Tom no longer has to hassle with long bus rides or audition nights. With much of his time claimed by back-to-back engagements, he can afford to fly from gig to gig.

If his music at all reflects the changes in his lifestyle, it indicates a desire to ignore them. In his songs, Tom remains preoccupied with the way of life he experienced while working late nights at Napoleone's Pizza House and roughing it on the job-go-round.

He also evidences a continuing fascination with the ephemeral ecstasies previously explored by such writers as Jack Kerouac, Lawrence Ferlinghetti, Allen Ginsberg, Ray Charles, and Mose Allison.

Like the Beat poets whose readings were accompanied by unobtrusive jazz, Tom utilizes a simple, jazz-flavored instrumentation. On his albums, he plays a soft piano and is backed by a small, bass-dominated ensemble. Onstage, he performs solo, incorporating a minimum of music and sometimes none at all.

"I'm doing spoken word now," he explains over a second beer at the luncheonette. "I'm considered a songwriter so it's something I gotta watch. But I'm getting tired of hearing myself sing and I like talking bits. I don't call them poetry, 'cause there's too many poets I admire; but they're in an oral tradition. I call 'em 'metropolitan double-talk.'"

Tom pulls a sheet of paper from his pocket, announcing, "This is called 'Easy Street,'" then drops the paper and recites from memory.

Recitation over, Tom lights an Old Gold and leans back in a satisfied pose. In front of him on the Formica tabletop are an empty beer mug, a full ashtray, and a few sheets of paper containing his handwritten poems. Tom surveys the scene for a second and says that he has to be going.

You might think he was headed off to ride the freights, read poetry with Ginsberg in some all-night jazz club, or get drunk with Kerouac. But Tom has never ridden the freights; he doesn't know Ginsberg; and Kerouac, of course, is dead.

Tom's world is not the one he lives in but the one he reads about and imagines and describes in his songs and poetry. And his friends are not the publicists, writers, bookers, and club managers who now surround him but the Jack Kerouacs, Allen Ginsbergs, and Lenny Bruces who people his mind's landscape.

Tom's recollection of an article by Nat Hentoff seems to sum up the singer's temporal displacement. "Hentoff was talking about the old days," Tom explains, as he reaches in his pocket for change to leave the waiter. "He said he ran into Miles Davis on the street; he hadn't seen him in several years and he was wondering how Davis would react to him 'cause they had been close before. He said they embraced and everything and Davis said, "We're from another time, Nat, and we need our old friends.'"

Tom leaves the restaurant booth, pulls on his coat, and looks up reflectively. "We need our old friends," he repeats. "It was just real touching, I thought."

NIGHTHAWKS AT THE DINER (1975)

In the weeks following Waits's important *Melody Maker* interview with Jeff Burger, he rigorously rehearsed his band for the recording of his third album, to be titled *Nighthawks at the Diner*. Bones Howe recalls in *Sound on Sound* (January/February 2004):

> We did it as a live recording, which was unusual for an artist so new. Herb Cohen and I both had a sense that we needed to bring out the jazz in Waits more clearly. Tom was a great performer onstage—Herb had him out there opening solo with an acoustic guitar for the Mothers of Invention, so that was a baptism under fire for anyone, having to yell back at the hecklers and do your show. I told Tom that he should use a piano instead, and he says back [*and Howe can almost perfectly mimic Waits's trademark growl and inflections*], "There's never one up there!" So we started talking about where we could do an album that would have a live feel to it. We thought about clubs, but the well-known ones like the Troubadour were toilets in those days.
>
> Then I remembered that Barbra Streisand had made a record at the old Record Plant Studios, when they were on Third Street near Cahuenga Boulevard.

The Record Plant was large enough to accommodate an orchestra with the mobility of recording consoles on wheels. Cohen and Howe came up with the idea of bringing in tables and chairs and filling up the extra room with an audience. "I got Michael Melvoin on piano, and he was one of the greatest jazz arrangers ever; I had Jim Hughart on [upright] bass, Bill Goodwin on drums and Pete Christlieb on sax. It was a totally jazz rhythm section. Herb gave out tickets to all his friends, we set up a bar, put potato chips on the tables, and we had a sellout, two nights, two shows a night."

Four shows were spread through July 30 and 31, 1975. For the proceedings Waits brought in a stripper named Dewana as a warm-up act. When Waits appeared, he began rapping out "Emotional Weather Report" before facing the band and reading the classifieds as they played. Hughart told *Bassics*, "Preparing for this thing, we had to memorize all this stuff, 'cause Waits had nothing on paper. So ultimately, we spent four or five days in a rehearsal studio going over this stuff. And that was drudgery. But when we did actually get it all prepared and go and record, that was the fastest two days of recording I've ever spent in my life. It was so fun. Some of the tunes were not what you'd call jazz tunes, but for the most part that was like a jazz record."

Asylum released *Nighthawks at the Diner* in October 1975. Asylum ads set the tone for the poetic booze-fueled themes of the double-LP, an anomaly for so young and unestablished an artist:

> *"Tom Waits. A day late. A dollar short.*
> *His lips around a bottle, his foot on the throttle.*
> *Music underneath a muscatel sky."*

For Michael Melvoin, Waits's songs were a force to behold; they were a form of "top-rank American poetry." Elaborating to Waits's biographer Jay S. Jacobs for his Waits biography, *Wild Years: The Music and Myth of Tom Waits* (2006), Melvoin stated, "I thought then, and I still believe, that I was dealing with a world-class poet. My degree from school was in English literature, so I felt that I was in the presence of one of the great Beat poets. Tom's work was a counterpoint to that experience. I was amazed by the richness of it. The musical settings that he was using reminded me of certain roots jazz experiences that I thought were very, very appropriate for that." The cover art depicted Waits staring out the plate glass window of an old diner, a photographic concept inspired by the Edward Hopper painting, *Nighthawks* (1942).

Shortly before *Nighthawks*'s release, Waits began a music tour to support it. On August 30, 1975, he opened for Judy Collins at an outdoor concert, an untypical venue for Waits. *Billboard* took notice: "Tom Waits, with his dark rumpled suit and dark rumpled stories, was quite definitely out of his element in the brilliant afternoon sunshine, although he did take the occasion to offer some of his new work, which had every bit of the idiosyncratic genius of his previous stuff."

For the bulk of the tour, Waits supported singer Bonnie Raitt as a warm-up act for numerous shows extending through November 1975. At times, Waits still had a difficult time delivering his music to audiences impatient to sit through a warm-up act or his at times incoherent and mumbling monologues. When he appeared at Red Rocks Amphitheatre in Morrison, Colorado, as warm-up act for the Eagles, Waits was booed midway through his set. To the displeasure of the Eagles, they revealed the identity of the gentleman as the composer of their hit single, "Ol' 55." This did little to rattle Waits's Spartan reserve, for he had made an art form of testing his audience's expectations, and he had developed ways to deal with unruly hecklers.

In October 1975, writer Todd Everett caught up with Waits for another interview for the *LA Free Press.* "I have to thank Roger Perry, who was running the Monday night hootenannies at the Troubadour, for tipping me off to Tom Waits," Everett recalls. "While Waits's influences were obvious, he put them in a context—where the rest of the world was revering long-haired, sensitive singer-songwriters—that was bracingly unique. Plus, he wrote songs that were admired and recorded by Bruce Springsteen, Rod Stewart, and [the] Eagles without diluting his own vision."

"Tom Waits: In Close Touch with the Streets"
Los Angeles Free Press
October 17–23, 1975
Todd Everett

Although he will take great care to avoid the term, Tom Waits is a poet. He'll admit to being a songwriter: he's certainly that, and a fine one.

To his detractors, who can't seem to make a thing of him, Waits is a mumbling sot onstage: a performer who wanders to the stage drunk and mutters meaningless multisyllables at the audience. To his fans, who safely outnumber his detractors, Waits is that "something different" that we've all been waiting for. Many will tell you that the goateed street rat is a talent far too great to be ignored: the source of the first successful attempt to bring the Beat culture of the Greenwich Village fifties into a form meaningful to today's listeners.

Waits, in his early twenties, has absorbed this rich, influential culture with the zeal of a religious convert. He came to it in his mid-teens: a time when some of us discovered Dylan, some of us discovered swing, and when some of us are discovering Bruce Springsteen. The mid-teens are an important, impressionable age. Waits discovered Jack Kerouac.

"I guess everybody reads Kerouac at some point in their life. Even though I was growing up in Southern California, he made a tremendous impression on me. I started wearing dark glasses and got myself a subscription to *DownBeat* . . . I was a little late. Kerouac died in 1969 in St. Petersburg, Florida, a bitter old man.

"I became curious about style more than anything else. I discovered Gregory Corso, Lawrence Ferlinghetti . . . Ginsberg still comes up with something every now and again."

The sources became more diverse. Comedian Lord Buckley. Ken Nordine, whose "word jazz" was a unique combination of spoken stories and improvised jazz background. Ray Charles. Mose Allison. And James Brown.

"There's a fascinating album that came out in '57 on Hanover Records: *Kerouac/Allen*. It's Jack Kerouac telling stories, with Steve Allen playing piano behind him. That album sort of sums up the whole thing. That's what gave me the idea to do some spoken pieces myself."

Spoken pieces are what immediately sets Waits off from most contemporary nightclub performers. It's the same discovery that Bob Dylan made some years ago: that one didn't necessarily have to set all of one's words to music. ("If I can sing it," said Dylan at the time, "it's a song. If I can't, it's a poem.")

"Poetry is a very dangerous word," says Waits, "It's very misused. Most people when they hear the word 'poetry' think of being chained to a school desk, memorizing 'Ode on a Grecian Urn.' When somebody says that they're going to read me a poem, I can think of any of a number of things that I'd rather be doing. I don't like the stigma that comes with being called a poet—so I call what I'm doing an improvisational adventure, or an inebriational travelogue, and all of a sudden it takes on a whole new form and meaning.

"If I'm tied down and have to call myself something, I prefer 'storyteller.' Everybody has their own definition of what poetry is, and of who's a poet. I think that Charles Bukowski is a poet—and I think that most will agree to that."

Waits, raised in various Southern California suburbs, was a frequent commuter from San Diego to the Troubadour's Monday night hootenannies when discovered by Herb Cohen. Cohen once managed Lord Buckley and currently handles the affairs of Frank Zappa as well as Waits. "You arrive at the Troubadour at ten in the morning and wait all day. They let the first several people in line perform that night. When you finally get up there, you are allowed four songs—you can blow it all in fifteen minutes. I was scared shitless."

Nevertheless, the first night Cohen spotted Waits, a contract was offered to the starving storyteller.

Within relatively short order, Waits was signed to the then new Asylum label, his first album produced by former Lovin' Spoonful member Jerry Yester. *Closing Time*, the album's title, accurately reflected the disc's overall mood—late night in a smoky, all-but-empty barroom. Tinkling piano, discreet rhythm and Waits's growled lyrics.

One of the songs, "Ol' 55," was picked up and recorded by another Asylum act, the Eagles. That and other Waits songs have subsequently been recorded by Tim Buckley, Lee Hazlewood, Iain Matthews, and Eric Andersen. John Stewart and Bette Midler include Waits's "Shiver Me Timbers" in their stage acts.

A second album, *The Heart of Saturday Night*, produced by Bones Howe, was released, winning even greater critical acclaim than did the well-received first ("I've never gotten any real strong verbal insubordination from any reviewers"). The after-hours mood persevered and strengthened.

Waits's third album, a double "live" set, *Nighthawks at the Diner*, was recorded at the Los Angeles branch of the Record Plant recording studios, decked up to simulate a nightclub atmosphere, before an invited audience. Instrumental accompaniment is by a well-rehearsed band of local jazzmen, including former Mose Allison drummer Bill Goodwin, pianist Mike Melvoin, bassist Jim Hughart, and tenor saxist Peter Christlieb.

The reedman, who regularly plays with Doc Severinsen's band and leads his own group at North Hollywood's Donte's nightclub, seemed particularly stricken by Waits's gifts. "I'd been going to the club for some time to hear Pete's band. After he played on my sessions, he asked me to come down to the club and sit in on vocabulary. I was very flattered."

Waits describes his relationship with his record company and fellow artists as "all right. I don't invite them over to my house or anything, but I don't really know very many of them. They have a lot of faith in me over there, with the idea that sooner or later I'll do something significant." His sales are, he admits, "pretty catastrophic," with the income "barely paying production costs." Thanks largely to a constant series of barnstorming personal-appearance tours, the audience is growing. "In cities like Minneapolis, Philadelphia, Boston, and Denver, I'm a very bizarre cultural phenomenon."

It isn't all that smooth, though, even with the exposure. Waits recalls with a sure shudder a series of tours opening the show for Frank Zappa and the Mothers—whose audience, sophisticated though they may be, were not ready for Waits and his "stories."

"I did three tours, until I couldn't stand it anymore. It's very difficult for one man [Waits usually plays alone] to come out in front of between five thousand and ten thousand people and get anything but visual and verbal insubordination from the audience. I wouldn't do it again—it makes me look bad, and scares me. People will come and throw produce at you—literally. I could say that I don't mind, that you can throw it at me and I'll pocket the money and run to Venezuela. But after a while, it creates a very bitter attitude. It's excruciating."

Waits did learn, though, and his present old-suit-and-loose-tie stage costume dates from those tours. "There was no way that I could wear anything and stand out onstage. So I just did a complete 360 degree. They started calling me 'the wino.'"

How about the rest of the onstage attitude: the shuffling gait, the ad-lib appearance? "I know what works, and what doesn't, strictly by trial and error. People who like what I do have come to expect this narrative; this I-don't-give-a-shit shuffle that I've been doing for a few years. I'm aware that I cut a certain sort of figure onstage. It's the difference between lighting up a cigarette in your living room and lighting one up onstage—a whole different attitude takes over. Everything is blown up beyond proportion. I want to be able to go up and be a caricature of myself onstage."

Caricature, perhaps. But that's not at all to say that Waits has sold out. He lives in one of Los Angeles' less expensive districts (Silver Lake) in a home that could be classed by any standards as "modest." When on tour, he tries to stay in the least expensive hotels in town, avoiding his business associates ("most of those places don't even have telephones") and keeping in close touch with the street.

At home Waits drives a huge, black 1954 Cadillac, which, he confesses, "costs me more than a new car probably would. I get six miles per hour long distance, three driving around town. It eats, drips, and burns oil like crazy. It's comfortable for me, though; it's roomy, and I can put all of my garbage in the backseat. I've always had old cars and always enjoyed Body by Fisher and other fine automotive structure."

His friends include his father and drinking buddies at the local bar. For a while, Tom was getting along fine with his landlord, too. But now, there's more than a hint of suspicion in the old man's eyes. "Before, I was at home all day and paid the rent on time; he thought that I must be collecting unemployment insurance. But since I've been touring, I'll pay my rent in advance and leave home for a couple of weeks at a time. He can't understand that; thinks that I must be involved in something illegal."

Has success spoiled Tom Waits? Hardly spoiled. But, says Tom, hardly "success" either. "I'm not concerned about financial success. I just don't think about it. If anything, I've become more comfortable, knowing that I can sleep until two and hang out until ten in the morning and don't have to worry about losing my job.

"But I'm not a big star. I'm not even a twinkle." Waits's eyes dance.

"I'm just a rumor."

Waits now made the first of a lifelong series of charismatic television appearances. However, some of his bookings were as unlikely as his sharing an onstage bill with Buffalo Bob and Howdy Doody in previous years. CBS Studios lured him to Hollywood on January 13, 1976, to appear on *The Dinah Shore Show*. Waits's discomfort was obvious, as he told the BBC that same year: "I must admit that I hoisted up six tall, cool ones in the back with the stage crew before I actually went out into the limelight, and I got to sing one song and sit on the panel. She had a good personality. It was a little awkward, I must admit. I was at the end of the couch, but they talked to me, they tolerated me."

It was Waits's affection for maintaining an image most of American society found abhorrent that both attracted his core fan base while piquing the curiosity of his detractors. Undeterred, he intuited that it was the right direction for him. In a *Los Angeles Times* interview (March 14, 1976), Waits expressed this to Richard Cromelin:

> There's not much difference between what I appear to be onstage and what I am. I think people like that, that I'm not trying to pull a caper. It's

easy for me, 'cause it's not such a large jump. I don't have to get into a costume. I'm in contact and I'm in context . . . but all of a sudden it becomes
your image, and it's hard to tell where the image stops and you begin or
where you stop and the image begins. Any image I have, it's just what I do,
but it comes off as being very pretentious. When you're a bit in the public
astigmatism, anything you do seems like you did it so somebody would see
you do it, like showing up at the right parties.

Perhaps his stage routine was one-upped by Charles Bukowski in March 1976
when they shared a bill together at the University of Pittsburgh. Waits explained
his admiration for "Buk" in an unidentified European interview in 1976: "I was
real fortunate to be able to run into Charles Bukowski. We did two shows. And
that was probably a highlight of the tour so far for me. I mean as far as joining
somebody that you admire and enjoy playing with. I've seen him in L.A. He's
certainly a pioneer of contemporary poets. He's on Black Sparrow [Bukowski's
publisher], and I've been reading him for a long time."

Between the end of May and June 12, 1976, Waits was booked for two weeks
at Ronnie Scott's Jazz Club in London's Soho district as a warm-up act for Monty
Alexander. Waits got into an altercation with Ronnie Scott's manager, Pete King,
before he was ejected from the premises. The performances he was able to fulfill
only resulted in lukewarm reviews. Peter O'Brien, writing for *ZigZag*, met up
with Waits, who, quaffing from a pint of lager, was understandably bitter. Despite
his disastrous European visit, he did find his visit there productive. During his
free time he began writing new material for a forthcoming LP, tentatively titled
Pasties and a G-String.

Tired of being misrepresented as nothing more than a drunken-troubadour
lounge act, Waits devised a new strategy of interaction with his interviewers. To
Karl Dallas from *Melody Maker* (June 5, 1976), he disavowed being called a
"poet," much like Bob Dylan had in the mid-sixties: "Poetry is something that is
kicked around a lot and the word is used loosely. Loose as a goose. I don't have
enough of a thoroughbred pedigree to consider myself a poet."

To Fred Dellar of *New Musical Express*, Waits dismissed the artists performing cover versions of his songs. The Eagles were "about as exciting as watching
paint dry," their albums only "good for keeping the dust off your turntable."
Musician Eric Andersen of Arista Records, who recorded a well-received cover of

"Ol' 55" in 1974, was also the object of Waits's pointed criticism. When Dellar handed Waits the album sleeve of Andersen's newest LP, Waits brushed it off: "I still don't like him. I wish he didn't like me. We had a fight once because he was messing about with my girl. Y'know something? . . . it's really difficult to hit a guy who likes you, so I wish he didn't. I guess I shouldn't bad-mouth anybody though. I mean, who the hell am I? Still, I've got my own tastes and I have to say that most of the performers currently on the circuit don't, with the exception of a few, fall into that category." Waits saved a final volley of contempt for country rock. In 1976, Donny and Marie Osmond, on their popular prime-time weekly television show, opened with a catchy yet cheesy duet, "I'm a Little Bit Country, I'm a Little Bit Rock 'n' Roll." Waits, however, didn't buy it, like the rest of America seemed to, and perhaps he was reacting out of his foundation as a folk purist: "Those guys [most likely he was referring to the Eagles, who were based out of Los Angeles] grew up in L.A. and they don't have cow shit on their boots—they just got dog shit from Laurel Canyon. They wouldn't last two minutes in Putnam County, that's for sure. If somebody gets shot and killed there on a Saturday night, the Sunday papers say he just died of natural causes!"

In June 1976, Waits returned stateside. Some noticed that his voice sounded different. Musician Paul Body theorized to Barney Hoskyns that it seemed to happen upon Waits's return from Europe, as if he had caught a cold affecting his throat. His sandpaper rasp became an instantly identifiable aspect of his sound identity, much as a throat surgery accident would cause Miles Davis's voice to change him into the rasping Prince of Darkness.

"Play It Again Tom"
New Times
June 11, 1976
Robert Ward

Scat-singing, dice-rolling, songwriting Tom Waits is on the road in his '55 Cadoo. And in his suitcase of songs are the ghostly tunes of old cocktail piano players and the jazz riffs of Beat poets.

Tom Waits is crushed. The eclectic singer-musician is sitting in the stale-aired dressing room of the Unicorn Club in Ithaca, New York, and he can feel the whole damned room pressing in on him. He's tired and his mouth is dry, in spite of the Heineken brought to him by the nice waitress in the black tights. He's feeling spaced and dizzy, and he's coughing like a seventy-year-old wino stevedore down for the last stroke. Frank Vicari, Waits's tenorman, and Chip White, the young Cherokee drummer who is always awake and excited, and Dr. Fitzgerald Huntington Jenkins III, the bassist, are bopping about the little cell of a room like a trio of mad bats. Waits is watching them from between two fingers he has pressed over his eyes, watching them as if he were staring through Venetian blinds in the potted palm lobby of some cheap hotel. Is this what stardom is all about? Is this all there is? Is this like "anywhere"?

Waits's road manager, John Forsha, introduces me to the band and Tom Waits, Asylum's new big hope, a cult figure for the seventies. Little and savvy and street-tough. Like Springsteen, he oozes punkdom, but a slightly different brand. Literate, intelligent, Waits is musically influenced by old cocktail singers like Mose Allison, eloquent songwriters of the forties like Johnny Mercer ("One for My Baby and One More for the Road") and swing blues masters like Count Basie. He also manages to sound like Dave Van Ronk (the gruffest street-voice Jack, whoa), Louis Armstrong, and Frank Sinatra (catch Waits's song "Drunk on the Moon").

Waits stares up at me and nods his head.

"How you doing?" I say, gazing at this skinny, little multivoiced, multiselved and multitalented twenty-seven-year-old jive artist.

Waits looks at me again, one eyeball opening.

"I'm a success," he says. "Success without college. Driving twelve hours, the bus breaks down. . . ." He shakes his head, and his rakish po' boy cap falls over his closed eye.

"Where did you break down?"

"By the side of the road. By the side of the road. Always by the side of the road . . . the side . . ."

Waits is scat-singing, scratching his crotch, still sitting slumped like the last Korean War vet left in the VA hospital. Twenty-seven going on fifty-two. "I was hoping we could talk."

"Yeah, great . . . in between shows. Just remember, I'm a rumor in my own time. Or is it a tumor in my own brain."

Waits smiles and shuts his eyes.

I wonder if there will be a show. The kid looks too small, too weak, too ane-mic to get up on a stage; what he needs are urgent glucose shots, not a three-hour two-set gig. The lights go down and the band members stroll onstage. Not jumping like the Stones, not strutting confidently like the E Street Band, but as if they were out for a walk on a breezy, late afternoon. And then the spot is down, and then, and then . . . Tom Waits is bopping out front while Frank Vicari, who says he used to "like blow with Maynard, Woody, Diz and Prez, you know what I mean, Joe," very coolly puts the reed into his mouth and sucks in air, his graying electric Afro standing on end. A cool breeze of sound wafts across the spacious wood-paneled hall.

In Waits's hand is this old suitcase with its fashionable travel stickers fash-ionably half torn off. The kid is almost as beat looking as he was in the dress-ing room, with his belt sort of crooked, his brown tie so cheap it glistens and his threadbare black sport coat, also glistening. CHEAP, baby. This boy is a Bible salesman on a cheap shot to nowhere. At least that's the bit, and it all depends on whether this fellow with a half-assed scraggly beard can put it across.

Waits stands at the mic and goes into a little soliloquy. Behind him the bass player is uprighting right along, so very coooool, Jim, so very fine, Jack—boom-boomboomboom, whapwhapwhapwhap—and Waits is snapping his fingers and popping his body in time with the beat. That scrawny, wasted, pasted, sparrow-boned body jerks and moves, and the crowd sits there looking at one another, and then Waits starts in with his lines, half-talking, half-singing, sounding like Louie Satchmo, like Dave Van Ronk—like Tom Waits.

"We been on the road." "Boomboomboomboom!" "We been on the road so long, man, you get home and everything in your refrigerator looks like a science project." "Boomboomboomboom!" The bass player is smiling, the tenorman aloof and blowing. "It's good to be busy." "Boomboomboomboom!" "It's good to be busy, and we been busier than a pair of jumper cables at a Puerto Rican wedding, Jack. You know baby, ahooooo." "Boomboomboomboom." And the sax does his thing. "Wah oh wah oh."

And it's a bit like sitting in Birdland listening to Prez and Diz and Bird blow, baby, while outside it's drizzling muck and fifteen dudes with runny junkie noses and trench coats slouch next to the big doors with the stars' eight-by-ten glossies slapped on them.

The lights go down and the band goes into "High on the Moon," a soft, lyrical ballad. Waits plays his piano, and while this isn't Thelonious Monk, it's not pedestrian either. Nice touch, nice feel, nice pace, very nice all around. But Waits's real forte is words. The man can write lyrics:

> *Tight clad slack girls*
> *On the graveyard shift 'neath the cement stroll*
> *Catch the midnight drift*
> *Cigar chewin' Charlies*
> *In their newspaper nests*
> *Grifting hot horse tips*
> *On who's running the best*
> *And I'm blinded by the moon*
> *Don't try to change my tune*
> *I thought I heard a saxophone*
> *I'm drunk on the moon.*

On the word "saxophone" Frank Vicari blows, man, and Waits shuts his eyes and rocks back and forth, and the listener's transported right out of the room to Rick's Café where Sam is hunched over the piano, the cocktail man, urbane and chic and beautifully ruined.

The music calls forth a vision found in movies of the forties and fifties. It's a vision of all-night talks among would-be novelists and poets in New York cafeterias, of lonely World War II sailors standing out on Front Street hoping for love but settling for a pint of rot-gut rye and a flophouse floozy—the stuff mined by novelists like Nelson Algren, directors like Elia Kazan. And yet, that's not all there is to Waits's music. He takes the American loser/hero—the cocktail piano player, the wise-assed smacked-around rogue who plays the nags and loses the winning ticket—and infuses the figure with new life, in a style that is at once nostalgic and completely contemporary.

Of course, everyone doesn't think so. In *Rolling Stone* and other journals, Waits has been given a bad rap because he likes to do scat songs, because, with near free-verse poem-songs like "The Ghost of Saturday Night," he is consciously reviving the old Beat poet–jazzman's collaborations. It's true that hearing the tunes makes one think of Gregory Corso or Allen Ginsberg reading their poetry while Philly Jo Jones lay down some drums and maybe Gerry Mulligan blew sax; but why should anyone criticize Waits for wanting to revive that form? The question, after all, isn't whether it's NEW NEW NEW but if it's authentic. And Waits's music is authentic.

In his Unicorn performance, Waits's version of "The Ghosts of Saturday Night" and a long talking number that appears on his new album, *Nighthawks at the Diner*, are superb. The jazzmen obviously love the kid. They play in perfect sync with him, and as he sweats and shakes and lets the words fly, there is a moment when the stage is magical, spinning not out of control but pleasantly and beautifully like a great patched-up lyrical balloon.

The solitary sailor who spends the facts of his life like small change on strangers,
pauses in a peacoat jacket for a welcome twenty-five cents, and a last bent butt of a
package of Kents

As he dreams of a waitress with Maxwell House eyes, with marmalade thighs,
and scrambled yellow hair . . .

Great wordplay and great energy combined perfectly with the sax and bass create a hypnotic, joyous floating sensation. Waits has an advantage over his Beat predecessors, because he is first a songwriter. He makes the words and music fit. The Beats, in spite of their claims to spontaneity, had very little feel for words put to music. For the music of language, yes, but one or two listens to any of the old Beat-jazz combos tell you that Tom Waits is not merely cashing in on nostalgia. He is improving on the form.

Tom Waits cruises through his first set and bops off to the dressing room. When I enter to say hello he is shaking his head:

"Where are we?"

The voice is gruff and strangely mannered, as if Waits were in practice for old age. One feels it cannot be his natural voice at all.

"You're in Ithaca, Tom," someone says.

"Good, just wanted to make sure. Was anybody out there?"

"They liked you, Tom."

Waits smiles and shakes his head. "No, they didn't, man. They didn't know where I was coming from. They only laughed when I got dirty."

Frank Vicari ambles back and sits down next to Waits. In the tradition of the coolest bebop musicians, he is "under control."

"It was like an oil painting out there," he says hoarsely.

"Not that bad," says manager John Forsha.

"They didn't understand where I was coming from," Waits says. "Reminds me of Mose Allison. He's great, right? But he just got dropped from his label at Atlantic because people couldn't put an easy tag on him. Well, he's not a blues singer, exactly. And he's not really progressive jazz, exactly, and he's not pop. So they get nervous and drop him."

Waits shakes his head, curls his feet under him, and looks for all the world like a boozy leprechaun. I sit down, accept a smoke, and we talk.

"I started listening to music at a very young age," Waits says. "In fact, I was born at a very young age." He smiles, nods his head and furrows his brow. "Very young—and it was like George and Ira Gershwin, Jerome Kern, Cab Calloway, and the old Nat King Cole Trio—I always liked that sort of trio sound."

"Some critics I've read put you down for being part of the nostalgia market."

Waits shakes his head again.

"I remember that interview in *Rolling Stone*. It's OK. The guy who wrote it has two broken arms now. Of course, I had nothing to do with it. I can verify my whereabouts every moment of the night and day. But, really, that article's not fair. I like this style of song. I dug the old songs by Johnny Mercer. I always played them. But I do other stuff, too. Take a song like 'Ol' 55.' That's not just nostalgic, I drive a '55 Cadillac. That's the car I've always driven. It has nothing to do with nostalgia. That's why I never do any oldies. You can't improve on 'Minnie the Moocher.' Cab Calloway did it best. I'm not going to do anything old until I think I can do it better. I'm not at all into the musical retread tire scene, like say The Manhattan Transfer or The Pointer Sisters. They're just ripping off the past."

I ask Waits about his use of jokes.

"Well, jokes loosen everybody up. That's what was disappointing about them out there tonight. They only related to my crotch jokes. You bring them out if nothing else is going over. Hell, I like jokes, and I even like hecklers . . . they get things cooking sometimes. If somebody is screaming at you, you can say, 'Say, mister, are you married?' He says yes. And then you ask him if he has a picture of his wife, and if he says no, you say, 'Well, would you like one?' and reach for your wallet. Something like that reminds you you're in a club. I love the glasses tinkling, the lights, the whole scene. I don't like it if there's just the arteest and the audience."

Waits smiles, puts out his cigarette on his prop suitcase and winks. A young boy comes into the dressing room and introduces himself as the brother of another musician. Waits is delighted.

"Sure, I remember you. What's happening with Bill? We were on the road together in Buffalo and I talked him into getting tattooed."

"Let's see yours," the kid says.

"Naw, not right now." Tom replies. "I'd have to undress. It's across my shoulders and chest. An American eagle, though with this body it looks more like a robin."

The band breaks up, and Waits is rambling again.

"Got a bad taste in my mouth. I been drinking anything, man. Sucking on cleaning products, slurping down Janitor in a Drum."

I ask him if his lyrics are influenced by the books he reads.

"Yeah, well, I was always a reader. That makes me a little different, I guess. I love Nelson Algren's work, and I love Charles Bukowski, the poet. He has this new novel out, *Factotum*, and it's terrific. Talks about all the lousy jobs he had to take to be a poet. Lemme see. Oh yeah, I like Johnny Rechy: *City of Night*, *Numbers*, and *The Fourth Angel*. Rechy is writing a script based on *City of Night* and I might get involved doing the music. He's another one who was never fairly appreciated."

A student reporter with an oversized notebook comes in, sits at Waits's feet and asks Tom where he got his first break.

"My first break was a set of disc brakes," Waits says. "No, really, I started out playing a country club in Los Angeles. The golfers would come in wearing their double knits and saying stuff like, 'Uh, got me a twenty-two handicap and shot a double birdie on the rise, er ahhhhh,' and I'd be over there in the sand-trap piano bar trying to play original tunes. I lasted one night, and made ten bucks because one lady asked me to play 'Stardust,' which I happened to know. A bad start. I slept a lot after that. Slept right through the sixties. Never went through an identity crisis, never had no Jimi Hendrix posters on the wall, never ate granola, never had any incense. I was like a lion ready to pounce on the music scene, but I ended up being a short-order cook and janitor in San Diego . . . good day job, real steady . . . sweeping every day, just lucky, I guess."

"Do you get depressed when people misunderstand your music?" I ask.

"Well, no, if you mean do they have to know my musical traditions. No. Music, thank God, ain't school. There are no prerequisites. You either get it or you don't. Last night they loved us in Willimantic, Connecticut. I guess the people around here must be into the Blue Oyster Cult."

As he continues it becomes clear that, like all good monologuists, he is really talking to himself, working out which riffs to use onstage, sorting through a mental junk pile for the right lines. Waits is a natural wordsman and everything about him—his taste in literature included—stems from the forties. But he admires some of his contemporaries in the rock scene, particularly those who emphasize lyrics.

"I like Martin Mull. I like his whole bit with the easy chairs, and I like his music. He's an ex-teacher. I have some of that in my family—my father teaches Spanish at a high school. Bonnie Raitt, Jerry Jeff Walker, Guy Clark . . . all good songwriters. The song is very important, and I don't relate at all to disco, which is barely music. I'm not out to get on the stage and be a spectacle; it's the work that's important."

Another student comes in and stares at Waits adoringly.

"Is your life different now?" the kid asks earnestly. "I mean since you had a hit record."

"Which one you talkin' about son?" Waits says in a perfect Southern accent. "The last album, *Nighthawks*, was booming along the charts and it got to 169, and then I got real excited when it hit 200 until someone told me it was supposed to be going the other way."

Waits smiles and curls up in his chair. He's loose and enjoying himself, yet he looks as though he's going to collapse.

The waitress, a nice girl who says she is an anthropology major, comes in and gives Waits a beer. He offers to shoot her craps for the tip, and she blushes when he starts juggling a pair of dice.

Waits springs up and rolls the red dice on her serving tray.

"Seven," he says. "You lose."

Quickly he fishes in his pocket and gives her a dollar.

"Just a lit-el joke, love," he says in a perfect Mayfair accent. "You know, we are taking the whole bloody band on a trip to the continent. Going to be staying at mother's summer palace. A modest palace, merely one and a half turrets."

The band breaks up again and peeps out the door.

"Big crowd," says Vicari.

"Yeah," Waits says. "We'll give Ithaca one more chance."

Outside, the crowd is bigger than before, and a lot drunker. There are Cornell and Ithaca college students, and some older people, many of them the type of mustachioed men who may have once dug Oscar Peterson, bebop, and the cool piano voice of Hoagie.

This time when the band appears there is a good round of applause, and when Tom Waits bops onstage there is shouting and laughing.

"Uhhh, I say, it's been cold on the road," Waits says, the bass starting behind him. "Colder than a Jewish American Princess on her wedding night. Colder than a flat frog on a Philadelphia highway on the fourth of February. Cold, uhhh . . ."

He pulls up his coat collar, reaches into his pocket for a Heineken, lights up a cigarette and gets the fingers snapping . . . and this time the audience is with him. Next to me a couple of young guys start laughing, slapping hands, snapping their fingers.

"Oooooh, that wind, ole Mr. Nighthawk," Waits growls. "It comes up to me and says, 'Waits, you got to move, boy,' and the moon, the moon is rising out of a manhole cover and we . . . we talk on a reg-u-lar basis."

And the crowd is starting to yell a little, like in the old days of fifties jazz.

"Yeah, yeah, and go," and Waits's body, tired and small, is suddenly trans-formed, and he looks like the roughest, wiriest newsstand boy on the block, and he's cutting into his late-night flying freeway song, and the boys behind him are smiling and leaning into it, and it all keeps coming on through the night, one good tune after another, and when he tries to leave his fans are on their feet cheering and screaming, so he's back, doing up "The Heart of Saturday Night," and we are all out there in the audience rooting for him because he's made the leap over the edge. He's not a nostalgia hype and he's not a mere cocktail singer. The audience's enthusiasm and his own radiant, wiggy energy have fused and he has become fully himself. And there's a lot there, a lot of Tom Waits. If he has any luck at all, and if the audiences catch up with him, he's soon going to be the front liner wherever he plays. He's got one vote here, dads, 'cause Tom Waits is . . . if you can dig my drift, Charlie . . . ah, like copacetic!

Waits on being the voice of everyman:
Excerpted from "Sweet and Sour," Newsweek
June 14, 1976
Betsy Carter with Peter S. Greenberg

Critics call his style affected and his poetry puerile ("A yellow biscuit of a buttery cue-ball moon rollin' maverick across an obsidian sky"). But Waits sees himself as the voice of everyman. "There's a common loneliness that just sprawls from coast to coast," he says. "It's like a common disjointed identity crisis. It's the dark, warm, narcotic American night. I just hope I'm able to touch that feeling before I find myself one of these days double-parked on easy street."

Waits on developing new material:
Excerpted from "Bitin' the Green Shiboda with Tom Waits," DownBeat
June 17, 1976
Marv Hohman

Marv Hohman: Some guy sitting in front of me during your set the other night said, "Where does he get all those one-liners?" It seems to me I've heard some of them before, yet others seem like they might be your own.

Tom Waits: Yeah, I steal a lot of them from somebody else. There are a lot of tired, old one-liners hangin' around that aren't being used; it all depends on whether you can make 'em palatable for what you're performing and who you're performing for. I like to get a chortle or two from the crowd on occasion . . .

MH: Do you think you'll always rely on the same sources for inspiration? Can you keep hanging around greasy spoons and Greyhound terminals and turning what you see and hear into fresh, vital material?

TW: What you essentially do is just look around you, take the raw material and forge it into something meaningful. It's as much the way you deal with what you're dealing with as what you choose to write about. *Nighthawks* was a result of spending eight months on the road; it's just a lot of travelogues strung together.

When you're on the road doing clubs, it's hard to stay out of the bars in the after-noons. You got time to kill before the show. Then you hang around the club all night and you're up till dawn, so you hang around coffee shops. It stops being somethin' you do—it becomes somethin' you are.

SMALL CHANGE (1976)

In September 1976, Waits released *Small Change*, featuring drummer Shelly Manne, Jim Hughart on bass, Lew Tabackin playing tenor sax, Jerry Yester as arranger-conductor of the string section, Harry Bluestone on violin, and Ed Lustgarden on cello. Shelly Manne's contributions (he did not join the band for the tour afterward) gave *Small Change* an authentic jazz sensibility. Manne had performed with the best—Thelonious Monk and Charlie Parker, among scores of others—and was a prominent star in his own right with Stan Kenton's orchestra. His understated playing suited Waits's needs, because he never threatened to drown out the delicate harmonic/rhythmic interplay between the band members (to superb effect in "Step Right Up") with a powerhouse approach.

In the studio, Waits had prepared his material by strewing lyric sheets on the floor. By day's end of his efforts he was still tackling mere fragments of songs. In the evening he met with producer Bones Howe in greasy spoon diners, endlessly conceptualizing the process of the album. The experience bonded Bones more closely to Waits, enough so that he began to feel a genuine affection for this wayward artist.

Small Change is Waits at his most pessimistic, for he has conjured the pitfalls of his ardent subject matter—perhaps channeled through the spirit of Kerouac, who had died from a "Bad Liver and a Broken Heart (in Lowell)," to name one of the songs on the album. There is also the tragic demise of "Small Change," or Waits's carnival barker rap persecuting soulless American commercialism in "Step Right Up." Waits considered the album the apex of his songwriting skills up until then. To Francis Thumm in *Interview* (October 1988), Waits confessed that he "didn't feel completely confident in the craft until maybe *Small Change*, when I first put a story to music. I felt I was learning and getting the confidence to keep doing it. 'Tom Traubert's Blues,' 'Small Change' and 'I Wish I Was in New Orleans' gave me some confidence." To obtain inspiration for "Tom Traubert's Blues," Waits went to L.A.'s Skid Row with a pint of rye wrapped in a paper sack. After imbibing, he got sick, returned to his Tropicana bungalow in a dazed state of waning intoxication, and wrote the song. The startling revelation, as he revealed to Howe afterward, was that every one of the homeless men he had met on the skids was there because of a woman.

Unlike previous albums, *Small Change* was a personal and musical sea change for Waits. He had been drinking heavily throughout the album's development, which began an eventual reappraisal of his musical process and public image. In January 1977, Waits revealed to *Rolling Stone*'s David McGee: "I was sick through that whole period [. . .] It was starting to wear on me, all the touring. I'd been traveling quite a bit, living in hotels, eating bad food, drinking a lot—too much. There's a lifestyle that's there before you arrive and you're introduced to it. It's unavoidable." Its result is a trajectory of songs effectively conjuring a harsh, lonely world spun out of an alcoholic vortex.

In support of *Small Change*, Waits tirelessly took to the road once more, bringing the Nocturnal Emissions (Frank Vicari on tenor sax, Fitz Jenkins on bass, and Chip White on percussion and vibes) to a number of small venues around the country. Along with the success of Asylum's promotional campaign for the new album, the tour also brought the artist into a wider scope of attention. Despite the number of music acts that relied on flash and props to augment their stage presence, his was a smaller, more intimate affair. By interacting with his audience like he was working a small pub, Waits brought an element of familiarity to his stage presence. *The Houston Post*'s was one example of the overwhelmingly positive press reports of the tour: "You can go out and boogie in hundreds of places tonight if you want to, but if you'd rather see somebody original, somebody important—possibly even somebody touched with genius—you owe it to yourself to catch this crazy anachronism of a hipster."

Tom Waits, a pair of pasties, and a g-string:
Excerpted from unidentified interview with Chip White

"One night is Tom Waits's birthday and we had been playing 'Pasties and a G-String'—you know, that song on his album, and the road manager decided to hire a lady to come onstage in the middle of that tune and he didn't tell Tom about it. So we got to that part of the concert, we played the tune and this lady comes up, looks like out of the audience, you know, he thought she was just somebody coming out of the audience, and she begins to take off her clothes and she gets down to pasties and everybody's like . . . this is in Cleveland, a club called the Agora in Cleveland, Ohio. It was 1976/77 in there, probably '76. So she came onstage and began to dance with him and he got into it right away 'cause he thought 'wow, this is just somebody out of the audience.' He didn't know that she was really a professional dancer; so she started dancing and then she started to take off her clothes and she unzipped her dress, man, and she stepped out and she had pasties and a G-string on. That was a funny night. So after that, every town that we played, he had the road manager call up a stripper and she would come up out of the audience. We started to rate the strippers. We played about fifty or sixty cities, so there was one every night. Madison, Wisconsin, actually was the best stripper. We had Los Angeles and San Francisco, Salt Lake City, Chicago, Phoenix. We did it across the country in every town so we were kind of like judging, checking out to see who was best."

At the Shaboo Inn in Willimantic, Connecticut, on November 9, 1976, David "Lefty" Foster, a vocalist for The Foster Brothers, recalled one memorable Waits performance.

Tom Waits, a piano, and a cat:
excerpted from "Memorable Nights at the Shaboo—Concert Saturday Marks Twenty-Fifth Anniversary of Roadhouse's Closing," *Hartford Courant*
August 12, 2007
Eric R. Danton

"There were like twelve people the first night we booked him, and in the middle of the show—he's chain-smoking at the piano, and the bass player and the drummer are there, and all of a sudden, one of the Shaboo cats—we had cats—jumped up on the piano and started walking across the piano while he was playing, and Tom was enamored by the cat," Foster says. "At the end of the night, he's up in the office, he's kind of mumbling and chain-smoking, going, 'Lefty, this is a great place. I really dug it.' I had my head tilted, going, 'Tom, there was nobody here. What could possibly get you off about the place when there was nobody here?' He goes, 'Man, the vibe, the cat—everything was just great.'" Waits's booking agent sent the singer back to Willimantic eight weeks later in the tour, after the album had attracted more attention, and this time the one-thousand-capacity

Shaboo sold out in advance. Foster recalls, "At the end of the night, I'm paying him again up in the office, and I said, 'Tom, a little better this time,' and he goes, 'Nah, it was better the first time.'"

Waits's television appearances continued to be uniquely rewarding, even if the core demographic of prime-time television often miscalculated the depth of Waits's talents. Emmy-award-winning television director Don Roy King, then director of *The Mike Douglas Show*, remembers one booking in 1976.

Tom Waits and the Mike Douglas show:
excerpted from **open e-mail to Blue Valentines (Italian Tom Waits Fan Club)**
Don Roy King

It was a great hook, I thought. He started his set in character, sort of a half-buzzed derelict with the voice of a bulldozer, slurring his way through a metaphor-rich stream of semiconsciousness. It was 1973. Reno Sweeney's, a small club in Manhattan. "Tom Waits" the program said, the opening act for a lovely, thin-voiced flight attendant turned cabaret singer (turned flight attendant, I'll bet). I couldn't wait for him to drop the act, to see what he was really like, to hear how he really sounded. Well, song after song went by. Each rich and gutsy. Each with its own syncopated stutter-step of urban images and dark-side tales. Some were brash. Some were tender. All were captivating. The moods swung and flipped and flayed. But Tom never changed. He played the role straight through. He never looked at us. Never smoothed out the gravel. Never put out his cigarette. (He did balance it on his stool once when he sat down to play the piano.) The whole set as that derelict. A gutsy, shrewd act, I thought. Fast-forward. 1976. I was directing *The Mike Douglas Show* in Philadelphia. The name Tom Waits came up in a booking meeting. He had a new album, I think. A press release had been sent to our head booker. I was the only one on the staff who knew the name. "He's great," I said, "the night I saw him he played this character onstage, sort of a beatnik street poet. Let's give him a shot." We did. One week later during rehearsals, I got a panic call. "Tom Waits isn't here yet. The car picked him up but nobody's seen him!" Well, someone had seen him, actually; and that was the problem. The security guard at the door wouldn't let him in. "There is no chance," he thought, "that this guy is on the show! Our guests own combs, razors, and shoes, well, at least shoes with laces!" My stage manager rushed out to get him. Tom was asleep in the lobby. Now it was my turn to panic. Tom Waits shuffled into the studio, mumbling something about South Philly, scratching a three-day beard, balancing an inch-and-a-half ash on a nonfiltered cigarette. "Oh my God," I thought, "it wasn't an act! I pushed for this guy to be on our national television show, and he's going to panhandle the audience!" We didn't have time to rehearse. I sent Tom up to the bandleader, Joe Massimino, to go over his charts; we opened up the house, and set for the show. Ten minutes later, Mike Douglas stormed into the control room. "Who is that?! I just stopped in the green room to say hi to the guests and there's some homeless guy in there asleep! Don't we have any security here!" "It's OK, Mike," I blustered (in a tone that is now known as "Clinton Under Oath"). "He is a guest. That's Tom Waits. Jazz singer. It's just a role he plays. You'll love him." Mentally, I was typing my resume. The first half of the show went by in a blur. I can't remember who the cohost was that week—Shecky Green, Red Skelton, perhaps. Maybe Joey Heatherton, Robert Goulet, Roy Clark—some name of '70s popular culture. I can't remember any other guests either. Could have been Professor Irwin Corey, Shari Lewis, the Amazing Kreskin, I don't know. But what I do remember is Tom Waits. And I'll bet every member of that staff and crew, every member of the studio and home audience remembers him, too. Tom knocked 'em dead! Mike introduced him. "A new talent on the cabaret scene, blah-blah-blah." Something like that. And then suddenly, there was Tom and all the regular rhythms of television talk skidded from 4/4 time into some beat only three-armed drummers could play. Mike was asking simple "how did you get started" kinds of prewritten questions, but Tom was answering in this otherworldly, or rather underworldly way. He was sputtering and wheezing and barely intelligible but genuinely poetic. Street poetic. His answers sounded like quotes from some Clifford Odets Depression play. Mike was getting nervous. I was holding my breath. "Well, why don't you sing for us, Tom," Mike said, after a quick glance to his floor producer who suddenly didn't know which cue card to hold next. I'd never heard the control room so quiet. Tom got up, lurched to the performance area, and began. "Small Change got rained on with his own .38 and nobody flinched down by the arcade. . . ." Right there on the chirpy, sparkling, squeaky-clean *Mike Douglas Show*, some urban lowlife named Small Change died in the street, shot by his own handgun, left to lie in the gutter. "Small Change got rained on with his own .38 and no one's gone over to close his eyes and there's a racing form in his pocket, circled 'Blue Boots' in the third." There were "naked mannequins with Cheshire grins," "raconteurs and roustabouts" saying "Buddy, come on in." Cops telling jokes about "some whorehouse in Seattle." It was a first for national daytime TV. "Small Change got rained on with his own .38. and a fistful of dollars can't change that and some- one copped his watch fob and someone got his ring and the newsboy got his porkpie Stetson hat." I glanced over at Mike's monitor. He was hooked. I saw that small, crooked smile of his, the one that meant he liked what he saw. I always believed that Mike's success was due mostly to his unselfish love of performers doing well. He didn't mind being upstaged by his guests. If they got big laughs or standing ovations he was thrilled. They'd scored on his show, and he loved it. Well, he was loving this. Tom was mesmerizing and he knew it. We all knew it. "And the tuberculosis old men at the Nelson wheeze and cough and someone will head South until this whole thing cools off cause Small Change got rained on with his own .38." In three riveting minutes the painting was done. It was harsh and hard-edged and very real. But there was an abstract rush to it, too. Some steady hand had splattered reds and blacks and yellows in a way that opened up a dark and unknown world and let us in. We'd been escorted to those back- streets we fear, those alleys we've never seen after dark. And there we met and almost got to know some poor loser named Small Change. I almost sent flowers. Mike jumped up at the end, rushed over to Tom. I could tell he was surprised and happy and relieved (not nearly as relieved as his director, however). I seem to remember Mike putting his arm around him, probably catching his ring on the rip in Tom's jacket. Tom mumbled a thank-you, and the show went on. The next day we had another ninety minutes to fill. I'm sure we did it with Dolly Parton or Dom DeLuise or Rosemary Clooney. But things were never quite the same. Every camera operator, every band member, every writer on that show did Tom Waits impressions for weeks. I heard Mike himself break into a "Small Change" refrain at least twice. And to this day, I'll bet fifty people tell this story as one of their highlights from the good old days.

Tom Waits on his seamy listening pleasures:
Excerpted from The Mike Douglas Show, **KYW Studios, Philadelphia, PA**
November 19, 1976
Mike Douglas

Mike Douglas: All of us, when we're growing up, we love music, I particularly did. Who were you listening to when you were thinking about this?

Tom Waits: Oh, I liked Mississippi John Hurt, I like Hubert Selby Junior. I like Chuck E. Weiss and I like Lord Buckley, Neal Cassady and George Shearing, and Symphony Sid. I listen to Cole Porter, George and Ira Gershwin, Irving Berlin, Jerome Kern, Johnny Mercer . . .

MD: Wait, wait, wait. You just hit upon a guy I think had a special quality. Even when he got "fat," as they say, and successful, he still had that wonderful earthy quality about him. I was at a party with him and I was sitting with him, just like you are sitting, just singing. That was marvelous. Johnny Mercer, boy he was a giant. He . . .

TW: Yeah, I agree. I have a lot of the 78s of his as a matter of fact.

MD: You came from a middle-class background. Even though you sing about the seamy side of life. How did you learn about the seamy side of life? Did you hang out with some guys that were on their uppers, or what?

TW: Oh, I don't consider myself seamy, really. You know?

MD: No, I didn't say you were seamy. I said, you convey that. You know, in what you do.

TW: That's my own frame of reference I guess, you know. I played some real toilets.

MD: I did my share of that too! Believe it or not! I played some great ones, boy! Gussy's Kentucky Lounge in Chicago . . .

TW: Oh, I was there last night.

"Tom Waits for No One?"
Northeastern Ohio Scene
December 23–29, 1976
Jim Gerard

With this guy they call Tom Waits, the accent, of course, is on the bizarre. Bizarre was the word of the day when Tom Waits rolled into Cleveland to play to a sold-out Agora crowd two Mondays ago. The very minute he hit town people started acting strange, trying to change their modes of life to suit his fancy. Disc jockeys started talking all gravelly and hoarse, and everyone drank a lot. The music business felt his presence, and in short, people started acting bizarre. I walked around the early part of last Monday talking in bebop phrases and, generally, acting stupid.

The Elektra Record's Cleveland man, Fred Toedtman, had his hands full planning an evening nobody would forget.

First, he planned (with a little help from *Scene* Extra Curricular Activities Board) a prepress reception at the New Era Cinema for the guys in the record business. Then, there was a formal (brain damage) press party below the Agora before the concert began at 9 P.M. Then, of course, there was the concert itself and the finale of finales—a real, live stripper, Bunny O'Hare, bounded onstage during Waits's set, shook her stuff and danced with the seedy character in question. And on and on. . . .

It's too bad all of you couldn't have been in my shoes last Monday. Because if you had been, you would have been able to see several dozen normal people acting like fools and going out of their way to fit, somehow, into the general scheme of Tom Waits's existence.

The Agora management even visited every room and the Keg & Quarter (Swingos Celebrity Hotel on Eighteenth and Euclid) to pick out the most tacky and bizarre suite they had. It was a brash one with a round bed and really loud decor—rococo would be more the word. They were trying to give Waits what they thought he would want.

The joke was on them, on Elektra's Toedtman, and on everyone else who tried to pamper him that day. One gets the impression that Tom Waits would rather be left alone. When he has to deal with a lot of people, he hunches up and withdraws. A Bowery bum would be jealous.

As Tom Waits ambled into the lobby of the Keg & Quarter from the elevator, he was still miffed about his hotel room. He made them give him "a square room with a square bed. I couldn't sleep in that Marilyn Monroe Memorial Room they put me in," he had said. And, yes, the first thing you notice about him is that he smells stale—as funky as he dresses. When we got in the car to drive to WMMS (to tape Murray Saul's "Jabberwocky" talk show and do a short visit with Kid Leo on the air), I noticed that his street garb was wrinkled, smelly, tattered, and worn. If he's putting us on, I thought, he sure has gone the whole route.

We made some (very) small talk while in transit to WMMS. Upon arriving, Tom sat sucking piping hot coffee through the hole in the plastic lid of a paper cup and coughing while he chain-smoked Salems because he couldn't find Camels. We drifted into the control room where Kid Leo was playing a KISS record. After the song ended, an amiable Waits was handed a Budweiser and started talking to Leo about jazz. Then it was time for a few on-the-air comments about that night's show. However, Tom got distracted because he couldn't decide if he should put his cigarette out on the floor or not. He did and was asked to introduce the next cut being played, one from Waits's new *Small Change* album, entitled "Step Right Up."

Tom explained it as being a song about "the kind of guy who'd sell ya a rat's asshole for a wedding ring." End of the on-the-air interview. Time to tape "Jabberwocky" with Murray Saul.

With half of the WMMS staff huddled around the corridor, we were all ready for a hot discussion.

The first thing Murray asked the twenty-seven-year-old Waits (by this time on his third beer, with more at bay) was:

"The way you sing and the way you write, one wonders if you ever had a childhood? You're like a full-grown adult; the only thing there could ever be was a man. Was there ever such a thing?"

Waits: [*grumbles and chortles low*] "You, uh, mean did I have a childhood? Or was I ever a child hood? [*More grumbled laughter*] I grew up in a neighborhood. Well, I was, uh, born at a very young age and I was born in the backseat of a Yellow Cab at Murphy Hospital parking lot in Pomona, California. But I was actually more interested in where I was conceived than where I was born."

Murray: "Do you have any information on that?"

Waits: [*grumbled laughter again*] "No, uh, it's kinda hard to find that kind of thing out. But I was a kid, sure. My father's a Spanish teacher in a downtown L.A.

high school. I had a pretty normal childhood. I learned to handle silverware and all of that stuff. . . ."

And so it went for the better part of an hour. We then took Waits to his sound check where I would leave him until the Agora party.

So how does a normal kid with normal parents from Southern California grow up to be degenerate?

The answer, naturally, is that he doesn't. He isn't. No way.

Now, this doesn't mean that his voice is a fake, nor are his way of life and mannerisms. However, his stylized way of dealing with poetry and music comes from choice, not from being born into poverty. Pomona isn't exactly Watts, you know. If you had opened as many shows for The Mothers of Invention as young Tom Waits has in his career (the two acts have the same manager), you might get a little squirrelly, too. Seriously though, Tom Waits is a deliberate enigma.

He drinks beer instead of breathing air and totally engulfs himself in his image, but Tom Waits is by no means a derelict. His mind is razor sharp and his wit can be as charming as his coldness is disarming.

In an interview conducted about one hour ago before his rousing Agora set, Tom Waits proved to be less relaxed than he was earlier that day. And although we were in a quiet room above the Agora, Waits squirmed his way through the following dialogue—constantly complaining about it being cold up there and how he was nervous about the show and that he didn't know they were taping his show for radio and that he wanted to get back to the party and the bar and everything else he could think of to get out of it. Whereas the afternoon found him relaxed, he was all hyper about the show now, and his personality changed from clever to cold. But not without some valid explanations thrown in.

Below are the highlights of our discussion.

Jim Gerard: Most people are just catching on to what you are doing. I suppose the Eagles did a lot in getting your name around by doing "Ol' 55" from your *Closing Time* album.

Tom Waits: I recorded *Closing Time* five years ago, more than a year before the Eagles did that song.

JG: I know that, but most people don't, I suppose. Most people think you have two albums out instead of four.

TW: Yeah [*wipes his mouth nervously and lights another cigarette*].

JG: Your four albums are really very different from one another. You have really moved into a more jazzy style. Like the first album was very much a singer-songwriter album. *The Heart of Saturday Night* was a lot more street-oriented, but in a suburban way. Then, *Nighthawks at the Diner* was really funky and urban and very real. Now, *Small Change* is even heavier in that same way but with an even deeper accent on jazz and less production. Was all of this evolution intentional; was it a plan to get what you wanted gradually or was it just that you changed as you went along?

TW: That was one of the longest questions I've ever been asked and I'll guarantee ya that my answer is . . . I'm not gonna even touch that one.

JG: OK. How about this—your music has really changed a lot, right?

TW: I've been uh, writing songs for a while now and each album is, uh, it ends up being a separate project, you know. It's completely separate from the one before. *Closing Time* was the first album I ever recorded, and so it was a collection of a lot of old songs of mine. You know when ya go into the studio for the first time you get a little nervous and you don't know as much. Well, ever since *Closing Time* came out, I've been on the road ever since. Continually, I write all the stuff out here now and my schedule has changed a great deal. That is bound to have an effect on what I do and what I say.

JG: I would imagine that you try out your new material onstage before it gets recorded, if that's the case.

TW: I usually try to stay ahead of myself, yeah. In that case, it is sort of a blessing and a curse at the same time. The problem with that is . . . when you have a tune it is nice to be able to test it on the road. When I was playing small clubs and playing all by myself without a band and opening shows for people, it didn't much really matter what the hell I played onstage. I could have played "Fernando's Hideaway" and nobody would have batted an eye. It was entirely up to me what I played back then. See, nobody was really familiar with my stuff. Now it is a little different because I'm playing to people who come to hear me, and they want to hear specific stuff and certain tunes I do. That kind of ties you down a little. Up in Cleveland and around here I am doing a lot of stuff from the new album because that's what people here are familiar with more than anything I've done before.

JG: Tell me a little about *The Heart of Saturday Night*.

TW: Well, all of the material was written in a couple of weeks. Whatta ya wanna know about it? We recorded it in a recording studio. Did you wanna know if the engineer had a moustache?

JG: You used session people on that album like Jim Gordon and other well-known people.

TW: Who is people like Jim Gordon? He's a drummer, that's all.

JG: Most of the other session players on the other albums are great players, but they seem to be relatively unheard of.

TW: A lot of people haven't heard of a lot of other people. That doesn't hold any water or hurt their credibility. But, you know, when you decide to cut an album you sit down and decide what cast would be best to get a hold of. It has to do with availability and you see who is in town and who is not and who might be back and who is double scale and triple scale. Who is available has as much to do with it as who you would like.

JG: It has to do with practicality, I suppose.

TW: Practicality couldn't make it; he was out of town.

JG: Jerry Jeff Walker recorded "The Heart of Saturday Night" on a recent album. Have you heard it? It's sort of country, and I think a lot of your songs are able to fit into a country format, especially lyrically. Have you ever thought about that—I mean people doing your songs in a country style?

TW: Boy, you're long-winded all right. Let me see . . . NO! How do I answer all those questions? I heard Jerry Jeff Walker do the song when I opened up for him on a show once. I never heard the record or anything. What is country anyway? People categorize music according to their own frame of reference; they hear a pedal steel and it must be country. If they hear a sax, they think it must be jazz.

JG: Do you like country music? Ever listen to it?

TW: It's hard to avoid, isn't it? There always is that spot on your dial. Actually I like very little country music. I like some of the narratives, but country is a little maudlin for me. Musically, it gets a little insipid. I try and be as selective as possible with it. If you go into a bar or something and you wanna get drunk, it's OK though.

JG: Is that why you did "Big Joe and Phantom 309" on *Nighthawks*, because it was an old narrative?

TW: Yeah, I liked the story—kind of like a *Legend of Sleepy Hollow* or Ichabod Crane and that. It was one narrative I've always enjoyed.

JG: "Small Change" is one thing you've written that will probably stand out years from now. It's so cold and real. It's a true story of a murder, right?

TW: Yeah, in New York. It happens all the time. It's all over. I was there and some little kid got murdered. Stuff like that usually gets buried in the back pages of the papers. All I did was cover the homicide, so to speak.

JG: The *Small Change* album is really sparse, as I was mentioning.

TW: Well, it was all stuff I wrote in a couple of weeks. Real fast. It was recorded in five nights. The whole album was done live with no overdubbing. It was done on a direct two-track machine; everything was done on the spot while it was being recorded. I like the album. It's got spoken word on it, ballads, and a little comic relief here and there.

JG: On the first two albums you used overdubbing and a more elaborate method of recording.

TW: Yeah. The third, being a live studio album, had no overdubbing.

JG: Are you ever going to slacken your pace?

TW: Meaning what?

JG: I mean, will you ever tour less or record less ever?

TW: I don't think so. I got the writing covered as far as new musical fabric is concerned. I'm working on stuff for a new album now. Before *Small Change* was released I was out on the road, though. As soon as I get home in February I'm going to start another album.

JG: Does touring burn you out?

TW: Doesn't burn me out. I just wanna get home. I've been gone so long and I don't get any time to myself. I just wanna go home.

When our interview ended—he finally got too restless to continue—Tom Waits resumed his beer diet, enforcing each one with several cigarettes. His Agora set was everything people came to see; he put on the whole routine for them, always aware that he was the center of attraction, as he chose his phrases and one-liners carefully.

As Bunny O'Hare pranced onstage and began doing her (sparse) number, a surprised Waits played along. He put his coat around her and danced around with her as she shook her assets. When she left the stage for him to finish the set, he told the crowd: "That was great. I haven't seen my mother in years."

Some writers, like Rich Trenbeth, were impressed by Waits's grounded personality despite his blossoming fame. "I was a fledgling writer when I interviewed Tom Waits. He didn't act like a celeb at all, even though *Heart of Saturday Night* was a big hit. We became friends enough to hang in some seedy western bars together. He had an infectious laugh and we had one of the best nights ever." Even his band members were struck by Waits's humility. Chip White explained to

Barney Hoskyns that touring with Waits was a "traveling party" with a tour bus with all the seats removed, videotapes, and a kitchenette. At times the bus even picked up friends and fans as they traveled around the country. The refrigerator was always kept stocked with Heineken and they killed time with card playing. Waits threw his cards in like the rest of them (including the bus driver). "There was never any star shit with him."

Rich Trenbeth was one of the last journalists to speak to Waits before he left the country for an extended tour to the Far East in January 1977. On his return, Waits laid low for a while before resurfacing as a musical guest for the popular late-night television show *Saturday Night Live*.

"The Ramblin' Street Life Is the Good Life for Tom Waits"
Country Rambler
December 30, 1976
Rich Trenbeth

The shoes are those pointy, black Monkey Ward jobs of garbage-can vintage. The dark, narrow-lapel suit looks like it was pressed by a park bench. The skinny, crippled tie is barely identifiable beneath the food stains. The white shirt looks like it was packed in a back pocket. And the tiny, tattered burlap hat has trouble holding onto the thick patch of slippery, slicked-back hair. Out from under it all comes a voice that sounds like an old scratchy 78 record played at 33.

Tom Waits, the fast-rising street-rambling songwriter from L.A., is in Chicago for weekend shows at the Quiet Knight, a small, intimate folk club that once gave a boost to such names as Kris Kristofferson, Waylon Jennings, Carly Simon, and Jackson Browne.

Waits looks like he just stepped out of a shot-and-a-beer, factory-district bar, but his musical tastes dip heavily into country. He digs Red Sovine. Jerry Jeff Walker frequently uses Waits's song, "Heart of Saturday Night," as a stopper during his own shows.

The opening act is on and Waits relaxes backstage on a heavily bandaged crumbling-leather suitcase. A friend hands him a cold beer and he scarfs it down, chasing each swig with a long drag off a straight cigarette.

"You know I've been the opening act for a long time and now I'm just slowly starting to headline. It's another world. Used to open for groups like The Mothers of Invention and Cheech & Chong. I used to get all sorts of produce and crap thrown at me. Some nights I had enough to make a fruit salad.

"Since I was a kid I had an image of me in a dark sport coat and clean tie getting up and entertaining people," he says with a laugh that sounds like an old Ford pickup revving up. "Even though I've had to do a lot of other things to make a buck, this is what I've always wanted to do."

Waits is twenty-seven, but you could guess anywhere from twenty-three to fifty. With the lean look of a Depression-era down-and-outer and a gravelly Louis Armstrong voice, he doesn't fit into any particular slot. Or generation. He's a street man. But not a street punk. While the Dylans, Stones, and Springsteens meant youthful rebellion, Waits is just street life. Young and old, beginner and bum. Red, white, and brown. Down and out. The ultimate city-street rambler.

Waits already has several successful albums behind him, major appearances at top clubs from coast to coast, and a shot on the prestigious Chicago PBS Channel 11 *Soundstage*. He is just beginning to enjoy star status.

His act can't really be compared with anything that is or was. He looks like he should be standing in a breadline during the Great Depression. His music is a curious weave of 1950's jazz walking a thin line between music and early Greenwich Village poetry. He's as comfortable snapping his fingers for an accompaniment as he is playing the piano and guitar. His voice sounds like the end result of a weeklong drinking binge. And his poignant lyrics are not only from the street but from their debris-filled gutters. He sings of the blues. His lyrics describe the gritty reality of street life in a humorous way. He hits the all-night cafés and comes out with "enough gas to open a Mobile station." When he runs into a cold streak with the ladies, "even the crack of dawn isn't safe." And he's been stuck in small towns "where the average age is deceased."

Waits doesn't play the big concert halls because his music needs the mood-setting, small, intimate clubs. You must be close enough to catch the little nuances, like the way he works over a cigarette or shakes his head or laughs. You get the impression that you're in a neighborhood bar. In most performances when he forgets to light the cigarette dangling from his mouth, someone from the audience will casually rise to give him fire.

Unlike most of today's country and pop stars who prance about singing of the common man and life in the streets while they live the reality of champagne and thirty-room mansions, Waits prefers his pocket pint of whiskey, ham and hash browns in a greasy-spoon café. And it's not just publicity.

For the last six years, home has been a one-room $135 walkup on the outskirts of L.A., where he cooks on a hot plate and watches his old black-and-white Philco TV. When he's home, which is only about four months of the year, he spends his time mingling with friends in workingmen's bars. "Most of my buddies are regular workingmen, hacks. And many really don't understand why I'm gone from home so long," he says, guiding a drooping ash into a dead beer can.

If his songs capture the gut-feel of city street life, with its raunchy cafés and hard-luck hustling, it isn't because Waits is just a good voyeur. Since high school until his music began supporting him five years ago, he was in the thick of the hustling himself. His experience reads like a page from the want ads. He's driven a cab, worked in a liquor store, was a fireman, cook, janitor, night watchman, worked in a warehouse, jewelry store, and drove an ice-cream truck.

He was raised in L.A. in a heavily Chicano and Oriental neighborhood and admits with a long rumbling chuckle, "When I was a kid, I was pretty normal. Used to go to Dodger Stadium, was a real avid Dodger fan. I did all the usual things like hang around parking lots, had paper routes, vandalized cars, stole things from dime stores and all that stuff."

He admits he lives in self-imposed poverty and doesn't have much of a hard-luck story to tell about his growing up. His family didn't have a lot of money but they got along OK. His father was and still is a Spanish teacher in downtown L.A.'s Belmont High. But young Tom was more interested in learning another "foreign" language, the vernacular of the street.

"Street wisdom is something that for a lot of people is inherent. You build on it and become streetwise after awhile. You can usually spot somebody with it and somebody without it. I seem to fall in with people who I know have it. After awhile you learn certain things, certain expressions. You can communicate on a level most people don't understand. Expressions like 'Harlem tennis'—a crap game. And the highest hand you can get in poker is 'deuces and a razor blade.' A 'crumb crusher' is a baby. 'Face' is a good-looking kid or a nice-looking doll. A 'fat man' is a five-dollar bill. And 'He went up north for a nickel's worth' means he went up north to jail for five years—usually for armed robbery. I learned that when I was in jail. I go there a lot and they just know me. I go to the Barb Wire Hotel in L.A. for minor violations like drunk driving, being a public nuisance. Expired driver's license, jaywalking tickets."

Popping open a new beer, he continues. "A lot of the vocabulary is just inner sanctum—it stays in the streets, but a lot goes out to the suburbs. That happened a lot in the '60s with terms like reefer. Suburban parents started getting uptight about drugs all of a sudden. They had the attitude that we don't mind drugs, just keep them in the ghetto. We don't want them in our neighborhood—keep their vocabulary and problems out."

Rapping, Waits draws heavily from the streets, but musically his influences take some unexpected detours. He admires Jerome Kern, Gershwin, Irving Berlin, Cole Porter, George Shearing, Oscar Brown Jr., Lord Buckley, Peter, Paul and Mary, and Mississippi John Hurt. "My musical influences of songwriters were guys who are either old or dead and just not around anymore. They're a real incongruous group that somehow I had to fuse together," he says with an incredulous look.

The group's bus is impatiently revving, horn honking, because they were scheduled to leave immediately after the Quiet Knight show and head for the East Coast. Waits's manager saunters backstage to remind him that the guys have been waiting and are ready to go.

"We will but the boys will just have to be patient," he tells him and then returns to the conversation with *Rambler*. "I first got onstage in a small club in San Diego. It was a folk club where I got 'blue-grassed' to death. I was working the door, taking tickets at the time and listening to all kinds of groups. The reason I got the doorman job was because I knew I was going to play there. I was sitting there incognito—like in the inner sanctum of this club, hobnobbing, doing some low-level social climbing. I knew one day I would perform myself, but I was trying to soak up as much before I did so I wouldn't make an ass of myself."

Although he started as a solo act playing both piano and guitar, today he performs with a backup of stand-up bass, tenor sax, and drums. It provides him with a rhythmic, finger-snapping background that forms a perfect frame in which to place his quick-driving lyrics.

Waits traveled to New York to round up his group because he felt the West Coast was loaded with too many slick studio types, and he wanted musicians who lived and breathed the old club circuit. "In New York there's still a healthy club scene. These boys know how to wail in the blue smoke," he says, lighting another cigarette and appropriately blowing a lazy cloud toward the ceiling.

"I found myself with three previously unemployed bebop musicians. Except my tenor used to play with Maynard Ferguson and Woody Herman—he's been around the block several times. My upright player is Dr. Fitzgerald Huntington Jenkins III. It's nice to have something to fall back on. He was a doctor and went to a concert, saw an upright player and went out. He quit his internship, split for Europe, and studied bass with a guy. And my drummer grew up in Harlem in a drumming family. He was weaned on brushes. I got a black bass player, a Sicilian tenor, and a Cherokee and Afro-American drummer. We can go into any neighborhood in the world and hang out."

During another Chicago appearance Waits and the group stayed in the seedy Transients Welcome uptown hotel. And they could be found downing shots and beers in places where you take your life into your hands along with your drink. A heavily poor Appalachian and Puerto Rican area where you're liable to find as many sitting in the gutter as in the dingy bars and cafés, uptown gave Waits an abundance of material to put into a song. "I used to go to the Victoria Café, which was only half a block away in a Puerto Rican neighborhood. But half-a-block in a Puerto Rican neighborhood is half-a-mile. I was scared to death. Kept my money in my sock and walked quickly," he laughed, tugging at one of his socks.

"I don't do a lot of hobnobbing with household words. It's hard to keep one foot in the street because of how this business can be and this whole American Dream. There are different criteria for success—like the American credit card. But for me life in the streets is much more fascinating."

And if anyone should know, Tom Waits should. "I may go to fifty cities in four months and I got friends in Chicago, New York, Montana, Madison, Wisconsin, New Orleans, Seattle, Portland, San Diego, Phoenix, Philadelphia, Pittsburgh, Bangor, Maine, and oh, yeah, Texas. That Texas scene is something else these days. I love those Red Sovine songs."

Is Waits's rising popularity beginning to make the street man well-to-do? "I'm not on easy street by any sense of the imagination. I'm a rumor in my own time. I couldn't even begin to tell you how much I'm making, but I am making more than when I was driving a cab. I feel at times I'm residually in jeopardy with my record company. I don't pull in a lot of dividends. Most of the money I make is from personal appearances and I spend most of that on the band and the bus.

I made it to 169 on the record charts and figured if we could only get to 200 it would be great. But I found out it goes the other way. No I don't know exactly how much I'm making."

What would happen if all of a sudden Waits made it really big and started raking in the money? "If I had a lot of money I'd probably get even more eccentric than I am now. I'd probably have a complete reversal."

What would happen if he were offered his own TV special, like John Denver, with a multimillion-dollar contract? He didn't hesitate: "I'd move into the Apollo Hotel in Philadelphia and pay my room up three weeks in advance. I don't know what I would do with a lot of money. Well, probably the first thing I'd do is buy a new sport coat and a pair of shoes."

Tom Waits has a jazz moment at Ronnie Scott's:
Excerpted from "Tom Waits–Offbeat Poet and Pianist," *Contemporary Keyboard*
April 1977
Dan Forte

"The first night I was there," he recounts, "the club closed up, it was about two in the morning, and I was having a couple of drinks with the waitresses sitting around in their prison uniforms having a cigarette. Two old spade cats walked in off the street in trench coats and caps like mine. They spotted me immediately, came over, and sat down. We had a drink and were bullshitting. One guy was talking about Louis Armstrong, said, 'When Satchmo used to come over, we used to hang, we were thick as thieves.' I said, 'Yeah, right. I've got Charlie Parker's saxophone right out in the car. Give me ten bucks, I'll be right back.' Then his partner got up and went over to the piano—it was closed down and the lights were up. He started playing 'Muskrat Ramble.' Then the trumpet player, out of an old brown paper sack, pulled the bell of this old, bent, silver horn and put his hat on the end of it for a mute. You could close your eyes and swear to God it was Satchmo.

"Then the bouncer came over and started to try to physically remove these cats from the club. He'd seen them in there before, and they were 'unwanted guests.' I said, 'Wait a minute, man. Forty years of playing, and you with your gut, and your ink pens, and your cash register are going to tell these guys they can't play? These aren't a bunch of drunk hippies with backpacks trying to play Neil Young songs and get to Big Sur. This is a magic moment!' So I defended these guys like this: [*makes a fist*]. We got into a big scuffle and all got thrown out. The things that bug me about the music business came to a head right there."

Waits spent April and part of May 1977 touring Europe, concluding his stay with an appearance on the famed *Old Grey Whistle Test* for BBC-TV performing "Tom Traubert's Blues." Waits flew back to Los Angeles and once again made the rounds of his local haunts. On May 27, Waits and Chuck E. Weiss were arrested for disturbing the peace at Duke's Tropicana Coffee Shop. According to Waits, before they were arrested he and Weiss were handcuffed and held at gunpoint. As *Rolling Stone* reported, "According to the sheriff's report, Waits and Weiss came to the defense of a man who had crowded ahead of three plainclothes deputies in line at Duke's. The report states that "Suspects Weiss and Waits . . . yelled to the unknown male, 'Hey man, I've got these dudes covered . . .' and then told the deputies 'You guys want to fight? Come on.'" This resulted in a reported physical confrontation by the undercover officers who claimed that Waits and Weiss assumed a "combative stance." A further "sudden movement" by Weiss after the plainclothesmen had identified themselves resulted in arrest by gunpoint. Waits and Weiss were arraigned on June 8, 1977. They pled not guilty and insisted on a trial by jury in order to clear their names. After a four-day trial by a twelve-person jury in Beverly Hills, they were unanimously acquitted.

Waits promptly sued Los Angeles County for false arrest, false imprisonment, assault and battery, intentional affliction of emotional distress, malicious prosecution, and defamation of character. Waits's legal team asked for $100,000 in general damages and reimbursement of attorney costs and court costs. Waits won five years later, though for far less than what he asked for: he received a paltry $7,500 for his troubles. Yet, it did send out a clear message to those who attempted to engage Waits legally: that he was no pushover. Waits told the *Los Angeles Times*: "Now I pick up the pieces and go on with my life [. . .] But it was a long pregnancy. Our legal system is like asking a dead stranger to come back from the grave, find some money and leave it to you."

In August 1977 Waits returned to television, this time as a guest for friend Martin Mull, whom he had met when he was a warm-up act for the comedian in

1975. The resulting show, *Fernwood 2 Night*, featured Mull as the television host Barth Gimble and his Ed McMahon-knockoff sidekick, Jerry Hubbard, played by Fred Willard. Out of this appearance came Waits's most remembered and quoted television exchanges:

> **Barth Gimble:** Tom, where do you hail from professionally? Is it the Big Apple, as they call New York I think? Or is it Hollywood?
> **Tom Waits:** I live at Bedlam and Squalor. It's thataway.
> **BG:** I think we all lived there at one time. [Gimble glances at the bottle in front of his guest.] It's kind of strange to have a guy sitting here with a bottle in front of him.
> **TW:** Well, I'd rather have a bottle in front of me than a frontal lobotomy.

(Our research shows that Steve Allen had already used that joke, but it's associated more with Waits.)

Following this appearance, Waits focused on the recording of his next LP, *Foreign Affairs*.

FOREIGN AFFAIRS (1977)

Waits, it was obvious, was as prolific a songwriter and recording artist as he was a performer. He had been releasing one album a year since 1973, one of which was a double LP. Again Waits and Bones Howe brought in an orchestra, this time with arranger-conductor Bob Alcivar, to fully realize the ambitious scope of his new music. Shelly Manne, Frank Vicari, and Jim Hughart all returned.

Waits's method was a change of pace from previous efforts. This time he decided to record a series of demos first and spend time listening to them before committing more polished versions to tape. To Howe, the new batch of songs evoked a film noir quality, a concept that extended to the front cover of the album, photographed by Hollywood photographer George Hurrell. Waits sat for two portraits, one in the clutches of a passport-yielding damsel reaching from the shadows (she was actually a woman named Marchiela, an employee from the Troubador), and, on the back cover, alone, looking every bit the denizen of his own invention, "Bedlam and Squalor."

On September 18, Waits put in a hand for a cause when he agreed to make an appearance at the Hollywood Bowl for a gay-rights benefit concert billed as "A Star Spangled Night for Rights: A Celebration for Human Rights." The star billing featured performances by Bette Midler, Lily Tomlin, Helen Reddy, Tanya Tucker, War, and Richard Pryor. The audience was Waits's largest to date—approximately seventeen thousand—and he was scheduled to follow Pryor. Pryor, according to the *Los Angeles Times*, "jolted the audience, confused them, and in the end angered them." As *Jet* magazine reported, Pryor said, "They're not paying me anything to do this. Where were you faggots when niggahs burned down Watts? All of you can kiss my happy, rich, black ass!" According to Art Fein, who was there, "The audience at first laughed at his audaciousness, then let loose boos. The stage went dark. After ten minutes, someone gave the signal to get on with it. With people shouting 'Kill him!' and 'Fuck Richard Pryor!' the spotlight hit Tom Waits sitting on top of the wall. He was virtually unknown to this crowd, and decided it wasn't time to get acquainted. He wouldn't move. He just sat there smoking a cigarette for five long minutes. Finally they switched off the light, and a spokesman came out and apologized for Pryor's remarks." As the *Times* reported, "It was left to Tom Waits to recover the audience and he tried nobly with songs including the old Four Lads tune 'Standing on the Corner.' But his was an unenviable task—following Pryor and preceding [Bette] Midler. He finished quickly."

Bette Midler sang with Waits on *Foreign Affairs*. She had first met, and was instantly entranced by, Waits in 1975 at The Bottom Line. As she told Grover Lewis for *New West* in 1978:

> Tom lives . . . well, sort of knee-deep in grunge, so he was reluctant for me
> to see his apartment. . . . I kept after him till he finally invited me over. He
> acted ultra-shy at first, but he finally ushered me around, and he's got his
> piano in the kitchen, and he only uses the kitchen range to light his ciga-
> rettes, and then there's this refrigerator where he keeps his hammers and
> wrenches and nuts and bolts and stuff like that. He opened the fridge door
> and with an absolute poker face he said, 'I got some cool tools in here.' You
> ever hear a cornier line than that? I howled for an hour, and we've been
> buddies ever since. Tom can always get me tickled, and he really helped
> jack up my spirits after the disaster of that gay-rights benefit in Hollywood.

The promotion of *Foreign Affairs* left Waits physically exhausted by Novem-ber 1977. The stage now boasted a single prop, a street lamp, evoking Waits's lonely streetwise songs to great effect. The tour returned to Europe and Japan. Back in America, a music critic watching Waits perform at the Squaw Valley Ski Resort in Olympic Valley, California, wrote in the *Nevada State Journal*: "To grasp the Waits experience one must have total consciousness of lyric, look, and music. The singer drools his words through yesterday's beard, pouring them into the blur of an electronic hangover that smothers the ears with unintelligible metaphors. In the smear, the art of Tom Waits drowns."

Tom Waits on American street life:
Excerpted from The Planet Radio Show
Late 1977
Norman Davis

Tom Waits: Well, they're trying to keep people off the streets basically with all these police programs on the air now, and the image they are trying to create is that it is not safe to walk the streets. That's what they've done with this movie

The Good Bar, Looking for Some Good Bar. It would be frightening as a woman living alone in a major city, to watch a movie like that. It would feel as though it wouldn't be safe to go out anymore. Put four or five locks on your door, get a German shepherd, stay home and watch *L.A.P.D.* or *M.W.P.D.* I think it is damaging because it's destroying American street life, which is an integral part of our culture. It's scaring the pants off of most of us, and people stay in home more. . . . I don't like that. I don't wanna feel as though I have to be afraid to go anywhere at anytime. . . . They create the vicarious thrill of the streets, you can perceive it in a movie theater or on television, and they closely exaggerate the dangers and before you know it, people are huddled in the corner, like in L.A. with the strangler. First of all, they give him a name. That's exactly the way he wants it. He's been a nobody all of his life and now all of a sudden he's "The Strangler," and after every murder he goes and sits in a bar and he watches the 11 o'clock news and jerks off in a booth 'cause now he's *somebody.* I think the media does more to encourage violence than anything, 'cause it sells papers and it becomes a merchandisable commodity, you know? And then you go to a late-night café and the only people in there are cops and murderers.

Waits's self-effacing stage image was in part an attempt to shield his personal life from the public. However, the troubadour lush he portrayed onstage threatened to undermine the stellar reputation he was earning as a serious songwriter. Slowly he began to shed that image before he was regarded as nothing more that a second-rate Foster Brooks act. When interviewed by Bart Bull after the last show of a long tour, Waits attacked the absurdity of his alcohol dependence interfering with his work—after displaying an initial reticence to be interviewed at all.

"After a One-Night Stand"
Phoenix New Times
November 1977
Bart Bull

"Tom may be a bit . . ." and there were many long moments before he finished the sentence. John the road manager had a molded golden eighth note that dangled from a chain around his neck.

"A bit cranky . . ." he said at last.

Out of the elevator, take a left, first door on the right. John held the door open. Tom Waits was piled up on the chair next to the bathroom door and a couple of the guys in the band were on the couch. It was sometime after one. Waits had just played two shows in front of two half-empty houses and he had to pull his fingers out of the ropy lengths of his hair to shake hands. Then he headed for the bathroom.

While Waits was out of the room and my photographer friend Tim was retrieving the tape recorder I'd left in the car, I took inventory of the pile of stuff that Waits had dumped in front of his chair. There were matchbooks and a couple of packs of cigarettes—an obscure brand, smaller than most, called Delicados. Phone numbers with and without names scrawled on scraps of paper. A torn-off piece of the *Greater New Orleans Yellow Pages*. Half-buried beneath was a silver-scaled hip flask, the kind with curved sides to hide the bulge. It was all great material to toss in to a story about Tom Waits, and listing it helped keep me from dozing off to the lull of the musicians' voices from the couch. I hadn't been getting all that much sleep lately myself, and it was beginning to tell. I felt slow.

Earlier that day I'd gotten a message from a woman, a photographer who wanted to do some photos of Tom Waits. I called to see what exactly she wanted. "I'm not into taking pictures of rock stars or anything," she told me. "It's just that Tom Waits . . . he seems different." So OK, I can understand that, but I had a photographer already. I told her I'd see how Waits was, and if he really wanted his picture taken, I'd give her a call back.

Waits came back into the room, sat down and pulled off his shirt. His face was younger than any of his photos seemed to reveal; he was obviously tired and restless and none too thrilled with the prospect of answering some guy's questions while another guy stared at him through a lens. Anybody could have felt it.

My first thought was to call it, call a halt to the whole thing right there, get the hell out, get gone.

Can't do that, though. You've hung on this long, gone this far, so you might as well try to get him to open up, give you enough quotes to throw a story together, and get out of here. Try and start a conversation with him.

Except the answers came back in words of one syllable or less. I was trying to draw him out somehow, trying to get him to say things I could quote him on but no dice. Time to try a new tack. "I'd like to talk about Kerouac," I told him. Waits had obviously been influenced by Jack Kerouac, spontaneous prose-spewer, and one of the songs on his latest album, "Jack & Neal," was loosely biographical. Besides, Kerouac is about as close as I come to having a hero.

"OK, so you wanna talk about Kerouac." He'd pulled a deeply worn brown leather jacket from the floor onto his lap and was lost in contemplation of its every wrinkle.

Dead end. Things were beginning to look a little grim. "Anything at all you want to talk about?"

Waits jumped all over that one. "No. No! That's your job. You're the journalist. I've just gotta stay here and answer the questions, but you're the one that's gotta ask the questions."

I was tired. My feelings were hurt and I had no more use for this guy, no desire whatsoever to pull an interview of the shambles. "Look, if you don't wanna do it, let's not do it." I slapped my notebook shut and stood up.

"Well, I don't want you to ask me what I want to be asked—I can do that all by myself." He pointed to my notebook. "You obviously came prepared with some questions but . . ."

"I came prepared with some questions but man, you know—I'm not gonna . . . I don't want to sit here and beat my head against the wall." I don't know which one of us was glaring harder.

"Well, I'll . . . y'know, I'll answer your questions."

It got no better. I asked a long, vague, and rambling question about his stage persona as opposed to his personal identity, the image of Tom Waits as a late-night bar-crawler and how it related to his actual life—something like that—and he thought I was calling him a drunk.

"I'm not a drunk," he said, sucking hard on his Delicado, then shooting smoke out of the corner of his mouth. "I'm not a lush. I work real hard all year. If I was a drunk I don't think I'd have five albums out, I don't think I'd be able to stay on the road eight months out of the year." He was pissed.

"No, what I mean is . . ." I was trying to get things back on track. "Do people expect you to be Tom Waits the hard-living barroom character, do they meet you and immediately try and drink you under the table?"

He waved his cigarette in the air, a little streak of smoke in the room. "That's a line in a song. What does—"

"And it's an old phrase. What I'm saying is do people expect you to be just like the characters you write about, do they react to you or do they react to your image?"

"I don't know. Are you reacting to me or are you reacting to my image?"

"Hey, I don't know—that's why I'm asking."

"Do I look like a drunk?"

I almost hesitated too long. It would have been so easy to say yes, to say yes and piss him good and well and just get the hell out of there. With his hacked-off hair, his pale drawn face, his ragged black slacks, and his battered black shoes, he could have blended right into the scenery on the corner of any metropolitan Tailspin Alley . . . but the clothes and the hair were matters of choice and the paleness of the face was plainly exhaustion, not alcohol. I hedged. "How should I know? What's a drunk look like?"

Waits dumped back in his chair. "Look, why don't you ask me something about what I do, about writing songs or traveling on the road eight months out of the year. I've written a lot of songs." His voice was tight and pinched now, the coarse threads of his usual growl stretched taut. "Do you know anything about the tunes I've written, the . . ."

Up yours, Jack. "Yeah . . ."

"They're not just about drunks. They're about murder and car wrecks and love and . . . and. . . ." He sucked at his cigarette. "I write about a lotta different things."

OK, all right, let's talk about the songs. That's only fair. "OK, it seems as though your songs are all very American, very American subjects . . ."

"Which one?" he snarled. "Which song?"

"Your songs in general, your songwriting . . ."

"Which one?" We were glaring again. "Do you know 'em?"

"Yeah, I know 'em. It doesn't matter whether it's 'The Heart of Saturday Night' or 'Ol' 55' or . . ."

"That's two . . ."

"Or 'Pasties and a G-String'—look," I yelled. "What do you want? You want me to list all the titles?"

He was memorizing the ceiling. "Yeah."

I shut the notebook again and reached down to pick up my tape recorder.

"I can do it," he said in a low voice, just less than a whisper.

"Yeah, well, you know, that's great . . . that's swell . . ."

"And if you can do it, we all have to do it." It was John, the road manager. He'd come back into the room without me noticing it, and now he was making a valiant effort to josh Tom along, to lighten things up. "We will all write the Tom Waits songbook on the blackboard." Then he left us.

"Listen," I said, "let's just call it. I . . ."

Waits pushed his hand through his hair. "Look, I don't know what you want from me. I'm not a geek, I'm not a drunk, I'm a regular guy—"

"Hey, wait a minute, wait a—"

"—I take shits, I've got a girlfriend, I live in a hotel—"

"—minute, wait a minute. You know, I don't. . . . Either I . . . either I did a really poor job of explaining myself or you took it the wrong way. I don't know which, but I wasn't saying any of that shit. I was just trying to find out if the whole thing about Tom Waits being certain things, being a person who spends all his time in bars and stuff, if that really fits."

"I go to bars, I do all kinds of things. I do everything that you do. Except maybe a little more. And a little more often." He rubbed at his nose. "I travel a great deal, all over the United States and, uh, I'm in a nightclub every night. I play bars, mainly, still play bars. And it's got its moments, you know, and then again, you know . . . some nights, it's a pain in the ass.

"I get pissed off, I get tired, I get . . . y'know. . . ." His voice dropped off, still high-pitched and tight, just above a whisper. "Just a regular guy. . . . Right now I'm pissed off, I'm tired. . . . We had two half-houses out there, with a lame promoter who's obviously—" here he pointed to his forehead "—operating with an unfurnished apartment. I mean, the guy seems like he must be about a quart low to me," he said bitterly. "He had a very lame sound department and a real antiseptic little environment here . . .

"You know, I'm tired. I been on the bus. I don't sleep. I just got up. I haven't had a night off in three weeks. I've been entertaining and talking to journalists and getting my picture taken and playing in nightclubs and it gets to be a little too much." His voice was beginning to sound like a record being played while someone slowed it down with their thumb.

"I'm on my way home. I can't wait to get home and just get twelve hours of sleep . . . some twelve-year-old scotch and a twelve-year-old girl. That's what I want."

I wasn't so pissed off anymore. He was so obviously exhausted, I wanted to help out somehow. "Well, let's do one of two things then: Let's either start all over again and if I've been antagonistic, I'll cool out, or else let's just, you know, maybe we're better off just letting you get your sleep, whatever you prefer—but be honest."

"All right . . . why'ntchya go out and come back in, and we'll start all over again. We'll shake hands, you can introduce yourself, tell me who you write for and all that." He looked over at Tim the photographer. "You can just turn your back."

So I went out the door, shut it. There was reason to listen for the sound of the lock clicking but I opened the door again. Waits had his head turned away. "For Christ's sake what a fuckin' damn—" [*big fake voice*] "—Oh, hel-lo . . ."

Things loosened considerably. Tom started unreeling tales about buying hundred-dollar cars and testing them out by driving them to Arizona. "I've broke down in Gila Bend, Buckeye, Tucson . . . uh . . . Camp Verde—know that joint? Spent a night in Stanfield. On New Year's Eve. New Year's Eve. I went to a church, Pentecostal church, you know, Holy Rollers? And this old lady, Mrs. Anderson, put me up. I was in the back of this church—it was real cold and, uh, my car was busted and I had it at the gas station and she had me come to this four-hour marathon New Year's Eve church service, so I could stay inside. And afterward they took up a collection—the whole church took up a collection and gave me all the money to get my car fixed so I could get out of town. About fifty bucks—I got a new water pump.

"Yeah, I used to come here a lot—but I haven't been here for a while. I think the last time I was here was two albums ago. That's why I was really disappointed that nobody showed up." He was scratching under his chin with a matchbook.

It wasn't twenty minutes later that we wrapped it up. We made our good-byes, apologized back and forth for our initial fracas and then Tim and I headed for the door.

"OK, you take it easy now," said Tom.

But as it turned out, Waits and John the road manager came around the corner while Tim and I were still waiting for the elevator. "Looks like we're all going up together," said John nervously. I think he was concerned that Waits and I might start screaming at each other again.

No one said much as the elevator rose. I took one last look at Waits as he slumped back in the corner. He had his leather jacket on now and he'd acquired a matchstick between his teeth. It took us a moment to reestablish where we were when we got to the ground level, but then we were all walking the same direction—Tim and I to my car and Tom and John to the modified highway cruiser bus that was dieseling at the curb.

It was cold. I stuffed my hand into my pocket for my keys and pulled them out with a piece of paper that fell to the ground. As I bent to get it, I knew what it was, it was the phone number of the photographer who'd wanted me to ask permission so she could take pictures of Tom Waits too. I'd forgotten all about that.

"Later," called Waits, and the bus door closed.

Freelance writer Pete Oppel began his career during the early stages of the Vietnam War working as a Southwest Division Overnight News Editor for United Press International. He then joined the *Dallas Morning News,* where he became the first person to write about rock 'n' roll on a daily basis for a Texas metropolitan newspaper.

"A Rumor in My Spare Time"
Dallas Morning News
November 13, 1977
Pete Oppel

> *Never saw the white line till I was leavin' you behind*
> *Never knew I needed you till I was caught up in a bind*
> *Never spoke I love you till I cursed you in vain*
> *Never felt my heart strings till I nearly went insane*
> —"San Diego Serenade" by Tom Waits

Tom Waits, his shoulders hunched forward and swaying, his left foot tapping the floor, sat in an easy chair just in front of the only window in the room. The curtain was drawn across the windowpane. It was as if Waits was seeking the light, but afraid of it at the same time.

"That song was about a girl I knew once," Waits said about "San Diego Serenade," one of his few compositions that display any sort of personal reflection. "I was crazy about her," he said. "So was her husband. But that went the way of all flesh."

The moment was one of the few sentimental ones Waits shared. And it didn't last long.

"We're all going to check out of this hotel sooner or later," he said, casting his eyes away from the floor and peeking up out of the corner of his left eye. "I wrote that song because I wanted to show the guys down at the service station that I was good for more than just a ring and valve job."

Tom Waits is a full-blown product of the 1970s. He has no known musical background in the '60s like some of his Southern Californian counterparts—Jackson Browne, J.D. Souther, Linda Ronstadt.

"I had lots of jobs in those days," Waits said. "I was a labor organizer in a maternity ward. I rotated tires on a miscarriage. Then I saw this matchbox. 'Success without college. You, too, can attain the unattainable ICS high school diploma.' I also worked in a commissary on a Navy base and as a doorman. Had a job as a street sweeper. Best job I ever had. Chances for pay raises. Self-employed. I've worked a lot of different jobs.

"I was born at a very young age—I'll be frank with you. I was born in the backseat of a Yellow Cab in Murphy Hospital parking lot. I grew up in Los Angeles. My dad's a Spanish teacher and my sister's a Communist. And I'm an unemployed service-station attendant. My father got the chance to open a translating business so we moved to San Diego. Went to high school there, but got in trouble and dropped out."

Waits didn't seem to want to talk about the "trouble" except to say, "I'm a closet kleptomaniac."

Waits is the songwriter's answer to the newspaper reporter and his beat is the all-night cafés and bowling alleys, the strip joints, the tattoo parlors. Both offstage and on he dresses like the people who inhabit this world—a shirt that hasn't been ironed in months (if ever), a string tie with a knot that settles against his chest, a tattered sports coat, and a broken-billed cap. Waits said the man onstage is not a character he invented and developed.

"Sometimes it's hard to separate the two identities," he said. "I may exaggerate a little onstage, but I'm not trying to be anyone else but me. I try not to be compromising and condescending. I talk about things I know about. Deep down inside there isn't a man wearing a leisure suit.

"I live in a run-down hotel—the Tropicana. All room rents paid in advance. The other people who live there are four-speed automatic transvestites, unemployed firemen, dikes, hoods, hookers, sadists, masochists, Avon ladies on the skids, reprieved murderers, ex-bebop singers and one-armed piano players. The whole gambit—lock, stock, and bagels.

"But I'm big in Philadelphia. They keep putting me in Philadelphia. And Missoula, Montana, and Japan. I kill 'em in Japan. Little Japs with cameras go crazy over me. I'm also big in Brussels."

Although Waits has recorded five albums, he remains pretty much of a cult figure. His fifth album, *Foreign Affairs*, is only #120 after four weeks on the national charts. Really not that big of a deal and not as good an appearance as his last record, *Small Change*, which was #105 its first week.

"I'm proud of that record [*Small Change*]," he said. "As a merchandisable property with a residual future, it didn't have a Chinaman's chance. It reflects my passive-aggressive personality."

Waits, twenty-six, sang more on his first two albums than the last three, which contain more of a recitation style.

"My voice is changing, that's why," he said. "I'm just going through puberty. I'm a late bloomer, I'm developing a bit of a conversational style, but then I never was a Maria Alberghetti. Those efforts were thwarted by continuous self-abuse.

"But as far as my being the poet of the night—if you want to know about the night ask a cop, or a paramedic, a fireman, a night clerk, a newsboy, a bartender, a waitress, a club owner. They'll tell you about the night. Ask the people who sweep up after you. Or ask the people who sweep you up."

Tom Waits will be in Dallas Sunday night, playing shows at 9 and 11 P.M. at Faces. He has the perfect opening act—a stripper. But after this, and all the other clubs and all the other Saturday and Sunday nights?

"In January, I'm either going to Japan or star in a major motion picture," he said. "I haven't decided which yet."

When Waits was booked at the Memphis Ritz on November 2, 1977, his appearance caught the attention of the owner: "I thought he was a homeless man looking for a handout. He looked like one of the winos who would come in if somebody left the backstage door open. I said, 'Hey, what do you think you're doing,' and he looked up at me and said, 'Well, I'm performing here tonight.'"

It was this look that caught the attention of actor-director Sylvester Stallone, hot off of winning an Oscar for his self-penned and directed film *Rocky*. Stallone had been given carte blanche by Hollywood to pursue a similar film (he was a wrestler this time) as director, screenwriter, and actor. *Paradise Alley* featured Waits as Mumbles, a down-and-out piano player with ultimately little to no screen time (Stallone opted to feature his own vocals along with his brother, Frank Stallone). Waits's song contributions, "Annie's Back in Town" and "Meet Me in Paradise Alley," perhaps betoken the more positive elements of an otherwise lackluster affair. The film fared poorly at the box office and was panned by critics. It did, however, open doors for Waits, who had by then gained the attention of one of Hollywood's top film directors, Francis Ford Coppola.

BLUE VALENTINE (1978)

Tom Waits appeared on *Fernwood 2 Night* once again on May 25, 1978, hinting at the new material he was working on via a comedic twist. The mock host Gimble prodded Waits about his current music plans:

> **Barth Gimble:** Any new albums coming out, that kind of thing?
>
> **Tom Waits:** I have an album called *Music to Seduce a Divorced Waitress By* which will be out. . . .
>
> **BG:** That should be popular with a lot of people I know, yeah. Any seasonal hits, or anything like that?
>
> **TW:** Seasonal hits?
>
> **BG:** You know a lot of people do special albums; do you have a Christmas album by any chance?
>
> **TW:** As a matter of fact I am gonna be releasing a Tom Waits Christmas album, in the middle of August, it's coming out then.
>
> **BG:** Well look at that. The album will be in the stores. That's great. I've tried to find some of your records around and, I don't know, I thought it was interesting cause we were talking backstage about that plan your record company had for distributing them—hiding them in various fields around the country—but didn't seem to really turn the tide. Listen we could talk like this all night . . .
>
> **TW:** I imagine we could.
>
> **BG:** . . . except I just hate the prospect of job hunting. So we will be right back.

Though his newest effort was not titled *Music to Seduce a Divorced Waitress By*, the allusions to that element remain intact. *Blue Valentine* represents another musical tableau of low-renters, sociopaths, brooding loners, and the girl at the end of the bar. The songs strewn throughout the album's two sides are Waitsian paeans to a world gone wrong. They also addressed a lovelorn state, perhaps permeated by his recent affection for twenty-two-year-old singer-songwriter Rickie Lee Jones. Jones had met Waits in 1977 after she left school and became

intent on becoming a songwriter. Like Waits, her songs were tinged by a bohemian sensibility. Two years later, after meeting Lowell George, she accomplished
her songwriting objective; she ultimately earned two Grammy nominations in
1979.

Rickie Lee Jones on her new family:
Excerpted from Rock Lives: Profiles and Interviews
Late 1979
Timothy White

Rickie Lee Jones: I didn't have any real friends back then [1977] and I didn't
have any place to live. I didn't have any money. So I'd go sit over at the Tropicana
motel and rest. A guy I know, Ivan Ulz, was performing at the Troubadour one
evening and he asked me to come over and sing a couple of songs. This fella
Chuck E. was working back in the kitchen of the club, and that's how I met him.
I sang "Easy Money" and a song Ivan wrote, called "You Almost Look Chinese." A
little later on, Tom saw me there, and he and Chuck E. and I started hanging out
together. That was a high point in my life. Before that, I guess I had learned not
to depend on anybody else, 'cause once people start affecting what happens to
you, it's trouble. But I think Chuck E. and Tom have been my family for a while
now. It seems sometimes like we're real romantic dreamers who got stuck in the
wrong time zone. So we cling, we love each other very much.

Tom Waits on Rickie Lee Jones:
Excerpted from unidentified interview
1979

Tom Waits: The first time I saw Rickie Lee she reminded me of Jayne Mansfield. I
thought she was extremely attractive, which is to say that my first reactions were
rather primitive—primeval even. Her style onstage was appealing and arousing,
sorta like that of a sexy white spade. She was drinking a lot then [1977] and I was

too, so we drank together. You can learn a lot about a woman by getting smashed with her. I remember her getting her first pair of high heels, at least since I knew her, and coming by one night to holler in my window to take her out celebrating. There she was, walking down Santa Monica Boulevard, drunk and falling off her shoes. I love her madly in my own way—you'll gather that our relationship wasn't exactly like Mike Todd and Elizabeth Taylor—but she scares me to death. She is much older than I am in terms of street wisdom; sometimes she seems as ancient as dirt, and yet other times she's so like a little girl.

Waits's willingness to include Rickie Lee Jones and Chuck E. Weiss in his musical sphere, and to photograph them for the cover and inside sleeve, infers that they were important to its conception. Jones epitomized the holy trinity of wine, woman, and song, the embodiment of a free spirit not opposed to skinny-dipping in the Tropicana pool, or wearing a black beret, gloves, and vintage footware. Her friendship with Waits had metamorphosed into an affair that lingered beneath the public radar until the popularity of her debut album exposed it completely. Until then, she was hidden in plain sight as the "mysterious lady" depicted on *Blue Valentine*.

America's musical landscape was rapidly changing, leaving many of the songwriters who jumped on the bandwagon floundering in the dustbin of 1970s nostalgia. The Vietnam War was but a far memory for those who wanted to forget it; cocaine, not booze, was coming to be the drug of choice, especially in the advent of disco clubs and punk rock and its offshoot of New Wave music. Many of the stadium rockers were either resting on their laurels or had fallen off the horse completely, struggling to reinvent their sound despite opposition by their fans. Punk music took American youth by the collar and rubbed their faces into the hypocrisy of the Establishment. Dylan found God, Neil Young was consumed with caring for his disabled son, and Bruce Springsteen, the new face in rock, was brash, handsome, and blue-collar. Waits, intuiting the key to relevance was to strategize musical longevity, slowly began to reassess his tactics. For the remainder of his career, he made it a point to publicly advocate various genres of music as diverse as punk, rap, and hip-hop.

Tom Waits and the current music scene:
Excerpted from "The Slime Who Came In from the Cold," *Creem*
May/June 1978
Clark Peterson

"Blue Oyster Cult and Black Oak Arkansas stayed in the same hotel with me in Phoenix," Waits mumbled, scratching his furry skin and trying to sound sincere. "It was a real thrill for me, ya know, being only three doors away from your heroes." (He once said he enjoyed the Cult about as much as listening to trains in a tunnel.) "I like them," he continued. "Of course, I also like boogers and snot and vomit on my clothes." [. . .] [Waits] has an affinity for punk rock. "It may be revolting to a lot of people, but at least it's an alternative to the garbage that's been around for ten years," he said. "I've had it up to here with Crosby Steals the Cash. I need another group like that like I need another dick. I'd rather listen to some young kid in a leather jacket singing a song like 'I want to eat out my mother' than to hear some of these insipid guys with their cowboy boots and embroidered shirts doing 'Six Days on the Road.' I like Mink DeVille.

"I was on the Bowery in New York and stood out in front of CBGBs one night. There were all these cats in small lapels and pointed shoes smokin' Pall Malls and bullshitting with the winos. It was good."

Tom Waits on Fandom:
Excerpted from "A Rumor in My Spare Time," *Hit Parader*
October 1978
Deanne Zimmerman

"I ain't no prima donna. I want to keep one foot in the street; I think that's important. I don't like artists who have an image of themselves as a big shot. I'm listed; people know where I am and I get a lot of phone calls.

"In that sense my personal life hasn't changed very much. When I'm on the road it's different, but when I'm home I'm just like everyone else here.

"Right now I get up at three in the afternoon, go downstairs and get some eggs, hang out in the lobby of the hotel, watch *Days of Our Lives*, come back here, smoke some cigarettes and do a little reading. Then, as soon as it gets dark I usually go out to a bar somewhere."

Tom Waits on Bette Midler and recording:
Excerpted from "Nighthawks at the Chelsea," *Modern Hi-Fi and Musics Sound Trax*
October 1978
Larry Goldstein

One day Bette dropped by the studio during the recording of *Foreign Affairs* just to say hello. The topic of duets arose, and she asked Waits to try and write one for them. So Tom went home and went to work and came back the next day with a brand-new song, to be recorded that day, "I Never Talk to Strangers," which has become the most popular song on the album. When I asked him about the possibility of more collaboration between the two, Waits was intentionally vague and mysterious.

"We might work something out," he said.

He's eager to admit, however, that writing songs isn't always that easy for him. He explained that he found it the hardest, but most rewarding, aspect of his work. Recording studios, on the other hand, make him extremely anxious, and he considers them "cruel and unusual punishment. It's excruciating, like going to the dentist." In order to get the recording over with, Waits records directly onto two tracks with no overdubbing. It is essentially playing live in a studio. [. . .] In this way he can finish an album in four or five sessions. It also keeps the musicians happier, as he puts it, "knowing that they won't be mixed out or anything."

Tom Waits on suicide and sentimentalism:
Excerpted from "Tom Waits–Little Murders," *Twin Cities Reader*
November 17, 1978
Greg Linder

He sighs and although none of us in the room have heard the record, he's eager to explain. *Blue Valentine* is, characteristically, full of street bulletins. "See, I can't write about 'Dear baby, I love you and everything's gonna be all right 'cause we're gonna get married.' It's presented problems in my personal life as well. I've just developed a more and more grim attitude. I've got a song on the album called 'Sweet Little Bullet from a Pretty Blue Gun.' It's about a suicide on Hollywood Boulevard. About a year ago, this fifteen-year-old girl jumped out of a seventeenth floor window with a guitar. Never made *Crawdaddy* magazine. You never hear those stories."

Tom Waits and cynicism:
Excerpted from Direct News, WNEW
Late 1978
Scott Muni

"I don't know if I'm more cynical, I just . . . I don't live in a vault or anything. I mean, I could be driving by a church and I could see a guy in a tuxedo and a nice girl in a white dress and they're throwing the rice and they come down and the organ's playing and everybody's smiling and then they go 'round the corner. I would say that they probably got hit by a truck, ya know?"

"Poet and Person Merge into Paradox: Tom Waits Is Tired of the Life That Has Made His Songs Unique"
Dallas Morning News
December 2, 1978 (issue date: January 21, 1979)
Pete Oppel

Tom Waits was in a rotten mood. His show a few moments earlier at the Palladium had not been one of his best and he knew it. Not only was he sick, but some special effects, particularly a gimmick that gave the illusion rain was falling onstage, had not worked properly.

He sat in the corner of his dressing room, shivering slightly. Someone had been rushed to a nearby drugstore to get some medicine for the ailing Waits. He blamed his condition on too many nights on the road with too little sleep.

"This has been one long experiment in terror these last two weeks," Waits said. "The hardest part is no sleep and a lot of traveling."

It presented a strange paradox. Because too many nights and too little sleep are what earned Waits the limited reputation he has. Waits has been dubbed "The Poet of a Saturday Night." He writes and sings about the underside of life in a gravelly voice that has kept him off most of the nation's major radio stations. The closest he's come to having a hit record is a song of his, "Ol' 55," that was recorded by the much smoother sounding group the Eagles.

But Waits didn't sing "Ol' 55," a song from his first album, during his Palladium show that night. In fact, he didn't sing anything from the first four albums, concentrating solely on the last two. He bristled when he was asked why.

"I decide what I'm gonna play," he said, rocking back and forth in his chair, his arms wrapped around him as if that would protect him from the chills he was feeling. "I don't ask the audience [what I should sing]. I don't have any hits. Helen Keller gets more [radio] airplay than I do. I'll do whatever I want on the stage. They don't play me on the radio stations so when I get onstage it's my radio show and I'll do whatever I want."

But it seems illogical Tom Waits will ever have a hit single as long as he pursues his current musical style. He has a wide cult following (both of his shows with Leon Redbone at the six-hundred-seat Palladium sold out) and when he was asked whether he would rather have this following or "The Hit" he answered:

"I'd rather have twelve hours of sleep, that's what I'd rather have. I'd rather have twelve hours of sleep, twelve-year-old Scotch and a twelve-year-old girl. That's what I'd rather have. Right now!"

Waits said it's impossible for him to write on the road, although lonely people in strange towns are the subjects of the overwhelming majority of his songs. So when does he write?

"Well, first I inject a little marinated herring in my jugular vein, put on some Bermuda shorts, white socks, some wing tips, go out and sit in the yard with an umbrella," he says.

Waits has become so associated with the types of songs he's written, he's on the verge of becoming a caricature of himself. Tom Waits the person has created Tom Waits the character and the two are beginning to become indistinguishable. Waits, however, disagrees with this generalization.

"It's better than a career in air conditioning," he says. "I can do whatever I want. Nobody's telling me what to do. That's why I got into this. I can play an ax murderer or anything.

"Right now I'm doing my thing, writing and trying to develop—theatrically develop. Eventually I would like to go and do what I'm doing now—very disciplined—and do it, like, in New York, in a theater, on Broadway. I'm getting tired of playing beer bars. They all have bad plumbing, termites, and junk all over the carpet. I'm sick of 'em. I'd like to stay in one town for a couple of months. Go to work and do what I have to do and just walk across the street."

"Waits Bringing New Band, Same Old Clothes"
Santa Barbara News and Review
December 12, 1978
Charley Delisle

Tom Waits will make what is becoming his annual appearance in Santa Barbara at the Arlington Theater on Tuesday, December 12. Now on tour to promote his sixth album, *Blue Valentine*, Waits has made steady progress professionally since his earliest appearances in town at the Bluebird Café.

At twenty-eight, he remembers very clearly his own painful start in the business, coming up from San Diego on the Greyhound, working as a doorman in clubs, living out of his "Ol' 55" Cadillac (he recently sold it in favor of his dream car, a '64 T-Bird), before being signed by Herb Cohen after an appearance at Hollywood's Troubadour club, and then finally signing with Asylum/Elektra in 1972.

That Waits has arrived as an established performer and songwriter is evidenced by his work in Sylvester Stallone's new movie *Paradise Alley*.

"I was real proud that Stallone called me here at home," Waits told me recently. "Originally, he was just going to have me write a song. But he ended up creating a part for me, a character called Mumbles."

Waits has also completed the title song for a new feature movie by Ralph (*The Waltons*) Waite, entitled *On the Nickel*, referring to L.A.'s skid row, Fifth Street.

"I saw the final cut. It's a beautiful movie, man. It'll take your breath away. That man [Waite] doesn't fall into the category of 'bullshit artists' like a lot of people in this city. He's doing something with his conscience."

Most people who are unprepared for a Waits performance ask the Butch Cassidy question: "Who is that guy?" At first glance, he does not appear to be someone you would want to introduce to your friends: Five-day beard with goatee; black stovepipe pants that, ironically, would be in with the latest styles if they were longer; black, devilishly pointed shoes ("I got them in London. The guy that sold 'em to me swore these were the sharpest in town"); tight-fitting, black Our Gang hat; torn leather aviator jacket. Except for the jacket, all Waits clichés.

As it becomes apparent that the man is a talented artist, the question evolves to: "Is he really like that?" The crumpled, low-life look is an image Waits uses as a vehicle for his music. However, it is part of him too, "but with the ifs, ands, and buts removed. Onstage, you got no time for distinctions."

Waits and I have been friends since childhood. Before his current road trip, I spent some time with him in Los Angeles.

Waits at Duke's

Waits starts his day about 1 P.M., hunched over a cup of coffee at Duke's coffee shop on Santa Monica Boulevard, as if he is carrying the weight of the room on his sparrow-boned frame. The small, steamy room is packed full of struggling artist types and clattering dishes. Sitting piggyback on top of Duke's is the fashionably tacky Tropicana Motel. This is Waits's territory, his home.

After two and a half years, Tom has let go his old group and has a new band. "I'm changing my sound a little. Something different. I've got to keep it fresh. God, it was tough letting those guys go." Waits pauses and shakes his head. "It was tougher than that." Members of his old group worked with him on only three songs for *Blue Valentine*. All of the new people happen to be black.

"They," he says tongue in cheek, "are all Negroes. I'm the only spot in the group."

"I don't live in a vault. Everyone I see, I welcome." Waits speaks in a voice that has been variously described as a rasp, growl, and a bad exhaust. We are alone in Waits's famous room at the Tropicana, a room where your feet never touch the floor. Though some myths have been perpetrated concerning Waits, his apartment deserves everything it gets. Each step is supported by cigarette butts, magazines, album covers, Dixie cups, books, cardboard boxes, and every other product of pulpwood imaginable. All the horizontal surfaces are populated with empty old Bushmills and beer cans and bottles. He cautions, "Just walk where it looks trampled down."

There is a knock at the door. Waits yells, "Who is it?" A voice asks for Tom Waits. Tom calls back, "He's not here, try later."

He explains to me, "I live in a neighborhood that far from insulates me from life out there. I feed off it. But at one point, you really have to stop and go away and sit down and collect all of the things you've been through. So it's always done in stanzas. You have to be away to let your imagination work along with your memory."

Laying around the room are letters addressed to Waits that have been left at his door. They are from all over the country, and ask for autographs, personal meetings, or offer a place for Waits to flop if he is in town.

"I have a little room in Hollywood where I go—by Van Ness and Sunset, next to the Denny's. I wrote all the songs on *Blue Valentine* between here and there in three weeks." He rubs his hand across his face and shrugs, "It was a lot of work."

Waits thinks it is his finest album. He hopes it will do well enough to give him a break from the grueling road trips he is on eight months of the year and allow him more time to write at home. Radio airtime for Waits's music has always been lacking; his unique grumbly-growl voice and smoky jazz-blues, Beat-poet genre is apparently too foreign for the Pepsi Generation. Though Waits has long received critical and professional praise (Bette Midler, whom Tom is very close to, the Eagles et al. have recorded his songs), he still feels the need to prove himself.

"In this business, you're either moving up or down, no status quo. The album was a huge boulder I had to move. There was pressure, but it was my own pressure. Most people think, 'Oh yeah, he's the guy that writes about winos and hookers.' That," he says matter-of-factly, "is just not true. I've written a wide range of songs about different kinds of experiences. A writer should challenge himself with a variety of subject matter and be able to do that well."

Though Waits was on his seventh album, had been working like a dog performing for each, and had broken through to television and film, he still felt he had not earned ample recognition. The rise of Rickie Lee Jones made 1979 a discouraging year for Waits. Though it was his first film and he had earned entry into the Screen Actors Guild, *Paradise Alley* still reduced Waits's role to barely a cameo. Furthermore, his songs were barely represented and another film project had

fallen through. To add to Waits's disillusion with the music scene, a recent video for one of Jones's songs depicted him via a Waits look-alike as a seedy stalker shadowing the heels of a more innocent-appearing Jones. Waits was fed up with the trappings of the American music industry and by year's end he had moved on.

Many journalists faced with the task of interviewing Tom Waits in 1979 got an initial impression of a disgruntled codger getting old before his time.

Waits's concert props were a bit more extensive, with bursts of confetti (which didn't always work), a lamppost, gas pumps, and a tire, some of which were used to great effect in a December 1978 performance broadcast on PBS's *Austin City Limits* in the spring of 1979. Waits occasionally added an element of surprise to his shows; at Penn State he appeared onstage during a rendition of "Pasties and a G-String" wearing a bathrobe and dropping into a comfortable chair to watch an unplugged television.

"Tom Waits for No One"
Circus Weekly
January 23, 1979
Stan Soocher

Tom Waits is plenty pissed off. In the middle of a fifty-city tour in support of his new album, *Blue Valentine* (Asylum), he's been rudely awakened in his Knoxville, Tennessee, motel room by a persistent telephone ring after two days without sleep. Plus his wallet has been stolen, to boot.

"It took me six months to get my license back since I had so many tickets for parking and moving violations," Waits growls before he plunges headlong into a series of incessant coughs. "I was doing a show in Valparaiso, Indiana, [*cough, cough*] and some guy jumped onstage and stole my leather jacket [*cough*] with my license, letters, and money. You just can't trust anyone anymore. They're armed and they're dangerous."

Whether on the road or at home in West Hollywood, California, at the seedy Tropicana Motel, Tom Waits has had to learn how to deal with overenthusiastic fans and overripe fodder for the police file.

"Most of the stories on *Blue Valentine* took place in Los Angeles in the last few months," Waits continues. "'Romeo Is Bleeding' is about a Mexican gang leader who was shot and died in a movie house in downtown L.A."

Waits's songs are extended poems, each telling a story, backed by blues and jazz shadings and a minimum of instruments. His vocals closely resemble a young Louis Armstrong who's received a quick kick to the crotch.

Produced by Bones Howe, *Blue Valentine* was recorded in six sessions at Filmways/Heider Studios in Hollywood during July and August, with no overdubs. Waits plays electric guitar and acoustic piano.

Waits recently made his screen debut in Sylvester Stallone's latest film *Paradise Alley*. Stallone originally hired Waits to write three songs for the movie, but ended up creating the part of piano-playing barfly Mumbles for him instead.

Born in a Pomona, California, taxicab in 1949, Waits grew up in several Southern California communities where his father taught high school Spanish. At fourteen, he got a job as a dishwasher at Napoleone's Pizza parlor in San Diego. "Hookers would come in, grab and play with me. The point was to wash enough dishes so you could go outside and smoke a cigarette. I wish I had my old job back."

At seventeen, Tom took up the piano after he saved his first model from a junk pile when his parents threw it out in the rain.

Reading beatnik novelist Jack Kerouac and working as a night watchman, janitor, gas station attendant and doorman at an L.A. nightclub inspired Waits to write songs. He took them to hoot night at L.A.'s Troubadour in 1969 where he was discovered by current manager Herb Cohen, who remembers, "I was on my way to the toilet when I heard Tom sing that night. When I came out of the toilet, I asked him what he was doing and he said, 'Nothing.' So I signed him up."

Waits has just completed the title song for *On the Nickel,* a film about L.A.'s skid row, and is writing the profiles for *Rock Dreams* illustrator Guy Peellaert's new book, *Vegas*.

Now that he's making it, will Tom Waits be moving out of his low-rent Tropicana Motel room when he gets back to Hollywood? "I like it because I'm very accessible there, but sometimes that's annoying. It's not Disneyland, you know. I've thought about moving out, but I never seem to get around to it. Where would I go? Probably another motel somewhere."

By spring 1979, Waits was back in Europe and then toured Australia. He took a short break from performing to accompany Rickie Lee Jones on her own concert tour of Europe before returning to America to tour for the remainder of the year.

Waits, who knew all too well the humiliation of being booed onstage by intol-
erant audiences, had stuck up for his opening act (unlike Zappa). At Harvard
Square Theatre in Cambridge, Massachusetts, on November 3, 1979, the punk
band Mink DeVille opened for Waits and were promptly booed. Disgusted, they
put down their instruments and left. Expressing his own displeasure at the audience, Waits assured them that he would not come out any earlier than what had
already been agreed upon contractually. Instead, he made the entitled Ivy
League collegians sit and wait. Waits does not suffer fools gladly.

By 1979, an important chapter of Waits's life, musically and personally, came
to a close. He was finished with gas pumps, lampposts, confetti, strippers, the
Tropicana, and Rickie Lee Jones. He wanted to break through, to change out of
the routine he felt he was stuck repeating year after year. This time he contem-
plated a turn in theater, of branching his songs beyond their beer-puddle sentiment. To accomplish this, he had to make a change, and one way of doing it was
settling on a tentative move to the East Coast. When Waits was holed up in a
cramped Zoetrope office with Bones Howe, there had been a woman working as
an assistant story editor by the name of Kathleen Brennan. Waits was instantly
infatuated with this younger woman and they soon got to know one another. Eight
months later they were married. The year without an album, the first since Waits
began his recording career, seemed an uneventful disappointment to his fans. For
Waits it portended a future of sobriety, stability, and startling musical invention.

Tom Waits, Jack Kerouac, and Emmett Kelly:
Excerpted from "Wry and Danish to Go," Melody Maker
May 5, 1979
Brian Case

In the lobby, we talk across the tables and chain-smoke. Didn't Ann Charters's
biography of Kerouac prick the myth, the King of the Beats spending much of his
life in his mother's parlor?

"No. I actually'd prefer to see the other side. He wasn't a hero who could do
no wrong. He saw a lot, got around. He wasn't nearly as mad and impetuous as
Neal Cassady. Fact, after Neal died, Kerouac would not admit that he was gone.
'Neal's coming—Neal'll be here,' you know. Never admitted that he was dead.
Kept him alive.

"Jack was sittin' poker-faced with bullets backed with bitches, Neal hunched at the wheel puttin' everyone in stitches." [from the song "Jack & Neal"]

Tom drew an ace in a beer puddle on the tabletop. "Ace is a bullet, bitches is queens. He died in St. Petersburg. I was in St. Petersburg, played a concert, thought a lot about Kerouac."

He retreated back into a cloud of tobacco smoke. There was a long silence while he rummaged among his wreaths.

"Emmett Kelly just died," he announced. "Famous American clown. Sad clown. Sarasota, Florida. S'where all the old carnies live in the off-season. Ringling Brothers, Barnum & Bailey circus. Yeah, he died. He was taking the garbage out. Just fell down on the lawn, died. He was old vaudeville. [. . .]

"I don't know how I'm looked upon in the context of American culture. It has to do with how long you stay around. How long you're allowed to stay around."

Tom Waits on an ideal bar:
Excerpted from "The Neon Dreams of Tom Waits," New Musical Express
May 12, 1979
John Hamblett

"Here, take a look at these," says Waits, handing across what appears to be a clutch of loose pages from a black-and-white magazine. "I was reading a magazine on the plane coming over and I just had to tear out these pages to show you. The photographs are really great." The press manager examines the pictures and passes them round the creamily veneered café table to the blonde-haired photographer and the blonde-haired journalist. Everybody laughs and searches for a joke to crack.

The pictures document the inside of a rough-looking, harshly lit bar where various combinations of middle-aged, apparently working-class men and women are in various stages of undress, and are engaged in all manner of bawdy frolic. (Privately, the journalist thinks that it all looks a bit desperate.) "I don't know what language that's printed in, so I don't know where the bar is, but I sure would like to find out."

Waits takes back the magazine pages and folds them roughly into his pocket.

Trying to pierce the armor of the real Tom Waits:
Excerpted from **"A Sobering Experience,"** *Sounds*
August 4, 1979
Dave Lewis

[Waits] tends to hide behind a mixed barrier of terse grunts and mumbles and stock one-liners like "I'm swimming through the bowels of the fascinating world of entertainment. I'm enjoying myself under the circumcision and it's a real pro-phylactic experience" or "I only drink when I'm alone or with someone." [. . .] He now lives in a shabby hotel that he sums up as "Oh, how the mighty have fallen."

"The place has termites and bad plumbing, you know, and they've just painted the swimming pool black, probably so they don't have to clean it so often. But they take my messages at the desk and gather my mail and I don't have to pay gas or electricity, so it's not so bad." [. . .]

"I'm a little run-down at the moment and I apologize if I'm not as lucid or imaginative as you would like me to be. I find it hard to relax. Inside this quiet exterior beats the heart of a complete lunatic."

Tom Waits and the Big Apple:
Excerpted from **"Tom Waits Does New York Shuffle,"** *Los Angeles Times*
January 20, 1980
Richard Cromelin

"My instincts tell me this is the best move to make. I'll get a hotel for a week or so and find an apartment, and while I'm there I'll start writing a new album. I'm hoping that in New York I'll get a little more excited about the whole thing."

Will Waits—Southland-born and -bred—feel pangs of homesickness?

"This town's a real slut," he laughed. "Yeah, I'll miss the old whore now and then."

HEARTATTACK AND VINE (1980)

Elektra/Asylum's last album with Tom Waits was *Heartattack and Vine*. It is fitting that an album on the brink of musical change would be severed from its comfort zone. The expansion of the album's musical dynamism suggested the future of Waits's musical evolution.

Heartattack and Vine was recorded at Filmways/Heider Studios in Hollywood from June 16 through July 15, 1980. Though there were personnel holdovers from previous recording sessions, the number required to bring the album into fruition had expanded to twelve, suggesting a complexity of ideas Waits was conjuring for his sound. Bones Howe was once again brought onboard as producer, honing a gritty yet polished album that became Waits's bestselling LP to date.

Kathleen Brennan's presence served as a wellspring of ideas for Waits. Her enthusiasm for music Waits had otherwise not been exposed to enlightened him to a degree of fervor that is evident in parts of *Heartattack and Vine* as well as in some of the newer songs he was pulling into focus for a film soundtrack he was commissioned to complete. Waits's partnership with Francis Ford Coppola was integral, for it allowed him the opportunity to reinvent himself. The film gig was also teaching Waits more self-discipline in his songwriting, and that extended to cutting loose his addiction to nicotine and hard booze. Waits also joined a health club. "I tried to arrive at some level of personal hygiene," he stated in a promotional piece for *Heartattack and Vine*. "I thought the record deserved that."

Stephen K. Peeples, together with photographer Henry Diltz, visited Waits on the set of *One for the Heart* in the early afternoon of September 4. "It was a half-hour I'll never forget," he says. "Before my tape rolled, Tom bummed a Marlboro from me, asking me to keep it on the down low, because Kathleen would get mad. So I didn't front him off. Until now."

Heartattack and Vine
Elektra Records Promo Interview
September 4, 1980
Stephen K. Peeples

The interview that follows took place Thursday afternoon, September 4, 1980, in Tom Waits's two-room office on the old Hollywood General movie lot, now part of Francis Ford Coppola's Zoetrope empire. Waits was ensconced there while working on original songs for *One from the Heart*, a film Coppola is directing. He wanted to talk briefly about his seventh album for Asylum: *Heartattack and Vine*.

Notwithstanding his image as participant in and chronicler of urban America's seamy underbelly, Waits is apparently a changed man in a lot of ways, both inwardly and outwardly, as an artist and as a person.

We met in a Zoetrope hallway a bit less than an hour after the interview was set to begin, and he apologized for being late as he walked to his car—a dusty Monte Carlo—so he could get the keys to his office. He was wearing a skinny-brimmed black hat, white shirt, black pants, and black pointed roach-impalers.

Inside his office, through an anteroom where an uncased guitar and a four-by-four-foot painting of a butterfly leaned up against separate walls, Waits cleared his inner-office couch of assorted papers, joking about the paneled room's "David Niven feel" and then sitting down in a chair near one end of the couch. Opposite our seats, under the shaded windows looking out on a Gulf station that fronts on Santa Monica Boulevard ("makes me feel like I'm at the beach"), a low coffee table was loaded down with a pre-amp, amp, turntable and cassette deck, and speakers were on the floor on either side. In the corner was a grand piano, and a mic and stand were set up in front of the ivories.

The floor was littered only ankle deep with papers, notebooks, cassettes and album jackets, and over against one wall leaned a battered, splitting-at-the-seams leather briefcase with old Waits albums spilling out of it. On the back of his inner-office door (which he used only once during the interview, to bolt across the hall to the men's washroom) was a bulletin board sporting various-sized pieces of paper on which lyrics and song fragments were handwritten.

During the interview, one thing emerged as a probable cause for Waits's improved spirits and more presentable appearance; it had to do with his forsaking his usual post-album tour to work on the film project with Coppola; it's a challenge, and one Waits feels compelled to rise to. And he was just as determined to limit his comments about the collaboration until it's more fully baked.

Tom Waits: [*apparently checking to see if his interviewer had done his research*] What do you like about the new album?

Stephen K. Peeples: For one thing, your voice sounds like it was in better shape for *Heartattack and Vine* than it was for your last LP [*Blue Valentine*, October 1978].

TW: I quit smoking during the recording of the new one. Maybe that had something to do with it. I tried to arrive at some level of personal hygiene. I thought the record deserved that. I just tried to clean myself up a little. I think it helped, you know.

SP: What 'bout your drinking habits?

TW: I just drink wine now. My favorite is Carlo Rossi. Have you tried Carlo Rossi Chablis?

SP: No. You have any around?

TW: Ah, no, not right now. But it's a remarkable beverage!

SP: Let's talk about music now that we've got the tobacco and wine end covered. Last year, a writer quoted you as saying you'd reached a crossroads, musically speaking. Could you amplify that a bit?

TW: You just go through seasons as a writer. At this point, I'm trying to learn how to write faster. I just used to brood over songs for months and months. The writing for *Heartattack and Vine* was more spontaneous. And I let a drummer use sticks for the first time, instead of brushes [*laughs*]. I mean I used to hear everything with upright bass, muted trumpet, or tenor sax. I just had a sort of limited musical scope, so I wanted to try to stretch out a little bit on the new one. I think I've accomplished that to a degree. It's all part of an ongoing process.

SP: Another writer quoted you as saying you wanted to make more rock 'n' roll than most of your past albums.

TW: [*officious tone*] The subject matter that I was dealing with was caustic enough to require an ensemble that perhaps sounded a little more jagged, so I considered musicians and selected the band with that in mind. It's not Mahogany Rush, but it's the best I can do.

SP: After working with Bones Howe on every album since your first, I'd heard you were thinking about connecting with Jack Nitzsche for this one.

TW: Yeah, I had some plans to explore new producers. I'd moved to New York for about five–six months, wanting to challenge myself with an entirely new environment. But my relationship with Bones has been a very close and personal one. That for me is more important than anything when you're in the studio—to have somebody you can trust and who knows you, knows who you are and doesn't let you get away with anything. I didn't really want to disturb that relationship. But, at the time, I thought I wanted to change everything. Then I decided that the change was something that had to take place inside of me and with my own musical growth. I wanted to take some dangerous chances, and I felt Bones could best accommodate me.

SP: The press really made a big deal out of your move to New York. Why'd you return to L.A. so fast?

TW: Being there was more like a prison sentence [*laughs*]. Hard time. When I moved there I stayed at the Chelsea and then got an apartment nearby and joined the McBurney Y.M.C.A. . . . actually, I just went to New York to have a drink. It was a very expensive drink.

SP: A long one, too, evidently . . .

TW: Yeah, it was a tall one [*laughs*].

SP: So what prompted your return? Did they give you your release papers?

TW: Yeah, I'm on parole. I came to work on the film for Francis [Coppola] and to do this album. I'm now living in the Greater Los Angeles area.

SP: How did you put the *Heartattack and Vine* band together?

TW: I used my drummer from the road, "Big John" Thomassie, who's from New Orleans. He used to play with Freddie King, Dr. John, and Bonnie Bramlett. He's been with me on the road for two years now, and this is the first record he's done with me. Then there's Ronnie Barron on piano, who's also from New Orleans and is someone I've admired for many years. It was a real pleasure working with him. He played [Hammond] B-3 [organ] and piano. Larry Taylor, who's from Canned Heat, is on bass. On guitar we had Roland Bautista, who grew up on Slauson Avenue [in Los Angeles], and that was good enough for me. But he's played with George Duke and the Crusaders before and does a lot of session work in L.A. In addition to the quartet, I had Jerry Yester [producer of Waits's first LP, *Closing Time*, in 1973 and frequent string arranger on subsequent albums] write two arrangements, and had Bob Alcivar do another two. Bob worked on *Foreign Affairs* [1977] and wrote "Potter's Field" with me. He's done some other arrangements and things for me, too. He's also working as orchestrator and arranger on the Coppola project. He's had experience as a film composer himself.

SP: So once you had Bones and the players lined up, it's my understanding you moved into the studio for the duration of the sessions.

TW: Yeah, we worked in the RCA building on Ivar and Sunset, and I moved in there and lived there while we recorded. Everybody thought I was crazy [*chuckles in a "so what else is new?" tone of voice*], but it seemed to help me a lot.

SP: I understand also that little if any material was written until you went into the studio. I wonder whether you had the band there all the time so that when you hit on an idea, you'd all be able to get it on tape quickly . . .

TW: No, it wasn't like that. Our recording schedule was to begin about two every afternoon. I just wanted to stay there because I was writing about one tune ahead of Bones every day. I was writing each night and every day so when the band got there, I'd have something new for everybody. So it was valuable for me to be writing in the same environment I was recording in. I'd never tried to do it that way before. It's a lot of work, it's not a party. I don't invite anyone that's not directly involved in the sessions. I sweat bullets for a month and a half, but my relationship with Bones was very healthy during the whole procedure. He had a lot of faith in me, that I'd be able to work under those conditions. It would make a lot of producers very nervous to be working against a deadline like that with all that gold riding on it.

SP: Forgetting deadlines for a moment, would you do another album the same way?

TW: Yeah, I think so. I'd like to try it again maybe on the next record. Maybe force the entire ensemble to stay in the studio. Chain 'em up like dogs [*laughs*]!

SP: Were there any particularly funny moments during your stay at the studio, like did the night maintenance man whack your boot soles with his broomstick while you were racked out on the couch?

TW: No, the funniest thing was that that didn't happen [*laughs*].

SP: OK, let's talk about the tunes, starting with the title track. How'd that one come about?

TW: I was in a bar one night on Hollywood Boulevard near Vine Street, and this lady came in with a dead animal over her arm, looking like she'd obviously been sleeping outdoors. She walked up to the bartender and said, "I'm gonna have a heart attack," and he says, "Yeah, right, you can have it outside." I thought that was pretty chilly. So I re-named Hollywood Boulevard "heartattack."

SP: On to "In Shades."

TW: I always wanted to put out just a little straight R & B instrumental. Originally, it was titled "Breakfast in Jail." But we changed it.

SP: How about "Saving All My Love for You?"

TW: That's an old song, about four years old. It was scratched off of another album, I think *Foreign Affairs*.

SP: There's a line in that tune about a prostitute with too much makeup and a broken shoe. On your last LP, *Blue Valentine*, the tune "$29.00" talks about another lady of the night who had a broken shoe . . .

TW: [*laughs*] Same girl!

SP: Then we go "Downtown" . . .

TW: That's a first take. I was just running it down to the band just to learn it, but it became the record. We tried several other versions of it but this take seemed to be the one that took. I love Ronnie's organ solo. It's real amphetamine. The tune's just a fast story, like a fast news update.

SP: Who is Montclaire de Havelin?

TW: It's a name I came up with when I was on the road. I used to check into hotels and use my real name on the registration form. I had some unfortunate experiences because of that [*clears throat and smiles*], so I decided to change my name, at least on the road, so I wouldn't have people I didn't want to associate with trying to get in touch with me.

SP: And side one closes with "Jersey Girl" . . .

TW: I never thought I would catch myself saying "sha la la" in a song. This is my first experiment with "sha la la." It has one of them kinda Drifters' feels. I didn't wanna say "muscular dystrophy" in it or anything, 'cause I didn't think it fit in with the feel of the number. So, lyrically, I tried to do it straight-ahead, a guy walking down the street to see his girl.

SP: Flipping over to side two, you open with "'Til the Money Runs Out" . . .

TW: It's an old mambo-type beat.

SP: Do you know any of the Chinamen on Telegraph Road?

TW: It's just a line about some Chinamen on Telegraph Road. Got outta that one pretty good, huh?

SP: OK. Just curious. Then comes "On the Nickel" . . .

TW: That was written for the Ralph Waite's motion picture of the same name. I don't think it's still showing anywhere. It was released about the time I got back from New York, in April sometime. It was a wonderful picture, I mean it, but it didn't make it. It wasn't no *Towering Inferno*, just a small picture with a lot of feeling. It was set on skid row in Los Angeles, Fifth Street, downtown. The locals call it "the Nickel." The film was about a couple of old friends who were reunited after some years. One had cleaned up and moved off the Nickel and the other was still there, and dying from it. The one who'd cleaned up went back to find his old pal. It's a wonderful story.

SP: What happened at the end?

TW: You'll have to see it.

SP: Is the subject of the next tune titled "Mr. Siegal" anyone in particular?

TW: I'm trying to kind of refer to Bugsy Siegal.

SP: Several people who've heard this tune already think the line "How do the angels get to sleep / when the devil leaves his porch light on" was pretty good.

TW: I like it too.

SP: And the album closes with "Ruby's Arms" . . .

TW: I love Jerry's arrangement on it. He used a brass choir and made it sound like a Salvation Army band at the top of the tune. It really got me. It's a little bit like that Matt Monro thing, "I Will Leave You Softly" [*sings a verse*]. I was trying to visualize this guy getting up in the morning before dawn and leaving on the train, with the clothesline outside. I just closed my eyes and saw this scene and wrote about it.

SP: I found it extremely touching, if you'll pardon the expression.

TW: Thank you.

SP: The room you recorded in, Filmway/Heider's Studio B there in the RCA building, has a pretty healthy rock 'n' roll reputation. Did you know or find out anything about past sessions there?

TW: I dunno, to be honest. Yeah, the Stones worked there. I heard The Monkees did, too [*laughs*]. Oh, yeah, Ray Charles and Cleo Laine recorded an album in that room with Frank De Vol. They did excerpts from "Porgy and Bess" about '75/76. Martin Mull cut his last Elektra LP, the live one, there, too.

SP: Previously, when you've finished an album, you've hit the road. How about this year?

TW: I came right off of the album back into this office. This is a whole other world for me. Up until this point I've done an album and gone out of the studio and put together a band and rehearsed for three or four weeks and hit the road for four months. It's just an old hustle that I've done for the last seven years.

SP: It gets old, doesn't it?

TW: Yeah, it does. So I came off the record and into a whole other project, writing for somebody else's approval rather than my own. It's important, I think, to be able to write that way.

SP: You were billing your last tour, late last year through earlier this year, as your "breakeven tour." Did you?

TW: Just barely. But this year I'm doing this project for Coppola.

SP: How'd that one come about?

TW: I was still living in New York and he arranged a meeting with me. Later, I went to Zoetrope and discussed it further with him and made a commitment to begin work on it. So he gave me this office and piano. I took a month and a half off to write and record the album.

SP: One more question about the album. On the front cover, at the top right, the name "David 'Doc' Feuer" is printed along with a New York phone number. Whoever he is, he's going to get a lot of phone calls . . .

TW: That's not his real number. I'll give you his real one if you need it. He's a psychiatrist who needs the work. Actually, I put my phone number on the back of a record once and got lots of phone calls from people with real clinical problems. I never really knew what to say to them. So I told Doc I'd put his number on there and he could handle 'em.

SP: Are you getting any kind of kickback from those referrals?

TW: Well, not really [laughs]. But he's a frustrated musician and actually I've been considering a possible career in medicine. So we're gonna trade skills instead of money. It'll give me something to fall back on . . .

ONE FROM THE HEART (1982)

The music soundtrack for *One from the Heart* fared better than Coppola's film in terms of longevity. Coppola was embarrassed by the critical lambasting and consequently withdrew all of the film prints from theaters nationwide two weeks after its disastrous release. For his part, Waits's intense labor for the score earned him an Oscar nomination for Best Original Song. The soundtrack, since reissued on CD with extra tracks, featured an unlikely pairing between Waits and country and western superstar Crystal Gayle. It remains a favorite among fans.

One from the Heart was the last collaboration between Bones Howe and Tom Waits. According to Howe, the split was amicable. He told *Sound on Sound* in February 2004, "He called me up and said 'Can we have a drink?' He told me he realized one night that as he was writing a song, he found himself asking 'If I write this, will Bones like it?' I said to him that we were getting to be kind of like an old married couple. I said I don't want to be the reason that an artist can't create. It was time for him to find another producer. We shook hands and that was it. It was a great ride."

More to the point, Howe knew that Waits's marriage meant that the past was severed. Howe left with an open-door policy should Waits want to return to the old ways. Selflessly, Howe realized that Waits's new life with Kathleen meant that he was taking better care of himself and not living out his life from the confines of a motel room.

Waits also broke off professional relations with his manager Herb Cohen, sourly explaining to *Melody Maker* that he had "gotten rid of my ex-manager, and a lot of the flesh peddlers and professional vermin I'm thrown in with. My wife and I are taking care of all my affairs now."

"A Simple Love Story"
City Limits
July 1–7, 1983
Peter Guttridge

Tom Waits, gruff-voiced romanticizer of the seamy side of urban life, spent much of 1981 holed up in a two-room office off Santa Monica Boulevard working on the music for Francis Coppola's *One from the Heart*, which is released this week. On his last visit to London he talked to Peter Guttridge about writing music for the movies and the mogul.

With his obsessive interest in hookers, hoodlums, and wasted lives, Tom Waits might seem to have more in common with Scorsese than Coppola. But the collaboration on *One from the Heart* worked well artistically. It needed to. Coppola, with his customary brinkmanship, had gambled the future of his Zoetrope company on the success of the "simple love story." For Waits the movie offered an opportunity to reach a wider audience than the cult following his albums had garnered.

The film opened in the United States to lukewarm reviews. The soundtrack album sat on a shelf for months until legal wrangles were sorted out in Britain. The album was finally released by CBS earlier this year and the film has its long-overdue London opening this week.

"What's *One from the Heart*? Son-of-a-bitch is what it is," says Waits. "I've never been in that kind of situation before. Doing a film score requires an application to detail I'm not accustomed to. Plus I was working for someone else's approval, which was hard for me at first."

How did the collaboration come about? "Got a call in the middle of the night and went over. It was like having an audience with the pope. I used to think directors were genies with wings you know. . . ." Coppola had heard Waits's entertaining bar-stool duet with Bette Midler, "I Never Talk to Strangers," on the *Foreign Affairs* album and wanted Waits to duet with Midler on the soundtrack. Midler had other commitments so Waits worked with Crystal Gayle: an eccentric combination if there ever was, but one that works.

Waits was happy to get involved "since the project was so interesting and I was new to it. The money didn't matter—money's not a barometer for me, never has been." Waits and Coppola worked very closely together. Waits wrote about twelve different songs to be used wherever they were required. "I strung them together like an overture for a musical. What he wanted was a glass of music that you could add to or take from. Then we got together and made a scratch tape where we spotted the story for music. I was reworking themes so I got about 175 musical cues to be extracted from the score. It ain't fun doing that."

One from the Heart was to be a relatively low-budget musical, a "fable with music" set in Las Vegas, and featuring three of Coppola's repertory company—Frederic Forrest, Raul Julia, and Teri Garr—with the addition of Nastassja Kinski. But the real Las Vegas didn't suit Coppola's image of Las Vegas so he constructed a new Las Vegas on nine huge soundstages. The budget soared accordingly. Initially all the music was to come from a Las Vegas act—piano, bass, and drums (which, with muted sax, is Waits's favorite combination)—but that too changed.

"Francis was very open to suggestions. For example, there's a used-car lot piece conducted with a dipstick. The main lead [Forrest] owns a wrecking yard for abandoned cars. It's a perfect setup because he loves cars—he's a little mad but that's why he's in the business—then he has to sell his Studebaker—breaks his heart. So I came up with this idea for a used-car lot piece where the music is conducted with a dipstick. Coppola shot it. I gave him a few other ideas too.

"But you know that man is incredible. There's no distance for him between imagination and execution. It's devilish. I have an idea, Francis says great, starts working out ways to do it. I'm saying yeah well it's, em, only an idea just occurred, Francis—next day he's set up the machinery and doing it."

Waits thinks highly of Coppola: "Coppola is an angel, a man with vision. He wants to be one of those old moguls with big cigars but he's not your typical cigar—he really cares. I admire his courage because he's getting into a lot of trouble over his social conscience thing—he cares about cinema, where it's going."

Waits has had a nodding acquaintance with films before. Strangely a couple of years back he was touting around his own screenplay, *Why Is the Dream So Much Sweeter Than the Taste?*, about a used-car dealer in downtown L.A. "He was a guy who was a success at being a failure." All the action takes place on New Year's Eve, which makes the whole thing uncannily like Coppola's own movie, set on the eve of July 4.

"On the Nickel," a haunting song off the *Heartattack and Vine* album, was written by Waits for Ralph Waite's film of the same name. "It was a wonderful picture, I mean it, but it didn't make it. It wasn't no *Towering Inferno*, just a small picture with a lot of feeling. It was set on skid row in Los Angeles, Fifth Street, downtown. The locals call it 'the Nickel.'

"Nicolas Roeg asked me to write a title song for *Bad Timing* but I was busy. Roeg took some off one of the albums." What he took was "Invitation to the Blues," a drifter's paean to a roadhouse waitress, which might have fitted *The Postman Always Rings Twice* but certainly not Roeg's coffee-table psychodrama. What did Waits think of the film? "Well. I don't know anybody who wants to see Art Garfunkel with his shirt off." Sylvester Stallone hired Waits for a cameo role in the ill-fated *Paradise Alley* as a Hoagy Carmichael bar pianist. A few snatches of his music made it onto the soundtrack, though Waits did not score the movie nor write the main theme, sung over the credits by Stallone himself. Intended as a Damon Runyan comedy, the film didn't fare too well with either critics or the public. "I went and sat in front of a piano for three weeks and then I went home. I didn't go to see it after." Waits's appearance seems rather truncated in the film. He agrees. "I had more scenes but they got cut. I finally saw it on TV with my wife [a scriptwriter from Twentieth Century Fox he married in 1981 after breaking up with longtime partner Rickie Lee Jones]. I sat her down to watch it, got really excited—look honey, here I am—shit where'd I go?"

PART II

PART II

SWORDFISHTROMBONES (1983)

The musically rich 1970s were hardly over before American pop culture was utterly transformed. The time was ripe for reinvention, for the era of music videos ushered in new opportunities for reaching audiences. It extended the promotional possibilities of creating hit singles and broadened the identities of musicians beyond a faceless voice emitting from a transistor radio. By decade's end, the tie-in of music video with a single was the norm.

By the end of 1979, Waits's disillusionment had ended with a hasty departure from Elektra/Asylum for Island Records, a move that inspired his most groundbreaking music yet. All of a sudden, Waits was no longer relying on the traditional acoustic instruments of his 1970s records, instead favoring odd instruments that gave his new music a signature sound (replete with his ever-more gravelly voice).

Kathleen Brennan was integral to her husband's musical development. She was considered an equal collaborator, ultimately sharing authorship of Waits's songs. Brennan's alternative influences steered Waits toward cabaret and tango as well as a smattering of obscure European folk songs.

His first record for Island, *Swordfishtrombones*, was the breakthrough. Critics were beside themselves, breathlessly trying to gain a perspective on this puzzling new release by an artist whom they thought they had finally deciphered (as much as they were ever going to figure him out, that is). Released in the autumn of 1983, *Swordfishtrombones* was a full-fledged collaboration between Waits and Brennan. Waits expanded the possibilities of his instrumental repertoire beyond the Hammond organ and piano, playing such instruments as the harmonium, a freedom bell, and a synthesizer. To expand upon that, Waits brought into the fold a rich cabinet of diverse musical talent. The year without an album had paid off, with fans either embracing their hero's new direction, or rejecting it altogether in favor of *Closing Time* and *Foreign Affairs*-type fodder.

The lyrics of *Swordfishtrombones* boasted an abstraction absent from earlier songs. Indeed they hinted at the same *type* of characters, though some were less depicted in real-world scenarios but instead shone through a surreal prism of theatrical exaggeration. Frank can still burn down the house, but he has to do it with the dog in there: *he never liked that damn dog*.

In 1989, *Spin* named *Swordfishtrombones* the second greatest album of all time.

"A Conversation with Tom Waits"
Swordfishtrombones Promo, Island Records (audio transcription)
Late 1983

"Underground"

It was originally an opportunity for me to chronicle the behavior of a mutant dwarf community and give it a feeling of a Russian march. People banging on steam pipes, a thousand boots coming down on a wood floor at the same time. That chorus of men singing, kind of a *Dr. Zhivago* feel to it. It was the way I originally perceived it. I abbreviated some of the scope and wanted bass marimba to give it kind of an exotic feel. So, you get the note and you get that kind of a tall wood clang with the attack. That's Victor Feldman on bass marimba, Larry Taylor on acoustic bass, Randy Aldcroft on baritone horn, Stephen Hodges on drums, and Fred Tackett on electric guitar. I had some assistance from a gentleman by the name of Francis Thumm, who worked on the arrangements of some of these songs with me, who plays Chromelodeon with the Harry Partch Ensemble headed up by Daniel Mitchell. So he worked closely on most of these songs. But I originally saw this [as] the theme for some late-night activity in the steam tunnels beneath New York City where allegedly there are entire communities of ladies and gentlemen living under difficult circumstances beneath the subways. When I was a kid I used to stare in the gopher holes for hours and hours sometimes. I tried to think my way down through the gopher hole and imagine this kind of a *Journey to the Center of the Earth* kind of thing.

"Shore Leave"

It's kind of an Oriental Bobby "Blue" Bland approach. Musically, it's essentially very simple. It's a minor blues. I tried to add some musical sound effects with the assistance of a low trombone to give a feeling of a bus going by, and metal aunglongs, the sound of tin cans in the wind, or rice on the bass drum to give a feeling of the waves hitting the shore. Just to capture the mood more than anything, of a marching marine or whatever, walking down the wet street in Hong Kong and missing his wife back home. I worked in a restaurant in a sailor town for a long time. It's National City, so it was something I saw every night. It was next to a tattoo parlor and country-and-western dance hall and a Mexican movie theater. So I imagined this Chinese pinwheel in a fireworks display spinning, spinning, and turning and then slowing down. As it slowed down, it dislodged into a windmill in Illinois, a home where a woman is sitting in the living room, sleeping on chairs with the television on. When he's having eggs at some joint, you know, thousands of miles away.

"Dave the Butcher"

This is an instrumental piece. It's a . . . actually I tried to find a calliope. Was it possible? So I ended up playing on the B-3 organ. Well, I wanted that carnival feeling on it. Kind of a *Nightmare Alley* with Tyrone Power and Joan Blondell. Kind of a monkey on wood alcohol. It was originally inspired by a gentleman who did tremendous amounts of religious things in his house and worked at a slaughterhouse. I was trying to imagine what was going in his head while he cut up a load of pork loin and got completely out of his mind with a meat cleaver. I don't think it's going to get a lot of airplay, unless we put a nice vocal on it.

"Johnsburg, Illinois"

My wife is from Johnsburg, Illinois. It's right outside McHenry and up by the Chain o' Lakes. She grew up on a farm up there. So it's dedicated to her. It's real short. Somehow I wanted just to get it all said in one verse. There are times when you work on a song and end up repeating in the second verse what you already said in the first. So I thought it would be more appropriate if it's just like a feeling of a sailor somewhere in a café, who opens his wallet and turns to the guy next to him and shows him the picture while he's talking about something else and says:

"Oh, here. That's her," and then closes his wallet and puts it back in his pants. It relates in some way to "Shore Leave" in the sense that it talks about Illinois. So, thematically, I was trying to tie it into "Shore Leave."

"Sixteen Shells from a Thirty-Ought-Six"

I tried to get a chain-gang-work-song-feel holler, a low trombone to give a feeling of a freight train going by. It's Stephen Hodges on drums, Larry Taylor on acoustic bass, Fred Tackett on electric guitar, Victor Feldman on brake drum and bell plate, and Joe Romano on trombone. So, I wanted to have that kind of a sledgehammer coming down on an anvil. Originally I saw the story as a guy and a mule going off looking for this crow. He has a Washburn guitar strapped on the side of his mule and when he gets the crow, he pulls the strings back and shoves this bird inside the guitar and then the strings make like a jail. Then he bangs the guitar on the strings and the bird goes out of his mind as he is riding off over the hill. So I tried to make the story a bit impressionistic but at the same time adding some very specific images in there. I worked a long time on this. The feel of it was really critical. I added snare and we pulled the snare off 'cause it made it shuffle too much. I liked the holes in it as much as I liked what was in them. It was a matter of trying to get that feeling of a train going. Originally I tried it just with organ and bass. Then I was afraid to add too much to it 'cause sometimes you get a feel that's appropriate. If you try to heap too much on it then it crumbles into [unintelligible—"the strain"?].

"Town with No Cheer"

When my wife heard that for the first time she said, "Oh gee, you must have loved her very much." So I said, "Wait a minute. This is not a love song. This is about a guy who can't get a drink!" It's about a miserable old town in Australia that made the news when they shut down the only watering hole. We found an article about it in a newspaper when we were over there and hung onto it for a year. So I said, "Ah, I'm going to write something about that someday," and finally got around to it. That's a freedom bell up front. I was just trying to get a feel of a ghost town, tumbleweeds, and that kind of thing. It's basically a folk song.

"In the Neighborhood"

Side One closes with "In the Neighborhood." It has that Salvation Army feel. I was trying to bring the music outdoors with a tuba, trombone, trumpets, snare, cymbals, and an accordion, so it had that feeling of a Felliniesque-type of a marching band going down the dirt road and with a glockenspiel to give it a feeling of a kind of a demented little parade band.

"Just Another Sucker in the Vine"

Another instrumental. It's myself playing the harmonium and Joe Romano on trumpet. I tried to give a little Nino Rota feel to it. Kind of like a car running out of gas, you know, just before it makes the crest of a hill and it starts to roll back. And . . . all right, I tried to picture two Italian brothers in a small circus arguing on the trapeze. One of them with a bottle of Ten High and a leotard doing the dozens on each other and throwing insults as they cross each other in mid-air. Or the feel of a band on the deck of the Titanic as it slowly goes under. The title really has a kind of lyric to it, it's like, you know . . . actually I originally planned to write a lyric called: "It's more than rain that falls on our parade tonight." But I thought it was more effective as an instrumental and it also sets up "Frank's Wild Years."

"Frank's Wild Years"

Charles Bukowski had a story that essentially was saying that it's the little things that drive men mad. It's not the big things. It's not World War II. It's the broken shoelace when there is no time left that sends men completely out of their minds. So this is kind of in that spirit. A little of a Ken Nordine flavor. Ronnie

Barron, alias Reverend Ether from New Orleans, Louisiana, on Hammond organ and Larry Taylor, originally with Canned Heat, on [unintelligible—sounds like "doghouse"—he played acoustic bass]. I think there is a little bit of Frank in everybody.

"Swordfishtrombone"

That's the title song. It has kind of a Cuban nightclub feel to it. It's a story to try and give an overview of a character. We tried it a lot of different ways. It was arranged differently, with electric guitar and drums. We had trombone on it and trumpet and ended up discarding most of what we had done and completely rearranged it just to get it as simple as possible so that it just kind of rolled and allowed me to tell the story over it without any interruptions. Tenkiller Lake, that's in Tulsa, Oklahoma. So, "He came home from the war with a party in his head and an idea for a fireworks display."

"Down, Down, Down"

It's best described as Pentecostal Revlon man. I was stranded in Arizona on Route 66. It was freezing cold and I slept in a ditch. I pulled all these leaves all over on top of me and dug a hole and shoved my feet in this hole. It was about twenty below and no cars going by. Everything was closed. When I woke up in the morning there was a Pentecostal church right over the road. I walked over there with leaves in my hair and sand on the side of my face. This woman named Mrs. Anderson came. It was like New Year's Eve . . . yeah, it was New Year's Eve. She said: "We're having services here and you are welcome to join us." So I sat at the back pew in this tiny little church and this mutant rock 'n' roll band got up and started playing these old hymns in such a broken sort of way. They were preaching, and every time they said something about the devil or evil or going down the wrong path, she gestured in the back of the church to me, and everyone would turn around and look and shake their heads and then turn back to the preacher. It gave me a complex that I grew up with. On Sunday evening they have these religious programs where the preachers, they are all bankers, they get on with these seven-hundred-dollar suits and shake their finger at America. So this is kind of my own little opportunity at the lectern.

"Soldier's Things"

[unintelligible] The theory is that if somebody rides a bicycle long enough, eventually the bicycle becomes 30 percent human and you become 70 percent bicycle. It's like the things that you have in your pocket. If you are carrying them there long enough, they take on certain atomic human characteristics. Sometimes you go to a garage sale or you go to a pawnshop or anywhere and look through other peoples' things, shoes in particular, that have walked around with somebody else inside them for a long time, they seem to have . . . they seem to be able to almost talk. So, it's just trying to string together different items that . . . instruments are always like that. This guy comes home from the service and "everything's a dollar in that box," you know.

"Gin Soaked Boy"

It's a bit of a Howlin' Wolf feel. It's Fred Tackett on electric guitar, plays good slide. Tried to get that "rrrrr" thing. Tried to get the vocal to sit way back to re-create the recording conditions that existed prior to advanced technical capabilities. We had it recorded by one round microphone. So, your dominance on the track depended entirely on your distance from the microphone. It was also to get a room feel. So Biff Dawes miked the room with several of these contact mics on the glass-net type of thing. So it got a real sense of the air of the place. It has a bit of an old feel to it.

"Trouble's Braids"

It's Victor Feldman on African talking drum, Stephen Taylor on parade bass drum, and Larry Taylor on acoustic bass. It has a bit of a Mongolian feel. Try to get the image of trouble being this little girl and then pulling on trouble's braids.

Our hero is at this point being pursued by bloodhounds, so he stays away from the main roads.

"Rainbirds"

The final song on side two. It's myself at the piano and Greg Cohen on acoustic bass. It's a real pleasure to work with him. We have a mutual intuition and it's really good to hear him again. Francis Thumm helped me with the glass harmonica introduction. It's kind of an epilogue to the story. After he floats down the stream on an old dead tree. It's kind of . . . you know . . . it's morning and you hear the birds and it starts to rain and he's off on another adventure somewhere. I wanted to close the side with an instrumental to give the hero room to breathe. Yeah, that's all . . . the end.

"Skid Romeo"
Face
September 1983
Robert Elms

When you ring Tom Waits, you get an answer-phone, a short burst of congas, and a voice that drawls sleepily: "This is Tom, I'm at the beach." But there's no beach near his home in the barrio and like as not he's sitting listening to your message, deciding whether to give you a burst of the live performer. Tom Waits is a famously private person; the barrio is in East Los Angeles.

Waits is also a professional enigma. Despite ten years' worth of bitingly intelligent, funny, dramatic music; despite album after album of the most essentially American songs white America has to offer, he's still no more than a goateed curio. If you're a fan he's a myth, if you're not he's a nobody. From where I stand Mr. Waits is the only possible reason to leave the highly developed civilization of Manhattan and head for the soporific wilds of the far West.

Before leaving the island I popped into Island. Waits, so long on WEA, is now one of Chris Blackwell's boys. *Swordfishtrombones* is his first solo album for three years, and I sat in an office and listened. After two sides of a TDK I was even more excited about meeting the man. Tom has moved to a new motel, the Edward Hopper painting has become an Orson Welles picture. Oriental, disturbing, merry-go-round music with Hammond organ, electric guitar, tom-toms, chimes, bagpipes, and a series of dark, tantalizing scenarios sketched by a master storyteller. It's a soundtrack to a sad, unmade movie. Ben Gazzara should play the lead.

L.A. airport is in turmoil. The threat of next year's Olympics has turned it into a chaos of cement mixers and never-ending diversions. You may get lost in the airport, but you'll never even locate the city. "A city with all the personality of a paper cup," Raymond Chandler called it. I think he also said it was "seventy-two suburbs in search of a city." You can bet they never found it. Los Angeles doesn't really exist.

L.A. is a great big freeway, if you haven't got a car you can't live, if you have there's little worth living for. It's always hot and the scenery's very pleasant but you can drive for hours without hitting anything more exciting than housing estates, incredibly expensive housing estates. Hollywood's just a memory of a sign, a shadow on a hill populated by Californians. Californians are a breed together, united by the fact that they all wear shorts and all talk suntanned nonsense. When I told the girl at the car-hire company that I was there to interview a musician she was genuinely interested. When I told her it was Tom Waits she was genuinely disappointed.

"I like the ocean but I don't feel very compatible with the type of people who are attracted to it." —Tom Waits

To get from a hotel on Sunset Boulevard to the Travelers Rest Café, you get on the Hollywood Freeway and keep going east. L.A.'s east end is where they keep the "wetbacks," all the poor illegal Mexican immigrants who've crossed the Rio Grande in order to sit on doorsteps and ride around in old cars that scrape the road.

Tom Waits and his wife are the only white people on their block, but there's several Catholic churches and the best chili in the world. Around the corner is the Travellers, a Honduran diner with gray net curtains, a blackened plastic chandelier, and a large black-and-white TV in the corner. When Tom walked in he looked just like his photos, just like one of his songs.

For a start he does talk with that voice. It may have been affected at one time, but there's no doubt that it's now the only voice he has. A lot of the time it's a low gruff whisper, barely audible above the baseball pouring out of the corner. The TV couldn't possibly be turned down so we paid for a couple of beers and left. We conducted the interview in his battered, maroon Volvo parked out on the strip.

"This street's great, every day there's a wedding or a funeral. The weddings are like processions, motorcades of late fifties automobiles with huge Kleenex chrysanthemums strung across them. The men wear lime-green tuxedos and the girls are straight off the top of a cake."

Tom Waits doesn't like doing interviews, but he's certainly no slouch at them either. Dragging me down to the tawdry glamour of a ghetto was a sweet move. Parked outside Los Quangos bar, a vibrant, siren-punctuated Latin hustle is going on all around us. There's a mariachi band in the bar and a stream of macho, low-rider Romeros wasting away the night. Tom Waits is younger than you expected, not far past thirty. My guess is that he's always consciously made himself seem older than he really is. This is a man with a keen awareness of his image.

"I'm so broke I can't even pay attention."

It's hard to understand how he can be as skint as he looks and claims. He's never risen above cult status, but then he's just written and performed the soundtrack for Francis Ford Coppola's *One from the Heart*. He made a considerably better job of it than the director did, but it doesn't seem to have done too much for his bank balance.

"Anybody that's been in this business for more than ten years has got horror stories about where the money went," is all he's prepared to say about his finances. "Francis is an inventor, a visionary," is his comment on Coppola, a man he gets on well with and intends to work alongside in the future. He's already got a small part in a new Coppola film *Rumble Fish*, a gang movie currently under production in Oklahoma, as well as a role as a sideshow freak alongside Robert Duvall in a movie called *The Stone Boy*.

Movies or, more accurately, the mythology of movies have always played a central role in the world and characters Waits [has] created. And it was often difficult to tell whether Tom Waits was the writer or the plot. He seemed to be living out his storylines—onstage he became the man in the song. So it's no surprise to learn that acting and more film scores are a powerful aim.

We sat and whistled Bernard Herrmann's haunting theme from *Taxi Driver* while a series of rowdy epic dramas were being acted out on the street and Tom Waits got less and less guarded. When he's telling the truth he thinks for a long time before answering. When he's spinning an apocryphal one, they roll from his tongue:

"Lately I've found an appreciation of Harry Partch who built and designed all his own instruments and died several years ago in San Diego. His ensemble continues under the name of The Harry Partch Ensemble. A friend of mine, Francis Thumm, plays the Chromelodeon. I'm sure that many of your readers will be familiar with his work."

That was his answer when I asked what musicians he admired. When I asked how he met his wife, he didn't even grin: "We met at a miserable little funeral in a miserable little town called San Casedra. She was an aerialist with Circus Vargas and we were both standing under the same umbrella. It's a very long story, the guy was in his seventies, he choked on a chicken bone."

Questions about his private life tend to be met with refusals or yarns. But it seems a safe bet to say that he's the son of an itinerant schoolteacher who attended a mainly black junior high school in L.A. where he fell in love with James Brown, Wilson Pickett, and The Temptations. At fifteen he was in a school soul band called The Systems and later became a professional accordion player in a polka band. He became more and more interested in jazz and the various ethnic musics that abound in multiracial America and he ended up as an eclectic and eccentric solo singer-songwriter.

"In America you have to control your diet very carefully. If you feed on things that are easy and accessible, that's what you put out yourself. The kind of exciting chemical explosions which take place when you're experimenting are much more likely to occur if you make mad choices."

But mavericks who stray from the middle of the road tend to get very lost in the vastness of middle America's musical conservatism. It's surprising that Tom Waits with his sleazy barroom jazz, his earthy barroom imagery, and his beat-up barroom image has survived as long, become as successful as he has. For a son of the Golden State he's a very curious being, for a white American musician he's a literal one-off.

With his obvious talent as a songwriter and performer, a decision to appeal to the Springsteen-fed masses could have bought fame, acclaim, and x amounts of dough. But when I put that to him, Waits replied sharply to a question that has obviously been put to him a hundred times.

"There's nothing more embarrassing than a person who tries to guess what the great American public would like, makes a compromise for the first time, and falls flat on his face. I don't intend to do that."

And there's no way you can possibly doubt him. After ten years of record company pressure and critical acclaim followed by public apathy he really doesn't mind the fact [that] he's still more likely to play clubs than stadiums. As long as he can still play and there are people to listen then he'll carry on.

"I would rather be a failure on my own terms than a success on someone else's. That's a difficult statement to live up to, but then I've always believed that the way you affect your audience is more important than how many of them there are."

By appealing to people force-fed on rock instead of aiming at jazz purists, he's undoubtedly influenced his audience, introduced them to a style of musicianship and songwriting that most people never hear. Yet *Swordfishtrombones* marks a radical and intriguing departure from his warped Tin Pan Alley world of not-too-grand piano, walking bass, and wailing sax. It certainly isn't an attempt to hit the commercial mainline, but it's definitely a shot at a different vein.

"When you establish a neighborhood for yourself as an artist it's important to keep challenging that, to move on. So I tried to get a more exotic sound. It's a kind of Oriental cabaret."

And he's done it brilliantly. This isn't a new Tom Waits, there's the same challenging eclecticism, the same cynical romanticism, the same delight in words. But it's a new sound, a sound without real comparison. Tom Waits still stands alone.

"I feel I've shaken off an identity that was hindering me for some time. People thought I was some kind of a throwback, a time-warp demented oddity."

In real life he's neither demented nor that odd, but his music is still slightly both. Instead of a throwback he's a step forward. All in all he seems quite a happy man: "I still like music, it gives me a lot to complain about."

Waits on bagpipes and the writing process:
Excerpted from "The Beat Goes On," RockBill
October 1983
Kid Millions

Tom Waits: When I was a kid, I wanted to skip growing up and rush all the way to forty. . . .

It's hard to play with a bagpipe player. I had an opportunity to play with my first bagpipe player on this record. You can't play with them. It's like an exotic bird. I love the sound, it's like strangling a goose. I played the trumpet when I was a kid, but I gave it up. I liked it because it was easy to carry. It was like carrying your lunch. A piano, you have to go to it. You never hear anybody say "Pass me that piano, buddy." Composing on different instruments will give you different songs. So, I'm trying to get away from the piano as a compositional device and find something else to write on. . . .

The problem is that all these things pass through you all the time, and when you sit down to write, it's really just like purchasing a butterfly net. It's going on all the time, it's just that you're going to draw a frame around it now. You're going to reach up and grab some and swallow it.

Waits on memories:
Excerpted from "One from the Heart & One for the Road," New Musical Express (UK)
October 1, 1983
Kristine McKenna

Kristine McKenna: Much of your music exudes a melancholy sense of the past, a yearning for some intangible thing that seems to have been lost. Is memory a source of comfort and joy for most people, or is it more apt to be a source of pain?

Tom Waits: My memory isn't a source of pain. Parts of it are like a pawnshop, other parts are like an aquarium, and other parts are like a closet. I think there's a place where your memory becomes distorted like a fun-house mirror and that's the area I'm most interested in.

KM: Do experiences tend to be idealized by the memory?

TW: Some things, yes. It makes other things worse than they really were.

KM: What's your earliest memory fixed in your mind?

TW: I have a very early memory of getting up in the middle of the night and standing at my doorway by the hall in the house and having to stand there and wait while a train went by. And after the train passed I could cross the hall into my parents' room.

KM: Was there a train yard nearby where you grew up?

TW: Not at that particular house, but there were trains in all the places I grew up. My grandmother lived by an orange grove and I remember sleeping at her house and hearing the Southern Pacific go by. This was in La Verne, California. My father moved from Texas to La Verne and he worked in the orange groves there. I also have a memory of wild gourds that grew by the railroad tracks, and putting pennies on the tracks.

KM: What sort of music were you exposed to when you were growing up?

TW: The earliest music I remember was mariachi, ranchera, romantica—Mexican music. My father used to tune that in on the car radio. He didn't listen to jitterbug or anything like that.

Waits on why the dream is so much sweeter than the taste:
Excerpted from "Tom Waits for No Man," Melody Maker
October 29, 1983
Brian Case

On the road with him a few years ago—Tom, my nephew Tommy Sheehan, and I drinking at dawn with the lesbian chapter of the Eskimo Hell's Angels—he had spoken of high hopes for his screenplay, *Why Is the Dream So Much Sweeter Than the Taste?* The title turned out mainly prophetic.

"Never got off the ground. Hah! Actually, I told Coppola the story and he used a piece of it in *One from the Heart*. Where the guy conducted some cars and a woman did a tightrope walk across the junkyard. I was the music department on *One from the Heart*. It was a real collaboration. You have to write a piece of music of a certain length for a scene, and then you get the music to fit. It was my first experience with films, so I wasn't complaining. Francis'd come and play me some music and describe a scene and he'd get the musicians together in a small room and we'd start playing and he'd start conducting in his own way. I'd throw out song titles. Some of it works better than others. Putting music to film is an old problem."

Waits on hotels, dives, and being a lowlife:
Excerpted from Loose Talk, Channel 4 (UK)
October 18, 1983
Steven Taylor

Steven Taylor: I've read somewhere that you once lived in a brothel, is that true?

Tom Waits: I don't know, you must have me mixed up with somebody else.

ST: OK, well you've lived in some "dives," have you not?

TW: I don't know if that translates in my language. Do you mean like a place with a pool?

ST: No, not really. I'm thinking more of the other end of the housing scale, really, something you know, pretty rough. Low-rent? Is that an American expression?

TW: Low-rent. You mean like Rangoon? Or Iowa?

ST: I'm thinking of the seedier parts of Los Angeles probably.

TW: You mean like a farming community?

ST: No, not that kind of seed. Have a go, a guess . . . try and guess what I'm getting at . . . yeah?

TW: I think what you're trying to ask me is have I ever lived in a cheap hotel?

ST: Yeah, that could be it! Yeah!

TW: I have a lot of close personal friends of mine that have lived in that type of place, and I've heard all the stories.

Waits on hobgoblins and fame:
Excerpted from Saturday Live, **BBC-Radio 1**
October 22, 1983
Richard Skinner

Tom Waits: You try and continue to explore new musical geography. "Consistency is the hobgoblin of little minds." You hope you're moving onward and upward and into something different. It's just an attempt to chronicle things in a more impressionistic way. I think musically I made some small private breakthroughs. The next thing will be a different LP. Some of the stuff in this new one I like. But usually the things that you are most fond of are the songs that you have yet to write.

Richard Skinner: Do you work on songs all the time or do they come to you quickly?

TW: At gunpoint. You carry them around and then it comes out.

RS: Will we get the chance to see you perform any of the songs live over here?

TW: Ah, well, let's see. I'm currently putting [on] the other kind of a demented-dark-follies-cabaret-musical-revue type of a Kabuki burlesque show. I'm going to be the focus of it.

Waits on the darker regions of his memory:
Excerpted from "Swordfish Out of Water," *Sounds*
November 5, 1983
Edwin Pouncey

I'm more interested in how your memory distorts things. It's like an apparatus that dismantles things and puts them back together with some of the parts missing. When you remember something it's always a distorted impression, once the moment is gone the memory is very different to the actual moment itself.

It's like when you misunderstand somebody or you're eavesdropping and you only hear part of a conversation, you reconstruct the rest of it around that. Or you read a magazine article that says "continued page 23" but that page is torn out so all you had was those two paragraphs to go on . . .

My parents had a friend who was an Indian woman, she used to paint Christmas scenes on the store windows during the holidays. We used to take her milk and eggs in the middle of the night. Then she inherited a lot of money and moved away . . .

My father knew a couple who owned a chicken ranch, she was a hypochondriac and he was an alcoholic. She looked like an exotic bird, she looked like a canary in a wet suit and he looked like Errol Flynn. As I remember something though, I'm changing it too, I mean he probably didn't look like Errol Flynn at all.

Waits continued promoting *Swordfishtrombones* by once again appearing on *Late Night* with David Letterman. The television host's quirky humor was a perfect match for the similarly quirky musician, together formulating some late-night synergy for their respective fans.

Waits on show and tell:
Excerpted from *Late Night with David Letterman*, NBC-TV
December 21, 1983

Tom Waits: I got a letter from a little kid that was from somewhere in the Midwest who had been suspended from school for bringing one of my records into a share.

Dave Letterman: A "show-and-tell" deal?

TW: Yeah, it was that type of thing, and so it interrupted his curriculum, temporarily.

DL: What was the particular record and the song he was playing for the kids?

TW: I think there was some reference to underwear in the song and so the teacher thought it was inappropriate. He was seven years old. So I wrote a letter and I did what I could.

DL: Trying to get him off the hook.

TW: A lot of these things are out of my hands.

DL: But it's nice that you've made the effort! I mean, without that he might have gone on to a life of crime, you never know.

TW: Someone has got to stand up for him.

Waits finished the year of 1983 with a photo shoot in the middle of Times Square with rock photographer George DuBose. By early 1984, he and Kathleen once again switched residences from Los Angeles to New York City. During this time, Waits initiated important relationships with future collaborators John Lurie, Jim Jarmusch, and Robert Frank.

Waits on identity, the creative process, and *Swordfishtrombones*:
Excerpted from unidentified audio source
1983

Tom Waits: I remember I worked in a restaurant for several years and Sal Crivello, who I worked with for six years, I never saw him in anything but a paper hat and a white linen shirt and dirty apron and white socks and black tractor-tread shoes and one night, it was Christmas Eve I think, I stayed late, he left early and he changed. He went into the little closet and he changed; it was like watching Superman. He went into this little closet and he came out with a sweater shirt and a little gold pepper around his neck and slicked his hair down, tight, a stay-pressed slack job there, and loafers, wild socks, and apparently an unbelievable itinerary. He was going to a bowling alley with a girl who was about six foot seven, weighed about 220, and I always remember that, the thrill of seeing him dressed as somebody else. I thought he wore that little white uniform everywhere he went, just like I always thought jazz musicians slept in their clothes and stayed in four-dollar rooms, drank cheap booze, and lived this whole life of self-denial, kind of in the name of the music. I found out all these guys wear panty hose, sit out by the swimming pool, play golf in the afternoon; it was really hard for me.

Q: Now you personify that image. Is that true?

TW: Yeah, that's me.

Q: There isn't that separation, is there?

TW: Well, I think it's important at some point to make a distinction. I think that you can continue to write about certain things without staying overnight there. Yeah, I think that's possible, it's safer. Hubert Selby Jr. has a nice family and is very . . . he writes about the dark side. It all depends on how you handle it, I guess. The creative process is imagination, memories, nightmares, and dismantling certain aspects of this world and putting them back together in the dark. Songs aren't necessarily verbatim chronicles or necessarily journal entries, they're like smoke, it's like it's made out of smoke. The stuff that makes a song . . . well, usually a song will remind you of something, it will take you back somewhere and make you think of somebody or someplace. They're like touchstones, or a mist.

Q: Why do it?

TW: It beats working in a fish market. It beats working in a slaughterhouse, and you have to do something 'cause you have to do it. It's just a bad habit with me, I get nervous when I'm not writing, I'm usually working on something . . .

Q: *Swordfishtrombones* is a soundtrack?

TW: Yeah, in some demented fashion I've tried to knit the songs together. I tried to have characters reappear at some point or another so that there was some sense of a revue or follies, that it all had some type of logic. The stuff on the new record is more . . . there's no saxophones. It's tuba, trombone, trumpet, bass marimba, accordion, banjo, electric guitar, harmonium, bass boobams, metal aunglongs, African squeeze drums. I tried to find a more exotic orchestra. There is much more percussion than I'm used to in the past. I was trying to get it to imitate things that I'm already used to hearing rather than just being separate, so it's more like an organized automobile accident and it has some shape to it, but it also relates to the real event itself. Some of the stuff on "Shore Leave" is sound effects, the low trombone is like a bus going by. I got a little more adventurous, I'm still a little timid about it, but melody is what really hits me first, melody is the first thing that seduces me. "Underground" had some; I thought it felt like a Russian march, the music to accompany the activities of a mutant dwarf community in the steam tunnels. That kind of a feel is what I was after. Some of the stuff is familiar territory. "Frank's Wild Years" is Jimmy Smith organ, Ken Nordine–attitude, "Gin Soaked Boy" is some of that old New Orleans thing, "Down, Down, Down" is more of a Pentecostal reprimand. In "Sixteen Shells" I wanted a chain-gang sort of feel, banging a hammer on an anvil. I used a brake drum and bell plate and tried to take it outside; certain instruments bring you indoors, other instruments take you outdoors.

Q: The album is a dramatic expansion of sound.

TW: Just dramatic? I don't know how dramatic, I noticed places where I pulled back and other places where I stretched out, it's hard to tell immediately till you look over your shoulder and you move on and you say, 'Oh, yeah, that was the place where I went over there so I could come over here.' I tried to keep as much air in there as I could, so that there's a sense of the room itself. Biff Dawes and I worked on trying to get a sense of the room, using a lot of different microphones to that end . . .

I wrote everything very close together, all in about two weeks so the songs have a relationship. That's the one I wrote yesterday. Today I'll hitch this one to that one, so you usually try to leave an end of the one you wrote before open, so it can attach onto the one you're writing next, rather than just a random arbitrary collection of tunes. I tried to get 'em to knit. It's not entirely successful as far as a libretto. It's just one guy who leaves the old neighborhood and joins the Merchant Marines, gets in a little trouble in Hong Kong, comes home, marries the girl, burns his house down, and takes off on an adventure, that kind of a story.

Q: There's a strong military feeling, is that you or the character?

TW: It's more the character than me. "Soldier's Things" I imagined was like a pawnshop. It's raining outside, and a bunch of sailors with all the instruments hanging up, and a guy pawning his watch. I lived in National City, every night the place was loaded with sailors, so I at one point considered joining the navy, but a friend of mine talked me out of it. I guess what made it most attractive was the $38.00 a month. I wanted to go to Hong Kong. . . .

There was a time when songwriters were heralded and considered valuable. Writing is valuable and important. I think, it's what you do with it and where you take it, and how you get it to come off the page and into your forehead. I was never really part of that coffeehouse scene, I kind of missed that. I've always kind of been on the outside, so I started doing this because I didn't fit. So you kind of don't want someone to tell you that you fit in over here, 'cause that's why you started doing what you did before. The creative process remains, regardless of whether it's 1939 or 1979, it remains the same.

At one point, Waits almost worked in collaboration with singer-songwriter Marianne Faithfull. Faithfull recalled in her autobiography, "A project like this requires weeks and weeks of sitting around listening to old records, and the person you usually end up working with is the one who has the time. Tom wanted to do it, but he was busy having a life: getting married, having children, making records." Musician-producer Hal Willner also wanted to work with Waits, planning at times to do a whole album together. Instead they collaborated on one song, "What Keeps Mankind Alive" from Kurt Weill's *The Threepenny Opera*. It was released on the album *Lost in the Stars: The Music of Kurt Weill*.

Waits's new film with director Jim Jarmusch and actor John Lurie was titled *Down by Law*. Jarmusch recalled one telling incident during the filming: "There were a lot of student nurses living there at the time, which was kinda weird. I remember on Tom Waits's birthday, I remember him having a bottle of champagne in each hand and drinking alternately from each bottle, and he would go around knocking on doors saying, 'We're a party on wheels, let us in!' And the nursing students would open up the door with the chain still on, and they'd take one look at Tom and then slam the door."

Meanwhile, Elektra Records wanted to cash in on Waits's renewed attention and complete the terms of his contractual obligation. They released some demos and outtakes that were deemed less than desirable to Tom's perfectionist standards. The new LPs were *Anthology* and *The Asylum Years*, neither of which was promoted by Waits.

RAIN DOGS (1985)

Island Records released *Rain Dogs* in September 1985. The Waits/Brennan duo had pointed the way with *Swordfishtrombones* and bottled their unique brand with the forward-thinking follow-up. While the rest of the new 1980s acts were content to ration out their music with LinnDrum programming and synthesizers, Waits shunned all that, though he was impressed by musicians like Prince. His music could no more be labeled "'80's music" than his earlier releases were "'70's" music. It was and remains strictly "Tom Waits" music.

Rain Dogs' album cover was unconventional as well, passing on the obligatory slick graphics of other albums but instead featuring an eerie Waits lookalike resting on the shoulders of a guffawing woman. Was it an old girlfriend? His mother? The madam of a Danish brothel? Shot by famed Swedish photographer Anders Petersen, it actually came from a collection of photos he had taken over several years of the working crowd at the Café Lehmitz, including street people, cab drivers, prostitutes, and the sailors who patronized them on shore leave. The photo portented the album's contents, the veritable rain dogs left wandering the streets after a deluge of rain had washed them from the streets. Says Petersen about his art: "The people at the Café Lehmitz had a presence and a sincerity that I myself lacked. It was OK to be desperate, to be tender, to sit all alone or share the company of others. There was a great warmth and tolerance in this destitute setting."

Hard-core fans rank *Rain Dogs* the highest among all of Waits's albums. It is seated in the middle of a musical triptych, between *Swordfishtrombones* and *Franks Wild Years*. Musical peers took notice. Elvis Costello, who was riding a crest of popularity with his 1984 LP *Goodbye Cruel World* (and a starring turn on Live Aid on July 13, 1985—Waits did not participate), was impressed with Waits's evolution of sound. Costello told Patrick Humphries for his Waits biography, *Small Change: A Life of Tom Waits* (1989):

> When the records *Swordfishtrombones* and *Rain Dogs* came out, I thought
> it was a very brave move, because he had such a totally complete persona,
> based around this hipster thing he'd taken from Kerouac and Bukowski,

and the music was tied to some Beat/jazz thing, and suddenly it's exploring music that was something to do with Howlin' Wolf and Charles Ives.
I think I was envious, not so much of the music, but his ability to rewrite
himself out of the corner he'd appeared to have backed himself into. It
was an audacious thing to do, and I think that anyone who can't recognize
the quality of that music really doesn't have their ears on the right way
round!

Rain Dogs continues to live up to its solid reputation. It remained his bestselling album until the release of Mule Variations in 1999. Featuring Keith Richards as a guest artist, the one thing tying this release to Waits's past albums is
that it too was recorded under inauspicious, unassuming surroundings, giving
each song a raw, unpolished resonance reminiscent of the Rolling Stones' Exile
on Main Street (an album Waits ranks highly among his influences for this
period). Waits compared the Lower Manhattan basement on Washington Street
in which the album was recorded to a vault. To prepare for the sessions, Waits
conducted some location research by recording the sounds of the teeming city
streets for inspiration. Waits also played the songs solo on what Marc Ribot
described as a "ratty, old hollow-body" acoustic guitar, from which he would
"slap" out the groove of the songs in an effort to give direction on how he
wanted it to sound. Waits expanded the repertoire of his instrumentation, conjuring from potential cacophony a splendidly eclectic assemblage, including
banjo, accordion, and marimba. The results satisfied not only the band's leader,
but the musicians participating in the sessions (including Keith Richards, who
added his signature licks to "Big Black Mariah"). Once Richards tuned into the
"animal instinct" of Waits's musical vision, the composition was a lock. The nineteen songs of the album constitute a gumbo stew of cross-referenced genres,
including a polka, two folk-based instrumentals, and others hinting at country,
pop, and gospel. For poetic embellishment, he included his spoken-word paean
to the soul-scarred urban environment he was so much a part of, "Ninth &
Hennepin."

    In September 1985 Tom and Kathleen welcomed their first son (and future
drummer for his dad) into the Waitsian universe, Casey Xavier Waits, who was
born during the hectic rush of the new album's promotion and tour rehearsals.
Then, in October, Waits and his touring band took Rain Dogs to Europe. The tour

ended in November 1985 with final dates in New York City and Los Angeles. By year's end, *Rolling Stone* magazine had declared Waits "Songwriter of the Year."

If Waits had any reservations about the reception of his new material, it was dispelled by the time *Franks Wild Years* was released two years later. According to rock journalist Robert Hilburn of the *Los Angeles Times*, Waits really wanted (contrary to his deep-seated paranoia) to be remembered, despite not being on the tip of the tongue of the public as a famous recording artist: "It's a strange thing with Tom. One thing about him is he's got this obsession to be remembered, to be different, to stand out. He told me a story that one time when he was a kid he went to a used-record store and went through the 99-cent bin. All of these records that were made by these people, they were all forgettable. [He said], 'I never want to be another name in that forgettable list.' I think sometimes he even went out of his way to be different. ("Rock Critic Robert Hilburn Talks of Music That Matters," *Blogcritics*—November 2009, Donald Gibson)

"The Sultan of Sleaze"
You magazine (supplement in *The Mail on Sunday*)
Late Summer 1985 (issue date: October 13, 1985)
Pete Silverton

> *Well I got a bad liver and a broken heart,*
> *yea I drunk me a river since you tore me apart,*
> *and I don't have a drinking problem 'cept when I can't get a drink*
> —"Bad Liver and a Broken Heart"

"When I'm recording I have certain things I have to do. I wet down my hair, I turn my jacket inside out, and I undo the first button on my collar. I throw a rock through a window, I tear the head off a doll, I drink a bottle of Scotch and, er, I'm there.

"For some people to have to watch you go through that it's a little embarrassing. So you have to work with people you trust, people who won't turn on you."

Tom, be honest, do you always lie? "No, no. I always tell the truth—except to policemen. It's an old reflex." He coughed, light and dry, perhaps a nervous tic, maybe the legacy of years spent living down to his billing as a "lowlife poet."

Tom Waits is a singer, thirty-five years old. His triangular face is as pointed as his derelict English boots—"imitation alligator skin, no one died to get these on my feet"—and finishes in a wisp of a goatee showing the first traces of gray. His father, he said, was president of a small country in Central America and his mother was a dwarf. I didn't believe that one either. "I don't think it's that important to tell the truth," he once said. Like the boy who cried wolf, he is disbelieved even when he's being honest. Waits, I'd said, was an unusual name. "Well," he deadpanned, "my name was Waitsosky and then we dropped the -osky." Oh really, said gullible me. "No, Waits is a musical term. It's the guy that puts out the lights at the end of the day and sings all the stories of what's happened in the town." Disbelievingly, I laughed. The dictionary put me right.

It's also a fair description of Waits's stock-in-trade—"a latter-day vaudevillian who weaves folktale and street patois into a hip new suit of his own design," one enthusiast called him. His songs are romances of the gutter, inheritors of an American tradition that takes in Simon & Garfunkel's "The Boxer" as well as Kerouac and Raymond Chandler. "Vocabulary is my main instrument," he said.

His singing voice is like rusty nails in a bottle of cheap bourbon. Yet his last album, his ninth since his first manager discovered him playing piano to the drunks in a Los Angeles cocktail lounge, was a top thirty hit in Britain. He's promoting his new record, *Rain Dogs*, with eight nights at London's Dominion Theatre, beginning this week.

The restaurant where we met—all vinyl, Formica, and sachets of Sweet'N Low—was his choice. "Tom likes to meet people in places he feels at home," said his press agent. It was on Manhattan's Fourteenth Street, crowded with Saturday lunchtime shoppers delving through the market stalls as the traders boasted about how their goods were stolen. Down the road from the Fourteenth Street Underwear King and across the street from Cohen's Fashion Opticals, it's the kind of area Waits was thinking of when he wrote about where "all the donuts have names that sound like prostitutes."

Waits lived on the next block. But, as his wife was about to have their second child, they were all staying with their parents out in New Jersey, half an hour by train, changing at Frank Sinatra's birthplace, Hoboken. Soon after the birth, the whole family would hit the road, abandoning not only the family home but their own Manhattan apartment. For the foreseeable future they'd be living out of suitcases. "Suites, room service, dry toast, and keep the coffee coming."

Waits's marriage and fatherhood came as something of a shock to his long-time fans, who'd grown up thinking of him as just one step from the decrepit failures he wrote about. Although he exudes the dingy run-down air of New York's treeless canyons, he's in fact spent most of his life in Los Angeles. That's where he met his wife, Kathleen Brennan, when she was script-editing Francis Ford Coppola's *One from the Heart*, the studio musical for which Waits wrote the music.

That and his burgeoning career as an actor (*Rumble Fish*, *Paradise Alley*, *The Cotton Club*) aside, Waits's Los Angeles is a long way from Hollywood dreams. His was the world of massage parlors, pawnshops, and dope dealers; Fourteenth Street with sun, in fact. Waits also had a reputation as a heavy drinker. Was this true? "Well, that is what I call a direct question. I don't know how things like that get started. But you know how the press blows everything out of proportion. You know, you have a little glass of sherry before bed, read a little Balzac, hit the light about eight thirty. Before you know it they've got you with a case of Cutty Sark in a cheap room with a dirty magazine."

But you lived at the Tropicana, the city's seediest rock 'n' roll hotel. No one goes to sleep there before eight thirty in the morning. "Yeah, I did my time there. I left when they painted the pool black and drained all the water. They got tired of cleaning it. It's like black socks; you never have to wash them. I knew that was my cue."

Another reason for his departure was the phoning from insane people. Waits had put his address on the back of one of his albums, he said, to check up on whether the record was being properly distributed. The response arrived in sackfuls. "It got a little bizarre," he said.

"I'll tell you all my secrets but I lie about my past," he wrote in "Tango Till They're Sore." He evades questions with practiced ease and refuses to be drawn about his own little family, insisting that that's part of his life he doesn't want to use to publicize his career. Always a polite man, rather than bluntly stonewall, he switches subjects.

His parents were first generation Californians, children of Steinbeck fodder pushed by the Depression from Texas to the orange groves. His mother's family was Norwegian, his father's Scots/Irish. His grandfather was called Jesse Frank Waits, after the two outlaw James brothers. His father Frank, a teacher, left his mother when Tom was eleven. Tom and his two sisters grew up in National City, close to the Mexican border.

You got to tell me brave captain,
why are the wicked so strong,
how do the angels get to sleep
when the devil leaves his porch light on
—"Mr. Siegal"

Just once in our conversation he found himself talking about his father. Instantly he changed tack. He says he was something of a tearaway as an adolescent. "I enjoyed the thrill of breaking the law, stealing, you know. All kids like that. But what sort of a child was I? I can't really answer that point-blank. But, you know, I liked trains and horses, birds and rocks, radios and bicycles." Elsewhere, he's said he left school at sixteen, worked in a restaurant. He told me he studied medicine. "A lot of doctors in my family—and alcoholics." He abandoned what he called the certainties of a doctor's life for music. "It was something that I didn't completely understand. I thought: I'm going to ride this somewhere, it's going to take me somewhere. I couldn't go any other way. You're in the world of adventure. It literally takes you places. It's like you went to sleep in a small house on a quiet street and you woke up in New York. The idea that you can dream yourself someplace, can change your world." One of the few songs written by other people that Waits has recorded is Stephen Sondheim's "Somewhere."

His family hero was his uncle Robert, a blind organ player. He'd installed a church organ in his house, the pipes coming up to the roof. Didn't his neighbors mind? "I guess he had something on them and they had something on him, you know. That's part of living next door to somebody. I'd rather live next door to an organ player than a guy that's a member of the National Rifle Association." Would you like to live next door to Tom Waits? "Well," he said, stressing his words with his right hand, his gray eyes still as a lizard's, "I guess I'm one of those guys you better not throw your baseball into his yard or you'll never see it again. I sit on the porch with a bottle of sour mash, spitting tobacco out on the sidewalk and shooting birds out of the sky." In New York? "That's my dream."

He moved to Manhattan when Coppola—with whom he'd already worked on *One from the Heart* and *Rumble Fish*—cast him as the manager in *Cotton Club*. Filming took so long "it was like joining the army; it was like being shanghaied." Toward the end of this year, he'll take up movie acting again; five weeks in New

Orleans on a film called *Down by Law*, about three prisoners escaping through the swamps. Next year he should be in a New York "odyssey" written by Rudy Wurlitzer (*Two Lane Blacktop*, *Pat Garrett and Billy the Kid*) and directed by Robert Frank, whose 1950s book of photographs, *America*, depicted the same part of the nation's culture that Waits now sings about.

Next spring should see the premiere of his stage musical, *Franks Wild Years*. (We should not forget his father was called Frank.) It takes up where a monologue left off on his last album, with Frank having burned down his house with the dog inside while his wife was at the beauty parlor. "Basically, it's about an accordion player who goes out into the world to make his mark and ends up despondent and penniless, dreaming his way back home." Tom will play Frank; he's already brushing up on his accordion playing. Written with his wife, Kathleen—"her name comes first"—it will be produced in Chicago by Steppenwolf Company, which also brought Sam Shepard's *True West* to the stage.

His new record, *Rain Dogs*, is the first he's made in New York. It takes its title from the city's street population. "People who live outdoors. You know how after the rain you see all these dogs that seem lost, wandering around. The rain washes away all their scent, all their direction. So all the people on the album are knit together by some corporeal way of sharing pain and discomfort."

Helping him to establish that mood on the record are the stars of Lower Manhattan's avant-garde session circuit and Rolling Stone Keith Richards, someone who just never plays on other people's records. "I was really flattered." They share an attitude toward studio technology, bucking the trend of generating music with a computer. "If I want a sound, I usually feel better if I've chased it and killed it, skinned it and cooked it. Most things you can get with a button nowadays. So if I was trying for a certain drum sound, my engineer would say: "Oh, for Christ's sake, why are we wasting our time? Let's just hit this little cup with a stick here, sample something (take a drum sound from another record) and make it bigger in the mix, don't worry about it." I'd say, "No, I would rather go in the bathroom and hit the door with a piece of two-by-four very hard."

"On this one I took some chances. *Swordfishtrombones* was done in Los Angeles. It was much more relaxed, much more leisure-oriented." Still a record of some tension, though? "Yeah, well my wife says I take that everywhere." Waits sat there nodding, examining his cold whole wheat toast. "Was it all right," he kept asking as we searched for a taxi. "Did I tell you the right things for you to make an article out of it?" For Waits, an interview is as much a performance as a stage show.

How about a last message to England? He thought a second, tugged his gold wedding band. "In the words of the old show-business sage, 'Champagne for my real friends; real pain for my sham friends.'"

"Waits Happening"
Beat
Late Summer 1985 (issue date: March 1986)
Pete Silverton

Tom Waits chose to meet in the heart of his own territory, in a cheap restaurant just down the road from what he said was his eighth home in New York. Outside, the Fourteenth Street market was in full Saturday lunchtime swing. Like Petticoat Lane, it flourishes amid, or because of, rumors that most of the goods have been dishonestly acquired. It was easy to feel he'd have chosen it for the interview even if he didn't live close by. So Tom Waits. Or, at least, so like the backdrop of so many Tom Waits songs.

It's an easy distinction to blur. Waits encourages the blurrings. When his PR handed me a copy of "Tom Waits Talks about *Swordfishtrombones*," he advised me: "Full of tall stories, wondrous inventions, downright lies, and maybe the odd truth."

For many years a notoriously difficult interviewee, peppering long gasps in the conversation with the occasional grunted "Yes" or "No," he's now developed a Tom Waits persona he can wheel out for interviewers. Its only major fault, apart from saying "you know" too often, is a tendency to use the same set phrases in different interviews. "Champagne for my real friends; real pain for my sham friends," was his favorite this time around.

The new ease with the press seemed to coincide with two other big switches in his life: his marriage to Kathleen Brennan, whom he met when she was working as a script editor for film director Francis Ford Coppola, and the change in his music, which happened with his switch of record labels. Barfly groanings gave way to a music that encompassed everything from Charles Ives to Howlin' Wolf.

"Currently," he said, "I'm not operating with a full staff." No manager. He was hoping, he joked, that Bullets Durgom, an old-style showbiz manager, would take him up. I suggested Mickey Duff, the boxing promoter. He liked the name, promised to give him serious consideration. His favorite record of the moment was Agnes Bernelle's *Father's Lying Dead on the Ironing Board*. When the interview was over, he asked how he'd done, was it all right?

Pete Silverton: You've lived in New York a couple of years now. Yet, in most people's minds, you're still strongly linked with California. Not the Beach Boys' California maybe but Nathaniel West's. . . .

Tom Waits: Well, we moved here for the peace and quiet, you know. Somehow I was misinformed. I came here for a movie [*Cotton Club*] with a suitcase and everything's still in boxes. I've moved eight times since I've been here. New York is like living inside of an engine. Some of the simplest things require a great deal of concentration and patience. It bears no resemblance to any place on the globe. So it kind of gets you prepared for nothing else. It's like being on a ship. People are even terrified to go to Brooklyn. Like that's the water, this [Manhattan] is the ship and anything outside of this and you're in the water. It's very peculiar. But there is something interesting about Manhattan. Someone could stand out in the middle of Fourteenth Street stark naked, playing a trumpet with a dead pigeon on their head and no one would flinch. In fact, tomorrow there will probably be two guys like that. They'd be lease-letting, trying to get more subscribers. I wouldn't bring up a family here, not unless I had a whole lot of money. You can't really live in a completely civilized manner in New York unless you have a lot of money. Dead presidents [i.e., dollar bills]. Lots of dead presidents, please. Get them right over here. You see, I think the place that you write stuff about usually ends up in the song. I wrote most of *Rain Dogs* down on Washington Street. It's a kind of rough area, Lower Manhattan between Canal and Fourteenth Street, just about a block in from the river. I started sharing a rehearsal space with the Lounge Lizards. I had nights there in this boiler room and a Siamese cat would go by sounding like a crying baby, every night. And there was a drummer down the hall. It was a good place for me to work. Very quiet, except for the water coming through the pipes every now and then. Sort of like being in a vault. With music, it's difficult to talk about the writing of it. It gets so pedantic. It's all made out of smoke. When you really think about it, it's invisible. And you're afraid it's not going to come and sit next to you anymore. And that keeps you doing it. When I'm writing I have sort of waking dreams. I try to go inside, go through a window someplace.

PS: It's probably been said many times before but your songs remind me of Edward Hopper paintings, which also often look through windows. He'd ride the subway and look at the secretaries working.

TW: Oh yeah. Well, I like listening to music through the wall. I like hearing things incomplete. New York's a place to do that because it's an international city, a cosmopolitan city. There's Little Italy, Chinatown, Russian cabdrivers. You have a chance to hear a lot of different kinds of music.

PS: Keith Richards plays on three tracks of *Rain Dogs*. He hardly ever plays on other people's records. Did you just think of a particular texture he could provide?

TW: There was something in there that I thought he would understand. I picked out a couple of songs that I thought he would understand and he did. He's got a great voice and he's just a great spirit in the studio. He's very spontaneous; he moves like some kind of animal. I was trying to explain "Big Black Mariah" and finally I started to move in a certain way and he said, "Oh, why didn't you do that to begin with? Now I know what you're talking about." It's like animal instinct.

PS: How about your acting?

TW: I'll be going to New Orleans soon to work with Jim Jarmusch for about five weeks on a film called *Down by Law*. It's about three guys in prison who make a jailbreak through the swamps.

PS: How large a budget?

TW: It's under a million.

PS: So it's basically just a cheap film.

TW: I wouldn't say that to Jim if I were you. If you're not careful, I'll tell him you said that.

PS: That's a compliment. I mean, people waste so much. . . . You worked on *Cotton Club*, you know how money . . .

TW: Yeah, that was like *Cleopatra*.

PS: Did you meet Bob Hoskins?

TW: Yeah, he's great; he's something else. I liked him a lot. He kept wanting to go out to the bar. I think he felt a whole lot better once he located that tavern right down at the end of the block. A little beer bar. He was holding court down there. He had his own little film going on. I think it relaxed him a lot.

PS: How long did you work on it?

TW: About twelve weeks.

PS: Hoskins was on it for about eighteen months, wasn't he?

TW: Yeah, it was like joining the army, like being shanghaied. But that film was, er . . . I don't know what to say about it apart from that it dealt with a very important period of American history.

PS: Any other acting planned?

TW: I'm doing a film with Rudi Wurlitzer and Robert Frank. [Wurlitzer wrote the films *Two Lane Blacktop* and *Pat Garrett and Billy the Kid*. Robert Frank has been a photographer for many years. The Rolling Stones used some of his photographs of the ugly side of the American dream for the cover of *Exile on Main St.*, then commissioned him to film their 1972 tour of America. The result, *Cocksucker Blues*, has remained suppressed by the Stones to this day. Frank also took the portrait of Waits on the back of *Rain Dogs*.] It's an odyssey about someone in

New York searching for someone. I hesitate to say what it's really about; I doubt if it would be . . . you know, it's Robert's film. I'm just in it.

PS: Your musical, *Franks Wild Years*, is it ever going to appear?

TW: Oh yeah, in the spring. Chicago's Steppenwolf [a theater company] is going to do it. Terry Kinney is going to direct. They did *Orphans* and Sam Shepard's *True West*. My wife wrote the play with me. Her name's first on it, not mine. It still needs a lot of work but, I mean, it's finished.

PS: Does it bear any relation to your song of the same title?

TW: Yeah, that's the same Frank. Basically, it's about an accordion player from a small town who goes out into the world to make his mark and ends up despondent and penniless. I play Frank so I'm going to take accordion lessons. I'm ready. I love the accordion, I tell you. I think it's going to come back and it's going to come back big.

PS: At the end of the song Frank burns the house down with the dog inside. Does he get charged with arson?

TW: No, he goes to Vegas, ends up dreaming his way back home.

PS: And the dog's gone?

TW: The dog has disappeared.

PS: Did you like *One from the Heart*?

TW: Well, that's a loaded question. It was a two-and-a-half-year project and it had some real nice moments. What I got out of it was learning how to collaborate with someone who has a great imagination. Francis [Ford Coppola] was like a university for all ages to learn the craft of filmmaking. It was really something to be a part of. It was a great feeling. I had a little office with a piano.

PS: You once said "Success will kill you faster than failure," or at least it will kill your soul quicker. Do you think you'll ever get to the level where you'll be able to judge that for yourself?

TW: I think before I go to my reward I'd like to lie out by the pool with a cold drink and a couple of Egyptian girls fanning me. . . . Everything has its darker side. There are lots of places you can go to you can't get back from. I don't know . . . I guess you get what you pay for. Some people play it like a board game . . .

PS: Do you have any recurrent nightmares?

TW: I do. I'm in this music store. There are these wooden masks, medieval ones from Upper Volta. This guy slams the door and nails it shut from the inside and puts oxygen masks over my face. I wake up at the Taft Hotel and all the clocks are turned back, all the magazines are from 1959. I climb out the window on an old bedsheet. I'm dangling there and there's this little kid with a cigarette lighter flaming at my feet. I hang there and I swing and then I drop into a tanker car. It's full of flowers and I ride it all the way up to Seattle, Oregon. I see smoke coming out of the train. I can't seem to shake that one.

PS: What's the most scary part?

TW: The guy with the cigarette lighter at the bottoms of my feet.

PS: What kind of child were you? Your father [Frank] left your mother, didn't he?

TW: Shouldn't I be laying down for this? All of a sudden I feel like I want to see your credentials. . . . Oh, here it is: "Dr."

PS: Just a BA.

TW: Oh, just a BA. Then you'll get nothing but B.S.

Rain Dogs Tourbook
Late 1985
Tom Waits

My father played a little guitar and I had an uncle who played a church organ. They were thinking about replacing him because every Sunday there were more mistakes than there had been the Sunday before. It got to the point where "Onward Christian Soldiers" was sounding more like "The Rites of Spring" and finally, they had to let him go. They tore the church down and he took the organ and installed it in his house, he had the pipes going right through the ceiling. He was also a botanist, he lived in the middle of an orange grove where a train went by, and we used to visit him when I was very small and impressionable. I played a piano that had been out in the rain, of all things, some of the keys were stuck and didn't operate so I learned to play the black keys.

The earliest music I remember was mariachi, ranchera, romantica—Mexican music. My father used to tune that in on the car radio. He didn't listen to jitter-bug or anything like that.

It's true I'll never sing opera again. It is, however, an appropriate organ for conveying, uh . . . it's the right kind of horn for my car. People get out of the way when I blow it. It frightens children and gets me a seat at the bar. What more do you want from a voice?

Waits on the real test of a song's longevity:
Excerpted from "Dog Day Afternoon," *Time Out* (UK)
October 3–9, 1985
Richard Rayner

Tom Waits: I would feel like a success if I walked by a schoolyard and I heard kids going around a jump rope with one of my songs and they'd changed the words. 'Cos the real test of a song is if it can be a song for all seasons, in lots of different circumstances. I heard "Raindrops Keep Falling on My Head" a coupla days back. This woman, this bald woman, wearing nothing but a blanket, on the D-train, smoking a cigar, with a bottle of sour mash and a *New York Post*. She was singing:

"Raindrops *ya fuckin' mother* keep falling on my head *ya little cunt, ya pig* but that doesn't mean my eyes will soon be *what the fuck, ya fucker*." And then she just went out. Boom. I never liked that Bacharach tune before but now it's become a song for me. I'd never heard it handled in quite that way.

It's great when a song gets absorbed like that. 'Cos that's where you want to end up. To be part of the fabric, part of the life that goes on around you, with your songs. That's better than getting played on the radio. That's what I'd like.

Waits on the advantages of abnormal behavior:
Excerpted from "Subterranean Low-Life Blues," *Sounds*
October 19, 1985
Chris Roberts

Tom Waits: I'm still drawn to the ugly; I don't know if it's a flaw in my personality or something that happened when I was a child. It's like when you look out of the window: what's the first thing you notice? My wife says I look down, that's what's wrong with me. That's why I see the spit. I don't know—it's what you choose to take from your vision.

Chris Roberts: So you're a pessimist?

TW: No, I was raised a Methodist actually. But that'll change.

CR: You constantly draw on the potent and jarring imagery of "handicaps"— deaf, dumb, blind, lame—bandages—and the photo on the cover of *Rain Dogs* isn't exactly a Dagwood and Blondie cartoon.

TW: Ah yeah, it does kinda have that Diane Arbus feel to it. His name is Anders Petersen—it's a drunk sailor being held by a mad prostitute, I guess. She's cackling and he's sombre. It did capture my mood for a moment. It's just like—uh—isolated. Maybe this comes from living in New York a little bit—you kinda have to invent an invisible elevator for yourself just to live in. A guy goes to the bathroom on the tire of a car, then a $70,000 car pulls up alongside an' a woman with $350 stockings pokes her foot out into a puddle of blood and sputum, an' the rain comes down, an' a plane falls off the sky. [. . .] I always gravitate toward abnormal behavior.

Waits on *Rambo*:
Excerpted from "Hard Rain," New Musical Express **(UK)**
October 19, 1985
Gavin Martin

Gavin Martin: You worked with Sylvester Stallone once in the movie *Paradise Alley*. Have you seen *Rambo*?

Tom Waits: No I haven't. I don't want to get drawn into something here just because I did some work once because I needed the bread. America has been looking for somewhere to put the Vietnam War for so long. We're making movies to help us forget. You hear the budget for the film was so many millions of bucks and here's this guy with all his muscles and a big machine gun. But the veterans were treated like dogmeat, the film budget was so many millions of dollars, and they get $100 a month.

GM: How did you avoid the draft during the '60s?

TW: I was in Israel on a kibbutz. No, I wasn't, that's a lie, I was in Washington, sir. I was in the White House as an aide. I got excused, the way anyone would get a note from school: "Dear Mr. President, Tom is sick today and won't be able to come along."

GM: Can you remember why you became a musician in the first place?

TW: I couldn't get into medical school, the administration at the time made it difficult for me.

GM: I heard you wanted to do neurosurgery.

TW: I wanted to help out, I wanted to combine yard work and medicine. When I was young I wanted to be a policeman. I liked the uniform, I wanted a bit of authority but that changed too.

Waits on Waits:
Excerpted from "Lower East Side Story," *Face*
November 1985
Elissa van Poznak

Elissa van Poznak: What do you wish for your children?

Tom Waits: Military school immediately before they're old enough to fight me on it. I've enrolled them already.

EP: Would you be very disappointed if they grew up to be bankers?

TW: No, I think we need a banker and lawyer in the family because Dad's just impossible. He needs somebody to look after him.

EP: Why do you always write about life's suckers?

TW: I don't know . . . certain things you feel compelled to dream on.

EP: Do you have a social conscience?

TW: Nah, it's just where my eyes go.

EP: And rain dogs, what are they?

TW: It's a kind of word I made up for people who sleep in doorways. I mean, New York when it rains, all the peelings and cigarette butts float to the surface like in *Taxi Driver* when he says, "Someday a real rain's gonna come along and wash all the scum off the street." Looks better in the rain, like it's been lacquered.

EP: What's the first song you recall?

TW: "Molly Malone." I was tiny [*starts singing*]. "In Dublin's fair city where the girls are so pretty . . ."

EP: Ever thought of running your own nightclub?

TW: I don't have the discipline, I'm not organized enough, and you have to be at the register all night long. I don't have leadership qualities.

EP: You lead a band, don't you?

TW: That's different.

EP: How do you construct a song?

TW: I put on a skirt, drink a bottle of Harveys Bristol Cream sherry, go out and stand on Eighth Avenue with an umbrella and start reciting from the back of a parking ticket at full volume.

Interview with Tom Waits
CBC Stereo
Late 1985
Michael Tearson

It started with a phone call. Tom Waits, an old friend whom I'd not seen in several years, had a new album coming out, *Rain Dogs*, his second for Island Records. And of all people, he wanted to talk to me, Michael Tearson, about it! Well, on the appointed day I caught the train in New York and caught up with Tom around a friendly piano. See, he's a guy who often talks as eloquently with his fingers as he does with his voice. And all the time between just melted away . . .

Michael Tearson: The whole sound of what you've been doing has changed a lot since you got to New York City. I think it's a lot rougher, you get a lot more of that city sound and less . . . lushness since you left Los Angeles. That was evident on *Swordfishtrombones*, and it's surely evident on *Rain Dogs*. What are rain dogs?

Tom Waits: I don't know, you can get 'em in Coney Island. They're little; they come in a bun. It's just water in a bun, that's all. It's a bun that's been . . . it's a bun without a hot dog in it. It's just . . . it's been left out in the rain and they're called a rain dog and they're less expensive than a standard hot dog. . . . [*plays piano chords*] No, a rain dog is anybody who eh . . . people who sleep in doorways; people who don't have credit cards; people who don't go to church; people who don't have, ya know, a mortgage, ya know? Who fly in this whole plane by the seat of their pants. People who are going down the road . . . ya know?

MT: You might say people who live in the margins?

TW: In the margins, yeah, in the margins. Who can't afford margarine.

MT: I've had a chance listening to the record with nineteen songs in it. Do you see the thing as a whole story-type of an album?

TW: I don't know, because at first I thought there was some place where, ya know, all these people were held together with pain and discomfort and there was some imported and domestic place where they were all hooked up. I'm not sure, there does seem to be . . . for me there does seem to be some connection. I wouldn't say it's a linear story, it's more like an aquarium. So it's not really anything, ya know, that takes you from the beginning and drops you off at the end.

MT: I hear a lot of sounds, odd percussive sounds, that remind me of foreign talking, things you hear coming up from the street in the night.

TW: Yeah, I don't know, I tried. You don't always get as close as you wanted. Some of the things you hear, it's not just New York, the things that you hear when you open your ears. When I'm writing I just . . . I kinda give myself a downbeat and say "from this moment on the things that happen to me and the things that I see will somehow fall into this hole I'm digging, and the things that I'm dreaming, the blue shoes that fell off the green tractor, and the broken window that came out through the yellow floorboards, that fell through the ceiling and . . . I just kinda put it all together from one moment on. So it's like when it's raining, and you can't find enough things to catch it in. Ya know when it's not, you can stand out in the middle of the street in a dress and a funny hat and nothing's gonna make it rain. When you're writing, the ideas somehow seem to come to you and when you're not, they don't. Ya know? It's just always been like that for me. I go through periods of spells, or times when I'm more receptive.

MT: How much of a stretch of time does this album represent to you for writing?

TW: A couple of months. I worked on Washington and Horatio, a little basement boiler room, a place I was sharing down there with a couple of bands, The Lounge Lizards, John Lurie's band. John Lurie played on this. He played on that "Walking Spanish" tune and is an actor and a sax player. So it's a place where I can go at night and work and dream, so it's really fortunate to have that, to organize my thoughts. When you're writing you can bang on anything for an idea, ya know? [*a sound of metal striking metal*] So, a place that was quiet, except for the water going through the pipes.

MT: Let me ask you about some of the songs individually and get some of your thoughts about them. "Singapore" reminds me a lot of "Hong Kong Blues," Hoagy Carmichael's song, which he played in *To Have and Have Not*.

TW: Oh, yeah! Yeah, I love that song. I was thinking about what would happen if Richard Burton got stranded in Hong Kong somewhere or . . . ya know? He's this burly English with . . . you know [*unintelligible*] . . . somewhere in . . . somewhere off, ya know? Taiwan or Guam, Hong Kong, Canton, Shanghai, the Philippines, somewhere over there? So I tried to imagine what would be going through . . . make it like a Richard Burton number.

MT: With an exotic setting for immediate impact?

TW: Yeah. You just dream things.

MT: And also sets up the ambience that follows through the rest of the record.

TW: Yeah, well I hope so, a little storm at the end. I thought, "Oh, maybe that's a little pretentious to put a storm on the end of it," but I thought it worked.

MT: "Clap Hands," a violent little picture.

TW: Well, I just kinda embedded a nursery rhyme, you know? [*recites some lines for emphasis*] "Wine, wine / why the goose drank wine / the monkey chewed tobacco on the streetcar line / the line broke, the monkey got choked / they all went to heaven in a little rowboat." Yeah. "Shine, shine, a Roosevelt dime / All the way to Baltimore and running out of time." Same meter, same . . . I just tried to imagine all these guys going up the A-train, all the millionaires in tuxedos shoveling all the coal into the . . . ya know? Everyone's hanging out of the window, ya know? Just kind of a little . . . a dark little . . . a kind of a Ralph Steadman drawing.

MT: "Cemetery Polka" is kind of a peculiar family portrait.

TW: Never talk about your family in public! That's . . . I learned my lesson, but I keep putting my foot in my mouth. I'm gonna get calls from my auntie Mame. I'm gonna get calls from Uncle Biltmore, Uncle William, Uncle Vernon. All of them. You know, your Uncle Phil, ya know? It always happens, so . . . "Uncle Phil can't live without his pills / He has emphysema and he's almost blind / And we must find out where the money is / Get it now before he loses his mind." That's something I heard from the dining room during a family reunion and I never forgot it.

MT: So these are real people?!

TW: Yeah!

MT: Really? It's hard to tell sometimes . . .

TW: Oh, I don't know!

MT: Now, I wanted to ask you about the "Tango Till You're Sore" tarantella.

TW: Oh yeah.

MT: Now, that's one of these offbeat kind of off-center things that . . .

TW: Oh yeah. [*plays some chords on the piano*]

MT: It's also one of the only places you play piano on this record.

TW: It is. Yeah, I had . . . I didn't go there very often, ya know? I had a good band. I didn't really feel compelled to sit down at the piano at all. I played a little guitar and I had . . . the piano always brings me indoors, ya know? I was trying to explore some different ideas and some different places in the music and so the piano always feels like you know where you are. You can't imagine a piano out in the middle of the . . . out in the yard unless it's got some plastic over it, ya know? You can . . .

MT: There hasn't been a lot of piano in either of the two Island records really.

TW: No.

MT: Does that mean you have been writing more with the guitar?

TW: I guess it was some guitar and I rented a little pump organ. It's a little harmonium, and I've been playing the accordion a little bit. I don't know, I've been trying to . . . it's interesting to write on instruments you don't understand. You know, I pick up a saxophone and bang on a drum . . . or, ya know, a trombone. Anything that I'm unfamiliar with, that is always . . . it's always good for your process.

MT: You wind up with different ideas for melodies?

TW: Yeah, yeah, and kid's toys, you pick up the little instruments that kids have, ya know? Bang on those and it's . . . the piano always makes me feel like I'm . . . [plays "Tango Till They're Sore" on the piano]

MT: I wanna ask you about "Hang Down Your Head," it's a relatively straightforward kind of song.

TW: Yeah it's a pop song, a pop *tune* almost . . . yeah.

MT: Little looong ago echo of "Tom Dooley," I guess? I couldn't help . . . I couldn't avoid thinking of that, Tom!

TW: Yeah, "Hang Down Your Head," I mean it's "Please," ya know? But yeah, Kathleen was whistling that and I said, "What the hell is that?" She said, "Oh, I don't know." So I made it. I put it down and took it in the studio. While I'm writing and while I'm recording, everything you seem to pick up during the process somehow ends up in there. You know, it's like a big vat, you just start throwing things into it. So that's funny, yeah.

MT: It seems like a good time to ask you . . . there have been over the years some attempts of covering your songs. Other people have done them; "Ol' 55" has been done by a lot of people of course. Bruce Springsteen did that lovely version of "Jersey Girl."

TW: Yeah.

MT: Can you imagine anyone that you'd like to hear doing some of those things, or is that not even into your thinking?

TW: No, I don't think so much about it, but you like it when somebody does, ya know? The song is going out there and somebody's gonna hear them and it's a nice feeling. It's like holding pigeons, ya know? "In the Neighborhood" of *Swordfishtrombones* was covered by a Dutch group. It's called "In the Stromcafé," and it was funny!

MT: Did they translate it?

TW: Yeah . . . "Innnn de Stróóómcaféeee. . . ." It was funny, I liked that!

MT: You know I've always had this odd thought of someone like a Frank Sinatra covering something like "Tom Traubert's Blues," the Waltzing Matilda song. That always seemed to me like one that was perfect for Frank at this late day.

TW: At this late day!

MT: Well, it's not the same Frank Sinatra that we had on *Songs for Swinging Lovers* in the '50s, you know? He's not the same guy anymore, 'cause neither are we.

TW: Well, I don't know, I've been waiting to hear from Frank. He doesn't call anymore when he's in town, ya know? And I'm . . . I don't know, what are you gonna do?

MT: Well, he's a busy guy.

TW: Well, sure, I'm busy too! But come on Frank! We used to be . . . we used to be close. We used to be real close.

MT: "Blind Love" is a real cockeyed country-and-western song.

TW: That's a country song, yeah! My first! My firstborn country song I think, really, with violins and everything. I like Merle Haggard and those guys, those roadhouse guys, I like. Robert Quine played on that. He saved the song for me. I was about ready to dump it. Quine plays on albums, he plays with Lou Reed, and he came in and gave it that Jimmy Reed kind of a . . . a little bit of Jimmy Reed in there. And I was just "Goddamn, that's all right, 'cause I didn't know what the hell to do with it." It just had a bass and a guitar, ya know? I figured, "Well, maybe we ought to open this up and put a little story in here, a little spoken part." I thought I just played it a little straight. I thought it came off real straight. I was down in Nashville and asked them and they said, "Forget it, pal! You'll never get on the radio around here, pal!" So I don't know, I missed the mark. I thought "Gee, I've finally done it, we're gonna break out here and. . . ."

MT: That's another one that Keith Richards plays on.

TW: Yeah, he's a killer. Well, I always loved his songs and his voice. Ya know, "You Got the Silver," do you know that one?

MT: Yeah.

TW: Oh man! He has that fragile voice. [*imitates Richards singing*] "Baaaby!" And a real . . .

MT: He has always had the cracks built into the voice.

TM: Yeah, he's a real animal. He's a real gentleman. The way he moves and the way he . . . I really was just lucky. He was . . . they were coming here to finish up a record, to mix an album. So I just . . . I got lucky. I thought, "What have I got to lose?" So this would be a good song for Keith Richards. And he came! He came and did it! You know? I was like . . .

MT: It turned out he had been listening to your stuff?

TW: I don't know. He said he knew the last album, *Swordfishtrombones.* He knew that a little bit, yeah. You know, he's a giant, ya know? So you figure, this guy probably only listens to opera or something, ya know? Yeah like THAT. So how's he ever come across anything I've ever done, yeah?

MT: Well, he's always been one guy who takes in a lot of different kinds of influences.

TW: Well, he travels too. He's real international. The stuff that appeals to him and the stuff that he integrates into his own ideas, and he still stays in Kansas and Oklahoma and plays that real dirty, ya know? He's in St. Louis and Iowa and Bulgaria and Hong Kong and he's got it all in there.

MT: Well, it's all music.

TW: Yeah it's a place where Nigeria meets Louisiana.

MT: What kind of stuff does Tom Waits listen to, when he's not trying to write his own? What's fun listening for Tom Waits?

TW: Gosh, I don't know. Lots of different kinds of things. I mean I listen to the radio sometimes. You can learn from anything, I guess. I like songs when they come through a wall and you hear them wrong. You just pick up a piece of it, ya know? When you distort the things that you are hearing and . . . New York's good for that, things coming up out of the radio through the traffic and in the window and . . . that's good.

MT: Have you ever written a song with somebody else doing it in mind, directly?

TW: Oh yeah! "Blind Love"—I figured Merle Haggard could do that. "Say, send that right over to Merle!" . . . "Hey you! Get Merle on the phone for me!"

MT: Have you sent it over to him?

TW: No, I probably should!

MT: I think you should.

TW: No, I don't really think like that. I figure, you throw these things out there and you don't really know what they're gonna mean to who. You're usually wrong when you try and play them for something that you thought would happen. I hate to be disappointed. So I'd rather just say, "Well, here's some stuff that I scribbled down, we'll just throw it out of the window and see what happens."

MT: Anyone ever asked Tom Waits to do a commercial?

TW: Yeah, the money wasn't good enough, ya know? Yeah, they wanted me to do the one for American Airlines and I said, "Well, if I'm gonna sell out, you got to get the money up!" Ya know? "I got to be able to retire on this, 'cause I'm never gonna be able to work again."

MT: Let me ask about one or two of the songs on *Rain Dogs* again. "Gun Street Girl"—I hear a little bit of "Danville Dame."

TW: Oh yeah? That was a revelation. I tried to make it a "tale in a tale," ya know? Where is the end of this tale? There's "telling everyone they saw, they went that-away." There's this girl tied to a tree with a skinny millionaire and a guy coming into Baker with a pistol and a . . . so I just tried to throw it all in there and make it like "what the hell's going on around here?" It's like when you wake up in the middle of the night and you try to remember something that you don't, you remember just pieces of things, ya know? But yeah, I liked that, I liked that one too.

MT: "Union Square," right after, is kind of a real flip side to that.

TW: That's just real straight. Keith played on that too. He played that . . . that guitar, Jesus! You know? He leans forward at almost at like two o'clock. I mean if this was like ten until two, ya know? He leans so far forward, he must have a string attached to the back of his neck and it's run up and it's being held to the ceiling and it keeps him from falling flat on his face. It's unbelievable. He had these old shoes, looked like a dog chewed 'em up. He was drinking this Rebel Yell sour mash whiskey and he looks like a pirate. He's a killer.

MT: He's looking healthier. He went through a phase of course when he looked like death went over him with a match.

TW: Well, it's all part of the down-the-road, ya know? I mean, we all have that to look forward to. He's got it behind him!

MT: How many days of work did he put in the studio with you?

TW: Just one night! He came in but I guess about . . . I don't know. About nine o'clock and we worked till about four in the morning.

MT: "Downtown Train."

TW: Yeah, that's kind of a pop song. Or an attempt at a pop song.

MT: It's got some other people playing on it. G. E. Smith from the Hall & Oates band, Tony Levin on bass . . .

TW: Yeah . . . all nice guys.

MT: How did you bring those particular players into this one?

TW: Well, they were all well paid.

MT: That helps.

TW: Believe me, a triple scale. All real nice guys. I tried that song with the other band and then . . . it just didn't make it. So you can't get the guys to play like this on some of the stuff. I just couldn't find the right guys.

MT: It also gives the album a different kind of dimension there, a little bit of a different sound.

TW: Yeah, a little bit. Yeah, that was hard to do 'cause I wasn't sure where I was going. It was kinda unfamiliar.

MT: I have to ask you about the Springsteen cover of "Jersey Girl." How did you first hear that and how did you first react when you heard it?

TW: I don't know when I first heard that. Oh! I got a tape, yeah. I heard it on the . . . I don't know, I guess I heard it on the radio. Yeah, I heard it on the radio. I said, "Yeah, that's a pretty good song there." Yeah, I did what I could to help him out. As far as I'm concerned he's on his own now. I've done what I can for his career and . . . ya know? Well, I liked it, I really liked it, and I heard it a lot. It was on some jukeboxes and that's kinda nice too, ya know? Yeah, it was a good feeling. I liked the way he did it, I liked it a lot. Yeah, he's a real nice guy.

MT: He's always been a real down-to-earth kind of guy.

TW: Yeah, yeah.

MT: Now that *Rain Dogs* is finished, how do you feel about it?

TW: Well, there's some stuff I would have done different but, ya know, I don't know, I like a lot of the things on it.

MT: There's a lot of songs there. There's nineteen songs.

TW: Yeah, boy!

MT: And adds up to somewhat fifty to fifty-five minutes. That's a lot of music for your money!

TW: Yeah, well you got a good point there, Michael, yeah, I mean, you get more for your entertainment dollar. I think that's very American. I don't know. The songs, let's see what happens to them. My songs don't get on the radio a lot so it . . . I think that, you know . . . maybe people that are played a lot write different kinds of songs because you know your audience. You know your audience is very . . . everybody is meant to hear this, ya know? I don't know . . .

MT: But at the same time those people might tend to write songs to fit a mold and that's something that's clearly not happening with *Rain Dogs*. The songs take their own shapes and lengths to suit.

TW: Yeah, well I think that's good. I think that's because songs should have their own anatomy that suits the story or whatever, I think.

MT: You know, thinking back over the twelve years that we've known each other, I don't remember you ever being really completely satisfied with a record once it was out.

TW: Yeah, I don't know. I guess that you immediately, you start work on another one to try and correct the mistakes you made on the one that came before. I played with some people that I really liked very much. So I . . . the whole process was very enjoyable.

MT: And you got a real challenging record that can stand up to a lot of listenings and take people to a lot of unsuspected places.

TW: Oh, I hope so. I hope so. But the next . . . there were some songs that didn't make it on there that I liked too. One called "Bethlehem PA." "That was Bob Christ, of Bob Christ Chevrolet, right here in beautiful downtown Bethlehem PA." That didn't make it on there. Another one called "Dressed Up in Rags" and

"Skeleton Bones" that didn't make it on there. "Marie Antoinette's Famous Last Words." So, there were some that didn't get on there. I said, "Oh well, maybe we could build a fin on top of it." We could put those right there, but I don't know what it's gonna do. You just send it out there and make sure his tie is on straight and comb his hair, ya know? "Be sure to zip up your fly and polish your shoes . . ."

MT: That's one reason we've had this hour with a lot of the songs from the record, and I hope that people like what they hear and they wanna hear some more. Tom Waits has a new album on Island Records, it's called *Rain Dogs*.

TW: OK, nice talking with you, Michael.

FRANKS WILD YEARS (1987)

Waits's theatrical debut, *Franks Wild Years,* was scheduled to open to the public by mid-June 1986. Stage director Terry Kinney's creative differences with Tom Waits were a constant source of friction. Kinney was either fired or left on his own accord, and Steppenwolf actor Gary Sinise, who would later be nominated for an Oscar for his supporting role in the film *Forrest Gump,* took charge. Sinise pooled his resources and, with a budget strapped for cash, gelled the final phase of the production. *Franks Wild Years* had its world premiere with the Steppenwolf Theatre Company at the Briar St. Theatre in Chicago, Illinois, on June 22, 1986.

Waits had formerly made an attempt at writing an original screenplay in collaboration with Paul Hampton, a collaborator of Burt Bacharach. *Why Is the Dream Always So Much Sweeter Than the Taste?* was a mystery project salvaged for *Franks Wild Years.* Waits explained to *Melody Maker* that the car salesman in the script was a "success at being a failure, and a guy who's a failure at being a success." The challenge of completing it at that time was too much for Waits, and it was aborted in pre-production.

The show had a mildly received three-month run. It featured Steppenwolf regulars like Moira Harris, Gary Cole, Vince Viverito, Tom Irwin, and Randall Arney. Waits used his touring band to make up the constituents of Frank's ragtag band. Teller, of Penn & Teller fame, came up with some magic tricks for Frank, who was played to perfection by Tom Waits.

Waits's decision to flesh out the songs from *Franks Wild Years* into an album was more than wise resourcefulness—the LP was to be ultimately regarded as a sustained work of art. For Waits, the play and the ensuing studio album were two entirely separate entities. When the play closed its doors, Waits and his band stayed in Chicago for two more weeks to record the album. Waits put his band to the task of working outside of their respective comfort zones in order to bring a fresh sound to the songs. Comfortable that he was on the right track, Waits flew in Marc Ribot to incorporate his singular guitar work. The finished product was released to the public in August 1987.

Meanwhile, Waits continued appearing in films. This prompted his own movie project for the big screen. *Big Time* boasted a new brand of surreal cabaret. It languished in cult status and remains unreleased in DVD format.

Former *Spin* West Coast editor Bart Bull has a flair for seeing the humor in the absurd. This came as an advantage when he interviewed Tom Waits. Using his eye for detail, the following interview strays from the traditional journalistic Q&A by matching Waits's quirks with his own.

At this point, Waits had all but jettisoned his former barfly image to concentrate more intensely on the inner and outer dynamics of his songwriting and performance.

"Boho Blues"
Spin
September 1987
Bart Bull

Tosca, Tuesday, late, Columbus near Broadway, San Francisco. This is a fine bar, a lovely bar, loud but not too loud. The jukebox plays scratchy opera music. Francis Coppola is in back where the tables and booths are. He's listening to Lauren Hutton tell a story and when he laughs, so does everybody else. Sam Shepard stands up from his stool at the bar to pay his tab. His MasterCard falls to the floor, unnoticed except by the redhead standing nearby. She puts her foot on top of it and carries on her conversation. Shepard leaves. Lauren Hutton leaves. Coppola and his people leave. Almost everybody leaves. The bartender works a rag across the bar, and in the doorway behind him we see someone who looks just like Tom Waits. He peers in, squints, rubbing his head. A cigarette butt, stepped on but still glowing, trails smoke across the floor, left to right. He steps through the smoke and goes to the jukebox, searches. He finds a quarter in his pants, punches buttons. A tenor yelps. It's "Nessun Dorma," from Puccini's *Turandot.*

A pink paper cocktail umbrella, the kind that sprouts at the rims of colorful tropical drinks, blows across the floor at the foot of the stage, left to right, blown by an invisible wind.

Tom Waits wears black tie and tails, red socks, and railroad boots. A big barrel-bellied woman sits next to him, one leg draped over his knee. She's wearing a red flamenco dress and a black mantilla, and her name is Val Diamond.

She has eyeballs painted on her eyelids. She can see you with her eyes open; she watches you with her eyes closed. Polaroids are scattered on the stage at their feet.

Tom Waits: I don't understand golf.

Val Diamond: [*mutters sympathetically*]

TW: It needs to have more sex [*gleaming lightbulb appears directly over his head*]. Night golf!

VD: Somebody won a lot of money golfing recently.

TW: They get more money than boxers.

VD: That *doesn't* seem right.

TW: It doesn't seem right. Somebody gets beat up for an hour and somebody else hits a ball into a hole. Doesn't seem right.

From the floor, the director watches them through a little black lens, through his director's viewfinder. He hands the viewfinder to his assistant and walks off. The assistant stares carefully through the lens. Tom's zipper is at half-mast.

It's dawn. Bats are hurrying back to the belfry, and below, one hand on the rope that rings the bell, Ken Nordine waits. Nordine, the word-jazzed Voice of God as heard on Levi's commercials, has something he wants to say. This time it's Tom Waits's words and Ken Nordine's voice; sometimes it's the other way around. Here's how to tell: Tom Waits's voice sounds like he gargles with gravel; Ken Nordine's sounds like he's selling three truckloads of soft margarine in handy reusable plastic tubs. There is no devil (for our purposes here, at least), just God when he's drunk. Ken Nordine, God as we understand Him (for our purposes here), is not inebriated in the least, but he's willing to act (for our purposes here). He has something he'd like to say.

Ken Nordine: [*gritty voice*] It's like Jack Nicholson said to me one time—Continuity is for sissies.

We're in a nightclub, an empty nightclub. A nearly empty nightclub, with a camera crew setting up in the back. Ken Nordine's butter-flavored voice is the only light.

KN: For our purposes here, perhaps some explanation is in order. Perhaps not. Welcome, in any case, to Miss Keiko's Chi Chi Club.

We see the stage now, bulbs flashing in sequence across the proscenium.

KN: Proscenium. Butter-flavored proscenium.

We see Tom Waits in a tuxedo, slumped in a chair at the center of the stage.

KN: We have a purpose here. We are filming a video here, a video to accompany the tune "Blow Wind Blow," from Tom Waits's new album, *Franks Wild Years*.

As Nordine speaks, we see Waits rise from his slump (as it were) and sit stiffly upright. His lips move precisely in time with Nordine's words, and his arms deliver florid gestures.

KN: But *Franks Wild Years* is not merely an album. *Franks Wild Years* is also a play, a stage production. *Franks Wild Years* is two . . .

Val and Tom are holding breath mints in front of them. They click the packages together carefully.

KN: . . . two mints in one. And the video from "Blow Wind Blow" is not merely a scene from the play, but an all-new-and-improved production. Tom is Frank, as it were, or perhaps he isn't, but in any case, he's a ventriloquist. He casts his voice into the rest of the cast. And the rest of the cast is ably portrayed by Val Diamond and a prosthetic leg.

Waits reaches into his jacket pocket and pulls out a pack of those personal details that reveal so much about a character's character. He smokes prewar Lucky Strikes in the Raymond Loewy–designed green pack. Or Chesterfields, named after W. C. Fields's favorite son. In truth, they're Raleighs, and he takes a dramatic drag off the cigarette, makes nonchalant expressions as he holds it in, then looks off in another direction as Val, the ventriloquist's dummy, exhales a white cloud. Waits takes the pack, crumples it, flicks it into the wastebasket hidden in the wings. A pause, another pause, and then he leaps up, dumping Val to the floor, and we see him bent over the wastebasket, digging around for the cigarette pack. He finds it, tears a square off the back.

TW: [*turns to the camera*] I save the coupons.

He sits back down. His lips keep moving.

KN: In truth, he doesn't smoke anymore. That would be too much like the old Tom Waits. And the old Tom Waits is over, done with, defunct, finito. Aesthetically, at least. He made his bed and he slept in it until it was past checkout time. Writing songs about dead-end kids on dead-end streets became a dead-end street. Damon Runyon demanded royalties.

Waits is making nonchalant expressions up on the stage. Val is staring baleful and blue-eyed, her eyelids clamped shut.

KN: And yet here we are in a nightclub, a nearly empty nightclub. Have you noticed the postage-stamp cocktail tables? The chains of garter snaps that decorate the walls? The black Naugahyde banquette booths? Once upon a time, this was Ann's 440 Club, where Lenny Bruce got that illustrious start of his. Ah, but that was long ago, and for more than twenty years this has been Miss Keiko's Chi Chi Club. Welcome. Have you met Miss Keiko yet?

A yellow spotlight comes on in the back of the club, illuminating a black-and-white photo. A signature in black felt-tip pen reads, "Miss Keiko—1969." She stands forever on the toes of one foot, gazing over her shoulder, lifting her long dark hair above her bare back. Her costume is brief; her breasts are tassel-tipped projectiles. Tom Waits stands nearby, appraising the photograph.

TW: [*gravel-voiced*] If I was a girl, I'd want to look like that.

Francis Coppola's sergeant at arms drops by to let Waits know that Francis is dining next door at Enrico's. He's willing to wait until the video crew takes a lunch break if Tom would care to come over and talk. There's a part for him in an upcoming project. Waits is sitting at the Chi Chi Club bar with a guy called Biff, waiting for the crew to set up the shot. Miss Keiko gazes down at them from over her shoulder.

TW: Vegas. She worked the big rooms in Vegas. You know, I saw a guy go down with a heart attack at a crap table, and his wife was pounding on his chest, and the pit boss said, "New shooter coming up." I swear to God.

KN: [*sounding godlike*] Search me. Sounds like it could be true.

TW: New dice, new shooter, keep it moving. Cold. Cold-blooded.

Biff: How far away were you?

TW: I was the new shooter.

B: Were you wealthy when you left the table?

TW: Nah. I gamble with scared money. I'm a tightwad. Moths in my change purse.

He gets up to get some cigarettes from the machine, although he doesn't smoke anymore. Moths burst forth from his change purse. He buys Raleighs. Doesn't smoke any.

TW: So what do you think is suitable for manly footgear, Biff?

B: Roman sandals. And beads to go with 'em.

TW: I've been asking everyone I, uh, come into contact with, because I'm doin' a little survey. I'd say we're in a crisis in terms of American footgear.

B: Slip-on loafers.

TW: Nah, can't go that route. You can't go down that road, for down that road danger lies.

B: How come?

TW: I don't like the name. Loafers. For a guy that works as hard as you do, it's just not right.

B: You could call 'em slip-ons, but . . .

TW: That's even worse. That's worse than loafers. You wouldn't want me to call you a slip-on.

B: You got a point there.

TW: Points. I always gravitate toward points. Things are getting better—ten years ago, you couldn't find any points. Things are getting better, in shoes and music both.

Lunch comes, lunch goes. Coppola waits impatiently at Enrico's; Waits tells Biff of movie roles he's been offered. Coppola's fingers tap the tabletop.

TW: Satanist cult leaders. The Iceman. I could've been the Iceman in *Iceman*.

B: You turned that down?

TW: Yep. Big mistake. Look where the guy that took it is today. I could've been the hitcher in *The Hitcher*, too.

B: Jesus Christ! You turned that down? You could've had a career. You could be Boris Karloff by now.

TW: Yep. Big mistake.

Coppola, alfresco at Enrico's, fumes silently. Fumes loudly. Fumes. Vows revenge. One week later, Waits wakes up in bed next to the oil-splattered head of a 350 Chevy. He shrieks.

   A small pile of pink confetti blows across the floor in front of the stage, left to right, blown by a handheld fan.

   Tom Waits wears black tie and tails, red socks, and railroad boots. His sideburns are going gray. Val Diamond wears a red flamenco dress. Her ginger hair is piled high in Spanish columns. Her left leg is draped over his right knee. Black fishnet stockings.

TW: You know who Dick Shawn is? Was?

VD: The world's second-greatest entertainer? The guy who did that show called *The World's Second-Greatest Entertainer*?

Although he doesn't smoke, smoke rises from an invisible Raleigh between his fingers. He taps his ashes absentmindedly. They fall onto the brim of the top hat at his feet.

TW: I did a little show with him, played the Wall Street Wino. It never aired. He had a dozen midgets on it. Thirteen.

A pause.

TW: He died onstage. His son was in the audience. He was in the middle of a bit about death, and he threw himself to the stage in a simulated heart attack. And it was real. And everybody in the audience was laughing. Not a bad thing to hear in your last moment.

More ashes, real as life, fall into the hat; real smoke rises from the invisible Raleigh.

TW: Good way to go, I guess. Maybe now they'll air the show.

The Chi Chi Club is empty, near empty. One chair is at the center of the stage, one chair is set in the center of the floor below. From the chair on the floor, we hear the voice of Ken Nordine.

KN: Curious as it is that Tom Waits abandoned his signature style of writing, it's every bit as intriguing that he jettisoned the very sound of his established style at the same time. Once known as something of a jazzed-down Beat generation throwback, as the romantic street poet of the least romantic of unpoetic streets, as a narrative storyteller of the most talented sort, as a truly gifted liar, he suddenly and abruptly ceased spinning yarns. And as he did, his music itself came unraveled. Or if not unraveled, then . . .

A long pause. Long.

KN: Perhaps someone else would be better qualified to discuss what happened to the music of Tom Waits. Perhaps it would pay to introduce Harry Partch.

A small spotlight illuminates the chair onstage.

KN: Harry Partch, sadly deceased, was an American original. An eccentric, that is; a tinkerer, a free spirit, an inventor of instruments and of himself. A nut, in other words. A Californian, like Tom Waits, and like Tom Waits, a man who lived the hobo's life long before he captured it in music. He invented his remarkable forty-three-tone musical scale, and he invented gorgeous and monumental instruments specifically for playing his odd and glorious music. You may have to grant him a certain grandiosity, a certain tendency toward the making of Major Pronouncements, a certain self-centeredness, a certain extreme certainty. Harry Partch received so little recognition during life, and he required so much of it. He called his musical scale "just intonation," and he felt entirely justified in doing so.

The voice that comes from the chair onstage is deep and rugged and rigorously resonant. It sounds much like John Huston's acceptance speech upon his being unanimously voted God.

Harry Partch: As I understand it, this young Tom Waits fellow has had some small contact with members of the ensemble that serves the noble purpose of preserving my music and my instruments, the Mazda Marimba, the Marimba Eroica, the Cloud Chamber Bowls, and all the rest. This contact, however limited, can't have hurt him, although it's impossible to say how much it has helped since what I've heard of his stuff is not more than a literal-minded bastardization of the eternal principles behind my system of just intonation. He'd be best served to study a little closer if he cares to attempt any further homage. Still, there is some small sense of my own music's grandeur in the young fellow's stuff. Like me, he's interested in the largest and the smallest of sounds, and like me, he's heard the music of the highway and the resonant clang of the beer bottle tapped with a church key. IMAGINE the sound of a hundred Chinamen beating spikes into the ground with nine-pound sledgehammers, laying the rails of the transcontinental railway! And the scream of the steam whistle as a locomotive flies over those same spikes. Imagine the snores of hobos sleeping in the open boxcars. Imagine the contrapuntal snores of the conductor comfortably bunked up in the caboose. IMAGINE THE THUNDER, the mighty prairie thunder that wakes them all from their slumbers! And imagine the raw COURAGE a composer would need to even ATTEMPT to create such sounds! I wish the young fellow a great deal of luck. I admire his theatricality.

At the back of the club, at the bar, a light glows. Tom Waits and the guy called Biff are back there, a beer bottle in front of each of them. Tom is not smoking, yet smoke rises from between two of his fingers.

TW: I traveled with a gas pump for years.

He tosses back a little beer.

TW: I still have a nightmare where the whole crowd is moving toward me and then the keys are falling off the piano and the curtain rips and my shoe comes off and I'm crawling toward the wings and the crowd is moving toward me, hurling insults at me. And car parts. I played cow palaces, rodeos, sports facilities, hockey arenas with the ice beneath the cardboard. It cools off the place. It's all right in August, but it's a bitch in February. But if you can appreciate the rich pageantry of it . . .

Biff tosses back a little beer.

TW: Never have your wallet with you onstage. It's bad luck. You shouldn't play the piano with money in your pocket. Play like you need the money.

Tom tosses back a little beer.

TW: I don't play the piano much anymore. I don't compose on it. It's hard. Because sometimes it feels like it's all made out of ice. It's cold. It's square, so much about it is square, you know, and music is round. And so sometimes I think it puts corners on your stuff.

Tom and Biff toss back a little beer. Behind them, we see a single chair and a single spotlight on the stage, and now we can hear that Harry Partch has never stopped talking.

HP: [*from afar*] . . . the wrongheadedness of the chromatic scale of the Western world and the deleterious effect it has had on untold generations of innocent ears . . . a gang of Irishmen headed due west with nine-pound sledgehammers of their own . . .

A pink balloon blows across the floor in front of the stage, left to right.
   Tom Waits wears black tie and tails, red socks, and railroad boots. Val Diamond wears a red dress and a black top hat. "Blow Wind Blow" is playing frantically in the background, sung by Alvin of the Chipmunks. When the soundman has re-cued it, the take begins.
   A clapboard claps. A pink balloon blows across the floor, left to right.

TW: Welcome to Miss Keiko's Chi Chi Club. It's showtime!

Two pump organs, an alto horn, a glockenspiel. A gravel voice grumbles, singing. The voice comes from Val's mouth, and her eyes, clamped closed, stare blue ahead. Tom Waits, ventriloquist, nonchalant, takes a deep, dramatic drag on his cigarette; a smoke puffs from Val's mouth. Her lips grumble his song. He unscrews her wooden leg, pulls a pint of liquor from within it, swigs. He caps the bottle, puts it back, screws her leg back on. His cigarette rests between her fingers, his song sings off her lips. He takes his hand out from behind her back to scratch his head, and she slumps, but he catches her before she falls. The song grumbles toward an end, and as it ends, she pulls a dry-cell battery out of his back. He slumps, slumps and flops. He twitches in rigor mortis. Confetti falls free from his hand, gathers in a little pile. A handheld fan blows it, left to right.

Wrap. The crew ascends to the stage, leaves nothing behind but a steamer trunk and a sousaphone. Tom sits on the trunk; the sousaphone sits on its side. A member of the crew grabs it and leaves.

TW: Aw, bring the sousaphone back.

It comes back. Waits climbs inside it, adjust the mouthpiece. It makes hideous bleats, like someone is forcing it to watch its mother being turned into a coffee table. Waits's cheeks puff out; his face turns red. He hoists it off like a weight lifter. He leaves the stage with it under his arm, his tuxedo tails flapping behind. He puts his little finger in his ear and wrings it vigorously.

TW: What should I do with this thing?

No answer. "Nessun Dorma," from Puccini's *Turandot*.

Waits on voice control:
Excerpted from "Tom Waits Is Flying Upside Down (On Purpose)," Musician
October 1987
Mark Rowland

Mark Rowland: Do you feel by now you've got control of your voice? I don't mean literally your voice, but your ability to communicate.

Tom Waits: You always work on your voice. Once you feel as though you have one, whatever you tackle will come under the spell of what you're trying to do. You want to be able to make turns and fly upside down—but not by mistake. You want it to be a conscious decision, and to do it well. You don't want somebody to say, "Well, he went for the bank there and lost control and he went right into the mountain and thirty-seven people died." You want 'em to say, "Well, he decided to take his hands off the controls and sacrifice the entire plane and its passengers. And I must say it was a spectacular flight. The explosion set off sparks that could be seen all the way to Oxnard. Remarkable." I think you have to work on yourself more than you work on the music. Then whatever you're aiming at you'll be able to hit between the eyes.

MR: You did wait a long time before taking your musical leap. So maybe that was a crucial part of the process.

TW: It's strange. It's all a journey. You don't know where it's going to take you, the people that you meet and the changes your life will bring. I can say I wished I'd jumped off earlier, but I don't know if I actually jumped off anything or else, you know, just redecorated. But I know that the last three records are a departure from what I was doing; I'm very aware of that. I don't write the same way. I used to sit in a room with a piano, the Tin Pan Alley approach. I thought that's how songs were written.

"Better Waits Than Ever"
Music & Sound Output
October 1987
Bill Forman

This story begins with trains. "My father had a friend when he was a kid in Texas, in a place called Sulphur Springs," says Tom Waits, in a corrugated voice custom-built for tales of travel, tears, and two-bit hoods. "He was kind of the local James Dean, and he used to race the train to the crossing on an Indian motorcycle. He was always talking about getting out of town. That was his big thing: getting out of town. But he always went to the edge of town and turned around and came back. And whenever the train would go through, it would have to slow down to pick up the mail. They had a hook that would come out and catch the mail sack and then keep going. And one day he was racing the train and he met it right at the crossing, and crashed into it. And he was pinned to the hook." Waits pauses and stares up from the table. "But it did take him all the way to the next town."

Five years after recognizing his need to escape the confines of the fake cocktail-jazz aesthetic that first brought him to public attention, Waits has successfully skipped town without the assistance of an impaling mail hook. Still, it was a close call at the crossing. Determined not to continue life as a comfortably eccentric prestige artist made commercially palatable by a succession of producers, Waits entered the studio in 1982 and recorded his first self-produced album, *Swordfishtrombones*. The glorious result of painstaking reassessment and new-found inspiration, the record defied Elektra/Asylum's expectations. Waits was on his own.

"I was trying to incorporate a lot of musical things that I experienced, but didn't know how to embrace," he recalls. "It's like you start out with a few colors and a certain style and you kind of paint yourself into a corner. I didn't know how to break out, unless I just set fire to it all. And I was afraid to do that, because I didn't know where it would lead me. I thought I would be all alone and I had all these birds in my head and I didn't know how to get them out."

Today, the self-proclaimed Prince of Melancholy has just finished a new album, his third for Island, who also released *Swordfishtrombones* and its successor *Rain Dogs*. *Franks Wild Years* is a wildly eclectic, uniformly brilliant recording with a truly original sound and vision. First previewed in the song "Frank's Wild Years" on *Swordfishtrombones* and later in a play Waits and his wife Kathleen Brennan put on in Chicago, the tale of Frank's quest for fame appears to address the pros and cons of burning one too many bridges, or ranch houses, behind you. The music is loose and unpredictable, like 1985's percussion- and guitar-dominated *Rain Dogs*, though the instrumentation this time out is more heavily slanted toward accordions, an arcane collection of keyboards and a vast array of horns, including the ever-popular police bullhorn.

With a revitalized grip on recording, a burgeoning acting career (Waits starred in Jim Jarmusch's *Down by Law*, is in Robert Frank's new *Candy Mountain*, and plays opposite Jack Nicholson in the upcoming *Ironweed*), and his own film venture in the early planning stage, Waits has little incentive to retread old turf these days.

"It's like displacement," he observes over a formidable-looking dish at the Travelers Café, an all-but-abandoned Filipino restaurant (pig's head and black beans only $3.89) on the edge of downtown Los Angeles. "As soon as you put something down, something else jumps into your arms. You think that if you don't hang onto this you're going to drown, but you may drown if you do hang onto it. Growth is frightening sometimes. You think you're going to get too big, like you can't get back into your childhood or something."

Childhood is important to Waits, and not only because he now has two kids of his own. "Staying in touch with your childhood becomes more and more difficult, but also more and more important. You can pick up anything and play it—you just have to know what to consider valid and what to consider invalid. When we were doing *Down by Law*, John Lurie [Waits's costar who also leads The Lounge Lizards] picked up a big old drainpipe out in the swamp and started blowing through it. And it sounded like a didgeridoo, you know? If you can get yourself to that place where you can attack things like a kid and not be so adult about it, then it opens a window to things."

And, as Waits will tell you, it closes another. "I don't listen to the older stuff. It's like looking at old pictures of yourself. It's like, 'My ears are too big in that one. And, God, the lighting is terrible and I've got a double chin. And, Jesus, look at that shirt. What did I think I was? Who is this guy?'"

Fair question. Tom Waits was born thirty-seven years ago in Pomona, California. Ma Waits was an elementary school teacher, Pa Waits taught Spanish at Belmont High School, only a mile from the Travelers Café. Spanish was spoken at the dinner table, Mexican music came over the airwaves and into the Waits household. But Waits's parents weren't inclined toward music, any more than he was toward academics. "Too many teachers in my family," he growls. "Teachers and ministers. I wanted to break windows, smoke cigars, and stay up late, you know? My role model was Pinocchio, you know, the little kids that went to Pleasure Island and shot pool. That's what I wanted to do. I wanted to go to Pleasure Island."

Waits's real-life version of Pleasure Island was a long road of run-down hotels, cocktail lounges, and restaurants. "I loved working in restaurants most of all," he deadpans. "Wearing an apron, sitting back there, washing dishes, taking care of things. Feeling like I was in charge." All this eventually led to recording studios and larger venues, which were still workable settings for his collection of small-time hoods and restless souls. Like a gambler who repeatedly shows up at the track with no money and last week's racing form, Waits's tales of grand illusions and harsh realities chronicled the failed romantic in all of us, while the gravel-laced voice, dangling cigarette, and rumpled clothing personified the dilemma.

A half-dozen Elektra/Asylum albums in as many years presented a poignant collection of characters and emotions, fitting documents of the first stage of Waits's career. Small Change gets rained on with his own .38. Tom Frost calls Martha after forty years to ask about the husband and kids and to confess a still-burning love. And Tom Waits, barely distinguishable from his broken-down characters, sings West Side Story's "Somewhere," the idyllic paradise it conjures up all-too-heartbreakingly out of reach.

Or as Frank puts it in one of the three songs Waits wrote with his wife on the new album, "If I fall asleep in your arms / please wake me up in my dreams." Pleasure Island still beckons. "I think that's why people make up these little stories, in order to escape into them sometimes," Waits figures. "You become impatient with your life and so you find these little places where you can kinda move people around and change their names and alter things a bit."

Back when he was working on the score for Francis Ford Coppola's One from the Heart, Waits met his future wife, which began a stable family life and songwriting partnership, despite a half-dozen moves between subletted residences in New York and L.A. over the last few years (L.A. being home for the moment). "I'm beginning to create a world for myself that I can live in," says Waits, defying the belief that creativity dries up when comfort sets in. "Oh, I'm not happy or anything like that," he reassures. "I mean, I'm happy for a minute and then most of us are manic-depressive.

"Most of us are a little uneasy around people who are emotionally disturbed, but I think artists have to stay in some state of that in order to remain an antenna for the things necessary to receive from whoever's transmitting. And it makes you a bit of a . . . I don't know. And then there are the few that we kind of indulge, people like Salvador Dalí. But we don't want too many of those."

Eccentric though they were, Tom Waits's Asylum years were more easily pigeonholed, partly because of arrangements that leaned toward standard-jazz-combo instrumentation. It was a sound Waits decided to leave behind with Swordfishtrombones. He mourns: "With the exception of a few people—maybe Monk and Mingus, Bud Powell, Miles—a lot of jazz for me conjures up nylon socks and swimming pools and little hurricane lanterns and, you know, clean bathrooms and new suits.

"People want to get you to the point where they know who you are and what you are so they can just kinda bottle it, so you can have one of everything. And it's difficult to grow up in public and be allowed to change and experiment, you know."

As for the orphaned songs from Waits's days with Elektra/Asylum, few will find their way into the live tour he's planning for this fall. "Songs are difficult, because some of them only live for a day. Some of them you just use to prop the door open, and some of them are more of a centerpiece. Each one has its own life. It's hard to tell sometimes how long a song is going to live. You have to go back to them and bring them out and push them around and see if they can take it."

A similar process was called for in the recording of *Franks Wild Years*, since the songs first appeared in the context of a stage play of the same name. Waits describes the challenge as "getting them all to walk around in the same shoes," which took some six months in the studio. Sessions began at Chicago's Universal Recording and were completed at L.A.'s Sunset Sound, where Waits also oversaw the remixing—ready for this?—of his first dance single.

While *Franks Wild Years* successfully assimilates such obvious influences as Kurt Weill, Marty Robbins, and Ennio Morricone (while also paying heed to stray barnyard animals and the Balinese Monkey Chant), the transformation of "Hang On St. Christopher" into a dance-floor hit would be miraculous indeed. Like all of Waits's recording sessions, the remixing was off limits to family members, animals, and the press, but Waits seems satisfied with the result, especially the train sound he added. Can't wait to see those dance-floor stampedes when the track's muttered vocal, lurching beat, trash can cymbals, Hammond pedal bass line, repetitive horns, and twisted modal guitar wanderings segue from the dying beats of Stacey Q.

"I like the stuff that happens in the dance clubs," says Waits. "It's like, free associating, you know, some of these places will blend Filipino folk music with Oscar Levant and bring in the *Dragnet* theme and then slip into a Stravinsky thing and then on to Oscar Brown Jr. into James Brown."

Still, a bass line played using the foot pedals of a Hammond organ? "I used upright bass for so long, it's hard for me to find an electric bass that I like," he explains. "So that was the closest I could get. It's like a drum with a note in it, you know, real fat and out of focus. Bill Schimmel, the accordion player, played them with his hands. I'm thinking of taking them on the road and raising them to the level of a marimba.

"Things that happened in those sessions were really good. Especially when people were playing instruments they weren't familiar with. I had Ralph Carney, the sax player, on several cuts where he played three saxes at once. And then Bill Schimmel playing the pedals, Greg Cohen playing alto horn. . . . Sometimes approaching an instrument you're unfamiliar with, the discovery process is good."

And then there are those who make familiar instruments unfamiliar, a specialty of borrowed Lounge Lizards guitarist Marc Ribot. "He prepares his guitar with alligator clips," reports Waits, "and has this whole apparatus made out of tinfoil and transistors that he kinda sticks on the guitar. Or he wraps the strings with gum, all kinds of things, just to get it to sound real industrial."

Waits had his own arsenal of prehistoric keyboards, the type you don't find on records these days. There's his wheezing pump organ, his plodding Mellotron, his tacky Farfisa and, of course, the Optigan. "The Optigan is kind of an early synthesizer/organ for home use. You have these discs that give you different environments—Tahitian, orchestral, lounge—and then you apply your own melodies to those different musical worlds. It comes with a whole encyclopedia of music worlds.

"I've always liked the Mellotron as well. The Beatles used it a lot, Beefheart used it a lot. They're real old and they're not making them anymore. A lot of them pick up radio stations, CB calls, television signals, and airline transmitting conversations. And they're very hard to work with in the studio because they're unsophisticated electronically. So it's almost like a wireless or a crystal set."

Waits's unconventional approach to recording doesn't end with his choice of instruments. "Telephone Call from Istanbul" goes rollicking along with banjo, guitar, bass, drums, and the faint ghost of Waits improvising away on that cheesy Farfisa. When the track is nearly over, the Farfisa kicks in full strength, catapulting the listener into some hellish Turkish roller-skating rink. "I usually don't like to isolate the instruments," says Waits, explaining the appearance of the ghost early in the track. "On that song, I pulled out the Farfisa and then just put it in very hot at the end, just so it sounded kind of Cuban or something."

Likening the sterile confines of the studio to an emergency ward, Waits seems intent on performing some very unorthodox operations. Take "Innocent When

You Dream," which appears in two disguises on *Franks Wild Years*. The "barroom version" puts across the melancholy melody (reminiscent of a mournful Irish drinking song) by way of pump organ, upright bass, violin, and piano. A second version closes out side two, stripped down and scratched up enough to inspire visions of an ancient Victrola. Says Waits: "The '78 version' of that was originally recorded at home on a little cassette player ['the Tascam 244, the one with the clamshell holster']. I sang into a seven-dollar microphone and saved the tape. Then I transferred that to twenty-four track and overdubbed Larry Taylor on upright, and then we mastered that. Texture is real important to me; it's like attaining grain or putting it a little out of focus. I don't like cleanliness. I like surface noise. It kind of becomes the glue of what you're doing sometimes."

Another innovation on *Franks Wild Years* is the prevalence of the bullhorn, which Waits sings through on at least four cuts. "Well, I tried to obtain that same sound in other ways," he explains, "by using broken microphones, singing into tin cans, cupping my hands around the microphone, putting the vocal through an Auratone speaker, which is like a car radio speaker, and then miking that. Practically even considered at one point making a record and then broadcasting the record through like a radio station and then having it come out of the car and then mike the car . . . and then it just became too complicated, you know? So a bullhorn seemed to be the answer to it all."

Waits says obtaining altered sounds in real time, rather than creating them afterward through studio gadgetry, allows him to react to the effect and modify his vocal delivery accordingly. "Plus it makes me feel like I'm making the sound rather than finding the sound through EQ and whatever. I feel more like I'm building some kind of a little world for myself, my own territory.

"I used to just write songs and think that was enough. I used to be frightened of the studio. But there's a lot you can do if you don't allow it to intimidate you. It's a laboratory, whatever you bring into it you have to know what you want to do with it. I worked with a lot of good people that helped me. Victor Feldman, the percussionist who just passed away a few months ago, helped me a lot with instruments. I kinda wanted to get away from the standard fare and experiment with some other instruments—Balinese instruments and things like that, boobams and angklungs and African drums, that type of thing. So he helped me a lot.

"I try to stay open to as many choices as I can," he continues. "It can be thirteen bass players, it can be recorded outside, it can be done in the bathroom.

There's a lot of ways to skin a cat. Being in the studio is like organizing noise. I just had to learn how to know exactly what I wanted and not be satisfied until I heard it. It's a journey; it's like being a scavenger.

The artist describes himself as an "idiot savant" when it comes to things technical. "I'm still very—I don't know—primitive in the studio. It's not a science and I don't approach it that way. And I don't necessarily have a way of working now that I bring with me every time I record. Mainly I try to keep things spontaneous and live, full of suggestions. Keep it living."

Asked how he directs his musicians in the studio, Waits says, "You just have to develop a way of communicating. Just like a director talks to an actor, you have to know how to say the right thing at the right time to the right person that will have meaning to them. It's like calling a dog—what do you say? You whistle, you slap your thigh, 'C'mere, boy!'"

Waits laughs at his analogy. "That's terrible. No, it's not like that. Sorry, boys."

Lyrically, *Franks Wild Years* is a no less extravagant puzzle, from the good advice of "Telephone Call from Istanbul" ("Never trust a man in a blue trench coat / Never drive a car when you're dead") to the poignant assessment of "Yesterday Is Here" ("Today is gray skies / tomorrow's tears / You'll have to wait till yesterday is here").

The LP essentially takes up where the song of the same name left off. Frank has already burnt his suburban home to the ground while parked across the street drinking a couple of Mickey's Big Mouths. Now it's on to a series of less-than-glorious adventures that leave him on a park bench in the middle of a snowstorm.

"Well, it opens on a park bench in the play," says Waits, "with a guy who is having a going-out-of-business sale for his life. And he lays down on the bench and it's thirty below in East St. Louis and he kind of dreams his way back home, and that's where he relives everything that happened. So it's kinda putting the end of your life first and the beginning of your life second.

"It's really a simple story of a guy who is very near suicide, who has been allowed to kind of walk back through his life before he goes under. And he has a chance to turn the ship around, set a new course for himself. That's really all it's about.

"It just represents somebody who decided to make a change in his life, and in order to do that you have to cut some of the strings that are holding you there, that's all. And then he came back looking for some answers, because the road that he took led him down some very dark paths. So he came home to kind of purge himself and confess and look for some reasons to keep going. It's like going through your past looking for answers."

But Waits discourages biographical interpretations. "Usually you hide what everything represents," says the songwriter. "You're the only one who really knows. I don't so much chronicle things that happen to me as kind of break down the world and dismantle it and rebuild it and look at it that way. Pieces from a lot of different places.

"On this album, I've learned to try to approach each song like a character in a little one-act play. I don't feel like I have to be the same guy in all the songs. So in each one I set the stage for myself and I try to approach it in whatever way I have to in order to be living in the story. You know, method singing."

The method singer's acting career also continues to develop through a series of bit parts that culminated in last year's starring role as Zach, the melancholic DJ in *Down by Law*. "I was real nervous about doing that at first," he recalls. "I wanted to back out." But once Waits went on location in Louisiana, he became more confident. "Mostly I just tried to relax and be natural. As far as developing a detailed character filled with all the geography of the imagination, I don't think I covered it real deeply. But I had never really done anything that intensive. Most of the parts I had were just a couple of lines."

Director Jarmusch, who saw the Chicago Steppenwolf Theatre Company's production of *Franks Wild Years* three times, praises Waits's acting abilities and adds that Waits helped develop the part of Zach, originally written into the script as a musician. "Zach's very sullen and doesn't want to talk, and yet as a DJ he's someone who talks for a living," says Jarmusch. "And I think that's sort of about Tom too, in a way. Personally, he's contradictory in certain ways. Tom can have a hot temper, he can be kind of tough, but there's something very gentle at the same time. He doesn't really stop between those two poles, he's always sort of shifting back and forth between them. It makes me like him a lot."

In *Ironweed*, Waits plays Jack Nicholson's sidekick Rudy, a small-time hood (naturally), who dies in the end. "Nicholson's a great American storyteller," enthuses Waits. "When he tells a story, it's like a guy soloing, he's *out*, you know? Very spontaneous, thinks on his feet. I remember he said, 'I know about three things: I know about beauty parlors, movies, and train yards.'"

For Waits, beauty parlors are still something of a mystery. But he is planning
his own film project. "It's scattered now, maybe it's too early to talk about it,"
says Waits, giving in with little prodding. "It's about a bail bondsman who has
amnesia on this journey into the city with a kid who doesn't read or write. It's
kinda like a blind seeing-eye dog. You know, with music, narration, voice-over,
kinda Brechtian, you know?"

And what would the look of the film be? "Kind of like *Eraserhead.*"

There's more. An upcoming promotional video for *Franks Wild Years* will cast
Waits as a ventriloquist using a fat lady for his dummy. He also plans to contribute music for a country-and-western opera by Robert Wilson. "He said there'll be
like seven principal players and all the rest will be carrying spears," recalls Tom.
"It's a little oblique."

Waits also expects to contribute a spoken-word piece, excerpted from Charles
Mingus's autobiography, to an upcoming album project of Mingus interpretations
being compiled by producer Hal Willner. And he's also starting a new collection
of songs with the working title, "Nothing But Trains."

But don't expect "78 versions" of any of these new songs, for Waits's Tascam
four-track is gone, clamshell holster and all. "Stolen in New York," he shakes his
head, suppressing a smile. "That's why I left—they beat me up. So now I'm back
to square one. I don't know, I'm just learning about sound relationships and how
the circumstances under which you record something always color the work. You
do it at home, you're in a different mood than you are in the studio.

"It's like acting. There are certain relaxation techniques to get yourself to tap
into your unconscious. You know, it's like they say, certain things transcend culture and countries: insanity, animals, and music."

And exactly who says that?

Waits pauses before answering in a low voice.

"I don't know, uh . . . I said it."

BIG TIME (1988)

Tom Waits's first feature film production centered around his one-of-a-kind stage presence and the vaudeville/huckster vibe it suggested each night. Waits definitely had a concept in mind, as he shared with *Rolling Stone* in October 1988: "What we tried to avoid is having a concert film that felt like a stuffed bird. I tried to film it like a Mexican cockfight instead of air-conditioned concert footage. Some of it felt like it was shot through a safari rifle. You forget about the camera, which is what I was trying to do. But when you see yourself in concert, it rarely looks like the way you feel when you're up there. I thought I was much taller. I thought I looked like Robert Wagner. . . . If we had more money, we would have done the Rangoon gladiator sequences. And the shot of the audience holding up their matches and all that. We could have gotten the underwater ballet sequences, but it really would have been a different film, I think. . . . Now that it's completed, I would not have had my underwear coming out of the back of my pants like I did, but there's always something you want to change after it's over." No matter how he felt, his loyal fans felt he did just fine.

Waits on *Big Time*
Excerpted from *Big Time* Press Kit, Island Records
September 1988

Explaining the exotic flowering of his music, Waits says, "I was trying to get my music to be more like what goes on inside my head. For a long time I wrote in a very restricted world. I gave myself limited tools to work with. It got to a point where my life and what was really going on in my head, what I was really hearing, was very different from what I was writing.

"You get to an impasse with your work and you have to do something about it," he continues. "You can't go forward and you can't go back, and sometimes you feel like you have to break all your vertebrae and then reset 'em. That's what I tried to do, a little bit at a time. It's a *nose job*." [. . .]

"Kathleen was the only one who really pushed to have a film done," Waits says. "I'd get home from the road, and I wouldn't have any pictures of the band or anything. We'd talk about it like something that didn't really happen. It was the first that we pursued pulling it together." [. . .]

Before tour rehearsals began, Waits, Brennan, and [director Chris Blum] engaged in in-depth discussions about the stage set, which would have to be adaptable to filmic uses.

"The original stage set started out as a junkyard," Blum explains. "We had an idea for these huge plexiglass signs, like the ones you see in L.A.'s Koreatown—backlit, primary colored." Eventually Waits and lighting designer Darryl Palagi simplified the concept to the light boxes seen in the film.

"We designed everything else around the light boxes—it's like having an elephant in the middle of the room. Each band member in the film was assigned one. Even though they're supplemented by other sources, we wanted to give the impression that they were the only light sources. Then we developed the red-and-black-checked floor.

"The attempt was always to have things look non-art-directed," Blum concludes. "It took on a Count Basie-art-deco-Copacabana kind of look, in the end.

"The hitch about concert films is that they just are not live," says Blum. "I always use the analogy of standing next to a little babbling brook or a river or a creek, and then taking a picture of it and looking at it. It just is not the same. I had to take the show and put it in a dice box and throw it out. I had to get past the problem of that river—turbo-charge it, add some drive, some of the essence of the stage show."

Waits also realized the problem intrinsic to translating a live concert experience into a motion picture: "You want a concert film to have something other than just concert footage, but at the same time, it is that kind of animal. So Chris weaves in a subplot about a guy working in a theater—the usher, the ticket taker, the fella in the booth—who falls asleep and dreams about show business." Blum says, "In his own slightly warped mind, he's hit the big time."

Waits on being in the limelight:
Excerpted from *Morning Becomes Eclectic*, KCRW
October 3, 1988

Interviewer: Do you like being in the limelight?

Tom Waits: I guess I do. I do, I don't. Half of you is saying, "Notice me"; the other half is saying, "Leave me alone." It's a bit ambiguous. You want people to recognize what you do. At the same time you don't want to have to do it all the time every day. The idea with the film, *Big Time*, was you put the film out there, the film can go on the road and I can stay home. That was the idea, but then I end up having to go out and do interviews. It's getting mixed reviews, I guess that's what they call it—mixed reviews. One reviewer said, "Piano teachers will be shocked," which is one of my favorite reviews. Another guy said it looked like it was filmed in the stomach of a very sick animal. Now those were the good reviews. I recommend it.

Waits on the creative process:
Excerpted from "Eavesdropping on Elvis Costello and Tom Waits," *Option*
July 1989

Tom Waits: Sometimes I'll listen to records, my own stuff, and I think, God, the original idea for this was so much better than the mutation that we arrived at. What I'm trying to do now is get what comes and keep it alive. It's like carrying water in your hands. I want to keep it all, and sometimes by the time you get to the studio you have nothing. [. . .]

There's a certain kind of musical dexterity that you can arrive at that actually punishes a certain point in your development or moves past it. It happens all the time with me. The three-chord syndrome. And then you say, well, if you try to ask a Barney Kessel to cut a simple thing, just a big block brick of chords, just dirty, fat, loud and mean and cryptic—no, he's a handwriter, he's moved and developed to that level. Larry Taylor, this bass player I worked with from Canned Heat, if he can't feel it, he'll put down his bass and walk away and say, "That's it, man, I can't get it." And I really respect that. And I said, well, thank you for telling me. [. . .]

Elvis Costello: Did you ever think, though, that in your choice of musicians, several groups of musicians now, they would ever stop you going past that point, when you start to wander away from your own song? Is it ever something they play that puts up the roadblock?

TW: Sometimes it puts up a roadblock, but sometimes it opens a door. Like the stuff that people are doing in between takes or something, you have to always be aware of what's happening in the room at all times. Because as soon as the camera's not on and the tape's not rolling . . . the amount of time it takes to discover something, sometimes you discover it on the first moment, sometimes it takes two weeks to find it. [. . .]

Most changes in music, most exciting things that happen in music, occur through a miscommunication between people: "I thought you said this." Poetry comes out of that too. [. . .] But I love those mistakes. I salute them and encourage them.

EC: Did you have any bit of a feeling of coincidence that songs might be written in advance of the events? Or songs may be written with people in mind in advance of their hearing them?

TW: Absolutely. It's like dreams sometimes foretell a particular event.

PART III

BONE MACHINE (1992)

After the glut of publicity-related interviews and television appearances to promote the film and LP *Big Time*, Waits disappeared for four years in order to focus on his family as well as to connect with new ideas on the direction of his music.

Waits had been inundated with requests for appearances in theatrical films, and ended up accepting offers as diverse as Terry Gilliam's *The Fisher King* and Hector Babenko's *At Play in the Fields of the Lord* (1991), Jim Jarmusch's *Coffee and Cigarettes: Somewhere in California* (1993), and Robert Altman's *Short Cuts* (1993); he also composed the film score for another Jarmusch film, *Night on Earth* (1991). Most who worked with him were taken by his genuine, earnest nature.

Terry Gilliam was especially impressed, enough to bring him on to future projects. Gilliam shared his impressions of Waits in a December 1997 interview with Phil Stubbs: "He was a friend of Jeff Bridges, basically. He said, 'You ought to meet Tom.' It's funny because when I met him and even in the course of making the film, I'd never heard a Tom Waits record. I'd never listened to them at all. I just met him and liked him immediately. So into the film he went, and he was great. The studio was trying to cut him out. They felt it wasn't advancing the narrative in any significant way so they thought that was one of the things that could go. They were totally wrong."

Waits was also waging a battle against corporate entities trying to cash in on his unique voice and image. On principle, Waits refuses all requests to use his songs or even the sound of his voice to sell a product. His first successful lawsuit occurred in 1988 when Frito-Lay approached Waits to use one of his songs, "Step Right Up" (which is an indictment against advertising). Waits refused, and Frito-Lay countered by hiring a sound-alike to sing a blatant steal of the song refused to them. Waits's legal team turned to the Ninth Circuit Court of Appeals, who awarded $2.375 million to the artist. Waits's legal victory made him one of the first artists to successfully sue a company for using an impersonator without permission. Notoriously, he remarked to an interviewer, "If Michael Jackson wants to work for Pepsi, why doesn't he just get himself a suit and an office in their headquarters and be done with it?" In the following interviews, Waits made clear his stance on being perceived as a commercial sell-out. Refusing each and every request, Waits aggressively sought out and defeated those who dared to infringe upon his trademarks.

In early August 1992, after a five-year wait since *Franks Wild Years*, Waits and Island Records unleashed to the world what many consider his masterpiece, *Bone Machine*, a cacophonous symphony of metal and flesh syncopated to a grand piano of skeleton chords over and under junkyard missives. The progressive instrumentation gave no quarter to the uninitiated listener, even though it won a Grammy for "Best Alternative Music Album." The first rattling percussion sounds leading in the song "Earth Died Screaming" was one-upped by Waits's ragged vocals. Time had done less to mellow his vocal cords than to give logic to the discordance.

The themes of the album were homicide, mortality, and longing. A pool of musical talent was freely available for Waits to draw upon, including a return visit by Keith Richards, Les Claypool from the band Primus, and Los Lobos' David Hidalgo. Waits stayed close to his home, choosing to record the album at Prairie Sun Recording Studios in Cotati, California. The room he chose, Studio C, became known to musicians recording there as the "Waits Room." The studio chief, Mark Rennick, shared the details of his Prairie Sun studio with the *Sonoma County Independent* in 1999.

> Studio X and the live areas are down in the old cement hatchery rooms, one of which, now called the Waiting Room, is Tom Waits's preferred acoustic environment.
>
> "[Waits] gravitated toward these 'echo' rooms and created the *Bone Machine* aural landscape," Rennick says.
>
> On this day, occupying a full corner of the cavernous main room of Studio X is an enormous pile of exotic instruments used by Waits while recently recording his yet-to-be-titled new album. The array runs the gamut from the gauche to the ramshackle, the most identifiable objects being huge, old wooden drums, antique carnival pianos, guitars of all shapes and sizes, and a heap of rusty yard tools.
>
> "What we like about Tom is that he is a musicologist. And he has a tremendous ear," Rennick says. "His talent is a national treasure."

Jesse Dylan, Bob Dylan's son, took a series of photographs of Waits playing court jester replete with a leather skullcap and aviator goggles. One such blurred photo, giving a hint to the blur of aural stylings found within, made the cover of the album.

"The Lie in Waits"
Observer
July 1992 (issue date: November 23, 1992)
Pete Silverton

To converse with Tom Waits is to be lied to, consistently, determinedly, entertainingly. "I'll tell you all my secrets but I'll lie about my past," he once sang.

Take that 64-point comma of a scar in the middle of his forehead, which runs at a direct right angle to the normal creases. "Gee," he said—a word that has an innocence on the page that it didn't have in his mouth. He didn't know how that scar came about. He couldn't remember. Then he paused, giving his eyes time to roam around a little and his body to twist and untwist itself as he thought. And then he could remember. A bullet went right in there. The scar marked the entry point and the bullet continued its journey through the Waits cranium and gray matter till it re-emerged into the outside world from the back of his skull.

"And I never felt better in my life," he growled into his morning coffee.

Or take the tale of his first meeting with Joe Strummer, when Waits was playing Ronnie Scott's club in London in 1976. (It's a tale told to me by Glen Matlock, Sex Pistols bassist.) A then unknown Strummer having met Waits a few days earlier, he turned up at the club to claim his promised free entry. Waits came to the door in a long dark coat, stared hard and blank at Strummer, then reached into his coat and pulled a full pint of newly poured Guinness from an inner pocket. He drank it right off and told the doorman to let Strummer in.

It's a tale that evokes no echoes in the modern Waits brain, but he loves it, he warms to it. "Gee, it's a GREAT story.

"Yeah, the truth of things is not something I particularly like. I go more for a good story than what really happened. That's just the way I am.

"I'm a big liar."

And what doesn't he lie about?

"Er, er." And he paused for some time, perhaps searching for inspiration in the pattern of the tablecloth, perhaps just hoping I'd shut up and go away and leave him to enjoy the rest of the day with his wife and two children. "Whatever I tell you right now would probably be a lie."

Tom Waits has a new album and Tom Waits had to do some interviews so Tom Waits was sitting, on a warm, early summer day, at a table in a Paris street café—he was staying at a quiet, reserved, and expensive hotel across the way. For him it was an early breakfast. For the rest of the Place des Vosges it was a regular Saturday lunchtime.

Like the good American he is, he had Coca-Cola and a large white coffee in front of him, and didn't even make an attempt at speaking French. "Not a man's town, Paris, not a man's town," he'd chant now and again. As ever, he was scrunched in his chair, with that constant twisting and turning and scratching of his. His black motorcycle boots shuffled their way around underneath the table. The gray thumbprint of facial hair—which is all that currently remains of the variety of whiskers Waits has experimented with over the years—stayed pretty much where it always does, immediately below his lower lip.

It was a somewhat unlikely setting in which to find a man whose reviews seem inevitably to have been stained with the same clichés about cheap booze and nicotine stains and Edward Hopper paintings and Jack Kerouac novels. Here he was in one of the most distinctive remnants of pre-revolutionary Paris, a short walk from the Bastille—where now a glass-walled opera house dominates much as the prison once must have done.

Adhering to the clichés about Waits would, as a rule, mean that at this point the suggestion would be made that Tom would have felt more at home in the area back when the prison—and its most renowned inhabitant, the Marquis de Sade—were still alive and, if not well, then healthily sick. Mention would probably be made of his once announcing his address as the fictitious junction of Bedlam and Squalor, or perhaps his long-term, and factual, residence in Los Angeles' Tropicana Motel, with its fine collection of antique junkies and splendid black-painted swimming pool.

Just as possibly, he could even have been looking forward to a Sunday in the Place des Vosges, watching the French royalists all turn up for their weekly parade, in their neat blue suits and their small children in neat blue corduroy shorts—always corduroy because it's a royalist word, from *corde du roi* (king's cords).

Don't let anyone tell you otherwise: whatever his idiosyncrasies, and they are legion, he just isn't that early cliché. Even when he was most wrapped in it, Rickie Lee Jones—his then girlfriend—begged to differ. She believed what Tom really wanted was to live in a bungalow with screaming kids and spend Saturday nights at the movies. Which is, give or take a scream or two, more or less what he's got.

He's now a man of forty-two, with a wife of nearly twelve years who was once a script editor and with whom he now writes his lyrics. The former Kathleen Brennan has straight, fair hair and pale skin. She was once an Illinois farm girl who was familiar with the sight of dead cats hanging from doorways. Now she lives with Tom Waits in a small California town. And, no, she won't talk, although she will gossip and sip her tea.

But he'll talk about her help with songwriting. Difficult working with your wife, is it? "Sure, we beat each other up over stuff but when you got kids and you live together, you do everything together. So why not, you know, write together."

What does she bring to the lyrics that wasn't there before?

"A whip and a chair. The Bible. Book of Revelations. She grew up Catholic so all that, you know, blood and liquor and guilt. She pulverizes me so that I don't just write the same song over and over again. Which is what a lot of people do, including myself."

And he's now a man with two small children, although—well, true or false, let him tell the story. "I was in Memphis about three weeks ago, for a wedding. While I was there I went to Graceland. It's like a sideshow. It's like the ultimate sideshow on a carnival. Paying to go in and look at a room where people used to drink and get loaded. I would have rather seen his pickled head in a jar. Then I would have felt like I got what I paid for.

"We walked by the grave. My little boy said: 'I wish they'd dig him up and take all his teeth out so I can make a necklace.'

"I don't think anybody had thought of that yet. Elvis's teeth necklace."

And he is also now a man who's had an international hit record, thanks to Rod Stewart and his convincingly melodramatic version of "Downtown Train."

He was on a two-week trip to Europe, part holiday, part seeing a Seville production [July 8–10, 1992] of *Black Rider*, the opera he has worked on with Robert

Wilson and William Burroughs—a "contraption" he called it, using his favorite word of the moment; he usually has a favorite word of the moment, which he likes to sprinkle in a fair number of suitable sentences.

And then came promoting the record. "No, not this," he thought. "Oh Jesus, I should have been a butcher." He thinks he doesn't seem to crave attention and validation and support and affection and encouragement as much as he used to—which is always the kind of statement that should be doubted when it comes from the mouth of a professional performer.

But he did it anyway, pointing out his own contradictions as he went along. "At times, feels like a rain dance. But I don't like it when it rains anyway. So here I am trying to get it to rain."

And it's a long time since it rained. *Bone Machine*—its title a reference of sorts to the human body—is his first album for four years, his first album of new songs for five. "Never thought about it before. I don't know how long it's been.

"It takes a while to get started. I collect ideas and I usually got them on me somewhere. It's just a matter of getting them all in one place. The songs came kind of fast. If you think you've got one in you, you take a fly at it.

"I think recording can sometimes be a violent operation. I think recording studios sometimes can be like a slaughterhouse, where you have some ideas you want to try and wrestle with. Many times you end up with a lot of feathers. A dead bird and a mouthful of feathers.

"It's not easy for me. Music is like a living thing. You don't wanna murder it." He really does say "wanna." "You don't wanna splatter it all over the walls. You wanna go into certain worlds; you wanna go into a teardrop or go through a hole in the crack in the plaster. You wanna go someplace you've never been before and sometimes those journeys are successful and sometimes you're left with just dead bodies all over the meadow. Sometimes you realize you didn't bring enough supplies, you're outta water. But I love the process of it all.

"It's a bit like taking a pill. If you're doing it right, there's nothing in the world that's as thrilling.

"Songs are really simple. You hold them in your hand. I can make one right now and finish it. But because they're so simple, it's like bird-watching, you know. You gotta know something about birds or you won't see anything: just you and your binoculars and a stupid look on your face.

"You have to make yourself some kind of an antenna for the songs to come to you. So you have to make yourself a kind of a musical yourself. You have to be of music and have music in you—some way for songs to continue to want to live in you, in or near you. You gotta be real quiet sometimes if you wanna catch the big ones."

What were the signposts on the map for *Bone Machine*?

"Well, certain areas you wanna cover. There was a certain kind of end-of-the-world kind of aspect we wanted it to have." The first track, for example, "The Earth Dies Screaming." "Sometimes you think it's going to be seven feet tall with rocks glued to it and it turns out to be something else. You don't always come back with what you set out to find. You have an imagination about it and the reality is very different.

"Sometimes a song just comes out of nowhere. Other times you chase one song for like a couple of days and then you wind up with nothing. Then you have to bring them back from where you found them. And sometimes they escape. Sometimes they die. Sometimes they get sick first and then die. Sometimes they kill you."

It's a clattering, clanging, thumping album with a menagerie of percussion—a conundrum, for example, which is "like an iron cross with these metal things hanging off. You hit it with a big hammer. Real hard. It's like hitting a dumpster." Elsewhere the record features Keith Richards, co-author of one track—"He's a real gypsy. Music stalks him"—and the Chamberlin—an analogue forerunner of the synthesizer. "It's a contraption, you know," he explains, using that favored word.

If he listens to other people's music at all these days, it's old favorites or the rap stations.

"I love rap. It's raw and hollering and violent. Rap has a shape and a frame. Black music in America is the only music that's changing and evolving. Maybe that's not accurate to say. It just seems that black music is a living music as opposed to a dead music. It's growing and it gets angry and then it shuts up and it breaks windows and it disappears and it comes back. But it's living music, it has a job."

Truth or storytelling? "When I'm talking about ideas or music, I'm telling you how I feel. I'm very sincere about the things that I'm talking about."

To observe that there are two Tom Waits is scarcely original and maybe not even true, but it's not something he'd necessarily dispute. "Yeah. I'm like a ventriloquist. You end up doing it in order to survive. So you never have to be where you say you are. It's just simpler after a while. You have at least two rooms in your house. And you're never in both at the same time."

But there's also a third Tom Waits, the one who cropped up on an American TV ad for Doritos Fritos. "They imitated my voice. The guy who did the voice was like a fan of mine who does an impersonation of me and lives in Texas, plays in a band." Waits sued, eventually winning a judgment of $2.5 million dollars, but of course it's still in appeal. The impersonator was Tom's star witness. "He felt so bad that he did this. He knew when he did it he was doing a bad thing. It was like he was going to get nailed for it. And he did. But he vindicated himself by being our witness, helping us win the case.

"I haven't seen a dime. These things go on forever and forever. Never get involved in litigation. Your hair will fall out, your bones will turn to sand. And it will still be going on.

"It was like throwing a rock through a window—but you wait for five years to hear the sound. Litigation is like picking up a glass of water with a prosthetic hand. It's very frustrating, and you'll never get it to your lips.

"But when you have to, you have to. If somebody burned your house down, you'd have to do something about it."

But what about the future, what does that hold for Tom Waits?

"I think about: the worms crawl in, the worms crawl out, the worms play pinochle on your snout. A snake just crawled in your eye. I can't wait till the worms are eating me. That's a big dream."

Sweet dreams, Tom Waits. All three of you.

"Composer, Musician, Performer, Actor: Tom Waits Is a Renaissance Man Whose Musique Noir Captures the Sound of the Dark Age"
Pulse
September 1992
Derk Richardson

"What I like to try and do with my voice is get kind of schizophrenic with it and see if I can scare myself."

Tom Waits is stirring his third cup of coffee, pouring in the creamer from one of those little plastic thimblelike containers. Outside this truck-stop café, just off Highway 101 in Petaluma, the Northern California drought has taken a rare day off and a steady summer rain is falling on eighteen-wheelers, Ford pickups, and Waits's faded-gold 1964 Cadillac Coupe de Ville. It's four thirty in the afternoon and Waits, after half an hour of conversation, is just warming up to the task of doing his first interviews in nearly five years and talking about his new album, *Bone Machine* (Island/PLG), his first studio album of songs since 1987's *Franks Wild Years*. "I don't like to be pinned down," he mutters in the unmistakably gruff voice that has grown increasingly graveled and ravaged on record since his 1973 debut *Closing Time*. "I hate direct questions. If we just pick a topic and drift, that's my favorite part."

Glancing around the diner, where truckers are wolfing down pork chops and making calls from the red leatherette phone booths, Waits notices the clocks—on one, the hands sweep across the face of John Wayne; the other's face is that of Elvis Presley. The young, healthy, "Love Me Tender" Elvis. "I went to Graceland," he says in his rumbling whisper. "I had to pull away from the crowd about half-way through. My little boy said, 'Hey, why don't we dig him up and take his teeth out and make a necklace.' A lot of people on the tour act like they're seeing the place where Christ lived and they don't like to hear things like that. But I got a kick out of it. There was a bullet hole in the swing set where his kid used to play. I didn't like that; that was a little rough. A bullet hole in the slide. Even the way they discussed that aspect of it, it was like, 'Oh the boys, they were just having fun.' But you know what the scene was like—they were all liquored up and opened the back door and someone got the Carbine .410 and they had to shoot at something or they would've hit a neighbor, so they said, 'Try for the swing set.' The trip was a little rough that way.

"But it was a good eyeball on our country," he continues. "It has a hollow center, like those Valentine candies with a hollow center. Whoa. It was very much like a sideshow, and I'm always curious about those things—you know, two-headed cows and stuff like that. Forget about it; I'm there. I don't care what it costs. I'll pay, I'll go in, sit down. I'll see the three-headed baby and all that stuff. When I got it on that level, it made better sense."

Anyone familiar with the evolution of Waits's music has a sense of his fascination with society's underbelly and the modern legacy of broken American dreams. Such concerns have long since marked his output, from the introspective, bohemian singer-songwriter folk of his "Ol' 55" (covered early by the Eagles) and "San Diego Serenade" (recently recorded by Nanci Griffith), through the sleazy "Pasties and a G-String"/"Warm Beer and Cold Women" nightlife world of *Small Change* and *Nighthawks at the Diner*, to the sometimes murky and clangy, musically complex, urban soundscapes of *Swordfishtrombones* and *Rain Dogs* (commonly regarded as the first two parts of a trilogy with *Franks Wild Years*). As well, those preoccupations resonate in Waits's live performances, especially his theatrical *Big Time* tour of 1987, his film roles, his film scores (most recently for Jim Jarmusch's *Night on Earth*), and his choice of material for a variety of tribute compilations, including "Heigh-Ho!" for Hal Willner's *Stay Awake* Disney roast, Kurt Weill and Bertolt Brecht's "What Keeps Mankind Alive" for *Lost in the Stars*, and an ironic "It's All Right with Me" for *Red Hot + Blue*.

"I like things that are kind of falling apart," Waits says, "'cause I come from a broken home, I guess. I like things that have been ignored or need to be put back together." With *Bone Machine*, Waits takes everything—the themes and the sounds of breakdown and decay—to new extremes. The portrayals of judgment day, rural desolation, and various forms of betrayal, the rattling percussion, the grinding guitars, the wheezing saxophones and keyboards, and Waits's hoarse bellowing and sinister whispers flesh out the songwriter's vision of heaven/hell. "I have some new categories," he says. "The end of the world, that's kind of a new category for me. Suicide notes. Murder. 'Earth Died Screaming'—that's one of my favorites; it's got kind of an apocalyptic, I don't know, African thing." You can picture Waits, in his boots, jeans, and black leather jacket with a big rip under the left arm, rummaging through the rubble of a suburban neighborhood ravaged by the big earthquake or the nuclear holocaust. He's poking at things with a stick, looking for metal shards and bits of broken machinery that only he would salvage, whacking them to make them confess their innermost feelings.

"We're like bone machines," he says of the album title. "Most machines take on a certain kind of human quality, even a bicycle, particularly an old bicycle that's been ridden a lot, even when nobody's on it. I like that aspect of machinery. I saw a picture of a bottle-making machine and a guy working it, back in the '20s. It made like forty thousand bottles in like twelve hours, and there was something very human, something very animal about it; it looked like some kind of creature with the skin burned off. I like those sounds. I wanted to explore more machinery sounds."

So Waits commissioned a percussion rack called the Conundrum. "It looks like some kind of perverted giant Spanish iron cross or something." The results include "In the Colosseum," which sounds like someone's hammering and clamoring in the next room, and "The Ocean Doesn't Want Me," a Ken Nordine–meets–*Sea Hunt* recitation about a foiled suicide attempt, haunted by the muffled clang of a giant iron chain knocking against an underwater pier.

"On 'Earth Died Screaming,' we got sticks and we tried them everywhere," Waits says. "I wanted to try and get some of that sound of pygmy field recordings that I love so much, and we couldn't get it. We tried different places in the room, different microphones, nothing. Different kinds of sticks, sizes of sticks. And then we went outside and just put a microphone on the asphalt and there it was, boom, 'cause we were outside.

"I'm exploring more and more things that make a sound but are not traditional instruments," he continues. "It's a good time to do it, too, because there's a lot of garbage in the world that I can use that is just sitting out there rusting. I can't believe it. I think something is gonna come out of this garbage world we're living in, where knowledge and information are becoming so abstract and the things that used to really work are sitting out there like big dinosaur carcasses, rusting. Something's gonna have to be made out of it that has some value. What can we do? Bury it and live on it? Americans still have some sense of, 'What can I do with this now that it's no good anymore besides just leaning it up against the barn?'

"I've heard that trash day in Japan is pretty wild, if you want to pick up some pretty weird things that have become obsolete in just the last seven or eight days. So I think about those things. I go up and hit stuff a lot to see what it sounds like. Getting it to make sense in the studio is always something different—how it's miked, what kind of room it's in. You're always up against the physics of it. I'm interested in that. I get into absurd arguments with myself about sound and the texture of it, all these things that keep you up at night that just drive you nuts, which is why I'm glad that this record's finally gonna be released: get it out of my house! But I love the process, I really do. I like having music going through my fingers."

One of the dinosaurs Waits reclaimed on *Bone Machine* is the Chamberlin, a pre-synthesizer keyboard that taps into analog tape loops of prerecorded material. "It's stunning, really," he enthuses. "I have like seventy voices on the instrument, from horses to rain, laughter, thunder, seven or eight different trains, and then all the standard orchestral instruments. It's a good alternative if you don't like the sound of the more conventional state-of-the-art instruments—sometimes it's like they've had the air sucked out of them."

Most of the music on *Bone Machine* is, appropriately, stripped down to guitar and percussion, predominantly by Waits, with Larry Taylor (Jerry Lee Lewis, Canned Heat) on upright bass. Waits is self-deprecating about the extraordinary array of guitar sounds he has generated. "Actually," he says, "I had somebody else doing it and I paid them. I said, 'Well, listen, I'm not gonna use your name; do I have to pay you a lot more so I can say it was me?' And in a lot of cases they said that I could do that: 'Just pay me off and I'll disappear, and there'll be no suit or anything.' I can play guitar in a limited spectrum, but I can play anything within a limited spectrum. It's like if the leg of the chest of drawers is broken off, I can get four books at just the right height so it won't fall over. I can be those four books with a song. I can't be the chest of drawers, but I can be the four books.

"And a lot of times, that's what you're doing in a song. You're listening and thinking, 'What does it need?' Some of what goes into song-building is almost a medical Frankenstein process. What does it need? It's very beautiful but it has no heart, or it has nothing but heart and it needs a rib cage, or whatever. I'm usually good at the medical questions about music. Eventually I'll probably just be a medical consultant in music. I'll be called in to look at sick songs and I'll either say, 'Put the sheet over it,' or, 'Operate.' I'll have a little bag with my saw. Sometimes you have to break the leg and then reset it. I'm good at that. But it's painful. But if you didn't call me in early and you need me now, you gotta be willing to go through some discomfort. I like breaking songs, breaking their backs. I like songs with scars on them—when I listen to them I just see all the scars."

Instead of forming a band to fit the surgical needs of his new songs, Waits invited his favorite musicians to make guest appearances: saxophonist Ralph Carney, bassist Les Claypool from Primus, the Limbomaniacs' Brain on drums, guitarists Joe Gore (also senior editor at *Guitar Player* magazine), David Philips, and Waddy Wachtel, David Hidalgo from Los Lobos on accordion and violin, and, on "That Feel," co-songwriter Keith Richards.

"If I had started out in a band, if I was a band, I would have already broken up," Waits laughs. "But I've had great musical impulses and experiences with many people. I'm not a real gregarious type of person where I'm like some kind of magnet so that people are brought into my gravity. Although it would appear that music has a more social aspect than maybe bug collecting, people are still isolated regarding their own peculiarities. I venture out there very carefully and then have to shut my mouth a lot. But when you meet someone you have a rapport with, it's really thrilling. I like it when you soar after a session—your knuckles are bleeding and your butt hurts, you've got skinned elbows and knees, and your pants are wet and you've got blood in your hair. I consider that really great. It's not always the case but you hope for that, you work for that. The responsibility to whatever you're doing requires that you do take yourself into those kinds of configurations in order to remain some kind of meaningful antenna and to stay filled with wonder about it all."

If Waits had let himself go completely, he says, *Bone Machine* might have turned into a total experiment in sound. But in the process of putting it together, the album was taken over by the themes of the songs. That didn't make his work any easier, however. He waxes on at length about the struggle to bring new songs into the world. About half of them were cowritten with his wife, Kathleen Brennan. "Kathleen and I went into a room for about a month and banged 'em out," he says. "We started with nothing sometimes. One-on-one. It's a different kind of thing, writing songs with someone. But hey, we got kids together, we can make songs together. I fall into a groove too easily. I get in there and say, 'Oh, here's my place.' It's like a shovel handle. Even on the piano, my hands are at the same place every time, because your hands have an intelligence that's separate from your own. But sometimes you need somebody to say, 'No, put 'em over here and try this,' and she does that. She calls me on all that stuff. 'Oh, this again, oh Jesus! Oh, here's the hundredth one of those.' But, oh yeah, I beat her up, too. Not literally," he says, leaning into the tape recorder. "I don't really beat her up, don't misunderstand me."

Waits describes the agony he puts his songs through. "Some come out of the ground just like a potato," he says. "Others, it's like papier-mâché: I gotta get the flour out, I gotta get dirty, and it makes you mad. With some, it's like the good son. 'Proud of you son,'" he says in Jack Nicholson's *The Shining* voice. "'You've always been a good son. You, on the other hand, have always given me problems, you won't be going on our little trip east.'

"I get real cranky about the songs," he says, "I get mad at the songs. 'Oh, you little sissy, you little wimp, you're not gonna go on my fucking record, you little bastard. No way are you going, and we're leaving in about three days and you're not going with us, 'cause you're a sissy and a wimp.' And then songs start to get like, 'Oh, God, we can't go.' Toward the end it's always good to whip the songs a little bit, scare 'em, and then make fun of them. And then they change. You come back the next day and they're better behaved.

"You know who really does that great?" Waits asks rhetorically. "Keith Richards. He's real like voodoo about it. He circles it. He's like an animal, smelling it, kicking dirt on it. He's real ritual about it, real jungle. I had an experience writing with him for several weeks and it was really thrilling. He's written so many different kinds of songs. You identify him with that really dirty guitar and that ganglike stance, like a killer at a gas station—'Oh man, we better not stop for gas here'—and then you realize he's a real gypsy. We had some wild times. You can't drink with him—just forget about it, you'll be leaving early, he reduces you to something very embarrassing. You'll be the table—they'll put drinks on you. He toughens you up."

After spending the past five years on special projects, including the soundtracks, guest shots on word-jazz maestro Ken Nordine's *Devout Catalyst* and saxophone legend Teddy Edwards' *Mississippi Lad*, and a joint-effort operatic piece, *The Black Rider*, written with William Burroughs and Robert Wilson (staged in Hamburg, Germany, where he'll do *Alice* with Wilson as well), Waits may have needed to toughen himself up a little bit to face down those songs. "If you're writing for film," he says, "it's all collaborative and sometimes you're like part of an orchestra, you're the trombone, you're the percussion, or whatever. You're the pallbearer, that's what you really are! Most films and most records are like the tombstone beneath which is buried the real film or the real record. It's amazing how much of the project ends up buried—ideas that you had, things that could have happened but didn't, songs that didn't make it. You hope that in dragging it out of the hole, you don't tear its head off and you're left with fur. It's rough for me."

But what he loves about writing songs, he says, is the opportunity they afford for tinkering. "You can change everything if you want," Waits says. "If you don't like the way something is going, you can totally change the bone structure of a song, or three or four songs in the way they all work together. The thing I hate about recording is that it's so permanent. Ultimately you have to let it dry, and I hate that, 'cause I like to just keep changing the shape of 'em, and cut 'em in half and use the parts that I didn't want on that one on another one.

"That's the part that drives everybody crazy. I like to get in there with the songs and eat them up and push them around and explore all the variables. Sometimes it sounds Irish and then you tilt it a little bit this way and it sounds more Balinese and over here it sounds more Romanian. I like that part of working with music; you can find yourself in a different latitude and longitude. There's a lot of different coordinates for rhythm, and when you start exploring rhythms, you find that maybe it sounds Chinese, and then you realize it's just kind of like banging sticks on the ground, it's just something that comes naturally and you don't necessarily have to put it in a particular country. Some of these things come out of your own rubber dream."

Over the years Waits has grown more confident about his ability to bring what he hears in his head into being as music. "I like to think wherever I aim this thing, I can hit it," he says. "You get to where if you really know how to shoot it, you can pick anything off. But a lot of songs don't want to be caught, and they do get away. If you want to take them alive, you have to have something other than a conventional understanding of music. It's like anything else—what you put yourself through in milking it is what comes back to you, in direct proportion."

Then there's the issue of his voice, which he has disciplined and sometimes processed, with megaphones and other devices, into an extraordinarily expressive, if harrowing, vehicle. "What I like to try and do with my voice is get kind of schizophrenic with it," he explains, "and see if I can scare myself or go from one song to the next and see if I can like turn my head around on my body so my vertebra cracks. Or I put on lipstick and start screaming into a tin can. Oh, yeah, I'm happy with my voice as an instrument. I quit smoking and nobody noticed. Or I say, 'I lost my voice, I have no voice,' and they say, 'I didn't notice.' That really hurts."

Finally, after improvising at length on the riffs about the blood and bones of song-making, Waits leans into the corner of the booth and tries to place himself in the overall picture of American culture, a picture that doesn't have much room for someone who likes to walk into his neighbor's yard and bang on things. "It's hard sometimes if you're faced with having to deal with the traditional world of commerce," he says. "We seem to salute anything that you can make ten million of and sell to everybody; the fact that everybody's got one is a triumph, not the fact that you made ten great ones. I don't use that as a gauge.

"But there are parts of America where music is a living thing. In New Orleans, music is just like this Tabasco here. They just go get some and put it on their food. The only thing really vital in this country, that is constantly evolving and working very hard, the only real American music is America's black music. It's infused with something so important. My daughter listens to the rap station and it's a music that is like graffiti or jail poems, it's like a brick through the window. It's powerful and essential."

For Waits, making a culture of his own in the vast wasteland of middle America has been an ongoing project much like composing songs. "For me, white boy from California," he says, "I listen to things and break a piece off of this, and a piece off of this, and I tie this to that, put these two together and then I take them out to meet the pieces coming down from the top and wrap it all in newspaper and set it on fire. It's like making a record" (or maybe like doing an interview?), he concludes before driving off in the rain that nobody expected. "You don't really finish, you just stop. You just keep painting it and doing things to it and eventually, you have to stop."

Waits on the road, songs, instruments, and the crying room:
Excerpted from Evening Becomes Eclectic, KCRW
October 9, 1992

The road is always rough because it's different every night. [. . .] Some nights, it's like being skinned and dipped in lemon juice, and other nights it's like you're eight miles high and the world is covered with mattresses and you can't get hurt. [. . .]

My theory is the best songs have never really been recorded so we're all listening to used music. We're listening to things that made it through but there's so many songs that have never made it because they were scared of the machine and wouldn't allow themselves to be recorded. The trick is to get it in there, don't hurt the song when you record it. [. . .]

I think drums play a lot better when you're mad. I think unfamiliarity is good for your development, the mystery of musicianship. It's important to keep that alive. I like to do it with the band. I say, "Let's try this thing once all together and now let's switch instruments and let's get really off balance here and see if we can play it again with no coordinance and no center of gravity at all." Let's try it like that. Or you take it and say, "Let's cut the band in half. Half you guys play the song now, the other part of the group here, I want you to play it too but a little bit behind the beat so we get that kind of wobbly kind of Titanic feel." I think suggestions to groups are really important things that you say to them before you go into a song. I like to work with people who respond to those things. [. . .]

I remember when I was a kid in the movies, in the theater, there used to be a place called the crying room, do you remember that? There was a big yellow sign and it said "The Crying Room" and I used to think that was for people who were overcome with emotion from the film and they had to go into this room and they were all in there crying. There was always a lot of people in there. You heard crying coming out. When I got older I realized that was for mothers with their kids and their kids were crying and they wanted to watch the movie but they couldn't watch it with everybody else because it would disturb the audience, so they had to go to the crying room and take their kids there, but it always seemed that it was more crowded during the sad films, the real sad movies, there was a lot of people in there.

Interview with Tom Waits
Morning Becomes Eclectic, KCRW
October 12, 1992
Chris Douridas

Chris Douridas: It's really great to meet you, finally.

Tom Waits: Good to meet you, Chris.

CD: *Swordfishtrombones* marked a new direction in your work . . . it seemed to, it's almost like you suddenly took the bull by the horns and you began producing projects yourself. It seemed as though you kind of began a whole new adventure that we're still hearing chapters from now even with your new work, *Bone Machine*.

TW: Oh yeah, well I like songs with adventure in them. I think that's what every-body's looking for, songs with adventure and, you know, acts of depravity and eroticism, and shipwrecks, murder . . . I dunno, that was for me, I think up until that point I had been . . . I don't think I was done yet. I think at that point I tried to make songs that felt a little more handmade; experiments and expeditions into a world of sound and stories, so I mean, particularly with percussion, I was more interested in percussion in these Bermuda Triangles of percussion that you find and sometimes you drop off the edge of the world, and . . .

CD: Did that new need that you were having, did that warrant the label change?

TW: Actually, no, the album was made for EA [Elektra/Asylum], and Joe Smith heard it. He didn't know what to do with it. He looked at me like I was nuts. At first he said, "Produce your own record, go ahead, make your own record, you should be producing your own record." So I said, "OK, good." I made about three or four things and brought 'em in and he heard 'em and he said, "Well, I dunno. . . ." Then I made a whole record and played it for him and he said, "I don't know if we can put this thing out or not." So Chris Blackwell heard it, and I left EA through a loophole in my contract, and I snuck out. Chris Blackwell loved the album and said, "We'll put it out." So that's what happened. He was very in tune with it. Blackwell has great ears, you know? Because he liked what I did, so I guess that means he has great ears, you know?

CD: That also was the beginning of the appearance of Frank, who stuck with your work for a good while. Where did Frank come from? Where's he from?

TW: Oh gee, I don't know. It's like a ventriloquist act. "Frank's Wild Years" was just a little story about a guy from a small town who went away to try and make something out of himself. I don't know where it came from, it's just a little story that was on *Swordfishtrombones,* an oddball short story.

CD: Obviously, he kept you a little interested because it kept getting tinkered with and expanded, and turned into a stage production you had taken on tour.

TW: A good butcher uses every part of the cow.

CD: I dunno if it's just coincidental, but after Frank started lurking around, you began to get involved with film work. The acting side of your life started to grow and expand and I guess that came first through your contacts with Francis Ford Coppola.

TW: Well, let's see, I done a couple of films before I worked with Francis. My first project with Francis was *One from the Heart*. I was living in New York and he longed to do a lounge operetta, that's what he called it. It was kind of a step backwards for me a little bit 'cause I had already tried to break out of my mortuary piano-and-cocktail hairdos in the songs. I was really trying to shut the door on that whole obsession with liquor and my own perverted enjoyment of all that. He wanted cocktail songs so I came back to L.A. from New York and started writing in an office. I'd never really written in an office before with wood paneling and all that. It was good, it was very satisfying to work with him, and since we've done other things together. You meet people along the way you have a rapport with, that's really great.

CD: What of the acting work, so far, are you most happy with?

TW: I like *Ironweed*. I also had a part in this Robert Altman film, which isn't out yet [*Short Cuts*]. I play Earl Piggot, a limo driver who drinks, and I was married to Lily Tomlin. Robert Altman was great to work with. He's like a good sheriff in a bad town. I was in *Dracula*. That's coming out pretty soon. That was great. I had a really, really great time doing that.

CD: Now you're playing Renfield in *Dracula* which is just an incredible opportunity, I would think to just let it . . .

TW: Just go crazy? Well, you see a lot of people think that I ate these insects and I wanted to really set the record straight on that because I didn't actually eat the insects, you know, I put 'em in my mouth like I gave 'em a carnival ride like a fun house. I put 'em in the fun house and I let them move around in my mouth and then I brought 'em back out again. You know, I didn't actually murder them with my teeth.

CD: Eating them is too easy.

TW: Yeah, but I had a good time. I was . . . I had some frightening moments, when I was both frightened and exhilarated: being hosed down in an insane asylum [and] dressed like a moth. I also had to wear these hand restraints that were really painful. They were designed . . . they were based on a design they had for piano players actually in Italy, to keep your hands straight. They were metal braces, and they corrected anything that your fingers may want to do that's un-piano-like. They were like, I dunno, it was like having a corset for your fingers. It kept them perfectly like this [*gesturing to hands in position of braces*]. It was all metal, and then it had these caps that went over your fingers and it was really painful to your cuticles and it looked really scary. That was the idea.

CD: Yeah, I was gonna say, why would they have those on Renfield? I guess it must just look very bizarre to begin with.

TW: Yeah, it looks funny.

CD: In the film, though, don't we see more of the history of Renfield?

TW: I don't know, I haven't seen the movie, I don't know how much of Renfield that we get to see.

CD: So never before do you see Renfield before he got to the asylum?

TW: Yeah. There's a photograph of him in the hat and suit before he started to lose it.

CD: I guess he was a businessman?

TW: Yeah, a solicitor for a real estate outfit.

CD: He made house calls. It must be kind of strange for you. When you work on the music side of things, you're completely in control, producing it, every inch of it is you, and when you're working in film, it's almost like you're back to the Asylum years or something.

TW: Yeah. Film is difficult sometimes, because, well you know, they don't pay you to act, they pay you to wait. You do a lot of waiting. Somebody told me that acting makes a woman more of a woman and a man less of a man. I said, "Oh God, so that's what's been bothering me. Thank you." Fussin' around with your hair, you know, gettin' up six in the morning and having to, you know, all these people fussin' all around.

CD: That's a good point.

TW: But I like it when I can actually leave the ground. That's rare in film. It's more common in a play where you can actually experience flight. Film is so broken up, it's a mosaic. But in working with good people it's always enriching and always satisfying. Some films are like you bought the last ticket on a death ship. *And you'll never come home.*

CD: Do you think that you ever might take more of an in-control role in film work, maybe do some directing?

TW: Gee, I don't know. You got to know a lot about a lot of things to do that. It's a lot to do. There's paraventricular prosthetic titanium adapters and thermal decapitators and bio-flesh regenerators, that type of thing. You have to know a lot, and I'm not really at that point in my career. It's like you got to be like Tesla.

CD: What first strikes you about this new release, or it struck me, was the heavy percussive feel, and the raw and gritty textures that are so much a part of it. And a lot of violence . . .

TW: Well it's always good material for songs.

CD: Really. Seems there's more of a home-based project for you too. Closer to home.

TW: Well, you know, it was all done in a little room at the studio. It was not a room that was designed to be used as a recording studio, so I think that's what helped us. It was just a room that sounded great. A cement floor that wasn't soundproofed, a broken window, you know, it's great. It was just a room, a storage room.

CD: This is what? A shed on your property?

TW: No, it was at the studio. They had other rooms. We worked at it for a couple days in a real studio, and I was really upset, just depressed. "This room sounds awful," I said, "no music will ever grow in this room." I was furious. I was so down. So I went around, looking around the place, and I said, "What about this room over here, I bet this room sounds good." Everybody laughed. I said, "No, really, what's wrong with this room here? Feels better. Hot water heater, a door, a window, a table, a chair, some maps on the wall. Get all these crates outta here, and let's do it right here, just run the wires down the hill." It was rainy season. Everybody said, "Oh, sure." And they did, and we got in there, and everything started to come together, so it was good, the project had a flat tire on the first day. Out of that we invented a new place for it to happen.

CD: Well, you had lugged in there a lot of instruments that have that kind of found quality to them. There's actually a new instrument on the album, that um . . .

TW: Oh, a conundrum.

CD: Yeah.

TW: Yeah, Serge Etienne built that, a friend of mine. It was . . . it's really . . . it's just a metal configuration, like a metal cross. It looks a little bit like a Chinese torture device. It's a simple thing, but it makes . . . it give you access to these alternative sound sources. Hit 'em with a hammer. Sounds like a jail door closing behind you. I like it. You end up with bloody knuckles when you play it. You just hit it with a hammer until you just, you can't hit it anymore. It's a great feeling to hit something like that. Really just slam it as hard as you can with a hammer. It's good and therapeutic, and all that.

CD: Do you try a lot of different things when you're working out a song? The way I understand it is that you and your wife Kathleen had come up with about sixty different ideas for this album, and after whittling them down, you came up with what you have left on the album?

TW: You always throw out a lot of songs. Not throw 'em out, but you cannibalize 'em. That's part of the process. Frankenstein that number over there, take the head offa him and put it, sew it onto this guy, immediately. Keep him alive until the head has been severed. And it's part of song building. Kathleen is great to work with, she's a lapsed Catholic from Illinois. She's loaded with mythology and a great sense of melody. I spin the chamber and she fires it. It's Russian roulette, sometimes you get great things. The collaboration is great with her, and we did have a lot of songs that were discarded, but that's part of the process.

CD: Your kids actually contributed some to the record as well.

TW: Oh yeah.

CD: How does this come up? Is this like breakfast table conversation?

TW: Oh, you know how everybody gets in like Jimmy Durante: "Everybody wants ta get inta the action." Eh, my little girl said—she has a word called, the word is *strangels*. It's a cross between *strange* and *angels*. Strange angels. *Strangels*. They're called *strangels*. "Or," I said, "you could have *braingels*." Those strange angels that live in your head would be *braingels*. We just went around and around with it, and it wound up in "The Ocean Doesn't Want Me Today," that little suicide note on the album. Hey, kids write thousands of songs before they learn how to talk. They write better songs than anybody. So you hope you can write something a kid would like.

CD: Toughest audience.

TW: I got a fan letter from somebody in the Midwest. They said, "Well, my little girl is just coming around to your songs now, she . . . they scare her a little bit.

She thinks you sound like a cross between a cherry bomb and a clown." I like that. Yeah, kids. You can't fool kids. They either like ya, or they don't.

CD: When you finally get the songs down to where you want them to be, lyrically and musically, and you've got the band there, as you're trying things out, do you have the tape rolling, or do you wait until you've got it, you rehearse it, and then you get the tape going?

TW: Do you stir the milk in before you add the batter? Do you add the eggs before you put . . . when do you put the cinnamon in? Is it after the nutmeg? Or do you first put the scallions in and you dice? What, do you brûlée that? Sauté that? I dunno, sometimes. Do you lift the lid, or do you not lift the lid?

CD: How do you know when a song is dead, when it's just not gonna come to life?

TW: Well, some of 'em never come to life. Sometimes you have to be like a doctor. You have to look at them medically: "What's wrong with this?" You have to diagnose them. Some have maladies that are impossible to deal with. Some of 'em you can't diagnose. Some songs, you work on them for months and they'll never make the journey. They'll be left behind, and someone has to break the news. We had one called "Filipino Box Spring Hog," it was a song about this old neighborhood ritual, and the song didn't make it on the record, it broke my heart, but it just couldn't come. It was good, maybe it'll come out on something else. It was a song about a . . . kinda like jambalaya, you know? Jambalaya. Crawfish pie. Filet gumbo.

CD: So it goes back in the scrap heap if you don't use it? Back in the compost?

TW: Yeah.

CD: Are you a particularly religious person?

TW: No, I wouldn't say . . . no, I'm not religious.

CD: Were you brought up religious at all?

TW: Oh, I had church when I was a kid, yeah. My mom heard the title of the album and she didn't like it. *Bone Machine.* She says, "Why must we always degrade?" She says, "Remember, the devil hates nothing more than a singing Christian." So, I went to church when I was a kid, and one Sunday morning, I finally decided I wasn't gonna go anymore. So I stopped. I dunno what's out there, or up there, a little office, maybe a little office, like when your car gets towed in New York and you have to go down to Pier 74, and it's like four in the morning and there's a Plexiglas shield, it's like three inches thick with bullet holes in it and an old woman with bifocals, sitting there at a typewriter, and you realize that your car is . . . you can see it, along, y'know, chain-ganged to hundreds of other cars over there, and your car looks ashamed and embarrassed. And you realize she, she's got the whole . . . she's got your destiny in her hands. So it's probably something like that. I mean, after you die. People think it's gonna be simple, but, I mean, *please*. It's gonna be an organizational nightmare after you die. All these spirits. Who? Where? What? When? You know, what did you do? Do you have your number? It's gonna be hell. So you're gonna have to be really . . . and to be able to find somebody after you've died is really gonna be hard, because there gonna be people that can't identify their loved ones cause they're just little lights blinking. It's gonna be rough.

CD: What must your upbringing have been like? I mean were your parents musical at all? Were they funny people?

TW: Funny people?

CD: When you were growing up?

TW: My dad was very musical, my mother also. They both sang. We had music in the house. We had Bing Crosby. We had Harry Belafonte. We had Marty Robbins.

CD: So they sang along with the records, and . . .

TW: A lot of mariachi music my dad loved, and still loves. He's a Spanish teacher, so that's what we listened to more than anything else, really. I wasn't allowed to listen to any of that hot rod music. So, I don't know where your musical education usually comes from, a little bit you heard when you were a kid, and then you're off on your own expedition, and what you do with it is up to you, how you integrate it. I have always felt like I'd find things that have fallen off a truck. Like the sound of this, I'll find some way to integrate it. I go at it like the Eyeball Kid. I try to sort of annex this. Change this. I don't know how it all comes together, but once you have musical confidence, and that usually comes from being naive enough to explore without feeling self-conscious, 'cause you really do want songs to like you as much as you want to like them, and there are things about music that . . . there are places in music that you can only go if you're an idiot. That's the only way you can get in. You know, there's high music, there's low music. We put an orchestra together in Hamburg that was half guys in the train station and half were all orchestral guys, and they . . . nobody got along. You think, "Oh, great. Everyone'll teach everyone how to. . . ." You know, there were some places where it did come together great, but . . . I don't know, music is a living thing, and so it can be . . . you can hurt it, you can bruise it, you can bruise the gin if you're not careful. So I dunno, I love to . . . songs are strange, they're very simple, they come quickly. If you don't take them, they'll move on. They'll go to somebody else. Someone else will write it down. Don't worry about it.

CD: Tom, have you realized the music the way you've heard it in your head?

TW: Well, you know, I always make compromises. If I really put it down the way I really want to hear it, nobody else would wanna listen to it but me.

CD: Really?

TW: Yeah.

CD: So you mean the way you . . .

TW: I clean everything up within reason because I'm getting more and more, like I like to step on it. Step on the negative. Grind it into the gutter and put that through the projector. I always love it, it's what Keith Richards calls the "hair in the gate" at a movie. You know when everybody's watching a movie and all of a sudden a piece of hair catches in the projector and everyone's going, "Wow, look at that hair," and then *Whoooooh!* and it flies out. And that's like, that was the most exciting moment in the film. It's like orchestras tuning up, sometimes, are the most interesting point in the evening's performance. "You know when you guys were tuning up, you really, well you had something there. And when you started to play, the music left."

Waits on trains:
Excerpted from "Tom Waits Meets Jim Jarmusch," Straight No Chaser (UK)
October 1992
Jim Jarmusch

Tom Waits: A sound that I've become obsessed with [is] getting an orchestra to sound like a train, actual train sounds. I have a guy in Los Angeles who collected not only the sound of the Stinson band organ, which is a carnival organ that's in all the carousels, the sound from that we used on *Night on Earth*, but he also has pitched four octaves of train whistles so that I can play the train whistle organ, which sounds like a calliope. It's a great sound. You know, a lot of the first, earliest experiments in sound, in creating illusions with sound and manipulating sound, happened with mediums that created this matrix of pipe configurations in their homes. Mediums that were doing séance work, contacting the dead, and they would outfit the room where they would conduct the séance with this whole matrix of pipes and things they could send voices into and have come out in unusual places. All of a sudden the sound of an old man snoring would come from under your chair. And you're in a dark room holding hands, and this was all an elaborate ruse to convince you that the spirits were visiting the room. So a lot of the sounds that we know, the things we can do in the studio now, with changing the shape of the voice or the resonance or the tonality or the frequency response or the EQ of it was first explored with these pipes. You'd hear a woman singing, and it's coming from behind a picture that's on the wall. The pipe just came up through the wall, there's a hole in the wall, the pipe came out and the sound came out. Who would ever think that anybody would ever do that? So they actually believed that they were hearing the voice of their mother, or all of a sudden they're hearing a woman singing, or . . .

One film Waits appeared in, *Coffee and Cigarettes: Somewhere in California*, a 1993 short directed by Jim Jarmusch, has become a cult favorite with cineastes with a taste for gritty black-and-white indies. This particular role was less acting as it was a display of Waits's candor with fellow iconoclast and rock star Iggy Pop. When he was interviewed by *Village Noize* in 1994, Jarmusch recalled how it all came together:

> Tom was exhausted. We had just shot a video the day before for "I Don't Wanna Grow Up" and he had been doing a lot of press. He was kind of in a surly mood as he is sometimes, but he's also very warm. He came in late that morning—I had given him the script the night before—and I was with Iggy. Tom threw the script down on the table and said, "Well, you know, you said this was going to be funny, Jim. Maybe you better just circle the jokes 'cause I don't see them." He looked at poor Iggy and said, "What do you think Iggy?" Iggy said, "I think I'm gonna go get some coffee and let you guys talk." So I calmed Tom down. I knew it was just early in the morning and Tom was in a bad mood. His attitude changed completely, but I wanted him to keep some of that paranoid surliness in the script. We worked with that and kept it in his character. If he had been in a really good mood, I don't think the film would have been as funny.

Waits on being remembered and the sound of big insects:
Excerpted from "What Do You Say to Tom Waits?," Village Noize
1993
Bill Dolan

Bill Dolan: How would you want to be remembered? Wait, you're not going anywhere are you?

Tom Waits: Be remembered? Why, do you know something I don't? Gee, I dunno. Eccentric. Uncommonly smooth, yet mild. Not a cough in a carload. Have you seen those new Adolf Hitler toilet brushes they're selling in Germany right now? To raise money to fight against the resurgence of Nazi activity?

BD: It's not on my shopping list yet. The key word is *yet*. What kind of places are you going to play next tour?

TW: I dunno, small theaters . . . or just sports arenas. That's all I'm gonna do is arenas. I'll insist on arenas. [. . .]

BD: Do you think MTV has irreversibly changed music for the worse?

TW: Basically, it's commerce. An international channel. The electronic circus.

BD: What kind of consumer product would a *Bone Machine* be?

TW: I dunno, but the left-handed model is more expensive, that's the difference. Have you ever seen an old printing press? Have you seen them work? The sound they make? Thrilling! They make that clang, and that cling and that whoosh. That's like a *Bone Machine*. Always looked like a big insect eating ink to me.

Waits and his favorite songs:
Excerpted from "Tom Foolery: Swapping Stories with Inimitable Tom Waits," *Buzz*
May 1993
Tom Waits

I've always loved songs of adventure, murder ballads, songs about shipwrecks and terrible acts of depravity and heroism. Erotic tales of seductions, songs of romance, wild courage, and mystery. Everyone has tried at one time or another to live inside a song. Songs where people die for love. Songs of people on the run. Songs of ghost ships or bank robberies. I've always wanted to live inside songs and never come back. Songs that are recipes for superstition or unexplained disappearances.

"They Call the Wind Maria," "Teen Angel," "Bonnie Bonnie Bedlam," "Pretty Boy Floyd," "Springhill Mining Disaster," "Lonesome Death of Hattie Carroll," "Wynken, Blynken, and Nod," "The Sinking of the Titanic," "Three Ravens," "Zaz Turned Blue," "Pretty Polly," "Streets of Laredo," "Raglan Road," "John Henry," "Stagger Lee," "Ode to Billie Joe," "Frankie and Johnny," "Brother, Can You Spare a Dime?" "Volga Boatmen," "In the Hall of the Mountain King," "Goodnight-Loving Trail," "Strange Fruit," "Jacob's Ladder," "Spanish Is the Loving Tongue," "Lost in the Stars," "Sympathy for the Devil," "Auld Lang Syne," and "Jesus' Blood Never Failed Me Yet."

These are a few of my favorites.

Tom Waits on dead animals:
Excerpted from "Tom Waits," Thrasher
February 1993
Brian Brannon

BB: Do you think the Earth is dying and we're just living in our own little dreams and ignoring it?

TW: I guess, but I think the world is going to be here a whole lot longer after we're gone. I'm just waiting for the whole world to open up and swallow us all in, scrape us all off its back. I think the world is a living organism. When you stick a shovel in the ground, have you ever heard the earth go "Uhhgm"? And we're living on the decomposed remains of our ancestors, both animal, mineral, and vegetable. So it is a living thing. I don't think it's going to die screaming, I think we're going to die screaming, in the swamp of time.

BB: So I heard that you moved to the country and there's a lot of roadkill out there?

TW: Yeah, roadkill, gun racks, collapsing chicken coops, and organized vultures.

BB: And there's always some killing?

TW: There's always some killing you've got to do around the farm. Barns are painted red because that's where all the slaughtering is done. Originally barns were painted with the blood of dead animals. Before they had paint, there was blood.

THE BLACK RIDER (1993)

Though the gap between his releases had widened, Waits remained prolific by contributing his talents to other artists, and his collaborators were as diverse as his albums. He was open-minded about different music forms emerging in the 1990s, notably rap and hip-hop. He also continued his interest in theater. Using the German folktale *Der Freischütz* as its basis, *The Black Rider: The Casting of the Magic Bullets*, a musical fable, had its premiere on March 31, 1990, at the Thalia Theater in Hamburg, Germany. Its English-language premiere occurred in 1998 at the Edmonton International Fringe Festival. In 1993, Island released studio versions of the Waits songs.

The Black Rider was the result of a collaboration between Waits, Beat writer William S. Burroughs, and stage director Robert Wilson. The Island Records CD was a sort of mixed bag for fans who hoped Waits would follow up *Bone Machine* with material of a similar ilk. The instrumentation featured similar instruments such as the calliope, a saw, viola, banjo, marimba, organ, French horn, and Waits on Emax strings (for "Russian Dance"). For the sleeve art, Kathleen Brennan contributed one of her paintings.

Shortly after its release, the Waits family welcomed their third child, a son named Sullivan. Waits had finally achieved financial security and the ability to pick and choose his projects when and where he liked. For now, the rock world would see less of him until April 1999 when his next original studio CD, *Mule Variations*, was released in the United States; but in the meantime, Waits's collaboration with Wilson continued with two more productions, *Alice* (1992) (an adaptation of Lewis Carroll's *Alice's Adventures in Wonderland*) and *Woyzeck* (2000).

Waits on Burroughs—Burroughs on Waits:
Excerpted from "Tom Waits, All-Purpose Troubadour," *New York Times*
November 14, 1993
Robert Palmer

Mr. Burroughs still sounds enthusiastic about the collaboration.

"When Tom was here in Lawrence," he said recently by telephone, "and we were sketching out the basic structure of *The Black Rider*, he had some very good ideas. I had the idea of comparing the magic bullet in the original German story to heroin. Once you use one, you'll use another. Tom said, 'Yeah, and the first one's always free,' and of course that went right in."

Mr. Burroughs, Mr. Waits said, "was always the scary old man to me, and he was scary when I met him. But he let everyone be a part of his whole creative process." In Hamburg, Mr. Waits and Mr. Burroughs worked separately, at night, bringing their results to Mr. Wilson's rehearsals the next morning. "Because of the way we worked," Mr. Waits said, "the recordings naturally tended to be kind of crude, like work tapes, and I didn't realize at the time that a lot of these recordings would eventually be released. Which was great for me. I've always struggled with that; as soon as I think we're doing something for real, it just freezes me up. My favorite recordings tend to be those kind of uninhibited moments in music that had no idea that they were music."

Waits on the waterphone:
Excerpted from "The Music of Chance," Spin
June 1994
Mark Richard

The waterphone is from Waits's collection of exotic instruments. It looks like two pizza pans welded face together with a length of rope-wrapped muffler pipe fitted to the center. Varying lengths of steel rods are staggered around the edges. When water is poured down the muffler pipe into the pizza pans you rap the rods with a mullet or draw a bow across them to achieve deep-sea, science-fiction-movie sounds.

"Play it," says Waits. "There are no experts or beginners." He says you pick up the instrument and you are in the same place as everyone else. "I love the places in music where you don't bring your ego to the process. You just shake hands with your instrument. Sometimes music will like you better if you are more innocent, it will want to stay around longer. I'm disorganized and I lose some lyrics, and I think, 'Well, maybe I was supposed to lose the lyrics so I have to write another.' That's why I love to bring in new instruments I found somewhere, I love ghosts in the machine. You lose things. 'What happened to that trumpet? I thought we had that trumpet! Do we have to do it again? We can't, he's gone. The trumpet player is in Vienna. We can't reach him. I guess there's no trumpet on this thing, then. Maybe it's better without the trumpet. It is! I never really liked the trumpet. I'm actually glad we didn't find the trumpet player because then we would have felt obligated to put the trumpet in there. Now I can tell the trumpet player I didn't take the trumpet out, don't get your feelings hurt, we just lost it.'"

Waits on "Singapore," astronaut razors, Reed Ghazala, and Sammy Davis Jr.
Excerpted from Morning Becomes Eclectic, KCRW
March 31, 1998
Chris Douridas

["Singapore" is] an adventure song. [. . .] In the studio the drum sound that we used was a two-by-four attacking somebody's chest of drawers and the whole song played and all the backbeats were played with a two-by-four hitting the chest of drawers repeatedly and on the last bar of the song the whole piece of furniture had collapsed and there was nothing left of it and the song was over but it was just a . . . that's what I think of when I hear the song. I see the pile of wood and it excites me. Michael Blair was the percussionist. It wasn't a very expensive chest of drawers. It was just one that we'd found out on the sidewalk. [. . .]

Did you realize that when astronauts first shaved in space their weightlessness, their whiskers, they floated up into the ceiling? They'd shave and the air would be filled with their whiskers and they had to come up with a special kind of a razor. It's a vacuum razor. It just sucks. The razor sucks all the whiskers right off your face while you shave. They're not available in stores but they should be. I would buy one. [. . .]

I want to do a whole record of [Kathleen's] dreams. She has amazing dreams and it's just remarkable and I think they should all be turned into songs. [. . .]

There's a very interesting guy who lives in Ohio, his name is Reed Ghazala and he made something called the photon clarinet that is a box with a light-sensitive patch on the top and the tone responds to the intensity of light so if you aim a flashlight at it it goes crazy and it sounds like you just threw a lobster on a campfire and then if you bring the lights down it goes kinda *hoooooowaaaahhh* down in here. He takes apart toys and puts them back together and they're never the same. There's a lot more conventional guys up there that do, like, stuff from a hardware store, you know. It changes the way you see a hardware store when you start hearing these instruments. You go into a hardware store and you start thinking, God, I wonder what that bucket sounds like over there. [. . .]

Maybe I'll just do medleys, a little piece of everything. I had a dream the other night that Sammy Davis Jr. embraced me in a bathroom. It was one of those big bathrooms like at the movie theaters, you know? This big regal-looking bathroom and I was just leaving and Sammy Davis was there and he looked wonderful. He had a little tweed suit on and his hair was great and he gave me one of those big hugs, you know? Apropos of nothing, Chris.

MULE VARIATIONS (1999)

Fans of Tom Waits had gone without a full-length LP since 1992. During that time, Waits continued his work in film and theater, as well as stockpiling a new cache of original songs composed with his wife.

Bone Machine had established a precedent for him, perhaps bringing him a higher profile under the public glare when he was awarded a Grammy. Waits chose instead to go underground and stay there until he felt he had a piece of work worthy enough to reintroduce himself to the world.

Mule Variations was the title of his newest offering, and it was the first to be released under Epitaph's new sister label Anti-. It became both a critical and fan favorite as well as garnering him another Grammy—for Best Contemporary Folk Album (as well as a nomination for Best Male Rock Performance for the track "Hold On").

Waits chose to support the album with a full-blown tour stateside as well as in Europe during the fall of 1999. He hadn't toured on this scale since 1987, and he was received with mass adulation and sold-out shows.

Waits also appeared on VH-1's *Storytellers*, bringing to the television audience a taste of his traditional stories and jokes—and an impassioned performance.

"Hobo Sapiens"
Telegraph Magazine
April 10, 1999
Mick Brown

Tom Waits first made his name by singing songs about that area of town marked out by the pawnbroker, the tattoo parlor, and the Greyhound bus station. These were wonderful stories—funny, sad, and wise—in which hookers were saints and skid-row bums were lovingly depicted as "little boys," and which led Francis Ford Coppola to describe him as "the prince of melancholy."

Waits, who has just made his first album in six years, describes his songs as "little movies for the ears," and there is one song in particular on the new album which is more explicitly cinematic than most. "What's He Building?" is a mystery story of the suburbs. Against a background of scratchy, *Twilight Zone* sound effects, Waits assumes the role of a nosy neighbor, narrating a dossier of the strange goings-on next door:

"He has subscriptions to all those magazines. He never waves when he goes by. He's hiding something from the rest of us. He has no dog and he has no friends and his lawn is dying, and what about all those packages he sends? Now what's that sound from under the door? He's pounding nails into a hardwood floor, and I swear to god I heard someone moan low and I keep seeing the blue light of a TV show. What's he building in there?"

Superficially a parable of suburban manners, it can also be read as a satire on the media's invasion of privacy. "It's about thinking we have a right to know," growls Waits. "Y'know, he drives a blue Mazda and doesn't get home until three in the morning. He was karate-chopping his own shrubbery last night— in his underwear. So we put all those things together and we make up a story about someone that bears no resemblance to the truth, and then we make it a serial. And that's what happens with the media. We love looking at each other through keyholes. They ought to make keyhole glasses, they'd sell a million of 'em, because that's how we prefer looking at each other, down on our knees in front of a keyhole."

What's he building in there? It's a question that could reasonably be asked of Tom Waits himself.

Ever since he started making records in the seventies, Waits has been pounding the hardwood floor and karate-chopping the shrubbery to produce the most singular and unusual body of work to be found anywhere in popular music. Is he a musician? A poet? A storyteller? An actor playing a part, or a part playing the actor? Time has suggested that Waits is all of these things and more. Over the past twenty-five years, he has recorded fifteen albums; he has written operettas and film music; and as a screen actor he has worked with directors as various as Coppola, Jim Jarmusch, and Robert Altman.

What has made his work all the more compelling is the character of Waits himself. With his boho threads and graveyard pallor, he arrived on the music scene looking, and behaving, like a man who had stepped out of a story by Charles Bukowski—an inebriated barfly, down in the gutter but looking up at the stars, with a hatful of sad stories about life's losers and a withering put-down for anyone who tried to get behind the veneer.

Waits has always been a man who would rather tell an entertaining lie than a prosaic truth, who greets any direct question, particularly one pertaining to his personal life, with all the enthusiasm of a dying man who spies an undertaker brandishing a tape measure at the foot of his bed.

I remember meeting Waits in 1976, on his first visit to Britain, and making the mistake of asking him for his definition of fun. He examined the word as if he'd scraped it off the bottom of his shoe.

"I don't have fun. Actually, I had fun once, in 1962. I drank a whole bottle of Robitussin cough medicine and went in the back of a 1961 powder-blue Lincoln Continental to a James Brown concert with some Mexican friends of mine. I haven't had fun since. It's just not a word I like. It's like Volkswagens or bell-bottoms, or patchouli oil or bean sprouts. It rubs me up the wrong way. I might go out and have an educational and entertaining evening, but I don't have fun."

That interview, inevitably, took place in a pub. Waits was wearing a thrift-shop suit, blackened with neglect, and apparently hadn't caught sight of a razor in days. It was lunchtime, but he already seemed somewhat the worse for wear. He had come to London to perform at Ronnie Scott's club. For three nights he sat at the piano, peering out at the empty seats through a haze of smoke from the cigarette cemented to his bottom lip, performing his songs of wry and melancholic beauty. On the fourth night they threw him out. "I think it was my clothes," Waits says now. "Every time I tried to go into a restaurant, people would chase me out. I couldn't even get a sandwich."

Such is the mythology surrounding Waits that there is an Internet site—The Tom Waits Memorial Tour of Joints—dedicated to chronicling the various bars and restaurants across America where Waits either has or "would" spend his time. These are places whose very names suggest low life and tall stories: the Hi-Boy in Washington, DC; Rose's Night Life, "just north of the South Platte River" in Denver, Colorado; and the Uranium Café in Grants, New Mexico.

The China Lights in Santa Rosa, Northern California, can now be officially added to the list: a quiet, neighborly, and agreeably cheap Chinese diner beside the railway tracks.

Tom Waits has only ever given interviews looking down the barrel of a gun, and in recent years he has avoided the media altogether. It is only the release of his new album, *Mule Variations*, that has persuaded him to drive the twenty or so miles from his home in the heart of the wine-growing district—where he lives with his wife, Kathleen, and their three children—to take up temporary residency in a booth at the back of the restaurant, behind a plate of steaming chow mein and a bottomless pot of Chinese tea.

His beaten-up pickup truck is parked outside, laden down with bags of water softener for his swimming pool. This is more incongruous than it sounds: Waits is a man whose milieu has always seemed strictly nocturnal; he is not the kind of person, you would think, who would even recognize a swimming pool, let alone maintain one.

He is wearing heavy-duty jeans and a denim jacket, motorcycle boots and a trilby hat. His face is weather-beaten and lined: the crinkled eyes and the merest suggestion of a goatee shadowing his bottom lip lend him a curiously Oriental aspect. There was a period in his life when Waits's voice was most usually described as having been marinated in nicotine and cheap booze. He gave up smoking years ago and nowadays drinks only in moderation, but there is still something alarmingly tubercular in his rough, grumbling growl.

"I'll tell you some things I've been thinking about lately." He puts down his cup of tea, reaches into his bag, and pulls out a notebook, which he scrutinizes in a parody of academic seriousness. "Did you know that cockroaches can live for several weeks with their heads cut off?"

The delivery is perfectly deadpan. "Here's something else: People that observe ants closely say that they actually stretch when they wake up in the morning, and they yawn. Now a scorpion . . ."

A scorpion?

"If you put a minute amount of liquor on a scorpion, it will go mad and sting itself until it's dead. These are things I find interesting, to keep myself from going crazy. I have a radio show called *Strange and Unusual Facts*, and these are some of the things we talk about every week. We broadcast from a little town called Miner's Prayer, Nevada. It's a small station, a very limited range, but a lot of people listen in. They've moved there because of the show—that's what we've found."

Does Tom Waits really host a radio show in the Nevada desert? You might as well ask whether he was really born "in the backseat of a yellow cab in the Murphy Hospital parking lot at a very young age"—the answer he would traditionally give to inquiries about his birthplace. The reference books say that he was born in 1949, in Pomona, California. His parents were schoolteachers who divorced when Waits was young. By the age of fourteen he was working as a short-order cook in a pizza parlor, Napoleone's, in a small Californian town called National City—"a stone's throw away," he recalls, "from Iwo Jima Eddie's tattoo parlor and across the street from Club 29, Sorenson's Triumph motorcycle shop, and Phil's Porno."

"I thought I was gonna be a cook," he says. "That's about as far as I could see. But what also happened was that I was mystified by the jukebox, and the physics of how you get into the wire and come out of the jukebox. That's where that came from. I'd listen to Ray Charles singing 'Crying Time' and 'I Can't Stop Loving You,' and I'd think, goddamn, that's something."

After dropping out of high school, Waits worked in a variety of jobs—"a jack-off of all trades"—eventually finding work as a nightclub doorman, while living out of the back of his car. It was here that he started writing down conversations overheard at the bar, "and realizing they had music in them."

By then, he had developed a romantic fascination with the boho mythology enshrined in the work of such writers as Bukowski, the poet Delmore Schwartz, who died in a run-down hotel for transients in 1966, and, above all, Jack Kerouac. Waits discovered *On the Road* when he was eighteen years of age. "It spoke to me," he says simply. "I couldn't believe that somebody'd be making words that felt like music, that didn't have any music in it, but had music all over it.

"I was the bouncer in this nightclub—place must have been really hurting if they had me as their bouncer; everybody got in—and I'd bring my books and my coffee and my cigarettes and put my feet up, and I'd read my Kerouac, and watch the cars go by, and I just felt like I was on fire and I had a reason to live. Because he put some meaning on the most ordinary things. Sitting there, my own ordinary life was just lifted out of that and I was all dusted with something sparkling."

References to Kerouac have sounded intermittently in his work ever since: he once recorded a song, "Jack & Neal," celebrating the friendship of Kerouac and Neal Cassady, and he has recently recorded a song called "On the Road" for a tribute album, which incorporates snatches of the writer scat-singing at a party. But what he shared most with Kerouac was a sympathy for the outsider. Like Kerouac's books, Waits's songs turned loneliness into an adventure, being deadbeat into a state of grace.

Waits began his recording career in the early seventies, after being discovered singing at the Troubadour club in Los Angeles by a man named Herb Cohen, who

managed Frank Zappa and Captain Beefheart. (Waits would later recall that he
had met Cohen outside the club: "He was exposing himself. Actually, it was so
cold that he was just describing himself.")

His first albums were peopled with America's flotsam and jetsam: barflies
and losers, the stripper who makes you "harder than Chinese algebra," the small-
town studs who boast of getting "more ass than a toilet seat," low-rent hoodlums
and sad-eyed peroxide waitresses promising love over easy ("They all cooked
dinner on my stove").

These were songs that had a way of sidling up on you like a stranger in a
bar with a story to tell ("The dreams aren't broken down here," Waits croaked,
"they're just walking with a limp"), romantic celebrations of the bare and enduring fact of existence under even the most straitened of circumstances. The characters in his songs may have lost their shirts and their temper, but never their
human dignity.

Working on the principle that to write about something you must live it, Waits
cultivated the habits as well as the appearance of a skid-row derelict. He dressed
cheaply and made a point when on the road of staying only in the most insalu-
brious places. His "home" was a room in the notorious Tropicana Motel in West
Hollywood—better known as the place where the soul singer Sam Cooke was
shot dead. There was a piano where the refrigerator should have been, and the
gas stove was "just a big cigarette lighter."

For a long time, Waits admits, he was in danger of being overtaken by the
low life he wrote about. He drank too much. He made bad friends. "I wanted to
experience what it was like to be on the road the way I imagined it would be for
all the old-timers that I loved, so I would stay in these down joints because I was
absorbing all the atmosphere in those places; the ghosts in the room.

"You want to be where the stories grow, and you think if you live in those
places they'll come up through the sidewalks and out of the cracks in the wall—
and they do. But you have to be very clear about who you are and who it is you're
projecting, and there was a time when I was very unclear about who I was. I
became a caricature of myself."

Whatever the moment of truth, how far he fell and how he stopped falling,
Waits is reluctant to say. Interviews "aren't supposed to be depositions," he says,
"and they're not therapy. I'm not entirely sure how I want to characterize what I
feel about all that, because I'm still trying to figure it out.

"But I do know you have to protect yourself. Y'see, most of us expect artists to do irresponsible things, to be out of control. Somehow we believe that if you're way down there, you're going to bring something back up for us, and we won't have to make the trip. Go to hell with gasoline drawers on and bring me back some chicken chow mein while you're at it. This is part of the tradition of artists; the problem with that is that you have people who will write you a ticket to go to hell; they support your bad habits. So you got to be careful."

He pauses, reflecting on this. "The fact is that everybody who starts doing this to a certain extent develops some kind of a persona or image in order to survive. Otherwise it's very dangerous to go out there. It's much safer to approach this with some kind of persona, because if it's not a ventriloquist act, if it's just you, then it's really scary.

"The whole thing's an act. Nobody would really show you who they are— nobody would ever dare to do that, and if they do, they change their mind after a while because it gets to a point where you don't know what's true anymore. The dice is throwing the man, instead of the man throwing the dice."

It was the film director Francis Ford Coppola who was to prove the catalyst in Waits's life when, in 1979, he asked Waits to write a suite of songs as the soundtrack for his Las Vegas romance *One from the Heart*. Waits spent twelve months on the project, turning up each day at his office at Coppola's Zoetrope Studios. He fell in love with, and married, Kathleen Brennan, a script editor on the film. And the commission led to Coppola's casting Waits in his first film role, in *Rumble Fish*. Since then he has appeared in two more Coppola films and had starring roles in Jim Jarmusch's *Down by Law* and Robert Altman's *Short Cuts*. He has recently completed a new film called *Mystery Men*, with Geoffrey Rush and Eddie Izzard. "It's about low-rent superheroes; the guys who never get to save the day or win the girl or any of that," says Waits, who plays a weapons designer.

He once described the transition from music to acting as "like going from bootlegging to watch repair." "I usually play small parts," he says, "which is just as well. But a small part in a film is rather wasteful. You go and you sit and you sit. . . . The acting is free. You charge them for the waiting. That's the way I see it. I like acting, but it's not something I consider myself an expert at. When I'm recording music I can be uninhibited and I can sing a song seven different ways. There are actors that can do that with a director: the first take is like some kind of rant; the next take is a prayer; the next take is like some old black man. They can go through all these different moves. I'm not able to do that as an actor."

This is true. Whether cast as a small-time hood in *Rumble Fish* or a truculent limo driver in *Short Cuts*, Waits's characters always seem to be less roles that he is playing than different ways of playing himself.

"You could say the same thing of Gary Cooper and Cary Grant," says Robert Altman. "Tom is unique—completely his own person. He's bent, but in the right way. It's a good bend."

Altman describes himself as Waits's greatest fan: "I just love whatever he does. If I feel the need to cry, which I find it hard to do nowadays, I only have to put on one of his albums." And the feeling is mutual. Waits describes Altman as "a good sheriff in a bad town."

"Well, that's because Tom spends all his life in bad towns," Altman jokes.

Waits is the first to admit that his work has never conformed to the "cover-the-earth" theory of merchandising, "like shoes, hair tonic, or sunglasses." For years, his records were a well-kept secret. It was only with the release of *Swordfishtrombones* in 1983 that he began to attract a wider audience. By then Waits had all but abandoned the fake cocktail-jazz aesthetic of his early work. He incorporated wheezing accordions and pipe organs, vocals sung through a police bullhorn, percussion that sounded like something that had come up from the swamp, rattling its bones and chains—a process he once described as "taking things that don't necessarily belong together and forcing them to get stuck in the same elevator."

It's likely that he has made more money from other people's recordings of his songs—notably the Eagles' "Ol' 55," Rod Stewart's versions of "Downtown Train" and "Tom Traubert's Blues," and Bruce Springsteen's "Jersey Girl"—than he has made from all of his own albums put together. (Frank Sinatra's greatest mistake toward the end of his career was to ignore the advice of a producer who suggested he should record a collection of Waits's ballads.)

Probably the largest paycheck of his career came from a recent lawsuit against an American crisp company, Frito-Lay, which used a Waits "sound-alike" in an advertisement without his permission. Waits sued, winning more than $3 million in damages. "I think your music is a gift, and I don't do commercials," he says. "There are people that do that, but I'm not one of them and I don't want people to think I am one of them, hawking cigarettes or potato chips."

He has always been a man who works at his own pace, pursuing the projects he wants to pursue, making records when he, not the record company, wants. The pace has sometimes been frantic. In the ten years between 1983 and 1993 he made seven albums, produced three stage plays (*Franks Wild Years, Alice,* and *The Black Rider*—the last two with the avant-garde playwright and director Robert Wilson), acted in a handful of films and contributed music to several more. But *Mule Variations* follows a six-year period in which Waits has been all but silent.

"I just thought I'd let things stack up for a little while. Do other things," he says, dismissing the subject with a shrug of his shoulders. He moved to Northern California from Los Angeles and concentrated on bringing up his family. "You take a break and you get a new perspective, that's all. But I was tired of the old songs and needed some new ones. It's not like I couldn't record anytime I wanted to. It's not like moving from Chicago to Marrakesh and not having the money to get home.

"I've got a tape recorder that I carry 'round in my pocket; I record in the car, play it back. You bang out a rhythm on a chest of drawers with your fist in a motel room, record that. So in a sense I'm always recording things. It's like people that draw. Sometimes when I'm trying to get the kids to be quiet so I can think, I say, What do you like? When you're going to draw, do you like to start out with a piece of paper that's already scribbled on and find a little place down at the bottom to do your drawing? Or do you like to get a nice clean, white sheet of paper? Which do you prefer? 'Oh, I want a clean, white sheet of paper.' OK, well right now I can't hear; I'm trying to make up some songs. I need to have the auditory equivalent of a clean, white sheet of paper." He shrugs. "But they just carry on, throw things at me . . .

"They call me the preacher at home. Uh-oh, here he comes . . . the preacher. I yell and holler a lot. I rant."

A disciplinarian, then?

Waits arches an eyebrow. "Actually, I was raised a Methodist."

Mule Variations sounds like a reconciliation of all the various musical styles that Waits has explored over the years, as if the songs have been hammered together from the skin and bones of American myth: scratchy Delta blues, sixties R & B, vaudeville rants, and Salvation Army band hymns.

The cast of urban picaroons who peopled Waits's early songs has largely vanished over the years (he has long been, in his own phrase, "hanging off a different lamppost"). *Mule Variations* is an American gothic exploration of rural primitives, freak-show exhibits and back-porch romantics, leavened with a handful of heartbreaking love songs that leave you feeling, as Waits puts it, "like one eye is laughing and the other eye is tearing up."

He pauses, fork poised over his Chinese meal. "Do you know how many teardrops it takes to fill up a teaspoon? A hundred and twenty, actually. I tested it. I was very sad and I thought, I'm going to make some use of it, so I held a spoon at my cheek and I cried. This is my science project for the year."

Songwriting, says Waits, is like "bird-watching," or "looking for insects. If you don't know what you're doing, you'll spend all day and find nothing. Same thing with songs. You've got to sneak up on them."

And there's a particular recipe for making an album. "You write two songs, you put 'em in a room and they have kids. Songs travel along the same line that jokes and stories do. They get written down, forgotten, and resurrected. You tear the wings off them for a while and they grow new ones. Songs are kind of like your memory of something, your homeland, or what you had for dinner last night; something for your kids. We all do it naturally, and kids do it better than any of us. So in a sense, it's kind of like children's work."

Since his marriage, he has cowritten most of his songs with his wife, a process of collaboration which he likens, with characteristic quirkiness, to "two people making dinner or carrying a piano or painting a fence. You work out your rhythm." Kathleen, he says, "doesn't like the limelight," but she has been an "incandescent presence" in his life since the day they met. One of his most poignant songs, "Johnsburg, Illinois," is a tribute to her:

"She's my only true love, she's all I think of, look here in my wallet, that's her. She grew up on a farm there, there's a place on my arm, where I've written her name next to mine. You see I just can't live without her, and I'm her only boy and she grew up outside McHenry in Johnsburg, Illinois."

Nobody writes love songs like Tom Waits, but he is uneasy talking about such things. He shifts in his seat, rubs his chin, and says that his life is private and he likes to keep it that way. Waits doesn't want anyone looking at him through keyhole glasses.

He's tapping his fingers on the table. He's draining the last of his Chinese tea. He's turning the pages of his little notebook. "Did you know," he asks, "that there's a town in Chile called Calama where it has never rained. Never." He pauses. "They don't talk about a little rain. They don't talk about we'd like to have some more rain, or we're hoping for a little more rain. They've just given up the whole topic."

He turns the pages.

"Here's another one. In Viking times, it was humans who were sacrificed on the prow of a ship, and of course from there it went to a bottle of wine. But the first time it was human beings. They'd volunteer. It was a short line—that real short line off to the right, just on the other side of the wharf, just two or three people. Depressed people."

He scrutinizes me suspiciously. "You realize that all of this is on tonight's show. I'm trusting you're going to keep this between the two of us. And this is the lead story: Thomas Edison was deaf from the age of twelve."

There is no radio show, of course. But Tom Waits has always been a terrific act.

"Tom Waits for No Man"
Time Out New York
April 22–29, 1999
Brett Martin

Tom Waits may want to rethink the prank-call thing. Just before he's scheduled to call from his home in Northern California, the phone rings. Someone says, "Wrong number" and hangs up. A few minutes later, another ring: "This the Department of Motor Vehicles?" the person asks and then laughs. "This is Tom, I'm just playing with you." I don't have the heart to tell him that with a voice as distinctive as his, he's not fooling anybody.

In fact, "the voice" is the first thing most people mention when the eccentric entertainer's name is brought up. But the amazing thing about Waits has always been his many *different* voices. His albums are like theater pieces, with Waits taking on a whole range of characters from the seamier side of life. Taken together, they go a long way toward fulfilling what appears to be his ultimate goal: cataloging the American subconscious.

The effort continues with *Mule Variations*, the musician's seventeenth album and his first in six years. There's a good chance that Waits will embark on his first live tour since 1987. Maybe. It's not easy to get straight answers from Waits. "I don't like direct questions," he says, "so if you hit me with one, chances are you will get a very indirect answer." When faced with queries he doesn't like—ones that belabor a point, for instance—he tends to respond with factoids read from a nearby newspaper. It's a strategy as distinctively Waitsian as that rumbling voice.

Brett Martin: Where did the title *Mule Variations* come from?

Tom Waits: Well, people don't write a lot about mules anymore. Ever since Robert Johnson wrote about an automobile, it's kind of been rock's most popular vehicle.

BM: Do you use a title as a guide when you're writing songs for an album?

TW: Halfway through a record you start riffing on something, and titles emerge out of the work somehow. Some of the songs had what we started calling a rural quality. They're kind of sur-rural—a combination of surreal and rural. They sound like old songs. And I sound like an old guy.

BM: So would you call it a throwback record?

TW: Gee, I don't know. I hope people don't throw it back.

BM: I mean, a lot of the songs seem to look back at earlier parts of your career.

TW: Most writers end up trying to say the same things different ways. Sometimes you spin out to places you rarely visit, but for the most part, songwriters come back to a certain familiar turf. Mine is a small little place, I guess.

BM: Some would say that place is an America of another time. Is it harder to find the kinds of voices and stories you use?

TW: I don't think so. This stuff is all over the place. If by evening tomorrow you wanted to be by a campfire by a railroad track, you could do so. You'd be under a bridge somewhere, cooking beans in a can, with your boots sitting on the cold ground, watching a train go by. Everything is available if you're inquisitive enough.

BM: Do you still go out looking, or does that stuff reside in you at this point?

TW: That's a big question. I might have to refer to my manual for the answer to that [*rustles paper*]. Oh yeah, right here: some Chinese typewriters have 5,700 characters. The keyboard is almost three feet wide on some models.

BM: Is that what you mean by an indirect answer?

TW: Yeah.

BM: Fair enough. You use some pretty strange instrumentation here. Where do you find a good *chumbus* and *dousengoni* player nowadays?

TW: Oh, that would be Smokey Hormel. He said he was coming up to play on the record and that he was going to bring a station wagon, and I said, "Well, throw some stuff in the back—stuff I've never seen or heard before." [Those are] West African guitars.

BM: What about an Optigan?

TW: That's a mid-'60s keyboard that used floppy disks with optical filaments. It's like everything else in popular music: it finally washes up in the Salvation Army twenty years later, and someone picks it up, brings it home, and makes a hit record out of it. Bury me, then dig me up—that's like the code of popular music.

BM: Your wife, Kathleen Brennan, was heavily involved in *Mule Variations*.

TW: She's the sun, the seed, the soil, the leaf, the root, and the rain of our work together. I think this record has a certain balance and light that she put there.

BM: Some of the songs are among the sweetest and most optimistic-sounding you've done.

TW: Those are songs that, if I were left to my own devices, I probably would have junked for the sake of something rougher. I'm usually wrong about those things. She's the brains behind Pa—[we've] been working together since *Swordfishtrombones*.

BM: Well, that record was a pretty revolutionary stylistic break for you. What happened?

TW: I hatched . . . I hatched out of the egg I was living in. I had nailed one foot to the floor and kept going in circles, making the same record. Kathleen was the first person who convinced me that you can take James White and the Blacks, and Elmer Bernstein and Lead Belly—folks that could never be on the bill together—and that they could be on the bill together in *you*. You take your dad's army uniform and your mom's Easter hat and your brother's motorcycle and your sister's purse and stitch them all together and try to make something meaningful out of it.

BM: It's like you found a new language to tell the same stories.

TW: Yeah. I don't know. . . . Do you realize that the right lung takes in more air than the left lung?

BM: Right. Why did you stop touring?

TW: There are all these variables on the road. If you're [at home] with your instruments and a tape machine, you can fashion things how you want them. On the road, you're dealing with all kinds of wind and weather. You know, viscosity and thermal breakdown.

BM: Your lyrics always use the best place names—like Hushpuckena or Murfreesboro. Do you just sit around and study atlases all day?

TW: My theory is that songs have to be anatomically correct. They need to have weather in them and the name of a town and usually something to eat—in case you get hungry.

BM: Did you know there was a Danish Tom Waits Society? You're apparently very big in Denmark.

TW: Well, that's OK. In fact, I've had a Danish society here for years. I have my coffee and my Danish every morning.

BM: What's a question you never get asked but wish you would?

TW: How about the oldest rocks in the world?

BM: What are the oldest rocks in the world?

TW: The so-called St. Peter and St. Paul stones in the Atlantic Ocean. They're four billion years old. Can you just throw that in? I like to see these things in print.

"Wily Tom Waits's Barnyard Breakthrough"
Now
April 22–28, 1999
Tim Perlich

An ornery coot at the best of times, Tom Waits takes a special delight in confounding interviewers with outlandish allegorical fabrications peppered with seemingly unrelated factoids concerning tropical fish, insect behavior, and the number of teardrops it takes to fill a teaspoon.

From Waits's perspective, there's no reason to settle for the boring old truth when a preposterous tale, convincingly told, packs a far more potent entertainment wallop. And if you can see through the layer of bullshit, there's often a kernel of truth in each apocryphal invention.

A possible reason behind his baffling decision to release his fabulous new *Mule Variations* album on the corporate-punk outpost Epitaph, for example, might be found in a story Waits used to tell about growing up in Whittier, California.

He would supposedly go out into the desert with his buddies, where they'd bury themselves neck-deep in the sand and wait for the vultures to circle. When the buzzards moved in for an eyeball peck, they'd jump up, grab them by the necks and swing them around overhead.

In similar fashion, Waits maintained radio silence over the last few years, waiting patiently for record-company reps to swoop in. When Epitaph got close enough, he seized the opportunity by the neck.

"Oh, yeah, yeah," chokes Waits over the phone from what he claims is "Miner's Prayer, Nevada, just across the bridge from Rio de Janeiro," yet it's likely much closer to his Petaluma County homestead in Northern California. "I've passed that game on to my kids now, and we play it together around the holidays.

"On Christmas Eve, instead of having a tree and doing the stuff everybody else does, we bury ourselves in sand and wring the necks of vultures. It's become a family tradition.

"And, oh, those kids of mine—they're all bigger than me now. They're taller than me, smarter than me, too. They're pushing me around, talking back and telling me what to do. They know a lot of the groups on Epitaph, like Rancid, mmm . . . Pennywise. I think it's a good place for me. I don't know why, it just feels right.

"A lot of artists think, 'Gee, they signed that new group Mean Old Man Next Door, who have that great *Tijuana Moon* record out now. If they understand them, maybe they'll like my music, too.' I guess that works for some people, but for me, the folks at Epitaph just seemed like good people. They put together this whole big proposal, so we're giving it a shot with *Mule Variations*."

However anomalous the *Mule Variations* album may be in the Epitaph catalog, it's nevertheless a stunning work, on which Waits neatly sums up his career to date.

He's taken what he's learned from clanking on rusty gas tanks with busted crankshafts and tempered it with some of that barfly romance from his lounge-crooner past, to come up with a bluesy bounce that recalls the rollicksome side of his *Heartattack and Vine* phase.

More than any of Waits's Island-era studio experiments, *Mule Variations* has the kick of a plugged-in working combo.

"Music, by nature, is a collaborative endeavor—it's social. My wife [Kathleen Brennan] and I wrote the songs together, arranged them, and produced them in the studio with great musicians like Charlie Musselwhite, Marc Ribot, John Hammond, Larry Taylor, Greg Cohen, Andrew Borger, Smokey Hormel, the guys from Primus, and Christopher Marvin—Lee Marvin's real son—plays drums on 'Cold

Water.'" The involvement of Beck's blues-schooled guitar/Dobro hombre Smokey Hormel makes perfect sense, particularly on the gritty "Get Behind the Mule," but Waits's connection with Les Claypool's merry band of spaz-rock pranksters, Primus, isn't quite as transparent.

Evidently, before Claypool participated in the *Bone Machine* sessions and Waits provided the voice of Tommy the Cat for Primus' *Sailing the Seas of Cheese*, Waits had a chance encounter with the members of Primus on a fishing trip.

"I was over at Bodega Bay," recalls Waits, "and I wasn't catching a thing. I flagged these guys down and asked them if they'd sell me one of their fish to put on my line and have my picture taken with it so I wouldn't feel humiliated when I got home. It turned out to be the guys from Primus, and they said 'Cool' and sold me a big barracuda.

"They live nearby, and since they're all part of the volunteer fire department, I see 'em now and then at pancake breakfasts or the Gun & Doll show they have at the community center.

"Those Primus guys are very active in community events. When it's flood season, they're always out there sandbagging, and they bring their instruments with them. As for myself, well, I do what I can for the community but I'd rather just write a check."

Apart from fishing at Bodega Bay and attending pancake breakfasts, Waits seems reluctant to discuss how he occupies his time when not recording at his converted-chicken-ranch home studio. The uncredited rooster solo that appears on the track "Chocolate Jesus" indicates that raising chickens might be involved.

"I've been breaking in other people's shoes," he insists with all the seriousness he can muster. "People send me their new shoes, boots, or whatever and I walk around in 'em for three or four weeks—it's a holistic thing. Then I send them back their shoes for $29.95 a pair.

"Right now we've got a holiday special of $24.95, which is a pretty good deal because that includes a beautiful leatherette carrying case . . . personalized.

"My father-in-law has been trying to get me involved in this other business. He's got these little lozenges that come in different flavors and they have a cross on one side and a Bible passage on the other. He calls them 'testamints.' The idea is that if you can't make the church service, you meditate on the testamint passage, then pop it in your mouth. We took the idea one step further with 'Chocolate Jesus.'"

As Beefheart-wacky as "Chocolate Jesus" gets, it doesn't diminish the album's surprisingly strong spiritual component, which shows up in the deep soul ballad "House Where Nobody Lives," just as it does in the moving hymn that closes the album, "Come On Up to the House."

From the hysterically hunching roast-pork recipe "Filipino Box Spring Hog" to the unabashedly sentimental "Picture in a Frame," *Mule Variations* might appear to be a haphazard jumble of conflicting notions, but everything eventually falls into place. It's almost like Waits was working to some grand design.

"I usually try to put some weather on there, some names of places and people, and maybe a recipe or two, so my record becomes like a survival kit that people can take on camping trips.

"This is the kind of record you want to turn up full blast, put on those leotards, hip boots, and your bathing cap and do the frog right there in the middle of the driveway. I'd like to see more of that going on."

"Interview with Tom Waits"
NY Rock
May 1999
Gabriella

A lot of artists try to be eccentric, but for Tom Waits, it comes naturally. He's an expert of sorts on the most peculiar of subjects, like the daily lives of ants. As a musician, he's in a league of his own. His masterful, yet disturbingly odd, improvisations result in songs of sheer melancholic beauty—delivered by one of the raspiest voices in the business.

As an actor, his characters take on a life of their own. He's the notorious outlaw, the washed-up hobo with a rough charm. Who could imagine Jim Jarmusch's *Down by Law* or Robert Altman's *Short Cuts* without him?

Although in his early fifties, Waits manages to look like a hundred-year-old beagle. A legend in his own right, who shows us the crooked beauty of dissonance, Waits always comes across like the guy who's got the blues so bad, he's ready to sell his soul for another glass of whisky.

Gabriella: *Mule Variations* is an interesting title. I almost expected to hear a mule as a guest musician . . .

Tom Waits: My wife called me a mule. She once said, "I didn't marry a man; I married a mule!" I kept thinking about it. It was in the back of my head. I think it makes a good title for an album.

G: Sounds like you're pretty stubborn . . .

TW: Of course, I am. She didn't call me a mule for nothing. But I'm rather consequent in my stubbornness. I think they're pretty straight animals. They don't listen to anybody else.

G: Do you have a thing for animals? I heard that you confused one of my colleagues a few years ago when discussing insects with him . . .

TW: [*raspy laugh*] I like weird things, ludicrous things. I have a notebook full of eerie facts. Don't get me started on them. I could go on for ages and would confuse you—or probably even scare you.

G: Just one? And then I'll pester you about your work . . .

TW: OK, this will scare you. . . . If you decapitate a cockroach, a simple cockroach, it won't die. It's able to live for a couple of weeks without a head, but regular flies die after two weeks. Imagine that, just two weeks and they're dead. It doesn't even seem worth the effort it takes to kill them. Or there are four hundred million sperm in each ejaculation—and if you look around, take a look at some people, it's kinda hard to imagine that they beat four hundred million. . . . It makes one wonder . . .

G: Wow, where do you get your information from?

TW: I read papers. I read magazines, and if I find something that's worth collecting, I'll write it down in my little notebook. Just call it a hobby or a weird spleen.

G: You're signed with Epitaph now, the legendary punk label. How did that happen?

TW: I like them. I like them a lot, and I like their taste when it comes to music, barbecues, and cars.

G: Brett Gurewitz [owner] is famous for his passion for fast cars . . .

TW: He is, and he infected a lot of other people . . .

G: A lot of musicians claim that Epitaph is completely different from other labels . . .

TW: That's true. What I really like about it is that a lot of the people there are musicians. They're working for the label, but they're still playing gigs. It's not run like a business; it's more run like friends and partners who are working together. They're one of the few labels who give artists time to grow.

G: Between *Big Time* [1988] and *Bone Machine* [1992] were four years. Then you released *The Black Rider* [1993] one year later, but it was another six years until *Mule Variations* . . .

TW: Well, yes. I guess I took my time.

G: What was the reason behind writing new songs now?

TW: I think it's always the same reason. There's only one reason why you write new songs: you get sick of the old songs. It's not that I didn't do anything during the time when I wrote no songs. I was creative, but in another way. I had ideas for songs and collected the ideas.

G: Did you use all the ideas?

TW: No, of course not. Sometimes I didn't even use the songs I wrote. Sometimes we recorded as much as four or five different versions of one song before I decided that I wouldn't use it.

G: How do you view your old songs? Are they a part of you, or are you sick of them?

TW: It's different. Some songs became a part of me and some just don't fit any-more, like an old sweater or a pair of pants you've outgrown. You hardly ever know what's going to happen with a song and how you'll feel about it in ten years' time.

G: Are you going on tour?

TW: I think I will. I might go on tour, do a few shows, but I'm not really a fan of touring. It's just so inconvenient. You're far away from home. You're wasting a lot of time sitting around waiting. When I was young—oh well, younger—I toured a lot. I lived out of my suitcase, but now that I have a home, kids, a family, it's different. I guess I'm getting old.

G: You're always the strange character in a movie. Is that what suits you best?

TW: I think I get typecasted. A lot of actors are trying to avoid that. They're trying to avoid getting pinned down as always the villain, the cop, the pimp. . . . But I'm not a real actor. I don't care.

"The Man Who Howled Wolf"
Magnet
June/July 1999
Jonathan Valania

The Astro is a broken-down, drunk motel located about an hour north of San Francisco in Santa Rosa, near the arid, wine-growing region of the Sonoma Valley. It's Tom Waits country—he lives somewhere around here, although exactly where remains a closely guarded secret. *Magnet* booked a room at the Astro because the price is right, but upon closer inspection, it's the ideal setting to await an audience with the man who elevates the down-and-out in song. The bard of boardinghouse madrigals. The man who reads the lines in people's faces like a palmist, uttering the stories behind the wheelchair smiles and motel miles that map the crazy countenances of the characters that haunt his songs.

Our room, as Waits puts it in the song "Ninth and Hennepin," is "filled with bitters and blue ruin." It's a stomped-out cigarette butt of a place. The ventilator is broken, and it's clear the oxygen has left this room years ago. There's mold on the ceiling and a hint of urine in the air. A brick holds up the short leg of the bed, which is dotted with cigarette burns and mysterious stains. The faucet won't stop dripping, and there's a pubic hair clinging to the rim of the bathtub like a garnish. The swimming pool is filled with dirt and weeds. There is, however, free HBO. The only other guest amenity is the comfort of knowing that the woman who checks you in also minds the cash register at the liquor store around back. It's 10 A.M. and the residents are getting an early start, stocking up on their daily allotment of vodka, brandy, and cigarettes. A little girl stands out front mimicking the happy-hour wobble of a drunk ambling down the sunstroked street. "He bumped into a wall and now he's skipping," she says to nobody in particular. There are two kinds of guests at the Astro: those who are only staying for an hour and those who will never leave.

File our stay under "Accidental Tourism," a random touchstone to Waits's boozy, flophouse residency at the Tropicana Motel in the endless, doomed summer of Los Angeles in the 1970s. It was a simpler time then. A piano served as furniture, and down the hall lived Waits's partner in grime, Chuck E. Weiss, "the kind of guy that would sell you a rat's ass for a wedding ring," joked Waits to an interviewer at the time. Weiss brought around Rickie Lee Jones, with whom Waits shared a brief creative and romantic dalliance. It was at the Tropicana that Waits forged the image that would stick with him through the years: a rumpled, bourbon-fed balladeer, holding up a drunk piano, eyes-closed, eighty-proof chords dancing the tarantella with his bullfrog croak of a voice, pirouetting in the halo of smoke, and stubble ringing the low-slung, tweed dude cap.

Between regular tours opening for acts like Frank Zappa and the Rolling Stones, Waits would record the seven albums that would mark his early incarnation as a crushed romantic huffing the last remaining fumes of the Beat and jazz eras. On albums like *The Heart of Saturday Night*, *Small Change*, and *Nighthawks at the Diner*, Waits hung his weary, gonna-drink-the-lights-out persona on a dancing skeleton of upright bass and plaintive piano chords. It was a Tin Pan Alley full of hobos and drifters, dancing girls and desperate characters, barroom wit and gutter poetry. Waits was the guy playing piano in the corner of the coffee shop in Edward Hopper's painting *Nighthawks*. Unfortunately, it's the corner that you can't see.

Waits checked out of the Tropicana life years ago, though the image still clings to him like the stink of the cigarettes he doesn't smoke anymore or the scent of the bourbon he no longer drinks. In 1980, Waits married Kathleen Brennan (then a script reader for Francis Ford Coppola's Zoetrope Studios), whom he met while working on the score to Coppola's *One from the Heart*. Brennan, who doesn't care to be interviewed or photographed, has been his collaborator and muse—not to mention the mother of their three children—ever since. "She saved my life," Waits says. It was Brennan who helped steer his musical direction into the deep left field of what has become known as the Island Years. Albums like *Swordfish-trombones*, *Rain Dogs*, and *Franks Wild Years* play like a series of disembodied ham-radio broadcasts colored with otherworld instrumentation, clanking percussion, and surreal street reportage. With all the bare ruined choirs, Beefheartian sea shanties, and clubfoot klezmer orchestras wandering in and out, these records have that *Barton Fink* feeling in spades. The only element that remains from Waits's 1970s singer-songwriter days is his voice. A voice that sounds like he was born old, born smoking.

An outsider amid the facile pomp of 1980s pop, Waits stuck to the margins, striking up vital creative friendships with people like filmmaker Jim Jarmusch, downtown-NYC scenester John Lurie, and Marc Ribot, whose impressionistic guitar playing has been a fixture on Waits's recordings since *Rain Dogs*. In 1985, Waits acted alongside Lurie and Roberto Benigni in Jarmusch's excellent prison-break buddy saga *Down by Law*, effectively establishing an impressive acting career. "I wrote that movie with Tom and John in mind," says Jarmusch. "There's a lot of Tom in his character. That whole bit about kicking out the window of a police car—I think Tom has had some experience with that."

In all, Waits has appeared in more than twenty films, including Robert Altman's *Short Cuts*, Coppola's *Bram Stoker's Dracula*, and *Ironweed* (a costar billing with Jack Nicholson). Waits also tried his hand at theater, staging *Franks Wild Years* at Chicago's Steppenwolf Theatre in 1986. Recently, he reunited with Lurie for a highly amusing episode of cable-TV's *Fishing with John*.

By the early 1990s, Waits had moved his family to Northern California and released *Bone Machine*, a dark blast of rustic surrealism, apocalyptic blues braying, and killing-field hollers that won him a Grammy for Best Alternative Music Performance in 1992. ("He flipped out when he got the Grammy," says Jarmusch. "He hated that. 'Alternative to what?! What the hell does that mean?!'") During this period, Waits also scored two Robert Wilson operas, *The Black Rider* (which features William Burroughs) and *Alice*, as well as Jarmusch's 1992 film *Night on*

Earth. A six-year hermitage followed, presumably spent pursuing his own brand of rural domestic bliss and exploring his fascination with rare and experimental musical instruments. He penned the foreword to *Gravikords, Whirlies & Pyrophones*, Bart Hopkin's study of obscure and often homemade instruments, and contributed to Hopkin's follow-up, *Orbitones, Spoon Harps & Bellowphones*. Waits and Brennan also supplied the music for *Bunny*, an animated short that won an Academy Award this year. Recently, Waits collaborated with Mark Linkous on a track called "Bloody Hands" that's slated to appear on the next Sparklehorse album. He also produced, cowrote, and performed on Weiss's *Extremely Cool*.

In a surprise move, Waits left Island Records last year and signed a one-off deal with the punk-rock Epitaph label. *Mule Variations*, his first album in seven years and possibly his best, finds him moving full circle. The cubist blues of his Island Records is still there, along with the American primitivism of *Bone Machine* and the grainy flicker of his soundtrack work. Waits can still make the piano weep with just his voice, as he does on "House Where Nobody Lives" and "Take It with Me When I Go." And he can still kick like a mule, as "Big in Japan" and "Filipino Box Spring Hog" can attest. *Mule* is hardly *Franks Mild Years*. Some may complain that there are no great surprises here, but when you reinvent the wheel, well, sometimes you've just gotta ride on it awhile. This music is built to last. Who else is making recordings this harsh and masterful twenty-five years into a career?

Arriving at the Astro, Waits pulls up in a 1985 Suburban, an unlikely ride for a man known for driving cars made before Kennedy was assassinated. "I refuse to call it a Suburban—I call it a Bourbon," he says, and compliments *Magnet* on its taste in accommodations with a wry smile. He's dressed head to toe in dark blue denim, a lived-in pair of boots, and his trademark porkpie hat—a rabbit-fur Stetson he bought in Austin while in town for a rare live performance at the recent South by Southwest festival. We head over to the nearby Mission Café, an unassuming greasy spoon, for eggs and sausage. Still a bit morning-groggy, his voice sounds an even rougher grit of sandpaper than on record. Laughing easily with a chesty wheeze, a pair of reading glasses perched low on the bridge of his nose, Waits looks almost fatherly as he dispenses bits of folk wisdom, oddball factoids, and good old-fashioned horse sense from a beat-up notebook he brought with him. Though the camera tends to add a few miles to his face, catching the shadows in the lines, in person Waits looks younger than his forty-nine years. The advantage of being born an old soul is that you never really seem to age. You just become a classic.

Tom Waits: When I was comin' down here, I was thinkin' of all the cars I had in my life. I'm drivin' this '85 Suburban, kind of a *Men in Black* car. I started thinking about it because I got a letter from the daughter of my neighbor, who sold me my first car, a '55 Buick Special. From there, I got a '55 Buick Roadmaster. I had a '56 Ford wagon, beige. Somewhere in there I had a '59 Volvo.

Jonathan Valania: You don't strike me as a Volvo guy.

TW: No, it wasn't me, but somebody was trying to get rid of it, and he wanted $100 for it. And he was a cop, so I said, "I'll take it." Had that sloped back, that scoliosis back. I had four Buicks: a Special, a Century and a Roadmaster, and a '65 T-Bird. Had a '59 Dodge wagon; it was gorgeous. A '56 Mercury convertible, a '54 Caddie, black—they said it was in *The Godfather*, and I think I paid more for it because of that. Godfather prices, that's what they said. Had two Caddies, a '54 Coupe de Ville and a '52 Caddie, blue and white. A '64 Cadillac, champagne color—bought it in Montana. My wife drove it back out, no air-conditioning, it was 120 degrees. She's still mad about that. [*reading from his notebook*] Most American auto horns beep in the key of what?

JV: Key of C?

TW: You cheated! You were looking at my notebook! The key of F. [*reading from his notebook*] You know, more steel is produced for the manufacture of bottle caps than auto bodies. There's a national thirst going on here. When gentlemen in medieval Japan wished to seal an agreement, they would urinate together and crisscross the streams—that was an early contract. . . . Recently, a Korean fisherman was arrested for feeding his wife to a school of sharks after getting into a heated argument; it's still against the law to use your wife as bait in Korea.

JV: Let's talk about shoes.

TW: All I wear now is engineer boots. Before that, I only wore pointy shoes and I destroyed my feet. My feet are now in the shape of a pointed shoe. I have a lot of room on either side in these boots, and I have to put newspaper in there. But I lived to see the pointed shoe once again emerge as a footgear leader. That was exciting. When I started looking for pointed shoes, I used to go to Fairfax on

Orchard Street in New York City, one of those little pushcart guys. I'd say, "You got any pointy shoes?" They would go way, way in the back and come back with a dusty box, blow the dust off the top and say, "What do you want with these things? Give me twenty bucks. Go on, get outta here!" And that was the beginning. From there, I saw it grow into a burgeoning industry, a pointy industry. The ultimate was the pointy toe and Cuban heel. But I was younger then. Now, I go for comfort and roadability.

JV: What about suits?

TW: I still don't pay more than $7 for a suit. When I first went on the road, I was very superstitious; I would wear the same suits onstage as I wore off. A lot of times, we would leave early in the morning. I hated the whole ritual of getting dressed, so a lot of times I would just lay down on the bed in my suit and my shoes, ready to get up at anytime. I would just put the blanket over me and sleep in my clothes; I did that for many years. I stopped after I got married. My wife just won't have it. Whenever she goes away for a couple of days, I put on a suit and get in bed but she can always tell.

JV: Speaking of the road, are you going to tour for this record?

TW: [*assumes mock belligerence*] I'm not gonna tour. I want to be set up with a theater like those guys in Missouri, and people come to me. The Wayne Newton Theater. The Trini Lopez Theater. I want my own, a little tin shack with a marquee and a work light, six chairs, and a dirt floor. I can see it—I know exactly what it looks like. I'll play six nights a week. You come to see me. [*paging through his notebook*] I got some things for you—you'll like this. You ever hear of a bombardier beetle? A bombardier beetle, when disturbed, defends itself by a series of explosions. Actually five individual reports from his rear end, in rapid succession; they are accompanied by a cloud of reddish-colored, vile-smelling fluid.

JV: I'll have to be careful. Do you still smoke?

TW: Gave it up. I'm like everybody else, quit a hundred times. It's a companion and a friend. I would smoke anything in the end. I would take a pack of cigarettes and dig a hole in the backyard and piss on them and bury 'em. Dig 'em up and an hour later, dry them in the oven and smoke. That's how bad I had it.

JV: Do you still drink?

TW: Now, is this of interest to your readers? We talked about the pointed shoes, the smoking—I have a feeling you're trying to steer me into the bars . . . I just got an image of one of those emergency-wall things that says "Break in Case of Emergency," and inside is the beverage . . . I gave it up, gave it up. I haven't had a drink in six years.

JV: You have a new movie coming out called *Mystery Men*. What's the premise?

TW: It's about low-rent superheros. There's a guy named the Shoveler. And there's the Bowler, who has the skull of her famous bowler father sealed in this polyurethane bowling ball. There's the Blue Raja; they make their own costumes and never get a chance to save the day. I play Dr. Heller, a weapons scientist they come to for firepower. Sounds like a blockbuster.

JV: Who's in it?

TW: Ben Stiller, Janeane Garofalo, Hank Azaria, Paul Reubens, William Macy, Eddie Izzard, Geoffrey Rush. Directed by Kinka Usher, who was a prince. I don't know why I agreed to do this except he made the whole thing sound like a soft-ball game.

JV: By the way, great English accent as Renfield in *Bram Stoker's Dracula*.

TW: They say I should be doing Shakespeare instead of all this pop-music crap.

JV: How did you meet up with Jim Jarmusch?

TW: Met him around the time of *Rain Dogs*. He stuck out. His movies were like Russian films, like nothing anyone had ever seen before. For me, they were like the hair in the gate. You know when you used to go to the movies and a big hair would get stuck in the projector, and you would sit there and watch that piece of hair? You would lose the whole plot for a while. So, he was the hair in the gate.

JV: The episode of *Fishing with John* is a hoot. How did you hook up with John Lurie?

TW: John's an unusual guy. Met him in New York around the time of *Rain Dogs*. I did [*Fishing*] because of John. But once I got down there, I wanted to kill him. He knows this. It was pretty pathetic. A fishing show. High concept—the idea is that it doesn't matter if we catch anything, which is the whole idea of fishing anyway, getting out in the woods and being together. Just an excuse to hold something in your hand and look off into the distance and talk about life. We caught nothing, which is embarrassing. It got to the point where we bought fish from fishermen in a passing boat, which was humiliating. And I got seasick and sunstroke—I was an unhappy guy for most of it. But it turned out to be funny anyway. John is an excellent composer and musician, can pick up anything and play it. We'll be walking along and he'll pick up a piece of irrigation pipe and very seriously ask you to hold one end of it while he tries to get a sound out of it. He's like a kid, a cross between a kid and a wizard—a kizzard. Great nose, too.

JV: Let's talk about the new record. You told journalist Rip Rense that the title comes from something your wife says when you're being stubborn: "I didn't marry a man—I married a mule." And the fact that you were going through some "changes." What changes?

TW: Electrolysis. I had a lot of unwanted hair removed. Went through aromatherapy. I'm in third-year medical school now—love it!

JV: The first song on *Mule Variations* that struck me was "What's He Building?" I got kind of a Unabomber image. We seem to be living in a time when the guy next door may be building a fertilizer bomb in his basement.

TW: Guess it's the rat theory: There's too many of us, and we're going crazy because of the proliferation of the human manifestation. You go down the freeway, and all of a sudden there are 350,000 new homes where there used to be wilderness. They all have to go to the bathroom somewhere, they all want toys for their kids, they all want eggs and bacon and a nice little car and a place to vacation. When the rats get too plentiful, they turn on each other.

JV: In the song you mention a town called Mayor's Income, Tennessee.

TW: Came to me in a dream. Two towns. The other one, same dream, Miner's Prayer, West Virginia.

JV: You collaborated with Kathleen on most of the songs on *Mule Variations*. Can you describe how you two write together? Is she a musician?

TW: Excellent pianist, plays contrabassoon, classically trained. Used to play recitals with all the relatives around, and she would start the nocturne and then go off and everybody would cock their ears like the RCA dog: "That ain't Beethoven anymore." She's free-floating. She doesn't seem to be pulled in any one direction. You see, we all like music, but what we really want is for music to like us, because it really is a language and some people are linguists and speak seven languages fluently, can do contracts in Chinese, and tell jokes in Hungarian.

JV: Getting back to the names of places, St. Louis seems to pop up a lot, in "Hold On" from the new record and "Time" from *Rain Dogs* and you've mentioned it a lot in interviews. Ever live there?

TW: No, never lived there. It's a good name to stick in a song. Every song needs to be anatomically correct: You need weather, you need the name of the town, something to eat—every song needs certain ingredients to be balanced. You're writing a song and you need a town, and you look out the window and you see "St. Louis Cardinals" on some kid's T-shirt. And you say, "Oh, we'll use that." [*Paging through his notebook*] There is still a law on the books in Kentucky that says you have to take a bath at least once a year, so we left Kentucky. They were too pushy.

JV: I understand that you cover the walls of the studio with maps when you record.

TW: Makes it more like an expedition.

JV: Where is the "House Where Nobody Lives"?

TW: That was the house I used to go by when I would drive my kids to school, abandoned, and the weeds were literally as tall as the trees. At Christmastime, all the neighbors in the area kicked in and bought some lights for it. It was kind of touching. It was like the bad tooth in that smile of a neighborhood.

JV: What about "Big in Japan"? How big are you in Japan?

TW: Haven't played there in a long time. Last time I was there, I was on a bullet train, had my little porkpie hat, my pointed shoes, and my skinny tie. There was a whole car of Japanese gangsters dressed like Al Capone and Cagney, really zooted. Everyone says, "Don't go in there, don't go in there," but it was the only place with seats—everybody else was huddled together like cattle. And they ate in this huge air-conditioned car, with tea and little cookies and six guys sitting around talking with cigars. I said, "Fuck, I'm gonna go in there and sit down." And I did. It was like this big, heavy standoff, then they all started laughing, we all tipped our hats and did that little bow. It was pretty funny. Then I brought my guys in and we all sat down, my mob with the Japanese mob. They always want me to do ads for underwear and cigarettes, but I never did them. I did one and I'll never do it again. I used to see celebrities doing ads and my first reaction was, "Aw, gee he must have needed the money. That's tough." When somebody was on the slide, they would do an ad.

JV: You successfully sued Frito-Lay for doing a commercial with a guy who sounds and acts just like you.

TW: This guy from Texas got paid three hundred bucks to do me. That was his specialty, anyway, that he does this perfect impersonation of me. And they did this whole thing around "Step Right Up," and every now and then they would say "Fritos" or whatever. And afterward, the guy felt so bad, he came out as our star witness. We won $2.5 million. David beats Goliath.

JV: Let's talk about some of the characters in the songs on *Mule Variations*. Who is Big Jack Earl?

TW: Tallest man in the world. Was with Barnum & Bailey. If you see old archival photographs, they used to put him next to some guy that was like a foot tall. Big hat, tall boots. That's why "Big Jack Earl was eight foot one and stood in the road and he cried." Imagine a guy eight foot one standing in the middle of the road crying. It breaks your heart.

JV: What about Birdie Joe Hoaks?

TW: I read in the newspaper about this gal, twelve years old, who had swindled Greyhound. She ran away from home and told Greyhound this whole story about her parents and meeting them in San Francisco. She had this whole Holden Caufield thing, and she got an unlimited ticket and crisscrossed the US. And she got nabbed.

JV: What did they do to her?

TW: They took her bus pass, for starters. I don't think she did hard time. Me and my wife read the paper and we clip hundreds of articles, and then we read the paper that way, without all the other stuff. It's our own paper. There is a lot of filler in the paper and the rest is advertising. If you just condense it down to the essential stories, like the story about the one-eyed fish they found in Lake Michigan with three tails, you can renew your whole relationship with the paper.

JV: There's a line in "What's He Building?": "You'll never guess what Mr. Sticha saw."

TW: Mr. Sticha was my neighbor when I was a kid. He didn't like kids and he didn't like noise. All the kids would go past his house yellin' and making noise, and you would see his fist out the window and he'd threaten to call the cops. His wife used to say, "You're gonna give him a heart attack if you keep this up." And he finally had a heart attack and he died, and his wife told us that it was our fault, that we had killed him as a group. We all had to distribute that guilt and live with it, and it was upsetting: "Sticha died and we killed him." We might just as well have plotted his murder.

JV: "Cold Water" is a kind of a hobo anthem. You ever sleep in a graveyard or ride the rails?

TW: I have slept in a graveyard and I have rode the rails. When I was a kid, I used to hitchhike all the time from California to Arizona with a buddy named Sam Jones. We would just see how far we could go in three days, on a weekend, see if we could get back by Monday. I remember one night in a fog, we got lost on this side road and didn't know where we were exactly. And the fog came in and we were really lost then and it was very cold. We dug a big ditch in a dry riverbed and we both laid in there and pulled all this dirt and leaves over us like a blanket. We're shivering in this ditch all night, and we woke up in the morning and the fog had cleared and right across from us was a diner; we couldn't see it through the fog. We went in and had a great breakfast, still my high-water mark for a great breakfast. The phantom diner.

JV: In "Black Market Baby," you call the baby in question a "Bonsai Aphrodite." Great line.

TW: Kathleen came up with that. We know this little gal who's just a gorgeous chick, but she's about four foot ten, looks like she's been bound, like the Chinese do with feet. Kathleen said, "She's a Bonsai Aphrodite." It was Patricia Arquette. We told her about that, she said, "I love that, I'm gonna open up a flower shop and call it Bonsai Aphrodite," which she did. But, apparently, it didn't last, went under.

JV: There's a great line in "Picture in a Frame": "I'm gonna love you till the wheels come off."

TW: That's prison slang. Means until the end of the world.

JV: I notice that the Eyeball Kid has the same birth date as you.

TW: Just a coincidence. The Eyeball Kid is a comic-book character. Actually, it was Nic Cage that reintroduced me to comic books. I hadn't thought about comic books since I was a little kid, but he seemed to carry that mythology with him. It was inspiring to see him keep alive some of those principles that we associate with childhood, to the point where he named himself after Cage, the comic-book hero. But I was trying to imagine what it would be like for a person with an enormous eyeball for a head to be in show business. If Barnum & Bailey were still around, I imagine he would have thrown in with them.

JV: The tour would be sponsored by Visine or Bausch & Lomb.

TW: It's a metaphor for people that get into show business, because they usually have some kind of family disturbance or are damaged in some way or another. I had a manager when I was a kid, I threw in with a guy named Herbie Cohen, who worked with Zappa. I wanted a big bruiser, the tough guy in the neighborhood, and I got it.

JV: A knee-breaker?

TW: You said that, not me. I got to be careful what I say about Herbie. I'll wind up in . . . court.

JV: Speaking of the business end of things, why did you leave Island Records?

TW: It started changing a lot. [Former owner Chris] Blackwell's gone. For me, it's about relationships. And when Blackwell pulled out and started his own company, I lost interest.

JV: What do you think of all the consolidation that has been going on with the major labels, cutting staff and artists?

TW: I think you should fight for your independence and freedom at all costs. I mean, it's a plantation system. All a record company is is a bank, and they loan you a little money to make a record and then they own you for the rest of your life. You don't even own your own work. Most people only have a small piece of their publishing. Most people are so happy to be recording, which I was—you like the way your name looks on the contract, so you start signing. I got myself tied up in a lot of knots when I was a kid.

JV: Your deal with Epitaph is for one record, where you license the record to the label for a limited time and then ownership reverts back to you. I don't know how aware you are of the Internet, but there is this technology called MP3 that basically allows artists to put songs on the Net and people can download them and burn their own CDs, essentially cutting the record companies out of the equation.

TW: I don't know what I think about that. I don't know about the Internet. I'm not on that. I'm way behind. I have a rotary phone. Progress is compulsive and obsessive, I guess. I get the feeling that people aren't leaving their homes. They are sitting in front of their computer desks and everything comes to them from their screens. That's what the whole nation really wants, but anything that is that popular or easily accessible is usually not good for you. It's like tap water is not good for you; it's recycled piss and chemicals, that's all. There is a reason that a bottle of water costs more than a gallon of gas. And what's the biggest enemy of computers? Water. And the computers are trying to eliminate all the water. I don't know where I'm going with this. I guess we're in the middle of a revolution and nobody knows where the rocks are going to fall. The record companies are ter-rified. But I don't want to be a record company. Too much paperwork, and I get too many calls already. Plus, I have two teenagers, and if I was a record company, you would never be able to get through.

JV: *Mule Variations* is your first record in six years. There were rumors floating around that you weren't putting out records or performing because you were sick.

TW: No, I'm not sick, but it's interesting that rumors of that nature would circu-late. Rumors of my death were greatly exaggerated, as they say. The rumor was that I had throat cancer.

JV: *Bone Machine* had a lot of death in it. And there's that song on *Mule* called "Take It with Me." Beautiful song. This is an absurd question, but I'll ask it anyway: are you afraid of dying?

TW: [*with mock bravado*] Who me? Naw, bring it on! Come on! Who me? I don't wanna go. I gotta rake the leaves first. I got a lot of things to do. I'm like that guy who said on his deathbed, "Either that wallpaper goes or I do." Famous last words. My favorite epitaph is the town hypochondriac's: "I told you I was sick."

JV: In 1976, you were quoted in *Newsweek* as saying, "There's a common loneliness that just sprawls from coast to coast. It's like a common disjointed identity crisis. It's the dark, warm, narcotic American night. I just hope I'm able to touch that feeling before I find myself one of these days parked on Easy Street." Twenty-three years later, here you are with a wife and kids and a house in the country, a tidy nest egg from Frito-Lay—Easy Street by most any standard—and still you seem to be at the height of your creative powers and popularity. Your career strikes me as a model for how to do it the right way in a business cluttered with bad examples.

TW: OK, thank you. I'm just improvising, like everybody else. . . . I never thought I would live out in the sticks. But now I'm the mean old man next door. Voila. I'm Mr. Sticha. I got a whole collection of baseballs that have been hit into my yard, and I'm not giving them up for nothing.

On December 7, 1999, Tom Waits would reach a new milestone: he would turn fifty. But his age did not prevent him from acting out a touring itinerary that would exhaust a male ten years his junior. He had just taken his touring band to Europe, where he had premiered his new album to appreciative, adoring audiences in The Hague, Berlin, Florence, and elsewhere. Back stateside in July 1999, he played some dates in Toronto, Canada, and a handful of United States dates. After all of the publicity-related work was behind him, Waits did not stop, but continued on with a variety of new works he had planned, including another theatrical collaboration with Robert Wilson: *Woyzeck*.

Interview with Tom Waits
Studio C, KBCO
October 13, 1999
Bret Saunders

Bret Saunders: Hi, it's Bret Saunders here on 97.3 KBCO and on Channel 103.1 in Los Angeles. Glad that you could join us this morning. This is such a fantastic opportunity to have a gentleman in the studio who's been such a big influence on my life and my philosophy. And he's just given such fantastic music. His name is Tom Waits. He's appearing at the Paramount Theatre [in Denver] tonight. He appeared last night, and by all accounts it was a fantastic show. Tom Waits, welcome to KBCO's C Studio.

Tom Waits: Thanks, Bret. Thank you. Good to be here. Wow, haven't been up in Boulder in a long, long time.

BS: Yeah, how long has it been?

TW: I hate to say how long it's been. It's been too long. Let's just say it's been twenty years?

BS: Wow!

TW: Something like that—I don't know. I mean I played in Boulder in Tulagi's a long time ago. But that's been, you know, I don't have a lot of details about what happened during that period but I've been told we did well, we did rather well at the club, yeah.

BS: I'm sure you could sell out Tulagi's at this juncture, Tom.

TW: OK [*laughs*].

BS: Not a problem. So maybe you could play something for us? We got a piano in here for you.

TW: Oh boy, you just got right out of the box here, huh? Right into the . . .

BS: No, I mean, we could hear some music?

TW: I thought we were gonna talk over, I don't know, my choice?

BS: Absolutely, anything you like.

TW: All right [*performs "Picture in a Frame" at the piano*].

BS: Tom Waits here at Studio C. "I'm gonna love you till the wheels come off." Well that is devotion! Those are lyrics of devotion. It may be the strongest pledge I've ever heard. How do you come up with that?

TW: Come up with what?

BS: "I'm gonna love you till the wheels come off."

TW: Oh, that's an old expression, yeah. That's an old . . . one of those old jail-house expressions, yeah. I guess it means that you have to . . . you have to have your wheels looked at regularly [*laughs*].

BS: Rotated!

TW: Yeah, balanced and rotated! Yeah, check the rotors, have 'em greased.

BS: Tom, who do you make your music for, or for whom. Is it for an individual; is it for Tom?

TW: Oh, uh, I guess, yeah, it's for me. I don't know. That's an interesting question, because you know you write a lot of songs that just kind of pass through you and this is really kind of child's work, you know? Children write the best songs.

So you know you're writing for yourself. I don't know where they come from, they kinda come from all kinds of places. You build 'em out of things you see and remember and find and felt before and feeling now, you know? Take notes, you know? I don't know really who I write for. Sometimes I'm writing for my wife. Sometimes I'm writing for my kids. Sometimes my neighbors, my friends, my loved ones. It's like selling salve, you know? I sent away when I was a kid on the back of a comic book and I could get a signet ring with my own initials on it and I didn't read the small print. And then I got like twelve cases of salve that I was supposed to sell in order to get the ring and everything. It was a scary time for me. And I hid the salve and I wore the ring and then I got a letter from a lawyer saying that, you know, I was supposed to be in court that Monday and I was like seven.

BS: Right, you were seven years old!

TW: I don't know. I don't know who you're writing for. Sometimes you just write 'em for music. You just have songs that you remember and loved and you just kinda departed the whole thing. You leave in the little things for folks to discover later and, you know, they're kinda like containers. Songs are kinda like containers. So I don't know.

BS: Your latest CD is called *Mule Variations*, it's great. Great album.

TW: OK, yeah that's been out for a while now and it's doing good I guess. That's what they say. The title came from my wife, she always said that I didn't marry a man, she said that I married a mule. So these are *Mule Variations*. So that's where that came from. I don't know what else to play here. Do you have any requests?

BS: Yeah, I like the one on *Mule Variations* about the "Come on off the cross we could use the wood."

TW: All right, right, yeah. I probably ought to do that one with a band. Is the band here? No? We're all by ourselves here. Uhhhh let's see. . . . [*begins to play intro to "Broken Bicycles"*] Oh, let's not do that one. . . . Oh, here's kind of an obscure one! [*performs "The Fall of Troy" at the piano*]

BS: Tom Waits at Studio C here at 97.3 KBCO on channel 1031 in Los Angeles. Tom it's great to have you in front of me. The opportunity to just sit here and talk to you.

TW: OK [*laughs*].

BS: It's been a long time since we've heard new studio material from you. Since recent *Mule Variations* it had been quite a few years. You've had *The Black Rider* with William S. Burroughs.

TW: All right, yeah!

BS: Why, your fans want to know, why it's been such a long time since we heard anything?

TW: Oh I don't know, traffic school. I was in traffic school for a while. It was Harvard Traffic School, so it really . . .

BS: At least it's one of the best!

TW: I got a lot more involved than I ever imagined it would be and so . . . I don't know. You know I've been, I don't know what I've been doing. Ice sculptures, plumbing, electrical, Sheetrock, that type of thing.

BS: Taking care of stuff around the house.

TW: Taking care of things, yeah.

BS: Which is important . . .

TW: Fixing fences and all that. But you know, "time flies," you know? You wait till you got a bunch of stuff together and then you go in and lay it down, you know? Miles Davis always said that the "only reason to write new songs is cause you're sick of the old ones." That kinda happened to me. You play the old ones but you know . . . it's always much more interesting to play something new.

BS: Speaking of new, any new film projects on the horizon perhaps?

TW: Film? Uh, let's see what have we got there. Something's coming up . . . I get a lot of offers, a lot of weird offers.

BS: Is there anything you won't do and you say "that's repugnant—I'm not gonna do that!"?

TW: No, there's nothing I won't do! "Just get the money out, Bob!" That's what she said. No there's gotta be something I won't do . . . but I haven't encountered it yet because I don't get that kind of wide range, open latitude with offers, you know? I mean, I'm not playing romantic leads so . . . but you know, I do . . . you know film is weird. I'm not a real . . . I do some acting, you know? I mean it's on my card. The trouble with it is that you're caught there for a long time and you have to kinda bring a book . . . bring a library really, cause you wait around a lot.

BS: It's a massive process.

TW: It is. You're one violin in a very large orchestra. I'm used to conducting myself within my own group. So it's both, you know, healthy and challenging and a pain in the butt. Yeah.

BS: So you're gonna be performing at the Paramount Theatre tonight?

TW: Oh yeah, we'll be there.

BS: You're pretty happy with last night's performance?

TW: Yeah, it went OK, yeah. And the crowd was wild, so yeah, it was a good night and I hope we'll have as good or better an evening tonight.

BS: Well, we're happy to have you back in Colorado. I just wonder if we could coax one more song out of you if that's possible.

TW: I don't know what to play. I've done all these slow songs. I worked at a pizza place when I was a kid. It was next to a mortuary and there were a lot of jokes about the food. And anyway, I guess this is for all the restaurant workers out there in the world [*performs "I Can't Wait to Get Off Work" at the piano*]. [. . .] So you played that Chuck E. Weiss record?

BS: Yeah, Chuck E. Weiss from Colorado.

TW: Yeah, Chuck E.

BS: You and your wife were involved as executive producers on that?

TW: That's right, yeah. Of course I've known Chuck E., well I met Chuck E. in about 1974, you know, out in front of Ebbets Field. And so that record was really a labor of love. Chuck E. did most of the work, you know? We put up the money and my wife shopped it around and got a lot of interest. You know I'm glad it came out. Everybody seemed to love it. It got a lot of great reviews. He played a lot of shows and so I was real happy for him. It's really a bizarre combination of . . . it's just like Chuck, you know? So it's like sick and touching and loud and you know it's. . . . So I was real glad it came out.

BS: Now is it true that "Chuck E.'s in Love" is about him?

TW: Yeah right, it's supposed to be about him.

BS: Colorado guy.

TW: Yeah! Colorado guy! When I met Chuck he was wearing a chinchilla coat.

BS: Yeah.

TW: And real high platforms, like four feet. You know? That was the old days.

BS: Think he was working for the Reagan administration?

TW: No, he was walking in on the ice. He was trying to balance on the ice. It was like February and he was doing this kinda balance-dance, you know?

BS: Wow.

TW: But, yeah, the songs on there are great. *He* really produced the record. I mean, you know the music, worked with the band he'd been with for a long time, they played a lot of dates and really honed the songs and wrote a lot of stuff just for the record just before he went in and the other stuff was stuff that had been, you know worked on, on the road.

BS: One last question for you, Tom. Regarding your career and what you managed to do. I mean you first hit me with *Swordfishtrombones* when I was a teenager.

TW: Aha.

BS: The music has become progressively more and more interesting and complex. How do you manage to thrive with the major record labels and do what you have been able to do as an artist and do without any compromise? Because let's face it, your records don't sound like everything else you hear on major labels.

TW: Oh yeah. I don't know, I really don't know the answer to that, except that I would suggest that to others, you know? And there'd probably be more variety and more diversity. But you know when you start out, you really do have to come in on some kind of suggested music that's already out there, you know? I mean I'm not totally original. I draw from all kinds of sources and I listen to a lot of things and I don't see myself as completely original, you know? I would recommend that when you are starting out that you stay with your own stuff and find out who you are. And stay with you minding your own unique qualities and rather than trying to sound like somebody else . . . I mean you do start like somebody else and slowly you become so it's kinda like life, you know?

BS: Well, Tom, it's been a great pleasure having you here in the Studio C.

TW: OK.

BS: Can we get one more before you go?

TW: I'll play a little bit of that "Jesus' Blood" because I know you like that . . .

BS: Yeah, it's a great story too.

TW: Well this was Gavin Bryars and this was a song that was discovered through, um . . . they did a documentary on songs that people remembered from their childhood and they interviewed a lot of homeless people in England. They went under the bridges and out to the beach and downtown and they found people and asked them what are the songs they carry with them, what are the songs that mean something to them? And there's a lot of people [who] have lost everything and maybe all they've got is, you know, these memories and these songs and this was one that they found and so Gavin Bryars orchestrated it and it was called "Jesus' Blood Never Failed Me Yet" and he made a record with that title.

BS: It's a beautiful record too.

TW: But I heard it on my wife's birthday at about three o'clock in the morning coming out of the radio. And I didn't know what it was and it went on and on and on. So it's one of those . . . it almost sounds like a kid's song. I'll just play a little bit of it.

BS: Yeah cause it's seventy-four minutes long.

TW: It's seventy-four minutes and everything's in B-flat today [*plays "Jesus' Blood Never Failed Me Yet" at the piano*].

BS: Thank you. Tom Waits here at Studio C, 97.3 KBCO, and on Channel 103.1 in Los Angeles.

TW: OK, good to be here.

"Tradition with a Twist"
Blues Revue
July/August 2000
Bret Kofford

He's somewhere between George Gershwin and a carnival barker, somewhere between Leadbelly and a guy selling vacuums from the trunk of his car. And Tom Waits—playwright, well-known character actor, scorer of films, writer of stage musicals, Academy Award nominee (for the score to Francis Ford Coppola's *One from the Heart*), devoted husband and dad—is comfortable with that considerable breadth.

First and foremost, though, Tom Waits is a songwriter. He's had hit songs—they've just been recorded by others, including Bruce Springsteen ("Jersey Girl") and Rod Stewart ("Downtown Train"). Recording a Waits song is a badge of honor for musicians in the know. Artists such as Beck, Los Lobos, Ani DiFranco, A. J. Croce, and Eddie Vedder cite Waits as a major influence. He's won two Grammys, this year for best contemporary folk album for *Mule Variations* and in 1992 for best alternative album for *Bone Machine*. He also was nominated for a Grammy this year for best male rock vocal performance for the song "Hold On."

Yet Waits is, in essence, a bluesman. He cites Leadbelly and countless other blues artists as inspirations. Several songs on *Mule Variations* are well within the realm of the blues ("Get Behind the Mule," "Chocolate Jesus," "Filipino Box Spring Hog," and "Come On Up to the House"), and Charlie Musselwhite and John Hammond both appear on the album. Waits is in the process of producing an album for Hammond.

The son of schoolteachers from National City, California, has come a long way.

During his more than twenty-five years of recording, Waits, fifty, has had long stints with Elektra and Island Records. For *Mule Variations*, he moved to Epitaph, previously known for punk-oriented recordings. Still, Waits's mix of clanging rave-ups, spoken-word landscapes, sing-along romps, roaring blues, and tender ballads seems to somehow fit on the label.

The acclaim he has received over his groundbreaking and critically lauded career seems to have had little effect on Waits's ego. Waits was gracious, engag-

ing, and forthcoming with *Blues Revue*. When the lengthy interview ended, Waits
said he would call back "if I come up with anything else." He did so the next day,
and beautifully played a portion of Gershwin's "Prelude II" on his piano.

Bret Kofford: When you started working on *Mule Variations*, did you somehow
anticipate you would be nominated for best contemporary folk album?

Tom Waits: Well, I don't go into it like that, thinkin' that. It's a nice thing, but it
doesn't really drive me. Grammys are kind of like the Food and Drug Administration. People like to be USDA-approved, with the little sticker on it and everything.
It's safer. It's kind of people formulating their tastes for what they like. They like
the company of others. But it's a good thing.

BK: Do you think Epitaph is going to put a sticker on the album that says, "contemporary folk album of the year"?

TW: Oh sure, yeah. They'll probably do something like that.

BK: Would you even categorize yourself as a folk musician?

TW: Well, I don't know. That's OK, if you are going to call yourself something.
I'm folks. I'm among folks. That's not a bad thing to be called if you've got to be
in some kind of category. I have a kind of miscellaneous quality to myself, but
I'll take folk. I started when I was a teenager playing folk clubs. That's all stuff I
was listening to. I've gone a little bit far afield, but it still stays within that realm.

BK: Would you object to being called a blues singer?

TW: Well, I guess I would be flattered if someone said I was a blues singer. I'm
not *just* that, but I like that.

BK: Many of your songs could be classified as blues songs, right?

TW: Yeah, yeah.

(Soon the discussion wanders into the qualities of a good tape recorder and other matters.)

TW: We've digressed, haven't we? I'd just as soon we digress the entire time. I never like walking in a straight line. The one thing about getting older, you get taller. We're not as close to the ground, and you miss a lot up here. My little boy found a jewel that had fallen out of a cheap ring this morning. I never would have spotted it. But he's only six and he was right down in there. I miss that proximity to the ground sometimes.

BK: One of the good things about getting older is you start heading back to the ground again, you start shrinking.

TW: You start bending over. [*laughs*] Yeah, right.

BK: Do you think your albums reflect where you're living at the moment? Your latest album, *Mule Variations*, has a rural feel. Would you agree with that?

TW: Sure, yeah, it's definitely more outdoors, whatever you call it.

BK: And you're living in a rural area of Northern California?

TW: Yeah, it's a rural area, but. . . . It's like people say [they] want to record in this studio because it's part of Georgia or Texas or Louisiana. Recording mostly happens inside your head. When you get to that point it doesn't really much matter where you are because the song really is the landscape. It has a lot to do with what you've been listening to and what you've been absorbing.

BK: So what kind of stuff do you listen to?

TW: Well, I dunno. There's only two kinds of music: there's good music and there's bad music, I guess, without running the risk of being too cliché.
    Blind Mamie Forehand, "Honey in the Rock." That's the song. 1927. It's on the Victor label. There's a couple of mistakes on it, and it trails off. I like imperfections. I like things that have a little crack in them. That's how I get into a song. I

remember hearing an old demo Roy Orbison did years ago, a song called "Clau-
dette." He was just doing a demo at home and he got to a certain point in the song
and he hit the wrong chord and said, "Oh shit." So he started over again. And I
said, "Whoa, I can get in there." That's the thing with a lot of music. I think when
it's expensive and heavily produced it puts off people when they hear it. They
think, "Well, gee, my music is small and has bumps on it and has cracks in it."

BK: Do you put the bumps and cracks in on purpose or is that just the way it
comes out?

TW: That's kind of just the way it comes out. And I've just stopped caring about
it. It's gotten to the point where sometimes I do it or pursue it because it lacks
. . . what do they call it . . . "distressing." But that one recording of "Honey in
the Rock," when she stops and says, "Just taste and see." And someone sounds
like they are banging on a telephone bell with a pen or something. They're just
keeping time.

You know, we just buy music now. We don't make it anymore. And that goes
for just about everything. I think it's so important that people develop and sub-
scribe to and have confidence in their own ability to make music, however rough
it is. The rougher the better for me.

What have I been listening to? I've got all of those Lomax reissues, *Southern
Journey*, all that Library of Congress stuff that was recently released on CD, the
Georgia Sea Island Singers and prison songs and field hollers and a lot of Leadbelly. I was born the day after Leadbelly died. I'd like to think we passed in the
hall. When I hear his voice, I feel I know him. Maybe I was a rock on a road he
walked on or a dish in his cupboard, because when I heard him first I recognized
him.

You see, I'm like everybody else in music. I don't have a formal background.
I learned from listening to records, from talking to people, from hanging around
record stores, and hanging around musicians and saying, "Hey, how did you do
that? Do that again. Let me see how you did that." And then I kind of incorporated it into what I was doing. I have a good friend, Francis Thumm, who used
to play the Chromelodeon with The Harry Partch Ensemble and he has been a
music teacher for a lot of years, he has been a profound influence on me. He
is a river to his people. And Greg Cohen, my bass player for many years, is a

complete Renaissance man. He introduced me to everything from The Seeds to Arnold Schoenberg and everything in between. Mostly, I've depended on the kindness of strangers and people I know. Other musical teachers are Chuck E. Weiss, who knows everything, and Kathleen Brennan [Waits's wife], who knows everything else.

BK: I interviewed A. J. Croce recently and he cited you as an influence, and you can hear your influence on a lot of other people, like Vic Chesnutt. How do you feel when people cite you as an influence?

TW: That's cool. Why not? Everybody's still really involved in the folk process of listening to each other. Even if you really try to do exactly what you think someone else did the night before, you can't, unless you're some kind of impersonator or impressionist. When you hear breakthroughs in music, it was their attempt to replicate something incorrectly, and that's what puts a hole in the door and lets the light in. You know, Chuck Berry was trying to play guitar the way Johnnie Johnson, his piano player, played keyboards, with the same kind of stride feeling. When I was a kid picking up a needle and trying to learn how someone did something over and over again . . . it's kind of how it gets passed along, and I'm proud to be part of that whole tradition.

BK: Alan Rudolph has used your songs in at least a couple of movies, including your version of "Somewhere." Are you an admirer of Sondheim?

TW: Well, gee, I like those songs from *West Side Story*. I'm a big fan of Leonard Bernstein. Those are all great songs. That's a great melody.

BK: Speaking of beautiful melodies, I love the little piano part on "Take It with Me."

TW: My wife and I collaborated on most of the songs . . . and if it's really good it's probably her [*laughs*]. Obviously, she's more refined than I am. I'm more throw it against the wall. . . . Yeah, I like the little part, too.

My wife's like a cross between Eudora Welty and Joan Jett. Kathleen is a rhododendron, an orchid, and an oak. She's got the four Bs: beauty, brightness, bravery, and brains. She rescued me. I'd be playing in a steakhouse right now if it weren't for her. I wouldn't even be *playing* a steakhouse. I'd be *cooking* in a steakhouse.

BK: What was going wrong in your life at that time?

TW: What wasn't going wrong?

BK: What year did you meet?

TW: 1979. We met on New Year's Eve.

BK: But you did some good stuff before '79.

TW: But I was falling apart. I was all over the road.

BK: OK, what do you write first, the words or the music?

TW: That's one of the oldest questions in the book.

BK: I didn't want to ask it.

TW: But you did. And the thing is, words are music. If you have words, you have sound, and the sounds have a shape to them. And in that sense, in the broader sense, music is organized noise. Monk said there are no wrong notes. It all has to do with how they are resolved. That's how jump-rope songs were. They're a rhythmic phrase. As soon as you have that, you have music. So you don't have to wait for the words if you have music. And sometimes you don't have to wait for the music if you have the words. I don't know who said this, but they said all things aspire to the condition of music at its best. Everyone is looking for that in many things.

BK: Charlie Musselwhite plays a lot on the new album. Have you heard his Latin thing [*Continental Drifter*]?

TW: The Cuban thing? Yeah, I like it. It seems like it goes together. He was probably worried about translation, disparate musical styles, but there's always an overlap. At some point, Chinese music starts sounding Irish. Who knows why?

BK: So you brought Charlie Musselwhite in because you wanted to use the best harp player you could find?

TW: Yeah [*laughs*], he's great. He brings about three hundred harmonicas, microphones. And he's up for anything. Some stuff doesn't adapt to that cross harp, but the songs that we tried it on did. On "Chocolate Jesus" just before the song starts, you can hear him talking into the mic. He says, "I love it." That's my favorite part of the song.

BK: When you're playing with all these famous people and you hear all these things about people being your admirers, do you ever think, "I'm just another guy who plays music. I don't need all that"?

TW: Well, it's important to remind yourself of that. It's a balancing act. I really do want to stay humble.

BK: One more thing to shatter your humility. I love your song "Johnsburg, Illinois." It's such a beautiful song. Is there really a Johnsburg, Illinois?

TW: Yeah, my wife grew up there. It's by McHenry, near the Chain of Lakes. It's the last place you can get margarine before you cross over into Wisconsin.

BK: You can't buy margarine in Wisconsin?

TW: It's the Dairy State. Are you kidding me? If you're even caught with margarine on you . . . they search you at the markets.

BK: And at the border station they check you.

TW: Yeah, there's a margarine check.

BK: Tell me about blues artists you like, you grew up listening to.

TW: Well, I used to play on the bill with Sonny Terry and Brownie McGhee. That was a big thrill for me. The song I love the most is that Skip James tune "Look at the People." It reminds me of the Son House tune "John the Revelator," which I'm a big fan of. [I listen] to old field hollers and work songs and jump-rope songs and chain-gang tunes and call and response.

Let's see. What else? Sister Rosetta Tharpe. Of course, Ray Charles, Speckled Red, Koko Taylor, Big Joe Turner, Peetie Wheatstraw, Professor Longhair, Canned Heat . . .

BK: Is there anyone out there who catches your ear now?

TW: T-Model Ford. The stuff on Fat Possum I like a lot.

BR. You worked with David Hidalgo. Do you like his stuff?

TW: Oh, man, yeah, I love those guys. I love Los Lobos. Those guys out of Denver, 16 Horsepower. What about Sparklehorse? He's great. Lou Ann Barton, she's got a great voice . . . [Captain] Beefheart, of course. Elvis Costello. He's a Renaissance man, he's multidimensional. His song "Baby Plays Around" I thought would be a good song for Little Jimmy Scott, who is someone else I really admire a lot. Howlin' Wolf, of course. The 3M Corporation—Monk, Miles, and Mingus. Roland Kirk is up there really high. Sun Ra, Crying Sam Collins, James Harman, Tina Turner, Aretha, Daniel Johnston. And I like anybody with "little" in their name. Little Jimmy Scott and, uh . . .

BK: Little Charlie & the Nightcats . . .

TW: Little Charlie & the Nightcats . . . all the Littles, and I like all the Bigs . . .

BK: Big Mama Thornton . . .

TW: Big Mama Thornton, Big Joe Turner, Big Bill Broonzy, Little Anthony & the Imperials, Little Richard . . . Zappa, Nick Cave, and, of course, The Rolling Stones, can't leave them out. Bill Hicks, Johnny Cash, Ramblin' Jack Elliott, Guy Clark, Randy Newman. And Harry Belafonte. My dad had all his records. I just put him on the other night and said, "Man, Harry, you're killin' me."

The thing about recording . . . it is a pretty miraculous phenomenon when you think about it. You put something that happens in three minutes' time and someone can come along a hundred years later and hear what you did in those three minutes. It's rather mystifying. And you get a chance to shake hands with the future and be part of the past.

BK: Do you consider yourself a good piano player?

TW: I play fake piano. I'm a composer, basically. When I sit down at the piano I don't sit down to play something or learn something. I sit down to discover.

BK: So when you hear a really good piano player, like Gene Taylor, you say, "I could never do that."

TW: Jeez, man, get out of here. But that's not my thing. I took a different road. I used to dream about the Brill Building and to write songs in that manner. . . . I love the whole cabaret tradition. I liked listening to Sinatra when I was starting out. My friends thought I was crazy. They were listening to Blue Cheer and Leadbelly. It's like when I discovered Leadbelly I discovered mariachi music, Irish music, gypsy music. You make a connection with it and you don't know why.

BK: How's it working out with Epitaph?

TW: Good place to be, compassionate and young.

BK: They haven't had anyone like you before.

TW: No . . . they brought me in for adult supervision. Yard duty. They're honest. [Epitaph founder] Brett Gurewitz is an innovator and a visionary and an iconoclast. He's very fair in all ways. He's not a gouger. They see themselves as more a service industry. You make music and they put it out. They're not part of the long tradition of the rape and pillage of artists, and the servitude. You get a lot of respect there.

BK: I read another interview with you where you said the term "you gotta get behind the mule and plow" from *Mule Variations* is something your dad used to say to you, an old saying about getting to work.

TW: No, that's what Robert Johnson's father said about Robert. He said he wouldn't get up in the morning and get behind the mule and plow. Robert wanted to have his own life and get out of the whole system there, so he flew the coop.

BK: What does Kathleen contribute to the writing process?

TW: We collaborate. Who knows how it really works, if it works? You know, you wash, I'll dry.
    She stays out of the limelight. That's what she prefers. I'm out there, I'm more song and dance, and she's more behind-the-scenes. She prefers it there.

BK: In retrospect it looks like she's added depth and textures to your albums that weren't there before.

TW: Well, you're married. You know how it is. She's the brains behind Pa [*laughs*].

BK: Do you ever listen to your old things and think "That's not very good"?

TW: Yeah, I do. I can't listen to the old stuff. I've got big ears and I dressed funny. And I have a monochromatic vocal style. I have a hard time listening to my old records, the stuff before my wife.

BK: Where's the threshold where you can say, "Well, I kinda like that one"?

TW: Oh, I dunno, *Swordfishtrombones*, and forward from there. That's a line of demarcation for me. And that's right around the time I got married, and my wife worked on that record with me. She's the one who said, "You can produce your own records, you don't need to go in with a staff and people telling you what to do." That started what became more of a mom-and-pop outfit. Till then I felt like I was trying too hard. You learn what not to play, what not to say, which is critical at all times. And in most cases that which is implied speaks volumes, in music particularly.

(The conversation returns to the blues.)

TW: Well I guess blues is in everything now. It's an ingredient that is so seminal and such a Rosetta Stone or wellspring, but now it's like that which was once a river becomes a road. The place where giant rivers cross, there's a great deal of electromagnetism. I love listening to old gospel stuff. You know that disc that came out that John Fahey's on, Charley Patton on the cover [American Primitive, Vol. I]? It's just a terrific collection, and the artists on it are just remarkable . . . prewar gospel, 1926–36. You can hear that Blind Mamie song on there.

BK: If fifty years from now you're remembered for writing ten great songs, would that be enough for you?

TW: Well, I've still got some time [laughs]. I think what it does come down to, because we're just plain human or we're so product-oriented, we like our products, and we want access to our goods and services, and we want to know what's best. That's what I hate about those "best of" records. You have to see most of this work in context.

I dunno. I think you're being a little generous.

ALICE, BLOOD MONEY
(2002)

Not content to sit upon the laurels of *Mule Variations*, Waits chose to stay active following the erratic spirit of his Muse (wheresoever his Muse chose to take him). In 2001, he appeared as an interviewee and performer in *Freedom Highway*, an Irish documentary concerning politics and art, directed by Philip King. King detailed to the *Irish Times* in 2004 his experiences working with Waits:

> Tom Waits walked into the room with the barn door and he threw it onto the ground and he threw a chair on it and he sat up on it. And the door creaked and the chair creaked and he threw that tambourine into the door and he put his foot on it and a banjo in his hand and he said: "I'm ready." I knew he was ready, but I wasn't ready. Because his voice was like a whirlwind that just blew me across the room when he started to sing. He was consumed by the act of doing what he was doing. . . . It's at those times that you feel the five-year wait is worth it. The 117 phone calls were worth it. The cajoling, the knocking on the door, the inevitable rejection, which is a constant part of this work, is worth it.

The documentary premiered in Europe in April 2001. Waits's abilities as an "extraordinary musical storyteller" were honored by ASCAP at the Beverly Hilton Hotel. Dean Goodman of ASCAP stated in his press release: "Tom Waits was awarded the American Society of Composers, Authors and Publishers' prestigious Founders Award Tuesday, at the eighteenth Annual ASCAP Pop Awards in Los Angeles. Before the performance, Keith Richards appeared larger-than-life in a video message recorded at his Connecticut estate. Dressed like Columbo in a grubby coat and hat, Richards staggered from thick brush and embarked on a generally indecipherable speech in praise of his one-time collaborator. He recalled buying ten thousand worms, on Waits's advice, to help aerate his lawn."

In September 2001, Waits returned to the world of musical theater. It was his third such venture, and for this outing Tom and Kathleen tackled the familiar ground of a disenchanted outcast.

Woyzeck, the progenitor of the album *Blood Money*, was written by Georg Büchner in 1836 and is considered by many to be the prototype of modern plays. The story (based on a true incident of 1821) concerns the slow uncoiling of one soldier's sanity as he is stripped of his identity by the military, ultimately committing murder for his troubles. Says the program guide for the Waits/Wilson production:

> With insight and social indignation Büchner portrays a man who is subject to the laws and rules of a merciless society, and in a series of surreal snapshots he shows us a man who is completely subdued by the will of society and his superiors. Woyzeck is seen and treated as a social experiment. He is alternately employed, unemployed, and employed again. Only one thing is certain: his desperation, social as well as emotional, and his isolation from the rest of the world grows bigger every day. Woyzeck is "only made of sand, dust, dirt, and filth," as it is said in the play—and in a relentless society he learns this bodily. Woyzeck is a very modern, political drama, which tells the story of how all human values are destroyed when society pushes the individual to the brink of survival. The tightness and linguistic expressionism of the text are an obvious takeoff for Wilson's abstract idiom and imagery.

These are all the hallmarks of a typical character in the Waitsian world of American desperation and longing. Waits explained to Edna Gundersen of *USA Today*: "It's a story that continues to surface in Europe. Wilson told me about this lowly soldier who submitted to medical experiments and went slowly mad from taking medications and herbs. He finds out his wife is unfaithful. He slits her throat and throws his knife in the lake, goes in after it and drowns, and then his child is raised by the village idiot. I said, 'OK, I'm in. You had me at "slit her throat."'" It was the fact that the play dealt with the working class that drew in Waits, who first heard of the story over eggs in Boston some years back.

The Waits songwriting team wrote the lyrics and composed the music while another collaborator, Wolfgang Wiens, adapted the splintered fragments of the play into a full-fledged work. The work progressed well, duly fleshed-out and realized in all of its entitled intensity. Remarked one journalist who witnessed the rehearsals: "By the end of the rehearsal period Büchner's *Woyzeck* was transformed into a mythical world interpretation that is even more abstract than the original, whose system of symbols is based on the interplay of the two elements representing male and female principles."

Woyzeck premiered at the Betty Nansen Theatre in Copenhagen, Denmark, on November 18, 2000. It toured throughout Europe in 2001 and 2002. For the first tour, the dialogue was spoken in Danish with Waits's songs sung in English. The second tour was entirely in English. The album, *Blood Money*, with songs from the production, was released in May 2002.

The same year, Waits decided to release his songs for the 1992 stage production of *Alice*. The original tapes, Waits told Margaret Moser of the *Austin Chronicle*, had been stolen:

> When we were doing the songs, all the tapes were in my briefcase. My car was broken into and someone stole the work tapes of the show. They realized they had something that might be worth some dough so they ransomed it, and I paid $3,000 to get it back. Not a lot of money, was it? I was a little insulted. . . . I think they wanted fast cash and no arguments. Along the line, the tapes got copied and the bootleg got out. At the time, I wasn't interested in recording anything at all. I was taking a break from the whole damn business, so it went south. The songs sat in a box, and I thought they were worth looking at again.

Alice was looked upon as the sister album of the darker and sinister *Blood Money*, an unintentional balancing of light and dark. Both featured compelling artwork on the cover reflecting in *Alice* the surreal meltdown of the play, and in *Blood Money* the blood-red internalization of a man gone mad with despair and delusion.

"Grimm's Reapers"
BlackBook
April 10, 2002 (issue date: June 2002)
Terry Gilliam

Set to release two new albums, *Alice* and *Blood Money*, legendary musician Tom Waits talks with visionary director Terry Gilliam. Carnivals, crows, and freak shows aside, they speak in tongues.

Terry Gilliam: How have you been, man?

Tom Waits: I've been OK, staying out of trouble.

TG: Why have you decided to be in competition with yourself?

TW: The reason no one does two records at the same time is that it's just too damn much work. It [was] really a question of making sure both of them had diverse textures and subject matter.

TG: Did you do them back-to-back, or did you swap between one to the other, back and forth?

TW: Back and forth, depending on how I was feeling. Most of the musicians drove up [on a] two-hour drive from San Francisco, and I instructed them that they were not allowed to listen to any music in the car on the way up, and I wanted them there by 10 A.M., so they were clean, you know? Their heads were clean. And we could start fresh. It's like actors . . . you know, you want people [who] will throw themselves down in the brook and drink with their hands.

TG: Yeah, these people have no shame; it's clear.

TW: You have to be able to melt yourself like candle wax and vanish into the picture.

TG: I'm just curious how you build those tracks. Does everyone play at the same time, and then you just start laying layers after that?

TW: Well, sometimes it comes out of the ground just like a potato, as you must realize yourself, and then other times you have to go in and use physics and math and finance and threatening remarks or embarrassing them.

TG: Do you actually arrange the parts and write them first?

TW: Well, I try to work with people who . . . will go anywhere, and then use meta-phor. . . . I go in with a certain number of experimental musical instruments. I try to use unusual sound sources, so that I'm putting on record things that may have never been used as an instrument before, and [songs] always get an unusual texture from that.

TG: That's what always gets me with your stuff. It gets my brain and parts of my body to vibrate differently. And it really thrills me—it scares me and thrills me at the same time, and it triggers all kinds of resonances in my own brain.

TW: Yeah. I like old records. I think what I like about old records is . . . the surface noise sometimes more than I like the music itself, or the two combined that creates some kind of a ghost. When you're listening to an old, scratchy recording of Caruso, it always sounds like he's trying to reach you from far away and you want to help him. You kind of lean into the speaker.

TG: [Your music] is exotic, even if it's talking about some shit-kicker in . . . in Missouri, somewhere in the country. Nineteenth-century Grimm's fairy tales are the things that keep coming to mind.

TW: Well, I'm flattered, Terry. I'm glad it penetrated your ears. Your films have taken me into another world for many years. I've seen [*The Adventures of*] *Baron Munchausen* probably—I don't know—probably fifty times. . . . Which I guess is a test of a good piece of work—that it can endure and grow with you, and you can continue to rediscover it, and it rediscovers you.

TG: I agree with you. I mean, whether it's a painting, a piece of music, a poem— it just keeps resonating.

TW: And, of course, I always love seeing a nun float by—and your relationship with little people. It's better than going to the circus!

TG: You're obviously obsessed with that, aren't you? Carnivals and circuses and freak shows?

TW: I think I ran away and joined the circus. I think that was what I wanted to do in music, and I guess at certain points I think we discovered that we have something peculiar . . . that makes us different.

TG: And no one is celebrating uniqueness—or bizarreness or weirdness or wonderfulness.

TW: I agree.

TG: I mean, I don't know how we bring that back and separate. I suppose we just keep doing what we do.

TW: I think the world looks like it's owned by three or four different cartels at this point, and it seems like eventually we're all going to be working for one or two of them.

TG: Who's [your] record company . . . Anti-?

TW: Epitaph is the name of the record company. And the group that I'm with is called Anti-. That's this collection of artists—Joe Strummer . . . Tricky . . . Merle Haggard.

TG: Right.

TW: So, it's an unusual place. It's a bit of an asylum for damaged artists, I think. Because it's also very just and sane and fair. You know, you take your suit to the cleaner's and you actually get your suit back.

TG: These are strange people to be working with [*laughs*].

TW: Are you sensitive to how the world collaborates with you . . . is it like *Fitzcarraldo*, where you're literally taking a boat over a mountain, or does the world want you to make the movie?

TG: Well, I'm not sure if the world wants me [to], but I think it's—I think I sort of believe in the platonic ideal of each film. It's up there pulling the strings, trying to make itself, and I become the hand that writes.

TW: I see.

TG: And it's purely that. And you find events start collaborating, mistakes . . . all sorts of things happen, and in most cases, [they] improve the film. I think the end result, I look at the stuff and I think, "Yeah. That's better because of the mistakes or the calamities that occurred."

TW: It's like life.

TG: I think that's right.

TW: My wife and I collaborated on all the songs, and we produced the record together, which was a feat unto itself. And we're still speaking to each other.

TG: I love collaborating. I mean, I have very firm ideas, but then, at a certain point, they kind of start boring me. With a collaborator, we can start leapfrogging. It gets much more exciting.

TW: Well, you want someone you can dig to China with, you know?

TG: All of your stuff, it always comes out as paintings or little films to me.

TW: Songs are movies for the ears or jewelry for the ears.

TG: What you do and hopefully what I do is we keep painting these pictures of the world, and hopefully one or two people notice that that is in fact what is going on around them. Because I find we're fighting the other forces. Whether it's publicity, advertising, movies—normal movies—which are so busy painting a completely fraudulent picture of the world.

TW: There's a battle going on all the time between the light and the dark. And I wonder sometimes whether the dark side doesn't have one more spear.

TG: Because the dark side—they present it as lightness and fun and entertainment.

TW: And that's the flimflam.

TG: Yeah! Flimflam is exactly what it's about. Everybody says my stuff is dark, and they probably say your stuff is dark, and I don't think it is. I think it's closer to the light than what is being presented out there.

TW: The tail has been wagging the dog for a long time now.

TG: Sometimes I listen to your stuff and I don't even know what the words are—I just know the sounds.

TW: Well, sometimes that's how they began. And then slowly the words were evolved out of the sounds. In fact, that one song, "Kommienezuspadt," is a completely invented language. And there's something thrilling about spending almost four minutes with the confidence of a language that you're discovering a word at a time.

TG: It's interesting that you've done an *Alice* because one of the projects I'm working on now is from a book called *Tideland*, written by a guy who lives out in Tucson. . . . It's about an eleven-year-old girl who is an Alice of sorts, whose parents are junkies. And she ends up with her father who is—well, we find out later—has been sitting there dead for some time. And she starts creating a world around her in a similar way. I've always been drawn to the Alice story because [Lewis Carroll] inverts the world all the time, and it's the power of that little child.

TW: Well, it sounds . . . wonderful—it sounds almost like a Grimm fairy tale.

TG: When I get this *Tideland* thing off the ground . . . I keep thinking of you. I've been thinking about you for quite a while on this one.

TW: Well, I'm ready.

TG: I'm looking down at [lyrics I've written] here and I keep seeing things like, "On the porch, geese salute." Is that the way the lyrics go?

TW: Oh no. That's even better. "In a Portuguese saloon." But I like that better. I'm going to write that down. [*Terry repeats as Tom writes*]

TG: What makes me crazy is that surrealism has been completely prostituted—it's used for advertising and selling shit now.

TW: I know. I hate that.

TG: It has no content anymore. It has a lot of the imagery but none of the content. [Crows] keep appearing in these albums a lot.

TW: Oh, crows. Well, crows are the teenagers of the bird world. And they say the trouble with crows is that by nine o'clock they've done all their work and they've got too much time on their hands. And they will spend the rest of the day playing a primitive form of rugby. Or playing keep off the nest. Or they'll sit and yap and chat. And they've discovered that there's no biological reason for this . . . but a crow will sit on an anthill until he's completely engulfed by the ants within and be in an almost hypnotic state during the sitting. They said that the only answer they can come up with is that it's pleasure for them. That it's a form of drug abuse.

TG: I'll bet!

TW: And their eyes roll back in their head and they tip their head up to the sky. They said it's part of a crow's destiny, because they've got the largest brain in proportion to their bodies of any bird and they have a lot of time on their hands. It's inevitable there'd be a descent into drugs [*both laugh*].

TG: That's quite wonderful.

TW: Have you ever eaten crow?

TG: No. Is it good?

TW: I haven't either. Well, I have—symbolically. A pretty steady diet of it for a number of years.

TG: Yeah. It keeps me healthy [*both laugh*].

Tom Waits on making sounds:
Excerpted from **"Never One for the Conventional,"** *Inpress* and *X-Press*
May 2, 2002
James Nicholas Joyce

James Nicholas Joyce: The music for *Alice* is now nine years old. Has it changed a lot?

Tom Waits: No, it's all the same stuff. It's like giving away a box of clothes and then you get them back. Hey, those pants, I like those pants, that shirt. I always liked that shirt. I never really recorded them, we just did rough demos and then you give the songs to someone else to do. And they either do them in a delight-ful way or they particularly butcher them and you're not having much say one way or another about it. [. . .] I was glad to get them back. I had forgotten I liked the tunes. My wife had been dripping on me for years, let's record those, there's some good tunes, baby. [. . .]

JJ: Has the fact that you've encountered your audience on tour changed anything in your music?

TW: I appreciate having an audience: it's kind of shocking sometimes. Like this group in Warsaw that wouldn't leave the theater, and I was already back at the hotel getting ready for bed. They were just screaming and stomping and I was like, what do we do? Isn't the evening over? Or do we go back and play more? That was an odd kind of moment, a tribute, I guess. They wanted to hang out and be in the place where it happened, that was cool. [. . .]

JJ: People feel this really strong link between you and the songs. Do you think that leads them to feel a certain closeness to you that isn't given?

TW: Well, I guess, because songs are these vessels, containers of emotional infor-mation. It's like getting a letter from me, maybe. It's understandable. [. . .]
   I like to use my voice like a drum, you know. [. . .] I'm always making sounds for the sake of making sounds. Before you have words you just make sounds. In fact as soon as you make any kind of sound, you've got music, really. In

the beginning there was the word. So you've got this kind of [*begins to chant*] *deshaggabon, deshaggabon, deshaggabon, deshaggabon, deshaggabon, deshaggabon, deshaggabon,* you've got something right there. [. . .] Whatever the hell a *deshaggabon* is. I don't know and I don't give a crap.

JJ: It's like kids' talk.

TW: They make the best songs. Nobody makes better songs than kids.

JJ: And they have intrinsic rhythm. But they lose it.

TW: Yeah, right. Then we lose it. We're born knowing everything. And our whole life is a process of forgetting everything.

Russell Bongard calls *Big Brother* "the best and stupidest skateboarding magazine of all time." He was a regular contributor for seven years. "I'm not really sure how, but I ended up as sort of a music editor for a while. My paychecks were signed by Larry Flynt."

"Tom Waits"
Big Brother
May 2002 (issue date: July 2002)
Russell Bongard

Tom Waits is fun to talk to. He has the kind of voice that would sound like anyone's voice who just swallowed a mouthful of broken glass and was trying to wash it down with a glass of cobra venom. He agreed to this interview because his son, Casey, is a fan of the magazine. When the publicist found out I would be doing the interview, she got very disappointed because she thought she had made it very clear that Casey would very much like to have his father talking to the one and only Dave Carnie, who he thinks is just peachy. Dave gave me the interview because he thinks that publicists are smelly and does not care to be anyone's peach.

Russell Bongard: What do you know about *Big Brother*?

Tom Waits: Oh, my boy reads the magazine. He's sixteen.

RB: Are you aware of the contents of this magazine, sir?

TW: You mean there's things in there I'd have no idea about?

RB: It is full of naughty articles. A potty-mouthed-based magazine, if you will. It definitely encourages a lot of pooing.

TW: You mean you're giving me an opportunity to jump ship right now?

RB: No. I just wanted you to know about the types of things your child has been reading.

TW: Well, then from now on he'll only be able to look at it from across the room. But to be honest with you, I've had people call me and criticize the magazine for some of its content. But I realize that boys will be boys.

RB: So you've been telling all your friends that you're going to do a *Big Brother* interview?

TW: Oh, yeah, everybody knows.

RB: But isn't your son the same kid who once mentioned something about digging up someone's corpse and using the teeth to make jewelry?

TW: Well, you know, the way I look at it is that when you're sixteen, lots of things pass through your mind, but I think he has an adequate filtering system.

RB: OK, speaking of sixteen-year-olds, have you been watching *The Osbournes* these days?

TW: You know, I haven't seen it because I don't have a TV.

RB: They had six million viewers last week tune in to watch that old man.

TW: I don't know what to say about that. The only thing I can think of is why would you want to submit your whole family to something like that?

RB: Well, it's MTV. It's like the education network.

TW: But a man has to value his privacy. If you don't know where to draw the line, then you won't have any life at all. Now, why he'd want to do that, I can't imagine, unless he's on medication.

RB: Well, he's the same guy that snorted a line of ants off the rim of a swimming pool if that's any indication. Have you ever met him?

TW: Yeah, I've met Ozzy.

RB: Is he cool?

TW: Oh, he's a gentleman. Very informed. Well mannered. Never says bad words. We've discussed mostly physics and high finance, so go figure. He's not the guy you think he is. I actually met him over at Nic Cage's house.

RB: Speaking of Nic Cage, I understand that you're friends with him. Does he take your advice?

TW: I can't be absolutely sure of that.

RB: Well, this is just my opinion and the opinion of a million other people, and that is that he needs some good advice from a close friend on picking better roles these days.

TW: He's made a lot of great pictures.

RB: I agree, but it's his choices lately. I mean *Captain Corelli's Mandolin* versus *Wild at Heart*? I mean, c'mon. That is not the same person.

TW: Easy, easy. There are many rooms in the house of madness, you know? Enter them all, son, before you finish.

RB: I suppose I can't argue with that. OK, so you're releasing two new albums this month, *Alice* and *Blood Money*, correct?

TW: That is correct. I got tired of carrying all those folks around in my head without paying rent, so I said, go out there and make Dad some money.

RB: That's very Guns N' Roses of you. Are you going to tour at all?

TW: I'm not up for that.

RB: I'm not either. When was the last time you had a booger on your sleeve?

TW: Is that one of Larry's questions?

RB: No, he was out tuning up the golden wheelchair when I came up with that one.

TW: Did you know that the male spider, after he strings three strands on his web, goes off to the side and reaches out with one leg and strums them? The sound that it makes attracts the female spider.

RB: No, I didn't know that. Is the sound recordable? Because if anyone can do it, it's you.

TW: Well, we can only imagine and dream what the sound might be like.

RB: Seductive, I'm sure.

TW: Well, isn't that what we're all doing? Putting out mating calls?

RB: Do you think that was what Frito-Lay was thinking when they messed with you a while back?

TW: Oh, right. That was a long time ago. Yeah, we nailed 'em. It was David and Goliath.

RB: I heard the numbers were quite astronomical at the end of the day.

TW: Well, they should be when you bring down a big cartel. They were lame. The problem with a big company like that is that its hands don't talk to its feet, and nobody knows what anyone else is doing. In this case, it was an ad agency that hired a fan of mine actually, in Texas. And they paid him like sixty bucks to come in and do an impersonation of me. Then, a little later, I was doing a radio interview, and the guy says we have to break for a commercial, so he punches that ad in.

RB: I'm sure that was an early-morning wake-up call for you.

TW: Well, yeah, I said that guy sounds just like me. I mean, there's a lot of things I can't remember, but I think I would have remembered doing that. I had an excellent attorney that went to bat for us.

RB: What is your recipe for a gravelly voice?

TW: Well, my son, you scream nightly into a pillow.

RB: Tell me a story about Frank Zappa.

TW: Well, I was just starting out, and I was his opening act for a few years. It was a difficult gig because I had to come out into a chrome forest of equipment at rodeos and hockey arenas by myself, prior to Frank, and if you've ever been to a Frank show, you know that he has rabid fans that want red meat. So Frank would refer to me as "the rectal thermometer." I was the one who had to go out before Frank and basically take the temperature of the crowd.

RB: When did your problems with Korean people begin?

TW: Are you trying to get me in trouble?

RB: No! I heard that there was a press release put out by someone in the Korean government stating that your albums were inflammatory and that basically you are no longer welcome in their land. So what did you do to them?

TW: Hey, I'm hearing about it for the first time.

RB: Stay out of Korea, I'm warning you.

TW: Did you realize that mosquito repellents don't actually repel? They hide you. The spray blocks the mosquito's sensors. They don't even know that you're there.

"Tom Waits"
A.V. Club
May 29, 2002
Keith Phipps

Tom Waits was born on December 7, 1949, in the back of a truck (or a taxi, depending on which account, if any, is to believed) in the Los Angeles suburb of Pomona. True or not, it's an appropriate origin for a man whose music contains so much transience and questionable sanitary conditions. Waits began performing Beat-inspired songs in clubs around the time he reached legal drinking age, though his gravelly voice seemed incongruous with his youth. Experience and albums followed, as he became a sort of hipster outsider cousin to the 1970s California music scene. After meeting frequent collaborator Kathleen Brennan, who eventually became his wife, Waits adopted a more experimental approach only suggested by his previous work. His cluttered, clamoring new style, first fully developed on 1983's *Swordfishtrombones*, led him to a new audience and a new label. Around the same time, Waits began curbing the lifestyle detailed in his gutter-trolling songs, tried his hand at acting, and found new collaborators, most notably director Jim Jarmusch and Robert Wilson, a longtime fixture of avant-garde theater. After a six-year silence following 1993's *The Black Rider*, Waits returned with *Mule Variations*, then disappeared again. From a carefully guarded location somewhere in rural California, Waits spoke to the *Onion A.V. Club* shortly after the simultaneous May release of *Alice* and *Blood Money*, both soundtracks to Wilson works.

Keith Phipps: When you do theatrical projects, do you worry at all about them translating to albums?

Tom Waits: Gee, I don't know. What do you think? How did it go? I don't think it really matters much. I mean, by the time it's a record, it's just a record. It either works in that way or it doesn't. I don't think the backstory really dignifies anything, or solves any problems that you tried to solve during the recording. "Oh, this is all based on the John Wilkes Booth story, and that third song is when he was trapped in the barn." I mean, I could tell you anything. "Helen Keller made an appearance in the last tune, and it's sung by her mother." "Oh, OK." Your mind will make sense of anything. The fact that *Blood Money* is about Woyzeck . . . I didn't know anything about *Woyzeck*. Kathleen knew more than I, but I didn't really know the story or anything. I was just told the story in a coffee shop in Boston over eggs a few years ago. You try to create some sort of counterpoint for this story, but you're still dealing with song logic. When people listen to songs, they're not. . . . It's like a form of hypnotism that goes on during the listening process, so you're taking it up through a straw. It's like a separate little world in the world. You go in there and then you pop back out. Those musicals always sound so corny when somebody stops and thinks of something and goes back to life.

KP: You've said before that the stories behind songs are less interesting than the songs themselves. Have you ever written a song where the opposite was true?

TW: Oh, gee. I don't know. Most songs have meager beginnings. You wake up in the morning, you throw on your suspenders, and you subvocalize and just think. They seem to form like calcium. I can't think of a story right off the bat that was that interesting. I write things on the back of my hand, usually, and sing into a tape recorder. I don't know.

KP: Many of your albums are filled with references to sailors and the sea. Do you think there's a reason for that, beyond growing up in San Diego?

TW: I think all songs should have weather in them. Names of towns and streets, and they should have a couple of sailors. I think those are just song prerequisites [*laughs*].

KP: For yours, or for all songs?

TW: Oh, all songs. Most of them fail miserably. I go looking in other people's songs for their sailors and their towns. I don't know, everybody has things that they gravitate toward. Some people put toy cars or clouds or cat crap. Everybody puts something different, and it's entirely up to you what belongs and what doesn't. They're interesting little vessels of emotional information, and you carry them in your pocket like a bagel.

KP: When *Mule Variations* came out, it seemed like the first question most people had for you was, "What took you so long?" Does that annoy you?

TW: Well, I submitted myself to the questions, so it's hard to be annoyed. But, yeah, when people want to know what you've been up to, how can you possibly explain to a stranger what you've been doing for seven years? Would they truly be interested? [*laughs*]

KP: It seems artists with a devoted following are under pressure to turn out albums regularly. Does that pressure ever get to you?

TW: Not really. It's not like I'm one of those expensive, high-powered pop groups on the road eight months out of the year, talking to *Teen Beat*. I finally discovered that my life is more important than show business. But, yeah, people are curious about all kinds of things, which takes your mind off that which is really important. They usually ask questions about things that don't matter to them, or to me, or to anybody else. Just to take up time, I guess, and distract them from the important questions, like "Who won the World Series in 1957?" or "Who said, 'Today you will play jazz, tomorrow you will betray your country'?"

KP: Is there an answer to that one?

TW: It was on a Soviet propaganda poster in the '30s. Did you know that honey is the only food that won't spoil? They found it in King Tut's tomb. Jars of honey. They said it was just as fresh as it was on the first day.

KP: Did they actually try it?

TW: They tried it, yeah. Wouldn't you? If you found a jar of honey in a thousands-of-years-old tomb, would you put your finger into it and taste it?

KP: So, why did it take you so long to record the songs on *Alice*?

TW: The songs were written around '92 or '93, 'round in there. It was done with Robert Wilson in Germany. We stuck 'em in a box and just left 'em there for a while. They were aging like the honey. And we locked in the freshness. They were hermetically sealed. You move on to other things, you know? And then you go back and say, "Well, this was OK."

KP: It was kind of developing a reputation as the great lost Tom Waits album.

TW: I bought a copy of the bootleg on eBay. 'Cause I didn't know where those tapes were.

KP: How does the bootleg hold up?

TW: OK. There was stuff that didn't make it onto the record.

KP: How many songs are usually left over on any given record?

TW: Oh, there's always a bunch of them that don't make the boat. That's normal. You just stick 'em all together later and put 'em out by themselves. Those *Alice* songs were all in a briefcase that got stolen out of the back of my car, and they were ransomed by these radicals who thought they really had something. We had to pay a couple grand to get the briefcase back, but I think they copied the tapes.

KP: What was the exchange like? Did you get to meet them somewhere?

TW: Yeah, some dark café, you know, everybody was wearing sunglasses, it was really cold. They said, "We're gonna leave the briefcase by the trash can. Put the money in a bag. . . ." It added a little intrigue to the whole project.

KP: What's your collaborative process like with Kathleen Brennan?

TW: [*chuckles*] Oh! Well, you know, "You wash, I'll dry." It all comes down to making choices and a lot of decisions. You know, are we gonna do a song about a cruise ship, or a meadow, or a brothel, or . . . just a rhapsody, or is it a parlor song or a work song or a field holler? What is it? The form itself is like a Jell-O mold. It's like doing anything that you would do with someone. "You hold it right there while I hit it," or the other way around. You find a rhythm in the way of working. I trust her opinion above all else. You've gotta have somebody to trust, that knows a lot. She's done a lot of things. I'm Ingrid Bergman and she's Bogart. She's got a pilot's license, and she was gonna be a nun before we got married. I put an end to that. She knows about everything from motorcycle repair to high finance, and she's an excellent pianist. One of the leading authorities on the African violet. She's a lot of strong material. She's like Superwoman, standing there with her cape flapping. It works. We've been at this for some time now. Sometimes you quarrel, and it's the result of irritation, and sometimes it comes out of the ground like a potato and we marvel at it. She doesn't like the spotlight. She's a very private person, as opposed to myself [*laughs*].

KP: You have kind of developed a reputation as a recluse. Does that bother you?

TW: Hell, no. I think that's a good one. It wards off strangers. It's like being a beekeeper. No, if people are a little nervous about approaching you at the market, it's good. I'm not Chuckles the Clown. Or Bozo. I don't cut the ribbon at the opening of markets. I don't stand next to the mayor. Hit your baseball into my yard, and you'll never see it again. I just have a close circle of friends and loved ones—the circle of trust, as they say.

KP: There's actually a section on your website about fans who have spotted or encountered you in public. Do you have a problem going out?

TW: I go where I feel like. Funny little story . . . I drove on a field trip once, to a guitar factory, to show all these little kids how to make guitars. So we're standing there, and I'm looking around, and folks are looking over at me, and I'm just waiting for someone to recognize me—you know, "Hey, aren't you that music guy? That singer guy?" Nobody. Nothing. We're there for, like, two hours, watching them put the frets on and all that, and I'm waiting and waiting. . . . A week later, I took the same group of kids on a field trip to the dump, and as I pulled up, don't ask me how, but my truck was surrounded by people that wanted an autograph. It was a dump, for Christ's sake. I guess everybody knows me at the dump.

KP: It kind of proves that you never know who your audience is.

TW: You don't really know. I guess one should not even assume that one has an audience, and allow it to go to your head.

KP: Your early stuff is influenced by the Beats, and your later stuff seems equally influenced by older, harder-to-define influences. Do you think you're slipping further back into the past as you get older?

TW: I don't know. I hope I'm not slipping at all.

KP: I don't mean that in a negative sense. I mean, do you think you're drawing on older influences as you get older?

TW: I really don't know. What you rely on . . . I think you kind of take the world apart and put it back together. The further you get from something, the better your memory is of it, sometimes. Who knows how that works? Those are big questions about the nature of memory and its influence on your present life. I don't know. Consider this: The number of cars on the planet is increasing three times faster than the population growth. Three times faster. I mean, there's eleven and a half million cars in Los Angeles alone.

KP: What are you driving these days?

TW: Oh, I got a beautiful 1959 Cadillac Coupe de Ville four-door. No one will ride in it with me.

KP: Why's that?

TW: It's unsafe. But it looks good. I take it to the dump. We spend a lot of time in our cars. You know what I really love? The CD players in a car. How when you put the CD right up by the slot, it actually takes it out of your hand, like it's hungry. It pulls it in, and you feel like it wants more silver discs. "More silver discs. Please." I enjoy that.

KP: Do you have one in the Cadillac?

TW: No, I have a little band in there. It's an old car, so I have a little old string band in the glove compartment. It's grumpy.

KP: You used a lot of unusual instruments on these albums. Can you tell me about any of them? I was intrigued by the Stroh violin [a violin with a trumpetlike bell attached to it].

TW: Well, you know, there were Stroh basses, and there were Stroh violas, Stroh cellos. Have you ever seen one?

KP: No, I don't think so.

TW: It's a horn attached to the bridge, and it has a hinge on it. It's like a brass flower designed in the same configuration or shape as the old 78 players. You could aim it at the balcony. The string players were disgruntled. They felt they were constantly competing with the brass. It gave 'em a little edge. I don't know, you don't hear it anymore. I guess because before the advent of amplification, you were dealing purely with physics all the time. It's an interesting solution to that problem.

KP: Are there any instruments that you've wanted to use that you haven't had a chance to yet?

TW: Well, we tried to find a theremin for *Alice*, but we were unable to find anyone locally that was really accomplished. The woman that played in the original *Alice* orchestra we found was the granddaughter of Léon Theremin. She was really amazing. You would imagine someone like that would have some really sophisticated instrument, but she brought this thing that looked like a hot plate with a car aerial coming out of it. She opened it up, and inside, all the connections between the circuits were established with cut-up little pieces of beer can wrapped around the wires. All the paint was worn off, but when she played it, it was like Jascha Heifetz. They're doing experiments with the theremin now. The sound waves you experience when you play it have therapeutic value.

KP: How so?

TW: I don't know, just the fact that you don't touch it—that you play the air and you're in contact with the waves—somehow does something to you on a more genetic level, and can heal the sick. Raise the dead. Apparently. You know the average person spends two weeks over their lifetime waiting for the traffic light to change?

KP: Really? I would actually guess a little more.

TW: I would guess more, too. I'm thinking, two weeks, you know . . .

KP: That sounds like a bargain.

TW: During your whole lifetime, though. You know mosquito repellents don't actually repel anything? They actually hide you because they block the mosquito's sensors. They don't know that you're there. It's like blinding them.

KP: It used to be that, like you, a lot of musicians took a hard-line stance against having their music used in advertising. That seems to have shifted. Why do you think that is?

TW: I don't know. They're all high on crack. Let's just say it's a sore subject with me. I went to court over it, you know. . . . You know, you see a bathroom-tissue commercial, and you start hearing "Let the Good Times Roll," and the paper thing's rolling down the stairs. Why would anybody want to mortify and humiliate themselves? Well, it's just business, you know? The memory that you have and the association you have with that song can be co-opted. And a lot of people are really in it for the money. Period. A lot of people don't have any control over it. I don't own the copyrights to my early tunes. So it is unfortunate, but there are a lot of people that consciously want their songs exploited in that way, which I think is demeaning. I hate it when I hear songs that I already have a connection with, used in a way that's humiliating. I mean, in the old days, if somebody was doing a commercial, you used to say, "Oh, gee, too bad, he probably needs the money." But now, it's like hocking cigarettes and underwear with rock 'n' roll. I guess that's our big export. It's like how a good butcher uses every part of the cow. I don't like hearing those Beatles songs in the commercials. It almost renders them useless. Maybe not for everyone else, but when I hear it I just think, "Oh, God, another one bites the dust."

KP: I still can't hear "Good Vibrations" without thinking of Sunkist.

TW: Oh, wow, yeah. That's exactly what they want. They want to plug your head into that and change the circuitry. While you're dreaming about your connection with that song, why don't you think about soda or candy or something? It's too bad, but it's the way of the world. They love to get their meat-hooks in you.

KP: Your kids are old enough to have their own musical tastes now. Do you approve of what they listen to?

TW: Oh, sure, yeah. As long as they're listening. You know, what happens is that as you start getting older, you get out of touch. I'm like a turtleneck sweater. And then your kids kind of enlighten you: "Dad, have you heard Blackalicious?" I take 'em to the show, but I drop them off. I'm not allowed to go in. It'd be too embarrassing.

KP: Do you have a favorite cover version of one of your songs?

TW: Johnny Cash did a song called "Down There by the Train"; Solomon Burke did one. But, you know, cover versions are good. I used to bark about it, and then

I said, "Oh, it's good." If you write songs, you really do kind of want someone to hear it and say, "Hey, man, I could do that." So if they're not doing your songs, you wonder, "Why aren't they doing my songs?" If it's too individual, too personal, then it can't be reimagined.

KP: What's the most outrageous lie you've ever told a reporter?

TW: That I'm a medical doctor.

KP: Did the reporter buy it?

TW: I started talking anatomy with the guy, and I think I strung him along pretty good for a while. But then I realized . . . he told me his dad was a doctor, and he tripped me up on something. I mispronounced "femur" or something. I do like books on anatomy. I have to say I'm an amateur physician, I guess.

KP: You've never practiced?

TW: I practice at home, on the kids. Interestingly enough, there are a lot of musicians who are also doctors, or a lot of doctors who are also musicians. There is a connection. Surgeons work in a theater, and they call it a theater. All medical procedures require two hands, so in a sense it's like when you play an instrument. That's what they call things that they use in their work: they call them instruments. I've played with a lot of musicians who are also doctors. I worked with a bass player who was a doctor. You know, I suppose there is a connection. A lot of people start out majoring in medicine and drop it and change their major to music. I don't know, it's just one of those things.

KP: Any last words for our readers?

TW: Famous last words? Lemme think here. All right, here we go. Um . . . I'm looking down my list. Never have I waltzed to "My Country 'Tis of Thee," nor met anyone who did. Still, it's a waltz, for it's written in waltz time.

"The Hobo Comes Home"
The Australian
June 2, 2002
Iain Shedden

Tom Waits is making a pot of soup. "Chicken," he says in his familiar growl, before going in search of cutlery. "I'll be right with you. It's dinnertime around here."

Domestic routine is hardly the picture one forms at the mention of Waits; rather, you imagine a dimly lit diner with some old hobo in the corner, or a wino in fingerless gloves shuffling along a back alley. Or, of course, a finely turned out figure sitting at the piano, gargling gravel and crooning sumptuous vignettes that portray America's seedy underbelly. That's Waits the musician, but, of course, there's also Waits the actor, exquisitely portraying trailer trash in Robert Altman's 1993 film *Short Cuts* or the world-weary con on the run in Jim Jarmusch's *Down by Law* (1986). There's also Waits the theater composer, collaborating with renowned stage director Robert Wilson.

All of these form the Waits curriculum vitae of the past thirty years or so. The fiction of his seedy-side songs even blends into reality, since much of his early material, fuelled by drunks, dames, and fellow nighthawks, was a portrait of the artist as a young desperado, following in the footsteps of Kerouac and Ginsberg and developing his poetic view of the world from the bottom of a bottle.

Nowadays there's not much left of the method muso. At fifty-two he no longer feels the need to live it as he writes it. He doesn't drink, rarely tours, has cut down the acting and enjoys a relatively quiet lifestyle in the remote town of Santa Rosa, 100 km north of San Francisco. This he shares with his wife and muse, Kathleen Brennan, and their three children, Kellesimone, eighteen; Casey, sixteen; and Sullivan, eight.

The Waits legend, however, lives on, and the success of his album *Mule Variations* (1999) has kept his name in the adult contemporary racks of CD stores worldwide. He and Brennan have now produced two additions to the catalog—*Blood Money* and *Alice*—that flow freely with the romantic, the dysfunctional, the lovelorn, and the world-weary; characters as vivid as any from his classic albums such as *Swordfishtrombones* (1983), *Rain Dogs* (1985), and *Franks Wild Years* (1987).

Those 1980s Beat music masterpieces are the benchmark of a genre that Waits pretty much invented, taking elements of blues, jazz, ragtime, and vaudeville and mixing it into a hotchpotch of bourbon-soaked storytelling.

The story continues. *Blood Money* and *Alice* were recorded at the same sessions last year and released simultaneously on May 6. The latter, however, has a longer history. It dates back to 1992, when much of the material formed the backdrop to the stage play *Alice*, American writer and director Wilson's avant-garde take on the Lewis Carroll classics *Alice's Adventures in Wonderland* and *Through the Looking-Glass*.

Waits's songs, such as "Lost in the Harbour," "We're All Mad Here," and the title track, are reflective of Wilson's cracked perspective on the classic children's tales. The pair's collaboration formed the basis of Waits's 1993 album *The Black Rider* and the trilogy is completed by *Blood Money*, based on their adaptation of the Georg Büchner play *Woyzeck*, which ran in Europe two years ago. It is more of a bleak study of hopelessness, with titles such as "Misery Is the River of the World" and "Everything Goes to Hell" setting the tone.

"They're completely different, unique collections of songs," he says. "*Blood Money* is perhaps a little rougher. *Alice* is more like taking a pill, I guess. They're completely different trips, but they both pretty much came out of the oven at the same time." The kitchen appliance wins the battle of these mixed metaphors, diverting him back to the soup at hand. "Sorry, got to get myself organized," he says.

As with his cooking, Waits has always taken a lengthy, some would say perfectionist, approach to recording.

"It's a lot of work, but by the time you're done . . . you'll never listen to it as many times or as closely as when you're working on it," he says. "You have to be in a certain frame of mind. It's like acting. You have to be making certain choices about how to approach the song. Sometimes it's hard to know when you're done."

"When they take it away from you," he reasons, "that's when you're done."

Interviewing Waits is a notoriously fickle affair. He is famous for deflecting questions with frivolous—if inventive—answers, or for simply not saying very much at all. Today he sounds mildly distracted but comes around to the idea of talking about himself, starting with the present.

"I find it easier now," he goes on. "I'm not as fussy." About writing, performing, acting? "About anything," he declares. "I think that everybody likes music but what you really want is music to like you. So . . . there you have it."

O-kaay . . .

"People who make up songs . . . the stuff you usually like the most is the stuff that refreshes you, the new stuff. Some songs you know right away that you'll never sing it again, others you know that thirty years down the road you'll still be trying to figure out what it means."

With *Mule Variations* the focus of his attention turned in part to the everyday, hidden eccentricities of middle America, particularly on songs such as "What's He Building," "House Where Nobody Lives," and "Hold On." The topics—and the tunes—touched a nerve. "Folks seemed to like it and I was happy about that," he says. "But I wasn't able to predict that. Some of it was to do with the fact that I hadn't recorded for a while and I had a new label."

He describes songs—his and everybody else's—as "just like people you hang out with. Some you hear once and throw them away."

Few American songwriters have drawn such colorful scenarios into the space of a three- or four-minute song. There's this gem, for example, from "Shore Leave" on *Swordfishtrombones*: "and so I slopped at the corner on cold chow mein / and shot billiards with a midget until the rain stopped / and I bought a long-sleeved shirt with horses on the front / and some gum and a lighter and a knife / and a new deck of cards (with girls on the back) and I sat down and wrote a letter to my wife."

"You just take it one step in front of the other . . . then you're up, then you're over, then you're in," he says, oversimplifying the procedure with a chuckle. "I like songs that have weather in them, and the names of towns and names of people. Then you can get a fire going, maybe a bite to eat . . . so, you got weather, you got wind, you got animals . . . it's all jewelry for the ears."

Tom Waits was born in Pomona, California, on December 7, 1949, and moved to National City when his parents divorced ten years later. The striking image that has stuck with him throughout his music and film career was forged in San Diego, where he worked as a doorman at a club in the late 1960s. He would jump up on stage to perform between the regular acts and attracted further attention at talent nights in a club called the Troubadour in Los Angeles. A recording deal with Asylum soon followed and with albums such as his debut, *Closing Time* (1973), and *The Heart of Saturday Night* (1974), Waits began putting together the elements that would serve him for so long.

It was in the 1980s, however, that the real turning point came. Switching record labels to Island and producing the album trilogy based loosely on the character of Frank in *Franks Wild Years*, Waits also discovered the art of writing music for film. Director Francis Ford Coppola invited him to write for his movie *One from the Heart*, released in 1982. The experience also led to him meeting his wife, [Kathleen] Brennan, who was a script editor at Coppola's Zoetrope Studios.

The writing discipline further developed his talent for creating vivid images with music. However, he believes there is plenty of license in fitting music to drama. "My theory is . . . if you were watching *The John Wilkes Booth Story* and all of a sudden you heard "Abeline" or "Crazy" or "I'm Forever Blowing Bubbles" or "We're in the Money," you'd make sense out of it, wouldn't you? That's the mind's job—to wrap yourself around it and make sense out of it. You try to have some idea in mind by juxtaposing, you know, a meadow with a brothel and a Cadillac and a rainstorm, but the people who perceive it are going to have their own interpretation and understanding of it. I don't deem it necessary that I be too specific because you want to leave room for your own ideas."

Waits's most recent film contribution was to last year's *Big Bad Love*, starring Debra Winger, which hasn't been released in Australia. He began his acting career in 1978 in the Sylvester Stallone film *Paradise Alley* and gained plaudits in the 1980s for starring roles in *Down by Law* and *Ironweed*, among others. In the '90s he garnered further acclaim in Altman's ensemble piece *Short Cuts* and for his brief portrayal of the insane would-be vampire R. M. Renfield in the screen adaptation of *Bram Stoker's Dracula*. Now acting is on the back burner, prompted, he says in jest, by his "classic" Renfield.

"Once you've played Renfield, they want you to be that," he says. "I had somebody tell me: 'Tom, it was really a mistake playing Renfield, man. You'll never come back from that.' What do you do for an encore?"

If there's suggestion of typecasting in his film work, there's also no escaping the fact that people have grown to expect a certain style from his music. "You mean if I don't give it to them they won't buy it?"

Well, yes.

"No. If I did disco or parlor songs or anything, it wouldn't matter. I don't feel chained to anybody's affectations of what they think I should do. I'm in a unique position. I pretty much do what I want. I'm not like the Backstreet Boys or anything. I don't have to live up to selling twenty-six million records, so that if I sell seventeen million I'm a failure."

This mention of the boy-band phenomenon betrays his disaffection with the mainstream music industry. "There are a lot of people who are in it for the money," he says. "There are record companies that are like behemoth cartels. They're like countries themselves. But that could be said of anything." You roll your own, is the Waits philosophy.

If record companies get up his nose, his worldview, somewhat prevalent in *Blood Money*, is even more despairing. "It feels like the whole world's on fire right now," he says, getting on a roll. "We're going downhill fast. It makes you wonder about what you're doing and whether it has anything to do with the rest of the world. It's a time for great men to step forward. I think we're all waiting for men of vision and passion to come forward and sit around a table and solve these problems."

We'll probably never see Waits in Australia again. He last appeared here in 1981, but the chances of a return are on the other side of slim. He no longer tours the United States (performing only in Los Angeles and New York for these albums), so will not be pressed into long-haul travel.

"Besides, I've got my ice sculptures to worry about," he says, throwing a curveball. I rise to it, almost, but I think better of it.

"It takes a lot to light a fire under me," he goes on. "I'm not going to tour but I'll do a few dates here and there. Living in hotels? Eating slop? Sleeping in the car? I don't know. I don't like it as much as I used to."

As long as his voice holds up, however, he'll keep making records.

"Well, whatya thinkin' of doin'?" he groans when I suggest otherwise. "I got Frank Sinatra's throat specialist. He said: 'You're doing everything right. Don't change a thing.' I figure if it's good enough for Frank, it's good enough for me."

"We're All Mad Here"
ANTI- Electronic Press Kit
June 13, 2002
Robert Lloyd

Robert Lloyd: Tom!

Tom Waits: Robert.

RL: Thanks for asking us into your house.

TW: [*laughs*]

RL: It's a rare treat!

TW: [*laughs*] You know, well, a lot of room. You know when you keep emus you know, you gotta have a lot of room.

RL: That's probably the cause of the lack of furniture.

TW: [*laughs*] Exactly! They'll eat anything, you know?

RL: Eh, we're here because you're putting out records. You're putting them out faster than anyone can believe. You're kinda like Greta Garbo.

TW: "Leave me alone," yeah.

RL: Yeah. Now you're putting out two records at once.

TW: Well, you know people complain when there's too much time between records. And then they complain when there's too many. The public is tickled. I can't be responsible for their feelings, I mean.

RL: So, is this a provocation?

TW: Well, you know, the idea of the two records is that you got the stove heated up and you might as well make more than one pancake because . . .

RL: People might be coming over.

TW: How often do you cook? You know? So you might as well make enough for the whole gang.

RL: Right, the whole gang. Today in your house here, you've been singing a song about God being away on business. Why is he away?

TW: I don't know, it's hard to say. It's song logic, you know. I don't know. Perhaps he's away indefinitely. Perhaps he was never here. You know, there are two different schools of thought on that I guess.

RL: And you called his office and got a message?

TW: [*laughs*] Yeah, well, no. It's just, eh, one of those things you say in order to explain the way that you feel in metaphor. I guess. It feels sometimes in the world that God is away on business and he's not coming back.

RL: And apparently he's left emus in charge.

TW: [*laughs*] He's been known to do that. You know he'll put an emu in the front office as a receptionist and a couple down there in the stockroom.

RL: Now I understand that emus are closely related, barely a fall, from the dinosaur. Is that true?

TW: They're direct descendants, yeah. You know scales are really feathers. Before they were feathers. If you look at a scale you can tell. It's about to become a feather. In about two million years. But eh. I know very little about emus, except that they are interesting to look at. According to the trainers here: birdbrains, you know.

RL: Which is, we've said before, really an insult to birds.

TW: [*laughs*]

RL: Tom, what is the world's smallest mammal?

TW: The world's smallest mammal? That would be the bumblebee bat from Thailand. It weighs actually less then a penny. You can imagine something that small, that still gives milk, you know.

RL: Well, that's correct! You got that right. We're gonna try a little harder one now. What bone in the human body is shaped like Africa? Now take your time, because it may not be the bone that you think. You probably were gonna say the pelvis.

TW: No, I wasn't gonna say the pelvis, I was gonna say the scapula.

RL: That's correct! The scapula is shaped like Africa.

TW: Did I win the Frigidaire?

RL: You did. I see you have a lot of room to put it in.

TW: [*laughs*]

RL: That's right, but why is it called the scapula, that looks like Africa?

TW: That's a whole other area. You know, Robert, I don't know what to answer to that.

RL: Shall we compare *Alice* to your record *Blood Money*? You have two records out. You have to give people some guidance I think, some consumer guidance, because they walk into the store . . .

TW: Because they're consumers.

RL: They're consumers, they have their $14.95 or whatever records cost now.

TW: It's gone up . . .

RL: Yeah? Well, that's odd to me. But help the people. They're looking at the covers and they can't choose. What would you tell them?

TW: Oh God. Well. *Alice* is kinda like taking a pill. It's a little more dreamier. It's a little more, I don't know, more druggy I'd say. Kind of an opiate and dreamy. More of a song cycle. And then what was the other one?

RL: *Blood Money*? Your record called *Blood Money*? I know you're putting out two. It's a lot to remember. Two titles at once, but really try . . .

TW: [*laughs*] Well, it's more rooted. You know more '*thum-thum-thum-thum!*' More rhythmic, I guess more real, more in the real world.

RL: Is that really more the real world, do you think?

TW: [*laughs*] Don't try that! I don't know, I'm oversimplifying.

RL: You are.

TW: I have a tendency to do that, you know.

RL: Yeah right.

TW: [*looks in the camera*] Who's watching anyway, right?

RL: [*lost in his papers*]

TW: Come here, let me help you.

RL: Tom, you did write all these questions!

TW: [*laughs*] I did NOT write all these questions!

RL: Well, you make sounds. Do you sometimes . . . do you ever find this happening to you?

TW: Yeah.

RL: You just suddenly make sounds with your voice that have no meaning?

TW: It happens a lot.

RL: Does it?

TW: Yeah it does. It's called subvocalizing. I don't know, I guess maybe it's part of the evolution of language. It's going backwards though, back to when sounds had just basic shapes to them and had yet to be applied to anything truly meaningful. And I guess I'm probably dyslexic and, you know, attention deficit disorder.

RL: Are there any examples on your new records?

TW: Actually, there is. One of the songs on there, that's on *Alice*, the "Kommien-ezuspadt," which is actually . . . there are a few words in there that have real meaning but the rest of it is just pure gibberish. But a lot of people when they hear it they say: "Gee I didn't know you spoke Romanian," or, "I didn't know you spoke the odd dialect of Finland." I have been known to tell them that I *do* speak those languages, but truthfully I don't.

RL: Have you ever put one over on the Romanians?

TW: No, not the Romanians specifically. No, I'm having a ball with just the sounds. It's kinda thrilling to invent a language and not know from one word to the next what you're gonna say. You have no idea what you're gonna say. It's free. It's a free feeling.

RL: In your head is there anything that you think you say when you speak these languages?

TW: Yeah, you go through a series of emotions. You're angry, you're compassionate, and you're sad. You go through a whole range, but you're doing it with just shapes. "*Ein-chon, fein-mon tein-shein fun-ka,*" you know? "*Hidda-minga, bolla-minga, bolla-monga, kille-monga, bille-monga,*" you know?

RL: That was Chinese!

TW: [*laughs*] See what I mean! It's really a language. Sid Caesar used to do it all the time [*laughs*]. But it's actually therapeutic. You ought to try it. If you're angry, don't say words. Just say shapes and sounds.

RL: When I'm angry I can only say shapes and sounds, I forget how to speak.

TW: Most lyrics and songs start just with the sound and somehow the meaning finds the sound and they join, and you get over it. That's the way I do it anyway, you know.

RL: Now with the song "You Haven't Looked at Me."

TW: All right.

RL: Now I think there might be a story behind that song, because it says so on the paper. You didn't begin with nonsense syllables with that?

TW: The story is . . . I guess it was that Oxford University had a celebration and they wanted Alice, the Alice of *Alice in Wonderland*, they wanted her to come and speak in front of the class because by then she was in her eighties. So she came all the way from wherever she came from, and it was a long journey, and she got up onstage and she walked up to the microphone, you know, and banged on the microphone and said a few words to the class, and this was kind of a hypothetical song that we created to cover a situation like that, that you might imagine one would be singing or thinking about. It's just kind of an odd situation to imagine a story with a little girl who is like nine years old, and then to see her as a grown woman walking out.

RL: So this is what she would have sung if she had burst into song at that moment?

TW: [*laughs*] Yeah, her musical, her Broadway, yeah.

RL: Now, I have another question.

TW: OK.

RL: And again, I want you to think carefully before answering it.

TW: OK, all right.

RL: What key do most houseflies sing in?

TW: Got it. Key of F.

RL: Key of F? One-flat key?

TW: Yeah, one flat.

RL: Now do they run up the whole scale?

TW: No. No, it's the middle octave.

RL: It's the middle octave?

TW: Maybe toward the end of their lives maybe they fluctuate, you know.

RL: There's no modulation in the lives of flies is what you're telling me?

TW: Well, I'm sure they have meaningful changes they go through but that can't be determined by the tone of their voice, but if there's a fly in the room now we can check it.

RL: There probably is a fly.

TW: I don't think so, not this time of the year. It's probably too early for flies.

RL: Especially when you keep the place this neat.

TW: [*laughs*] Any more questions?

RL: Yeah, you have fifteen out of sixteen. You left out six.

TW: [*looks to the camera*] I hate to burn up all this tape.

RL: What did Joseph Stalin say about jazz?

TW: You know what Joseph Stalin said about jazz? He said, "Today you play jazz and tomorrow you betray your country," and it was on a poster; I guess it was circulating in Russia at the time. It was in all the subways and theaters and beer halls. He wasn't a big fan of jazz apparently.

RL: Well, everyone knows about Louis Armstrong's treason trial. That's fine, I think.

TW: Yeah, he did like thirty years I think.

RL: Yeah, all these messages in his solos. "Lazy River," as I recall. It's a scandal!

TW: [*laughs*]

RL: Who do you go to for advice? Do you need advice?

TW: Who do I go to for advice? Gee I don't know . . .

RL: The Green Hornet? Fats Waller? Oscar Levant?

TW: [*laughs*] Actually, the Green Lantern I've gone to for advice in the past. And the Silver Surfer and, of course, the Eyeball Kid. You can always count on him for vision and clarity. But yeah, Fats Waller I looked to for guidance and Oscar Levant, if you can get him out of your medicine cabinet. But I don't know, I go to recordings, usually, when I need guidance.

RL: Would you recommend your own recordings as, you know, as a life plan for anyone, you know? To look into the song like . . .

TW: [*laughs*] I don't know, I don't know about that, Robert.

RL: Misery is the river of the world for . . . ?

TW: You mean *is* misery the river of the world?

RL: Well . . .

TW: Is there a real river called Misery?

RL: Is there an actual Misery River?

TW: No, no, no. There is not a Misery River. I got a letter from a nine-year-old girl in Illinois who said she brought a record of mine into school and got into big trouble and she wanted me to come out there and defend her. Would I call her teacher? She left her teacher's home phone number and everything. She said she loved my songs and tells me that for her my voice reminds her of something between a cherry bomb and a clown and I really liked that.

RL: There's a lot of room between a cherry bomb and a clown.

TW: [*laughs*] Yeah! So we corresponded for a while. But we've drifted apart. We've lost touch.

RL: What is she, ten now?

TW: [*laughs*] She's much older now. Probably outgrew me. I'm probably like a turtleneck sweater to her now, but there was a period there I had meaning for her.

RL: I'll try and stump you again here, one more.

TW: OK, I'm ready.

RL: Do giraffes have vocal cords?

TW: No, they don't [*laughs*].

RL: Why?

TW: Well, it must have been a choice you know? Because God must have said at one point: "You can either have, you know, like a twenty-seven-foot neck or you can have vocal cords." They made their choice.

RL: When you were given that choice with God, when he'd come back from being away on business, he got in touch with you and said, "Tom, neck or voice."

TW: I would have gone for the voice, yeah. Be nice to have both, you know. But I hear that they rarely offer the two of those together.

RL: Well, in fact not at all like your . . . no, exactly like your records that are coming out, because they are not being offered together.

TW: No, they're not, they're separate entities. Buy one, buy 'em both, but you're not obligated to buy them both. You're not obligated to buy either one of them for that matter [*laughs*].

RL: They must be members of your family, no?

TW: No obligation necessary.

RL: Do you dance when you sing?

TW: I *do* actually dance when I sing. Don't we all? I sing and dance. I guess I'm part of that whole tradition on a certain level. I'm like . . .

RL: Gene Kelly, Fred Astaire.

TW: Yeah, I'm in the circus business, I guess. This business we call show.

RL: And when you were on stilts you were very agile on them I must say.

TW: Thanks, Robert.

RL: Have you ever been on stilts before?

TW: No, only as a child and I haven't been on stilts since. But it all came back. It's like a stilt memory. I think we all have certain kinds of primal . . . like I thought I had forgotten all about how to fix a kite, and all that comes back. If you haven't flown a kite in years you'd be surprised [*snaps fingers*]. It comes right back.

RL: What is that phrase? It's like walking on stilts. Is that what they say? When remembering how to do things?

TW: Yeah, exactly.

RL: When do you know when a song is finished, Tom?

TW: You don't always know when a song is finished and I'm not sure if a song *is* ever finished to be honest with you. You know they're constantly evolving. It's like jump-rope songs you know. When are they done? They are never done. You know people are always changing them, changing the tempo, adding new verses, getting rid of old verses. So I mean, when you are ready to record there is a certain finality to that. It's time to . . .

RL: To commit?

TW: Yeah, to cut the head off the fish. That's not really the right analogy for that [*laughs*]. It's more like . . . a lot of people say, "You really captured something on that." There's something alive in a song and the trick to recording them is to capture something and have it be taken alive. So there's always a trick in the studio.

RL: The world is just a wild kingdom for you, isn't it?

TW: [*laughs*]

RL: I see you as the Euell Gibbons of songwriting.

TW: Oh thanks! [*laughs*]

RL: Up to your knees with nonsense syllables, grabbing them as they fly by.

TW: [*laughs*]

RL: Now Tom, if you didn't do this, and by "this" I assume that you mean sitting in a room talking to me, what would you do?

TW: Oh, Jesus, I don't know. You mean, what do I have as a backup?

RL: What's in the back pocket? What's in the backroom? What's down that hallway waiting?

TW: [*laughs*] Well, you know, I had a mail-order night crawler business when I was a kid. I sold night crawlers. I always think back on that and I think, well I can always get that cranked up again [*laughs*]. And, of course, there's motel management. Keep your present job!

RL: Well, I look around and I see that you have a gift for decorating.

TW: [*laughs*] Simple is best! Don't you think?

RL: I think.

TW: That eventually you are getting rid of it anyway. Just start simple!

RL: It's true. Start again.

TW: Yeah, that's what they say.

RL: I think I've asked you . . . oh no! I haven't asked you all your own questions.

TW: [*laughs*]

RL: You collaborate with your wife and you're still married . . .

TW: A very good question. No, that's not really a question, it's a statement in there.

RL: It's both a question and a statement . . .

TW: Okaaay, I . . .

RL: It's a statement in the form of a question.

TW: I *do* collaborate with my wife. I think that's why we're still married. She was a blackjack dealer in a card room out in Emeryville when we first met. She's done everything, really. She does motorcycle repair [*laughs*], she does it all, and high finance, you name it. Deep-sea fishing. Has a pilot's license. She's a barber, you know? Everything . . .

RL: When does she find time to work with you?

TW: Exactly! That's right. I gotta book early.

RL: Is that why it's so long between records then?

TW: There you go! Now you're starting to see the picture, yeah.

RL: When she's done with this Yamaha?

TW: [*laughs*] It works, I don't know how it works. I guess: "If it's not broke, don't fix it," right? It works, it's like . . . I don't know. Yeah, it just works. "You wash, I'll dry." We have a good rhythm together and I trust her opinion, you know. If you're not careful it gets like "The Emperor's New Clothes," you know? You have to have somebody to say, "Honey, what is this, is this hogwash, is this crap? What is this?" So it's good. She's got a great sense of melody. She's the only one who plays the piano actually and reads music, you know? So, yeah, she's excellent.

RL: How have you kept her from going solo?

TW: Yeah, exactly. She doesn't like the limelight. She doesn't like it. So it works, you know?

RL: Good choice of a partner there.

TW: Yeah, right . . . yeah.

RL: Stays in the background . . .

TW: [*laughs*] Stays in the background! Put a muzzle on her and chain her to the fire hydrant!

RL: Now these records that you've made seem to be full of different forms of music.

TW: Yeah . . . oh! Oh yeah!

RL: Like cakewalks?

TW: Cakewalks, yeah!

RL: No barcaroles.

TW: Like *barcwalks*?

RL: No, barcarole. I hadn't heard of anybody writing a barcarole since Offenbach in "The Tales of Hoffmann."

TW: All right, well, barcarole, it's just a ship's waltz. I mean "barc" can mean another word for ship, and then "roll." That's why there are so many waltzes written by sailors because they're always waltzing, you know? Moving from one side to the next. So barc-a-role, there you have it.

RL: And the cakewalk. What does the cakewalk mean to you?

TW: I don't know. I remember in carnivals when I was a kid there was always a cakewalk and then they put on a record and then you go 'round in circles and if you land on the right number you win a cake.

RL: Is that the term?

TW: [*laughs*] I don't know! Song forms are just like Jell-O molds. I don't know. I like goofing around with them.

RL: You pour a flavor in there . . .

TW: Yeah, and wait for it to set.

RL: Is there anything you'd like to say about any other member of the animal kingdom before we send you back to the emus?

TW: No . . .

RL: The crows? The . . .

TW: The crows?

RL: The termites?

TW: The crows? You mean the teenagers of the bird world?

RL: I've heard that they are.

TW: They are the teenagers of the bird world because they . . . what happens is that they got all their work done about 9 A.M. They have a whole day. So they play rugby with a white rock. Or play "keep off the nest" and have little races around town. Kill bugs. Have bug-killing contests, you know?

RL: Do they ever get in trouble with the bird authorities?

TW: [*laughs*] It's probably very likely. Yeah they do, but when they have time to themselves they'll sit on an anthill and they'll wait till all the ants in the anthill have completely engulfed them. They say there's no true biological reason for it except that it must give them pleasure. It's like their eyes kinda roll back in their head, and they tip to one side, ants crawling all over them.

RL: So there's no authority figures in their life to keep them in line?

TW: Apparently not, no [*laughs*], but they say it's understandable though, that they would choose something like that because they have a lot of time on their hands. They have the largest brain in proportion to their body than any other bird. It's kind of a slow descent into . . . it's almost like a form of drug abuse because they spend every possible moment on an anthill, after they've done their work in the morning though . . . and . . . you're looking at me like you don't believe me?

RL: I don't know . . .

TW: [*laughs*]

RL: I've seen crows . . .

TW: Yeah.

RL: I've seen them work . . .

TW: You've seen them with real jobs!

RL: I've seen them out there taking care of business.

TW: OK, well, maybe this was just a particular crow.

RL: More? Shall we . . .

TW: I think we're fine.

RL: Go on?

TW: I think we've covered it all.

RL: Well, this is something else [*looking in his papers*].

TW: That's something else, yeah.

RL: Here we go. Oh. "Any strange suggestions to musicians?" Do you wanna cover that one?

TW: Oh, musicians?

RL: When you're working with these musicians, that you hire to play on your records, do you have any strange suggestions for them?

TW: Well, I wouldn't call it strange, but I try to tell them, when you're going to be in the car for more than two hours, don't listen to any music, you know? 'Cause it's early in the morning and you gotta drive up here and record it at 10 A.M. in the morning. I tell them, if it's at all possible, turn the radio off and don't play any music, because I like to start fresh and clean. That's really the only real thing that I'm adamant about.

RL: If you really wanted to start fresh and clean, you would just play with people that never played.

TW: [*laughs*] Never played! Yeah, well it's just one of those things. It's like nice to know that whatever you're doing is the first thing that happened that day. I mean musically the first thing that happened.

RL: Right, some days you get up and you work with emus.

TW: Yeah.

RL: Other days you get up and you work with musicians.

TW: Exactly, very similar.

RL: I would think so.

TW: Thanks, Robert.

RL: Tom, no problem.

TW: [laughs]

In September 2004, the first-ever English-language production of the Waits/ Wilson/Burroughs musical drama *The Black Rider: The Casting of the Magic Bullets* premiered at San Francisco's American Conservatory Theater. Pamela Feinsilber got a chance to speak to Waits about Burroughs and the play.

"One Wild Ride"
San Francisco Magazine
September 2004
Pamela Feinsilber

For even jaded theatergoers, the event of the season has to be *The Black Rider*, a macabre musical set in a nightmarish forest. The play—a surreal imagining of a German folktale in which, to gain some magic bullets, a man makes a pact with the devil—is all distorted perspectives, exaggerated gestures, and sinister songs, with catchy melodies performed on unusual-sounding instruments. Critics can't help making comparisons ("Diane Arbus meets *Moulin Rouge*," "Gothic vaudeville," "a cross of *Cabaret, The Threepenny Opera*, and *The Rocky Horror Picture Show*") because the wild mind behind this spooky terrain belongs to Robert Wilson—a man so limitlessly inventive he's won theater, film, sculpture, and design awards and had his artwork displayed in major museums. His experimental theater work always combines media such as dance, painting, music, and text in adventurous ways. He's probably best known for the opera *Einstein on the Beach*, written with composer Philip Glass, and an epic play, *The Civil Wars*, created with David Byrne, though you could fill this magazine with his resume.

The Black Rider* was originally created with a theater group in Hamburg and performed, in the early nineties, only in German. Wilson used his own inky, childlike drawings to design the sets and the eerie Expressionist lighting. Since neither those sets nor the lighting program was saved, Wilson has dreamed up new staging and other elements for this, the first English-language production. (You can thank Carey Perloff of A.C.T. for bringing it to San Francisco, the only American venue.) All of which seems sufficiently exciting, but there's more: the songs are by the always original Tom Waits, and wonderfully scored, with his colleague Greg Cohen, using all manner of instruments—a little like some of the songs on Waits's 2002 CDs, *Alice* and *Blood Money*, with their decadent European flavor. (Waits, who lives north of San Francisco, is releasing a new CD, *Real Gone*, next month.) And the text came from the late Beat author and one-time heroin addict William Burroughs, famed for *Naked Lunch* and other stream-of-consciousness writings, as well as for his colorful life. You may recall that at a party in Mexico in the fifties, he tried to shoot a glass off his wife's head and accidentally killed her. Burroughs has said her death is what spurred him to write, and *The Black Rider*, with its echoes of his own story ("the gun turns into a dowser's wand, and points where the bullet wants to go"), was perhaps his last work. He died at eighty-three in 1997.

When I spoke to Tom Waits about seeing *The Black Rider* in English after all these years, he said, "For the first time, I can understand what they were saying, because I never really knew, you know?"

Pamela Feinsilber: You've said that you were trying to write music "that could dream its way into the forest of Wilson's images."

Tom Waits: He makes these dreamscapes up onstage, and you sit out there in the dark and you start hearing what could possibly be the accompaniment to what you are seeing. But to do that, you have to kind of fall into this liquid dream that he's making for you. I heard a saw [as musical instrument] and all this stuff—'cause you figure the forest, you know.

PF: Yes, and on your CD of these songs [*The Black Rider*, on which we also hear Burroughs], the saw isn't the least pedestrian or everyday; it sounds kind of creepy.

TW: It also has that theremin quality that most people associate with horror movies or space odysseys.

PF: And in terms of the lyrics, you said on the liner notes that Burroughs's language "became a river of words for me to draw from." Yet some of the lines sound so much like you. Can you explain to me how you fished in that river and pulled out some of your lyrics?

TW: Um [*thinks*] . . . "Beware of"—what is it? [*sings*] "There is a light in the forest . . . Beware of the telescopic meats." [*speaks it slowly, to emphasize*] Telescopic meats. "He'll find his way back to the forest"—wella, huh huh huh . . . "and the briar is strangling the rose back down." [*talks*] "His back shall be my slender new branch. It will bend, it will sway in the breeze."

And then I would add my little thing: "And the devil does his polka with a hatchet in his hand. There's a sniper in the branches of the trees." Someone gives you a bunch of words—like they give you a bunch of bottle caps, and you can glue 'em down wherever you want. And mix them with your own macaroni. It was good.

It also set the tone for the piece, 'cause Burroughs has plumbed the depths of so many levels of hell. Burroughs is kind of like a demonic Mark Twain. He's like the real dark heart of America. Comes from the Burroughs Adding Machine family, you know, and he threw off all the shackles of his inheritance and struck out on his own. Like they say, when you're in hell, keep going. So at times he was much more in the realm of Philip K. Dick in science fiction. Anyway, very inspiring. And I was very romantic about all the Beats when I was first coming on the scene myself.

And that voice. My favorite thing is [*quoting from "That's the Way," which Burroughs performs on the CD*] "That's the way the cookie crumbles, that's the way the stomach rumbles, that's the way the needle pricks, that's the way the glue sticks—" That stuff really killed me.

PF: You and your arranger and bandmate, Greg Cohen, and Wilson went to talk with him in Lawrence, Kansas, when you first prepared to work on the play. What was he like?

TW: Burroughs—yeah, he loves firearms and reptiles and . . . [*remembering*] the shotgun paintings. He would finish a painting—he painted on plywood—and then he would stand back from it with a 12-gauge shotgun and shoot a hole in it with buckshot. And then he'd say, "That's done," and in a way, ironically, he gave life to it, with all these splinters coming off of it. And around three, 'cause it was almost cocktail time, he'd start massaging his watch, as if maybe he could get that big hand to move up there a little faster.

PF: What was official cocktail time?

TW: Apparently, it was three in Lawrence, Kansas, which is maybe why he moved to that time zone.

PF: I've always wondered why he moved there.

TW: He probably went through there when he was young and traveling and said, "You know, I'm gonna buy a house here someday and settle down." You could hear the train tracks from there . . . Wilson is from Texas—lot of flat land in Texas. It's good for dreaming; you know, big-sky country. That's why Roy Orbison loved it. Roy Orbison got his voice from listening to the sound of a dance coming across the prairie from, like, a hundred miles away. There'd be a dance in another town, and everything sounded echoey. He wanted to sound like that with his voice.

PF: You once said about Wilson, "He changed my eyes and my ears permanently."

TW: I've worn glasses ever since I met him. He's like an inventor, you know, and he throws down the gauntlet for your own imagination.

PF: Now that there's finally going to be an English-language production, do you wish you were performing in it?

TW: It's just too much work. I think Wilson makes you change the molecular structure of your whole body and then builds you back up in his image. It's like being beamed up in *Star Trek*; you first have to be turned to dust. You know, I do some acting, but I'm not really an actor in that sense. I'm just acting with my songs. I feel safer there.

PF: But you've been in quite a few movies—Jim Jarmusch's *Down by Law* and his new one, *Coffee and Cigarettes,* and *Short Cuts,* and *The Cotton Club* . . .

TW: Yeah, yeah, but it's another thing to say I also do a little acting. I do a little car repair; I do a little lumberjacking. I'm a rock hound, or whatever. I would love to have Wilson take my songs and then build a world for me to live in for my act. 'Cause we seem to complement each other. There's talk about different stuff. But he's one of those people, he's busier than James Brown. He's a globe-trotter.

PF: So he doesn't really live any particular place.

TW: I think he lives in his head most of the time. When I worked with Wilson, I think I started understanding that there are portals you can pass through when you are working in the theater. He's always had visions and been different . . . and made a world for himself.

PF: Meaning that with artists, there can be a blurring of the lines between reality and—

TW: Insanity.

PF: It's a fine line, isn't it? If you can understand that your visions are visions—if you can use them as an artist would as opposed to fearing them or letting them drive you mad . . .

TW: Yeah, if you were in Pago Pago years ago, you might be a shaman. In another country, you'd be elected president.

REAL GONE (2004)

Throughout 2003, Waits was working on new material for a projected compilation project as well as an all-new original CD. On April 24, 2004, Anti- updated
fans on Waits's doings on their website: "Tom Waits has been holed up in an old
schoolhouse in Mississippi, recording a new album, titled *Real Gone* for Anti-.
Real Gone is primal rhythmic blues." These early rumblings set up a frantic state
of nervous anticipation for Waits's fans, who most readily checked the site (a
great marketing strategy!) for updates. Waits also contributed information
about the recordings via his tour manager, Stuart Ross, to the collective mem-
bership of the Raindogs listserv discussion list: "We are currently recording a
new record in an old schoolhouse in Mississippi because there's nothing like
fresh material . . . all new tunes by Kathleen Brennan and myself to come out in
September. No title as of yet. We worked with Larry Taylor on bass and guitar,
Marc Ribot on guitar and tres, Brain Mantia on drums, Casey Waits on percussion and turntables, Les Claypool on electric bass, and Harry Cody on guitar.
Feelin' good about it all. Songs about Mama, liquor, trains, and death. Politics,
rats, war, hangings, dancing, pirates, farms, the carnival, and sinning. In other
words, the same ol' dirty business."

The album was slated to drop in the fall of 2004. To feed the frenzy, Anti-
sent out a press release which promised in part: "*Real Gone* features fifteen
tracks of funk, Jamaican rock-steady, blues both urban and rural, rhythms and
melodies both Latin and African and, for the first time, no piano. The crash and
collide of rhythms and genres within a song creates a hybrid unlike any music he
has made before." With *Real Gone*, Waits would see an album peak higher than it
ever had before in the entirety of his career. It entered at #28 with sales of
thirty-four thousand, as well as reaching #1 on the Top Independent Albums
chart.

"It's Last Call Somewhere in the World"
Magnet
August or September 2004 (issue date: October/November 2004)
Jonathan Valania

When Batman takes someone other than Robin back to the Batcave, usually to extract some crucial information via one of his super-scientific mind-reading devices, he knocks them out with Batgas so as to keep the exact location of his lair a secret.

Something similar happens when you go to interview Tom Waits. You find yourself in some sleepy town north of San Francisco. He pulls up in his hearse-black, old-model Chevy Suburban, then takes you to some Waits-appropriate location—a greasy spoon, a truck-stop cafeteria—for a Q&A session that ends promptly when the check arrives. He is, without fail, charming, witty, odd, poetic, and often profound. Then he drives you back to your hotel, tips his porkpie hat and asks you to turn around. Before you can look back, he's gone, back to that someplace in the rolling pastures and pines of Sonoma County, where he lives with Kathleen Brennan, his wife, collaborator, muse, and mother of his three teenage children.

I first interviewed Waits for *Magnet* in 1999 in Santa Rosa. I had a room at the Astro, a broken-down welfare motel straight out of one of the bourbon-fed board-inghouse madrigals Waits used to pound the horse teeth to in the 1970s. This time it's the Metro Hotel & Café, a quaint bed-and-breakfast in Petaluma recommended by Waits. With its beguilingly appointed rooms—a blend of vintage-store Victoriana, bohemian bric-a-brac, and faintly Wiccan aura (if Stevie Nicks were a hotel, it would be the Metro)—it seems fitting of Tom Waits circa now. He's gone from the flophouse to the big house in the woods with the mysterious wife, three kids, the dogs, the garden, and a lot of funny ideas about what sounds good.

Upon arriving at the Metro, I check in with the *Magnet* office back in Philadelphia. It's a sunny, immaculate Northern California day, but the news on the line is cloudy at best. I'm warned that Waits is in a "weird" mood today. Not to worry, his publicist assures me, Waits is just a little nervous because this is the first interview he's doing for his new album, *Real Gone* (Anti-).

The man has nothing to be nervous about. *Real Gone* is Waits at the top of his game, another brilliant late-period canvas from an American master. It picks up where 1999's *Mule Variations*—with its perfect blend of what Waits calls "creepers and weepers"—left off, reflecting the midnight mood of the times. In 2002, Waits released *Blood Money* and *Alice*, two separate scores for theatrical productions by frequent collaborator and acclaimed avant-garde dramatist Robert Wilson. While those albums are prime examples of Waits's mastery of Brechtian burlesque and carny surrealism, they're more akin to 1993's *The Black Rider*, another Wilson theatrical score. As good as they are, you come away from *Blood Money* and *Alice* with the distinct feeling you kind of had to be there, with "there" being the Thalia Theater in Hamburg, Germany, where the pieces were staged. Unlike those scores, *Real Gone* isn't the soundtrack to some faraway show; it *is* the show, with all the drama and pageantry unfolding right between your ears. As ever, the music is otherworldly and full of dust-bowl sadness, somehow managing to sound both as old as an Alan Lomax field recording and as modern as tail fins on a '59 Caddy.

But where most Waits records seem hermetically sealed off from the world that does backflips over *American Idol*, *Real Gone* ripples in the same troubled waters we all find ourselves bobbing in these days. Waits directs a fair share of his hobo magic-realism at current affairs: rigged politics, imperial blood sport, humanity tattered under the grinding wheels of war, and the greed and hate that keeps them spinning without mercy. All of this is reflected in the sometimes somber and wistful conversation I have with Waits, a stark contrast to the left-field whimsy of the talk I had with him five years ago. But, as a wise man once said, those were different times.

Which isn't to suggest anyone will confuse *Real Gone* with *Sandinista!* The sociopolitical commentary is tinted with Waits's patented sepia tones, lending it both a currency and timelessness that manage to blend seamlessly with the standard Waitsian themes of love, dreams, circus freaks, and murder in the red barn. Nor is this *Mule Variations* part two. Piano, long a fixture of most Waits recordings, is nowhere to be heard. While there is, as per usual, plenty of bloozy abstraction, sad-eyed balladry, and organ-grinder-monkey dance music punctuated with odd conks of percussion, most of the songs are built around "mouth rhythms" Waits created by huffing and puffing into a tape recorder in his bathroom.

It's not for everyone. In fact, you can tell a lot about people from what they make of Tom Waits. His career is a musical Rorschach test: some just see spilled ink, others see fantastic chimeras. He's one of those love-'em-or-hate-'em artists, and the great divide between us and them is invariably Waits's worn-out shoe of a voice. If you like your singers to sound like a shiny new sneaker, well, there's always *American Idol*. Waits's frogman croak is a far more versatile instrument than he's given credit for, capable of morphing from lupine howl to grainy, heart-warming purr, from a devil-horned carnival barker to a three-pack-a-day Romeo wheezing sweet nothings that are, upon closer inspection, about everything. Everything that matters, anyway: life and death, love and hope, sex and dreams. And the infinite spaces in between that God fills.

It's hard to say where the public Tom Waits begins and the private one ends, and vice versa. Which is just how he wants it. It's how he maintains his aura. When Waits finally pulls up to the Metro in his Suburban, he's dressed exactly as he was for his last conversation with *Magnet*—rumpled porkpie hat, head-to-toe in ranch-hand denim—but he seems a little on edge. Chalk it up to opening-night jitters for a veteran performer pulling his public persona out of mothballs for the first time in a couple years. The suit still fits, but it's a little stiff from the hanger.

Yet the same old tics—the "walking Spanish down the hall" body language, the pretzeling of the arms—don't seem like affectations. There's something Lenny Bruce-raised-by-wolves about the way Waits carries himself: part wolf-man, part Wolfman Jack. It's really not difficult to imagine Waits out in the back-yard around midnight, howling at a full moon. At one point, he's talking on his cell phone to Brennan, leaning with one arm against the trunk of his publicist's rental car like an old man urinating or a chain-gang member getting patted down before being shipped back to the prison farm. Like the man's art, this moment seems at once highly theatrical and utterly natural.

Waits wants to go to his favorite Chinese restaurant in Petaluma, but he has some difficulty finding it. We pull up one street, and Waits looks around dumbfounded, like they'd moved the joint. Then he remembers that it is, in fact, located in a nearby strip mall. Charmless and antiseptic under a drop ceiling and fluorescent lights—not to mention completely devoid of other customers—the place has none of the Oriental opium-den vibe you can't help but imagine when Waits says, "We're goin' for Chinese." But he has a way of lending color and character to any room he walks into. Studying the menu, Waits makes a point of ordering some steamed vegetables. "If I don't eat something green, my wife will be very upset with me." When the food arrives, Waits seems more comfortable in his own skin. Full of green tea and sympathy, he shares jokes and fears, dreams and memories, does some sound effects, even sings a little Ray Charles.

And then he's gone again. Like, real gone.

Jonathan Valania: I'm noticing you have the words "diapers" and "fireworks" written on the back of your hand in magic marker. Would it be impolite to ask you why?

Tom Waits: Shopping list. Fireworks and diapers is all anyone ever needs. Life is what happens between fireworks and diapers.

JV: With age supposedly comes wisdom. What do you know at fifty-four that you didn't when you were younger?

TW: I've learned a lot. Most of the big things I've learned in the last ten years. Of course, I've been sober for twelve years. Let's see, what have I learned? As a nation, we are addicted to cigarettes and underwear. And it's getting harder and harder to find a bad cup of coffee.

JV: Let's go back to ancient history for a second.

TW: OK, don't go back too far. I get lost back there.

JV: When you were a teenager, you worked as a doorman at a nightclub in San Diego. What do you remember about that time?

TW: I don't know. I got paid $8 a night, and I got to hear a lot of great music.

JV: I've read that when you were young, you heard sounds the way Van Gogh saw colors. Even everyday sounds took on these hyper-iridescent tone colors.

TW: I went through a period like being color-blind with regard to your hearing. Or astigmatism of the ears.

JV: Then you would recite these little incantations that made it go away?

TW: [*goes into chant, which sounds like* "gila-monster-killamonster-chilla-monster-boom," *while tapping on a water glass with a spoon*]

JV: Do you still do that?

TW: I just did it.

JV: No, I mean do you still have those kinds of experiences with sound?

TW: I write music that way. It's sort of like automatic writing. Wouldn't you love to go into a darkened room with a piece of paper and a pen and just start drawing circles and wind up writing the great American novel? Recording for me is like photographing ghosts.

JV: How did you first encounter Captain Beefheart?

TW: We had the same manager back in 1975–76.

JV: You weren't acquainted with his music in the '60s?

TW: Nope. I became more acquainted with him when I got married. My wife had all his records.

JV: It's interesting you came to Beefheart so late considering how often critics compare you to him.

TW: Anything you absorb you will ultimately secrete. It's inevitable. Most of us are original paintings, and it's a mystery as to what is learned and what is borrowed, what is stolen and what is born, what you came in with and what you found while you were here.

JV: What do you know about this Waitstock thing in Poughkeepsie, New York, each year? What do they do?

TW: Incantations, speak in tongues, wake up at six in the morning and have whiskey and eggs, walk around in their undershirts. I don't know; it's just what I imagine. It's just some attempt at a worshipful homage.

JV: Do you still spend time scavenging in junkyards?

TW: I practically live at Costco. I am still a bit of a scavenger. I bring home useless things.

JV: Are you one of those guys who has a front yard full of car parts, old birdbaths and lawn jockeys?

TW: If I could find a lawn jockey, I would pay good money for it. As for my yard, I will leave that up to you to imagine because if I told you, you wouldn't believe me. Mostly medical supplies and Venus flytraps.

JV: I was surprised to learn *Mule Variations* sold a million copies worldwide. How does that feel?

TW: I guess it feels good. Isn't that supposed to feel good?

JV: But what does that mean when an artist like Tom Waits can sell a million copies of an album at a time when the music business is basically saying nothing but easy-sell artists are worth bothering with?

TW: I don't know what it means. If they were lawn chairs, what would it mean? If they were potted plants, what would it mean? If they were little poodles, what would it mean? It's America: free enterprise.

JV: There's no piano on *Real Gone*, was that intentional?

TW: No. I moved the piano into the studio, and we never touched it. We put drinks on it. I put my coat on it. Before you know it, I couldn't even see it. It just became an end table. Most of it was written a cappella. I started with these mouth rhythms, making my own cycles and playing along with them. That's fairly new. Sometimes when you just do sounds into the tape recorder, you don't realize it, but you're channeling something, like incantations or talking in tongues.

JV: Was this a real old, vintage tape recorder?

TW: No, a Fostex four-track with a Shure SM58 [microphone] in a really small bathroom with about a four-second delay and overload the hell out of it. . . . I'll tell you what else is new. There's an instructional dance number on there. When was the last time you heard an instructional dance number on a record?

JV: Which one is that?

TW: "Metropolitan Glide." It has instructions [in the lyrics] on how to do the dance. And it also has lots of other dances on there that the gentleman is able to do. It's a real dance. They used to do it in the '20s. It's kind of a revival.

JV: You sometimes use an instrument called the "bastarda." What the hell is that?

TW: That's something Les [Claypool] played. It's like an electric stick with four strings, like a bass without a body. *Real Gone* is definitely not a record filled with bizarre, left-wing sound sources. The idea was to go in and do something that was going to be bread and water, skin and bones, three-legged tables, rudimentary three-minute songs. That was the idea.

JV: When did you start working on the album?

TW: Gee, I don't know. A few months ago.

JV: Is that a new thing for you, writing and recording so quickly?

TW: We wanted to get it done before the summer began. When the kids are out of school, it's a whole new paradigm shift at home. They're everywhere.

JV: Where did you record it?

TW: It got misconstrued. It was recorded in the Delta, and everybody thought we were working in Mississippi. It was the Sacramento Delta.

JV: A lot of great bluesmen came out of the tar-paper shacks of Sacramento.

TW: I'm not pulling your leg. There really is a Sacramento Delta. We recorded in an abandoned schoolhouse. I don't like the politics of a studio. It's used as a studio all year long, and then you come in. I was looking for a place that might have an unusual sound.

JV: Let's talk about some of these obscure references in the lyrics on *Real Gone*. On "Sins of My Father," you mention a "Tyburn jig."

TW: When someone was being hung, the dance they would do at the end of the rope was called the Tyburn jig. It was also called "the dance upon nothing"; that kind of explains itself. The reason theaters traditionally have no performances on Monday night is because Monday night was Hanging Night, and nobody could compete with Hanging Night. To this day, theaters are dark on Mondays.

JV: I think most people would be surprised how recently there were public hangings in this country.

TW: Well, we still do it today. It's just a little more civilized: lethal injection. How long after the discovery of electricity do you think somebody invented the electric chair? Probably, the next day. How long do you think after they invented these picture phones that somebody put it in their pants? Less than a day. Crime is always way ahead of technology, waiting for it to catch up.

JV: What about some of these characters on the new album? There's the line "Jesus of Nazareth told Mike of the weeds."

TW: Well, if there is a Jesus of Nazareth, there had to be a Mike of the weeds and a Bob of the parking lot, Jim of the river, Steve of the backyard.

JV: Was Weeds the next town over from Nazareth?

TW: No, Mike lived in the weeds. Jesus lived in Nazareth. They corresponded.

JV: There was a guy back in Jesus's time named Mike?

TW: I don't know if they pronounced it like that.

JV: Who is Knocky Parker?

TW: Old Delta-blues guy.

JV: Bowlegged Sal?

TW: Singer. I think from St. Louis. Sorry, Bo [*laughs*].

JV: Who's Joel Tornabene?

TW: He's in the concrete business [*laughs*]. Mob guy. He was the grandson of Sam Giancana from Chicago. He did some yard work for me, and I hung out with him most of the time. He died in Mexico about five years ago. He was a good friend of [producer/composer] Hal Willner's, and he was a good guy. He had an errant—I don't know how to put this—he used to go around, and when he saw something he liked in somebody's yard, he would go back that night with a shovel, dig it up and plant it in your yard. We used to get a kick out of that. So I stopped saying, "I really like that rosebush, I really like that banana tree, I really like that palm." Because I knew what it meant. He came over once with twelve chickens as a gift. My wife said, "Joel, don't even turn the car off. Turn that car around and take those chickens back where you found them." He was a good friend, one of the wildest guys I've ever known.

JV: I love the line "I want to know the same thing everyone wants to know: how's it going to end?"

TW: What's it gonna be? A heart attack at a dance? An egg that went down the wrong pipe? Wild bullet from a conflict two miles away that ricochets off the lamppost and goes through the windshield and pierces your forehead like a diamond? Who knows? Look at Robert Mitchum. He died in his sleep. That's pretty good for a guy like Robert Mitchum.

JV: How about "My baby's so fine, even her car looks good from behind"?

TW: [*laughs*] I was following my wife home once, and I said, "I don't know where I am, baby." She said, "Follow me." And I remarked to myself, "My baby's so fine, even the back of her car looks fine." How about Ray Charles? What a shame.

JV: Did you ever meet him?

TW: I met Ray in an airport, and he had all his handlers around him like he was Muhammad Ali. And I knew I could never get through unless I looked really stupid, like I didn't know any better.

JV: It blows my mind what he overcame to get to where he was. To be a black man in America at that time, blind and a junkie.

TW: Well, *Brother Ray* is an excellent autobiography if you want to get all the dirt on Ray. The most commonly told story about Ray was about [his backup singers] the Raelettes. If you wanted to be a Raelette, you had to let Ray. . . . [*laughs*] My favorite image of Ray is this wonderful story of him touring North Carolina in the '50s as a rhythm 'n' blues act, playing empty tobacco warehouses. They would just call a dance and put out notices, and the place would fill up. People were dancing so hard that the dust from the floorboards made it so smoky in there that after a while you couldn't even see who you were dancing with, and Ray would just be howling. . . . You know, showbiz is the only place where you can actually make money after you're dead. And he'll also live on. You put those records on and he's here; it's really like a hologram of your spirit.

JV: If you go back through history, the rich and powerful would strive for immortality by building monuments so they would always be remembered. To a certain extent, there was some permanence, but only in that one place. You would have to travel to see it. A Ray Charles record is everywhere.

TW: And it's just as fresh as the day it was recorded. When I listen to old field recordings, maybe you'll hear a dog barking way off in the background. You realize the house it was recorded in is torn down, the dog is dead, the tape recorder is broken, the guy who made the recording died in Texas, the car out front has four flat tires, even the dirt that the house sat on is gone—probably a parking lot—but we still have this song. Takes me out when I listen to those old recordings. I put on my stuff in the house, which is always those old Alan Lomax recordings. My son Casey started doing his turntable stuff; he's upstairs listening to Aesop Rock, El-P, Sage Francis and all those kind of guys. So I get exposed to a lot at home, and then, you know, I weave it all together.

JV: Have you ever thought about messing around with electronics more, maybe deconstructing some of your old stuff?

TW: I don't know if that's my culture. Maybe it's more of your culture. You're younger than me. I don't want to get a weird haircut just because I saw it at the mall.

JV: Does Kathleen do the woman's voice on "Trampled Rose"?

TW: No, that's me. That's my female voice. I got a big girl in me. Don't you?

JV: Probably. Don't take this the wrong way, but on "Misery Is the River of the World" [from *Blood Money*], you sound like one of those Swiss Alps rescue dogs that got into the brandy.

TW: [*laughs*] Sometimes my kids will listen to something I did and say, "Were you going for a Cookie Monster-in-love thing on that, Dad?"

JV: You have a daughter who's in college.

TW: It was inevitable. I have a son who's eighteen, played turntables on *Real Gone*. As far as my kids go, it's the family business. If I was a farmer, I would have them out there on a tractor. If I was a ballet dancer, I would have them in tutus.

JV: What do they make of what you do?

TW: I'm their dad, that's really the extent of it. They are not fans of mine. Your kids are not your fans, they're your kids. The trick is to have a career and have a family. It's like having two dogs that hate each other and you have to take them for a walk every night.

JV: There's a line on *Real Gone* about "She was a middle-class girl / Thought she could stand up in the deep end," which struck me as something a father would come up with. Am I off base?

TW: No, but not consciously. It's one of those things when you're a dad. When I see these pictures of these kids coming home from Iraq, they're my son's age: eighteen, nineteen years old. That's who's over there.

JV: Let's get to that. I'm hearing a lot of echoes of life post-9/11 on *Real Gone*.

TW: Well, "Sins of My Father" is political. "Hoist That Rag" is. There's a bunch of soldier songs.

JV: "Sins of My Father": Are you talking about George W. Bush?

TW: I'm talking about my father, I'm talking about your father, I'm talking about his father. The sins of the father will be visited upon the son. Everybody knows that.

JV: On "Day After Tomorrow," which sounds like a soldier's letter home to his family, you mention Rockford [Illinois], near the Wisconsin border.

TW: I read an article about a soldier who died and was from Rockford. A lot of these soldiers come from the South and the Midwest. And these ads for the army? They're ridiculous. They all play rock 'n' roll, and it's turned up full blast; they all look so cool in their equipment.

JV: On that song, there's a line that goes, "I'm not fighting for justice, I'm not fighting for freedom, I'm fighting for my life."

TW: All the guys who come home on leave say that. That's why when you ask them why they just don't stay home now that they're safe, they say, "Because I've got buddies over there, and they need me. I'm not going over there for the government." Because in the end, it's just you and your rifle and your friends. They really are just gravel on the road. Do you think that a senator sleeping in a nice warm bed looks at a soldier as anything more than a spent shell casing? Nothing more. That's why we need more ammo, and the ammo is these children.

JV: How do you think the election is going to go?

TW: I don't know. I hope he gets voted out. I pray that we will be mobilized and it will be a landslide and everybody who's ever believed in these ideals that we're talking about will vote the bastard out. But now it's all done on computer, and there's probably somebody who's rigging the whole thing. It's such a huge thing. We're the United States of the World. It's not just a country; we're talking about world domination. Most of us aren't ready to absorb the truth about what's really going on.

JV: I don't know if you know about this, but there's a company called Diebold that makes the electronic voting machines used in Florida. One of these machines in Volusia County registered sixteen thousand negative votes for Gore in 2000. Here's the kicker: The CEO of Diebold [Walden O'Dell] is a major fundraiser for the Bush-Cheney campaign.

TW: [*sarcastically*] No connection.

JV: These machines can be hacked into and manipulated very easily; this is all well documented. Each vote is just a digital blip, really. There's this movement to make these machines print out a receipt of your vote, so if you wanted to have a recount, everybody could turn in their slip of paper. And Diebold goes, "That's just not possible." Well, you know what other machines Diebold makes? ATMs.

TW: Please. I'm thinking that this is the last of our civilization. I think we are all going into the crapper, waiting to be flushed. It just feels like the whole world's on fire right now.

JV: You could last a long time out here in the woods when it goes police state.

TW: It will get to the point where the only food you can trust is what's grown in your backyard.

JV: Are you against irradiated food?

TW: Oh, God yeah. I got a big garden in my backyard.

JV: What do you grow?

TW: Tomatoes, corn, eggplant, squash, beans, pumpkins.

JV: So how does it work with you and Kathleen writing songs together?

TW: We just throw out lines, it's like dreaming out loud. When we're writing, we kinda go into a trance.

JV: Kathleen goes into the studio with you, right?

TW: Oh, yeah. She and I produced the record. It's like she's tying a rope around my waist and lowering me down into the well, hollering "A little more to the left, a little more to the left."

JV: "Circus" is the kind of William S. Burroughs hurdy-gurdy narrative you've been honing to perfection your entire career. A lot of your albums have some great spoken-word pieces—"Shore Leave," "Ninth & Hennepin," "What's He Building?"—but I think "Circus" is the best. You've got Horse Face Ethel, you've got one-eyed Myra in her Roy Orbison T-shirt bottle-feeding an orangutan named Tripod. Is that because he's three-limbed?

TW: [*laughs*] Naw, naw. I think he got his name because he always had an erection.

JV: You've got Yodeling Elaine, the Queen of the Air with the tiny bubble of spittle around her nostril and a little rusty tear. And then over by the frozen tractor—I really love this phrase—"the music was like electric sugar."

TW: It's a daydream. We were just sort of dreaming of the place I'd like to work. If I was a kid and wanted to run away to the circus, this is the circus I would want to run away to.

JV: What about Poodle Murphy?

TW: She's a girl from Funeral Wells's knife act who was strapped to the spinning board. I don't know if I would want to work for a guy named Funeral Wells, especially if he threw knives.

JV: Another great line: "Damn good address for a rat."

TW: [*laughs*] Well, that's any ship, you know. They grab each other's tails when they cross the river, hundreds and hundreds of them. They're omnivorous. They'll eat anything. You put them in a room with an empty can, and they will eat the can, the label, the top and they'll digest and shit it out. The myth about rats is that they have to eat constantly or their teeth would grow too long and the bottoms would come out of the top of their heads like horns.

JV: That's not true?

TW: I don't know. I haven't spent that much time with rats.

JV: Let's talk about your scene with Iggy Pop in Jim Jarmusch's *Coffee and Cigarettes*. It was filmed a while ago.

TW: Ten years ago.

JV: I thought you were a natural. I love Iggy, but I think he made the right career choice going into rock 'n' roll instead of acting.

TW: Well, you know, they were vignettes. It wasn't an actors' thing; it was more like situation comedy. Jarmusch has been doing those a long time. When he's working on a project, he'll try and get people to go into the alley or the Italian restaurant and try and do something spontaneous. He really wants it to be like Beckett plays.

JV: Have you talked with him about doing another full-length feature along the lines of *Down by Law*?

TW: Acting is not something that I really pursue. I like to say that I'm not really an actor, but I do a little acting. I'm not really looking for something, but if something came along that I really loved, I would do it.

JV: Why don't you tour anymore? Is it just the stress and drudgery and "who needs it"?

TW: Exactly. Just the physics alone of going into a new hall every night. I'm a grumpy old guy. It doesn't take much to tick me off, I'm like an old hooker, you know.

JV: Why did you title the album *Real Gone*?

TW: That's Kathleen's title. I was going to call it *Clang, Boom, and Steam*. She said everyone's going or really gone, and there's a lot of leaving on the record. It's almost hard to get laughs these days; we are living in such a dark place.

JV: I don't want to sound like one of those people who whines about 9/11, but up until then, I was generally an optimistic person. There was that bubble of peace, hope, and endless possibility after the Cold War ended, that all of our energies as a civilization could be directed toward making the world a better place instead of just shooting at each other. But after 9/11, it occurred to me that I'll probably never see a time like that again, that there'll just be endless war.

TW: That's all you read about in the paper anymore.

JV: Well, that's why I think if you had to distill the essence of *Real Gone* down to one line, it's where you say, "I want to believe in the mercy of the world again." I think so many people feel that way right now.

TW: Do you know who said that? Bob Dylan. He didn't say it in a song; he said it in an interview. He was just talking about the state of the world, so I threw that in there.

JV: I was reading an interview you did with [director] Terry Gilliam, and at one point you said to him, "I feel like there is a battle going on all the time between light and dark, and I wonder sometimes if the dark has one more spear."

TW: Do you know who said that to me? Fred Gwynne.

JV: Herman Munster?

TW: Yeah. A good friend of mine. We worked together on *The Cotton Club*. We used to talk all the time, very deep guy. We rode to work every day in a van; we'd hang out for hours and hours. Sweet guy. Head bigger than a horse. I don't think they added any plaster when they made him up as Herman. But getting back to that bit about light and dark: I do believe that. But I also believe that when you do something really good, it goes into an account and other folks can write checks against it. I really believe that.

"The *Mojo* Interview: Tom Waits Speaks"
Mojo
September 2004
Sylvie Simmons

"He comes in for coffee sometimes. Reads some poetry. They told me he was a musician. Tom Wait. Never heard of Tom Wait." Little Amsterdam's elderly owner shrugs. "So someone gave me his record. He sounds just like Clemens van de Ven." He points out a photograph of De Ven behind the bar. "That's him. And that," he points helpfully at the picture next to it, "is Tom Wait."

You can see why Waits likes it here. An oyster bar so near the middle of nowhere it smacks of perversity (forty-five minutes outside sleepy Petaluma, California, former egg capital of America and the place they filmed *American Graffiti*), boasting a windmill, bullfighting trophies and pool tables, and run by an old Dutch seaman who takes it for granted Waits copped his licks from a guy in South Holland but still likes him well enough.

Sat at a table with a coffee mug and a bottle of water—"I haven't had a drink in twelve years"—Waits looks relaxed. Looks, in fact, like he came in from fixing a truck: short-sleeved shirt, dusty boots, a face that's seen the sun. "Well, I hate to overemphasize the importance of music sometimes because, as you get older, the more important question is, 'Can you fix the truck, Tom?' 'Can you fix the toilet?' 'There's some very strange sound outside, who's that weird guy at the gate . . . ?'" The sentence crescendos into a scary spoken-word piece. Waits is comfortable spinning yarns. Shy folk, eager to deflect attention, often are. When his answers are less anecdotal, more personal, his hand reflexively covers his mouth and the sentences lose their structure. He'll stop, tinker with the words and rebuild them as if they—like everything else about him—were a work in progress.

Sylvie Simmons: *Real Gone* is as different from *Alice* and *Blood Money* as they were from *Mule Variations*. Before you embark on a new album is there a deliberate process of deck clearing?

Tom Waits: Well, you do the dishes first. You want it to be fresh in some way. I don't want to repeat myself. It's always a little bit of something old and something new—except I don't record with great frequency so, with the time that's gone between records, you can't avoid having gone through some changes. I think you get more confident with your process—even though you're trying to *change* the process, you know? Because I don't cook the same way every time. Sometimes I put the turkey in one side of my mouth and the tomato in the other side and I just chew it up in the car. Other times you spend the whole evening making a meal and it's gone in fifteen minutes. I don't know, maybe it's—a different identity that you get? Everybody has a growing edge—you know, where the growth stops on the plant and the new branch comes out?

SS: Your branch seems to have grown backwards. Where your peers get cozier with age—less likely to fuck with things or scare their listeners—you, at fifty, get an indie deal, an alternative rock Grammy, and make increasingly edgy albums. Challenging yourself or your audience?

TW: Myself. Fighting against decay. We all die kind of a toe at a time. But, I don't know, some old fruit trees put out the best stuff. . . . It wasn't really a conscious thing, but I always figured that you get to be more eccentric as you get older and people have to endure it. "Old Uncle Al has spittle around his chin, but that's OK, he's old." I guess I've always admired people that are able to dance like there's nobody watching—that's kind of what making songs is trying to accomplish, to ignore the fact that it is being recorded.

SS: What is it with you and "old"?

TW: I wanted to be an old man when I was a little kid. Wore my granddaddy's hat, used his cane, and lowered my voice. I was dying to be old. I paid a lot of attention to old people. The music I listened to as a teenager was old-people music. Yeah, I heard The Beatles, but I didn't really pay attention. I was suspicious of anyone new and young. I don't know, probably a respect thing? My father left when I was about eleven—I think I looked up to older musicians like father figures. Louis Armstrong or Bing Crosby or Nat King Cole or Howlin' Wolf—I never really thought about it that way, but maybe it was that I needed parental guidance or something.

SS: Gerontophilia would have been a curious stance to take in '60s California?

TW: I was always kind of backwards in a lot of ways—in fact, when I was a teenager I tried to get a job at a piano lounge at a golf course in San Diego. It was a little pathetic. I put on a suit, I didn't even know enough songs to pull it off really; I learned some Frank Sinatra and Cole Porter. But it was interesting that that was the world I wanted to be part of, plaid pants and golf.

SS: And isolating in an era when the world was divided into "us"—young, long-haired, pot-smoking, guitar-playing—and "them"—old, suit-wearing, piano-playing, golf clubbers.

TW: I was a rebel. A rebel against the rebels. I discovered alcohol at an early age and that guided me a lot.

SS: Didn't the hippie culture intrigue you?

TW: Well, I had shot a friend of mine—by accident. I was shooting cans in a canyon and he walked in front of me and my gun went off and hit him in the hip and it came out the inside of his leg. He was fine—the first thing he said to me—his name was Pat Gonzalez—was "Tom, why did you do it?" like it was a Western. I picked him up—fortunately, he was smaller than me—and ran three miles, put him in the car, drove him to the hospital. While he was recuperating, he had people come and visit—a cousin who had been in San Francisco and he had hair down to here, an earring, everything—really bizarre to see. I became curious about San Francisco from that point on. But what happened, when I went up there, I went to City Lights bookstore, I was looking for Jack Kerouac. Determined to find someone at least who used to know him—I knew the bars he went to from the books, so I used to go look around. I remember meeting Lawrence Ferlinghetti, got his autograph on a book, and I would go and sit by the window with a cup of coffee and look out at the street and spend hours there trying to conjure up that world. I think that was my first entrance into youth culture—but I was a little late on that one.

SS: The right age for Vietnam though?

TW: It was weird. I had a very low lottery number and I wound up being a fireman for three years—in the forestry service, way out in the sticks on the border between Mexico and California. I learned how to dig a hole in the ground and bury myself so the fire would burn over me. Never had to use it since, but I'm ready.

SS: Your first record label, Asylum, represented the West Coast, post-hippie, singer-songwriter mafia. How did you fit into that clique and how did it inform your music?

TW: I was very suspicious of organized crime—or organized groups. Afraid of going in there. I genuinely didn't know where I fit in. I looked around me and saw the artists who most people would assume I should fraternize and create some bonds with, but I didn't know what to do. My manager worked with Zappa, so I went on the road and opened for Frank Zappa for a couple of years—really hard time, very disturbing, with 3,500 people united together chanting "You suck," full volume, in a hockey arena. But I think I *wanted* some resistance. So that I would really be genuinely committed to what I wanted to do. I didn't want it to be too easy. It wasn't.

SS: So you dug a hole and let the fire rage overhead?

TW: Right, that's what I did. I was the opening act for a lot of different people they assume you'll be compatible with—Martha and the Vandellas, Buffy Sainte-Marie, Bonnie Raitt.

SS: They must have had an odd idea who you were?

TW: I wasn't sure at that point if I knew who I was either. Even though I was recording by that time, I was flailing about, trying to find my own voice.

SS: When do you feel you found it?

TW: Hmm . . .

SS: By your second album, *The Heart of Saturday Night*, we got glimpses.

TW: It was very ill formed, but I was trying. There was spoken word on there. I don't know, in those days I think I really wanted to see my head on somebody else's body. It was that kind of deal. When I was writing, I kind of made up my own little Tin Pan Alley so I could sit at the piano, like a songwriter, with a bottle and an ashtray and come out of the room with a handful of songs, as they did.

SS: Why piano, not guitar?

TW: I don't know—my father was a singer, mariachi music was his big love, and Harry Belafonte, so I learned all these Mexican folk songs when I was a kid—Woody Guthrie too; he was from Texas. And music really is a language, so maybe when I was learning Spanish as a kid I felt at the same time I had a propensity for music, because he was showing me things on the guitar. My dad—his name's Jesse Frank, named after Jesse and Frank, a double shot there of rebellion, he was really a tough one—was always an outsider. He slept in the orange groves and learned Spanish at a young age. If you went to a restaurant in Mexico with my dad, he would invite the mariachis to the table and give them two dollars for a song, and then *he* would start to sing with them and he would wind up leaving with them, and we would have to find our way back to the hotel on our own, and

Dad would come home a day later, because he fell asleep on a hilltop somewhere looking down on the town.

SS: A very romantic picture.

TW: *Very* romantic—but it's in there with a lot of documentary footage as well where the lighting is not nearly as good. But my dad—I think it was a rebel raising a rebel. That's kind of what my kids are dealing with right now—when your mission is really to be immovable and filled with guidance and assurance and an ability to look over the hill and see what's coming? So somewhere in the conflict of all that is where I am.

SS: Mexican music rivals Jewish music in extravagant sentimentality. Fuse that with that cinematically romantic image you just painted of the past and you get a big part of your music.

TW: Maudlin and schmaltzy. Oh yeah, I'm aware of that. My wife [cowriter Kathleen Brennan] electrocutes me every time I do that.

SS: She has a schmaltz meter?

TW: She really does. And I have to be careful—"Am I slipping into self-parody here?" "Is this worthwhile or just a lame exercise?" The song she really hates is "Saving All My Love for You," off *Heartattack and Vine*. "What *is* this bullshit?"— I'm happy to have it pointed out. "If I have egg on my face, tell me," and she does. Because—I don't know where songs come from, some of it comes from incantations, some from talking in tongues. Writing songs, *you're* the instrument. You know, you're really working on yourself.

SS: Many of your songs exist in an idealized, romantic, neon-lit, pre-'60s America. Did you invent this world as a place to create your art in, or do you inhabit it as much as possible day-to-day?

TW: Gee, I don't know. The line is blurred sometimes. But I have a very different life when I'm not on the road or in the studio. My role in the family is very different to my role in that world—ball games, graduations, family reunions. I think perhaps when I was younger I was much more hesitant to leave my world that I drew nourishment from to write, and now I feel like I can go back and forth between the documentary and the romantic comedy, you know?

SS: *Blue Valentine* was your most mannered album, as far as that "Tom Waits'" world goes—a side effect of the film acting you started doing around then?

TW: I used to think I was making movies for the ears—writing them, directing them, releasing them. Kind of making a fiction in a nonfiction world. Taking the real world and then getting rid of certain things that I didn't want to be there and adding certain things that I hoped would have been there. I was overly maudlin and romantic and I really hadn't grown up, I still very much lived in a fantasy world. But I like that "Blue Valentines" song. Still play it sometimes. Somebody asked me to play that at a wedding recently.

SS: Do you hire yourself out?

TW: No, no, no, it was a friend's wedding.

SS: Just thought I'd clear it up in case you get bombarded with requests.

TW: I do. But it's hard even for my loved ones to get me to do things like that.

SS: When you're cast in a film, it's according to who and what the director—not you—thinks you are. What have you learned about yourself from the roles you're offered?

TW: I don't know. You see, I don't really think of myself as an actor. I do some acting, like I do a little plumbing, I do a little electrical, I do a little instrument repair. The only thing, when I'm making songs, is I'm the actor in the songs. "What's the voice for this song?" "What should this guy be wearing in this picture?" I have a few I try on and then I land on the right one.

SS: You said on *Blue Valentine* you hadn't grown up. On *Heartattack and Vine* you sounded like you'd aged thirty years. Were you trying to wear your old voice out as an excuse to get a new one?

TW: I didn't know any way of finding a new one, but I know I was anxious to reach a new channel, and sometimes we don't know how to do that. You're like a wound-up toy car who's hit a wall and you just keep hitting it. I was very self-destructive. Drinking and smoking and staying out all night long and it wasn't good for me so I sounded like I had been screaming into a pillow. You know, I needed to shift gears—I knew that I wanted to change but I didn't really know how to do it. I got married there, right after, in 1980, so that was really the kind of end of a certain long period of my life.

SS: In 1983 you released two albums that couldn't have been more polarized: the Tin Pan Alley sentimentality of Coppola soundtrack *One from the Heart* and the free-form musical madness of *Swordfishtrombones*. What was going on?

TW: That was my wife. She had the best record collection—she thought that I was going to have a really great record collection and was sorely disappointed. I hadn't really listened to Captain Beefheart before, even though I worked with Zappa. I was such a one-man show—very isolated in what I allowed myself to be exposed to. I *was* like an old man, stuck in my ways. She helped me rethink myself. Because my music up to that point was still in the box—*I* was still in the box; hadn't unwrapped myself yet. She let me take my shoes off and loosen up—back then I was still wearing suits to the park. I think from that point on I really tried to grow. Growth is scary, because you're a seed and you're in the dark and you don't know which way is up, and down might take you down further into a darker place, you know? I felt like that: I don't know which way to grow. I don't know what to incorporate into myself. What do you want to take from your parents? What did you come in with? What did you find when you got here? I was sorting all that out.

SS: When Keith Richards guested on *Rain Dogs*, what would a fly on the wall have seen?

TW: Oh man . . . ! I was going to work with the people I'd always worked with, but they were in L.A. and I'd moved to New York. I remember somebody said, "Who do you want to play on the record? Anybody," and I said, "Ah, Keith Richards"—I'm a huge, huge fan of the Rolling Stones. They said, "Call him right now." I was like, "Jesus, don't do that, please don't do that, I was just kidding around." A couple of weeks later he sent me a note: "The wait is over. Let's dance. Keith." And he comes in with a guitar valet, who brought in seven hundred guitars and three hundred amps. And I was "Oh Jesus. . . ." Shy? *Entirely* shy.

SS: You weren't tempted back to the bottle?

TW: Well, you really can't keep up with Keith. He's from a different stock. I didn't realize it at first, but then I met his father and I understood. His dad looked like Popeye. He had the little corncob pipe and the wink in his eye—oh man! I was real nervous and trying to not be afraid, but he's real regular, a gentleman, and we had a lot of fun. He just loves to play. He'll play at four o'clock in the morning, play until the bottle is gone, like an old troubadour, until they can't remember any more songs or they turn out the lights and tell us to leave.

SS: You worked with another one-off, William Burroughs, on *Black Rider*. Most vivid memory?

TW: Every day at about three o'clock he'd start massaging his watch, like he's trying to get the big hand to move with the heat of his fingers because around three thirty or four o'clock it's cocktail hour. We went to his house and hung out for a couple of days. I saw some of his shotgun paintings—he puts up plywood and shoots it—and we'd talk about the story and all these songs just started occurring to him, "Take off your skin and dance. . . ." From Burroughs I learned a lot about reptiles and firearms.

SS: Like you, his aim wasn't too good.

TW: Right! For me, working with him was a chance to go up on the wire without a net and you really find out what kind of resources you have. Because you're with someone who has a whole *community* inside of them. It was heavy.

SS: When you're writing for the stage rather than a record, do you keep in mind that it's something that will change, depending where and when it's staged?

TW: With an album, you fix it—you can wait until it's exactly like you want it and then freeze it in time—but doing a piece of theater is almost like putting a circle of rocks right here and then coming back in two weeks, expecting them all to be in the same place. But you still try to fix it, give it a skeleton—you should be able to know that it's an alligator or it's a flamingo even though it'll change position—and you work as if opening night is the night when it will all be fixed in resin forever, so you've got to have your whole look down and don't forget your hat. But as soon as you leave, everyone goes "I hate the way that fucker made me sing that song. He's gone now, so I'm going to do it how I want." That's human nature. I'm the same way if I'm in a play. I've been in some plays and when the director's gone it's "Whew, it's mine now, what's he going to do, come up in the middle of the show and take my hat off? Hell no!"

SS: Were you surprised to find yourself in middle age, signed to a young indie label and selling a million copies of *Mule Variations*?

TW: Oh yeah. It was my first record for them and I had no idea what was going to happen, I was excited but I wasn't really sure where I fit in—an almost exclusively punk label and here I am, like fifty, am I some old fuddy-duddy trying out a new haircut? But they convinced me that I belonged there and that what I was doing was perfectly valid, and that gave me confidence. Because what I do is kind of abstract—I work on things that are in some way invisible. Yeah the room's filled with instruments, but to process things that are invisible. So I break a lot of eggs. And I leave the shell in there. Texture's everything.

SS: There's some interesting textures on the new album—your vocal sounds like a loop impersonating a tortured rhythm instrument.

TW: Yeah yeah. But it wasn't a loop. The trouble with a loop is once your mind realizes that it's a loop it stops listening to it, just like you stop looking at the pattern on that tablecloth. There's no reason to continue to stare at that pattern. So every three or four bars you have to do something different. I would do it until my throat was raw—*Ook, kakkk kakk*—sweating, eyes all bugged out, hair sticking up, in the bathroom with a little four-track, singing in the microphone at night while everyone's asleep. I felt like I was talking in tongues because I was making sounds that weren't words, but once I listened back I could actually determine certain syllables. It was like going back in time with the language where the sound came first and then slowly it shaped itself around items and experiences.

I'm one of those people that if I don't have my knees skinned and a cut on my hand, I don't really feel like I've had much of a day's work. That's where the title came from—the blues thing, like I'm *really gone*.

SS: *Real Gone* is what *Mojo* calls the "obituaries."

TW: I'd better be careful then. Kathleen made up the title. She said: "All these people on the record are leaving. You're not going to be leaving, are you?"

SS: If you do, might you finally come back and play Britain?

TW: It's not that I don't like the UK, I just don't like to travel [*smiles*]. I'm a *really* grumpy guy.

"Tom Waits: Dancing in the Dark"
Harp
December 2004
Tom Moon

Undisguised glee creeps into Tom Waits's voice when he talks about the instructional dance song he heard on the radio the other day. He can't quite believe he stumbled onto such a thing, a hip-hop station in 2004 playing what amounts to the bling generation's Mashed Potato. It's Terror Squad, featuring Fat Joe, doing "Lean Back," but in his telling, the song it becomes a pearl on the order of "The Twist." "It was so wild, they're telling you how to do it. The only phrase I caught was 'lean back,' but you couldn't mistake it. I mean, I haven't had anybody tell me how to do a dance in a long, long time."

The wheels are turning because it just so happens that he, Tom Waits, has an instructional dance song on his new disc *Real Gone*. He's not going to delude himself, but the more he thinks about this the more he realizes that as a semi-obscure cult artist with limited commercial prospects, it's his duty to at least try to drum up business for the latest work—and his contribution to the storied dance-step genre, "Metropolitan Glide," a junkyard symphony of rattling skeletons, slurpy mouth percussion and urban-gangster fabulousness that harkens to a bygone era. No one will confuse it with "Lean Back," but still, he might just be on the front end of a trend. He says he's already placed calls to several executives at his label, alerting them about the Terror Squad track's prodigious airplay. "I said, honey, look into that, we gotta get on this station," he says in a tone that's death-letter serious and at the same time playfully self-mocking. "This could be the opening we need."

This unleashes a fantasy on the theme of Tom Waits Having a Hit. He's asked what might happen to him if "Metropolitan Glide" someday broke large. "You mean people from all over, Indiana to Hong Kong, out in the street doing the Metropolitan Glide? Poet laureate of America and all that? What would it do to me?" He pauses for a moment to contemplate such an oddity. "I'd get the truck fixed. Whatever came in on that net, we'd have to freeze. I'd have to get a freezer. I'm not twenty-one, I've got most of the stuff I want."

Yet try as he might to dismiss it, "Lean Back" won't leave him alone. It appeals to his sense of continuum, his belief that everything old can be new again. It's fuel for his argument that there is something intrinsically valuable, if not noble, about going back and doing the grimy work of transformation. In the Waitsian view, it was only a matter of time before those dance-like-this songs stormed back onto the airwaves—either as a viable commercial endeavor like "Lean Back" or more of a nudge-wink commentary, as on "Metropolitan Glide." During an extended telephone interview from his home in Northern California, the fifty-four-year-old singer occasionally refers to himself as "Recyclerman," or, less grandiosely, "Finderman"—the one to call when your car keys are lost in the couch. That's who he is in the studio: Waits's recordings proceed from the belief that any discarded spare-pan relic from the pop-culture heap can be found, dusted off, and repurposed. That the drivetrain from the old Rambler, long past its usefulness as a drivetrain, might just be the perfect authentic thing for some wood-grained Restoration Hardware contraption designed to look like a throwback and glide ever so subversively like a stealth bomber. Waits's musical repertoire/architecture is made exclusively from cobbled parts, some unfrozen from as far back as Louis Armstrong and others lifted from the Fat Joe production trick bag. He gets a certain delight in hearing how the discontinuous pieces coexist, how the bigfoot hip-hop backbeats rub against vocal phrasings he's borrowed from a time when the blues was new.

But the dance steps—the ones he talks about and the ones he doesn't—are the secret killers underpinning most of the transfixing *Real Gone*. It's the first Waits effort since *Rain Dogs* to benefit from the input of guitarist Marc Ribot, and not coincidentally, is the most rhythmically intense offering since that 1985 benchmark. There are moments when the music herks and jerks with the customary Waitsian sad-sack swagger, moments devoted to slow Afro-Cuban ritual processions and rock-steady grooves that won't let you sit still. The conventional reading divides Waits's oeuvre into the broad categories "grand weepers" and "grim reapers," and while both exist on *Real Gone*, the latest iterations of both archetypes aren't cut precisely from the old molds—this time Waits evidently believes both can benefit from a goosing on the dance floor.

Waits says that after the interior contemplations of his last project, the twin discs *Alice* and *Blood Money*, he wanted radical change. He avoided the piano entirely. At first he avoided even conventional instruments entirely. Seeking music that was less fussy, less European (though *Real Gone* does contain several parlor songs), with less instrumental elaboration, he began by returning to the organic mouth-percussion textures he'd experimented with in the late 1980s. He wanted, he says, to fly on instinct, and so he assembled hundreds of rhythm ideas generated on the fly and worried about the song forms later. He began to relate everything to dance. His acid test for ideas: Did it make you dance?

"The only reason people dance is that they're supplying with their body the missing syncopated notes," Waits says. "You know, raise your elbow, throw your head back and kick the dirt. That's a pretty great thing. You almost can't talk about it. It's just natural to do."

What Waits was after wasn't the line-dancing perfection found on MTV or the Super Bowl halftime show. Instead, he wanted real dancing abandon. "What I mean is dancing like nobody's watching," Waits says. "I heard that from [comic] Dave Chappelle, and I can't stop thinking about it. . . . Music right now is, you know people are going to be watching. Even when you make a record there are people watching what you do, and I'm not sure that self-consciousness helps anything. The other day my little boy [Sullivan, age eleven, is the youngest of the three Waits/Brennan kids] had a record on full blast, and he was dancing, totally in the moment. I saw him through a crack in the door. It was amazing how he believed in it. As soon as he knew I was there, he stopped. Turned off the music. Well, that's really what you're trying to accomplish in the studio. My job is to locate that mood, enlarge it, and then put everybody in the middle of it. You want them to dance like there's nobody watching. You want them to be talking in tongues."

Dancing while nobody's looking is not necessarily easy to capture on tape. It means suspending judgment, putting self-consciousness on the deep back burner. It takes a certain kind of person—someone with a highly developed ego and the ability to keep moving through what would be, for most people, embarrassing situations. It requires a bit of hustler chutzpah, and it is this last trait that Tom Waits has covered. He might not be the most ruthless operator, but inside him beats the heart of a sideshow huckster. His songs are full of schemes and scamming, of rigged games in shady parts of town, and frauds unraveled before they can begin. His favorite characters are broken-down show people with one good eye and the obligatory heart of gold, who are endlessly willing to proclaim undying love for romantic interests described as "Horse Face Ethel" and the like. His stories take place in the dusty open fields and back lots where the carnivals roll in and set up. He follows the road-rough types employed by small-time circuses, watches them doing their one sellable skill—sword-swallowing or the flying trapeze—and then follows them back into rattling trailers, where they medicate themselves with not-so-magic potions and face those nagging existential demons.

On *Real Gone*, there's an extended spoken-word reverie, "Circus," that Waits says came out in a daydream torrent. Running away with the circus, he says, was "a thing I used to think about in school. . . . I remember George Burns once said that after he saw some vaudeville show, he realized he wanted to get into show business as soon as possible. What is it about that? Some grand old tradition, I guess. Usually it's filled with people who are in some way fractured or bruised or chipping. It's the old irritation-in-the-oyster-making-the-pearl."

What he likes about the circus is the show isn't simply what happens in the center ring. "You think you're going to the circus looking at the show people? They're looking at you. You're just an extra in their show that night. Your being there is twofold—to be entertained, and as background noise, part of the strange pattern of faces in the crowd."

That awareness, expressed in a strange megaphone vocal that tells of music sounding like "electric sugar," gives "Circus" its poignancy, its energy. "Of course it's highly romantic the way I put it," Waits says, asked about his storytelling strategies. "It all has to do with what you leave in and what you leave out. There's an art to that, telling a story to make somebody split a gut. . . . It's 'How do you take a picture of your driveway and make it look like the road of life?'"

He doesn't provide an answer. There is no answer. But this is one of Waits's special niche skills. "Usually people who do that don't know how to do other things. My wife, she can take apart the truck, spread the parts out on a blanket, and put it back together with no parts left over. She's been a heavy equipment operator and a suicide hotline gal. She can fix the television set. So for everything you can do, there's something you can't do—otherwise, all of business collapses."

Leaving aside Waits's economic theories, there is a certain essential check-and-balance to his creative relationship with Kathleen Brennan, who has served as adviser, ear, lyricist, and copilot. She'll clip stories she thinks he might have missed from the paper. She'll toss ideas out when he's stuck. He doesn't like to break down the "who does what," but will say that Brennan serves as his bullshit detector and sounding board.

"Having someone to check your work is a good thing," he says in a grudging grumble. "Just to be able to say, 'Honey, is this crap?' Tell me. I think it's great, but I'm biased. I think everything I do should be for sale. But tell me, am I full of it? That's what you do when you collaborate. The doing of it becomes richer, and hopefully the work becomes richer."

It's been that way long enough for these two. Waits had already recorded several key albums when they met at Francis Ford Coppola's Zoetrope Studios where he'd come to write the music for *One from the Heart* and encountered Brennan, who worked there as a script editor. By then, Waits had played out the *Heartattack and Vine* boho thing and was ready to move on. The two married in 1980 and began collaborating shortly afterward—on the work that became *Swordfishtrombones*, released in 1983.

Around that time, Waits began to get serious about acting—he played the pool hall owner in *Rumble Fish* (1983) and a sharpie in *The Cotton Club* the following year, though his most powerful role was as Zack in Jim Jarmusch's 1986 road film *Down by Law*. He also wrote several plays, including *The Black Rider*. It's tempting to conclude that the theater work has influenced Waits's music since *Rain Dogs*—the themes have grown more universal (even as, perversely, the characterizations sharpened), the insights delivered in language that moves beyond circus-barker patter. But it's equally possible that the maturity and wisdom was Brennan's contribution.

Waits won't say. He describes the creative end of their partnership this way: "A lot of times, it's like lighting firecrackers—who gets to light, who throws. We take turns. Sometimes it's: I'll get the cherry bomb, you hold, I'll light!"

Most singing voices have one singular overriding characteristic—a honeyed purity, a porcelain sheen. Tom Waits's vocal instrument is a broad-spectrum assault weapon: sometimes when he sings, extreme high harmonics resembling the squeaks of a church mouse are audible, way in the ether. Running beneath them is a sawtooth snarl in the upper-midrange that sounds like paint being scraped from a ceiling. Along with that comes a touch of battery-acid bray, then down low, in the bass range, the formless howl of a marine animal. You hear him sing several of the demanding vocal things from *Real Gone*—the brutal "Hoist That Rag," the more mannered "Sins of My Father"—and there's so many textures coming through at once it sounds like Waits multitracked himself.

Then there's the phrasing. Though he's always been a student of the soul singers—Ray Charles is in his DNA, as is Solomon Burke—Waits affects not just the contours of soul, but its peculiar pacing; an ambling, tempo-defying slowness runs throughout his singing on the new songs. Recognizing, perhaps, that his voice is the ultimate manifestation of the word "jalopy," he lurches and putters and sputters along, and only in the album's mannered moments (the parlor song "Dead and Lovely") does he suspend the feeling of constant motion. Also more evident this time is a Louis Armstrongian tick, an appraising, murmuring curl that provides some phrases with world-weary finishing punctuation. Maybe he always had Satch in his sights, but now he's located the gravitas to pull it off.

Waits says he began *Real Gone* with hours of vocal percussion taped in his bathroom. The idea was to make little groove contraptions using his voice—on some tracks Waits can be heard chugging and spitting as the one-man-beatboxing foundation, popping out rhythms that might sound looped but were often recorded in linear fashion, from start to finish. ("I didn't want things to be so perfect," he says. "I did it for four minutes just like you'd do a drum part, get all sweaty, and that way it would feel like I was really inside the tune, with everything sliding a little bit.")

Then, after cobbling together basic rhythmic structure, he invited his eighteen-year-old son Casey (a turntable artist), Ribot, bassist Larry Taylor and percussionist Brain Mantia to play along. He expected some fireworks, simply because he'll set up a collision between modern cut-and-paste production methods and the old-school-all-live approach. Since *Rain Dogs*, Ribot's musical diet has included hard urban sounds and clever updates of Cuban guitar music of the 1950s. Waits suspects that Casey showed up because there was money involved—"He saw it as a new skateboard kind of thing"—but he found himself pleasantly surprised at the textures and energy his son brought to the music.

"What happened this time was there's one guy in my band who's eighteen and one guy's in his mid-sixties, and when everybody gets together you know they're gonna learn something—each wants what the other knows. . . . We'd used turntables before, but the techniques have changed all over the place— they've changed in heavy equipment and in bird sanctuaries. People are always saying, 'I remember when he used to go out with a shovel and a rag around his head to do the fields.' Everything is available to you in the modern studio, and that can be liberating. There were days when the decision was: 'Am I gonna put the mic in the bathroom and hit that trash can with a two-by-four, or am I gonna go with the Pearl snare?'"

Waits allows that the biggest mind-blower for him was singing on top of the percussive tracks he'd made with his voice. "When I do it, and then sing over it, it's like harmonizing with yourself in a way. There's already a rapport. It's like in science—they're injecting human genes into pig fetuses now, so that when the pigs come to maturity their organs will be accepted more readily in humans. The voice seems to sound different when there are all these other vocal things around it. We got at a whole different energy in the rhythm, too."

For much of the last decade, there's been a set of recurring complaints about Waits: That he's too obvious about recycling his tricks, that his chronicles of love undone and his almost-romantic odes pondering mortality have become boilerplate, that his sentimental stuff is sung by the same boho characters inhabiting the same vinyl-bar-stool, Schlitz-on-tap lounges. That the spectacular, almost shamanic street dramas of *Rain Dogs* and *Franks Wild Years* have lost a certain animating quality in subsequent iterations.

This much is indisputable: the avid recycler's characters are a dying breed, denizens of frontier America who've vanished since the time when Jack Kerouac, another great chronicler of dissipation, took to the road. There might be more Tom Waits songs immortalizing the doings of the small-time marginal schemers than there are actual humans living this way in 2004. Waits has painted himself into a curious cul-de-sac: he's scrounging the byways for rogue outlaw behavior now found mostly in theme parks, and so as much as the romantic in him wants to paint an outsized notion of circus life, say, he has to bring some sense of human truth, if not a human scale, to the enterprise.

Real Gone—the title, Waits says, appropriates the Beat phrase for "crazy" and also refers to the preponderance of characters leaving or dying—manages to thwart that recycling criticism in several ways, through its vivid, screenplaylike lyric images and the jackrabbit rhythmic urgency that carries them. The characters of *Real Gone* are normal-enough folks, bit players whose hopes and dreams are relatively unremarkable. Waits makes them seem almost heroic, however—on the ten-minute processional "Sins of My Father," he tells of a wayward son's urge to cleanse, if not rewrite, the past; on the poignant bewildered-lover ode "Trampled Rose," he follows the thoughts of a fallen dandy who realizes he's been betrayed when he spots a flower in the street. Once Waits could rattle off the disconnected observations of a prison dweller, and that was exotic enough to carry a song; now, with "Shake It," he ventures deep into that convict's dreams and drives, catching something almost universal about the living change he plans to do when freedom comes.

Waits has given some thought to this charge that he's just riffing. His conclusion is that there are no new notes. Everything in popular music is an update of something else, which is why he's so captivated by that instructional hip-hop dance step. No matter how much he wishes to be regarded as an innovator, his contribution is primarily as an assimilator. What he does is, to an extent, further refinement and refraction of what he's already done—sometimes incorporating different colors or ideas. Do not look to him for the long-awaited reinvention of the wheel.

"Most artists you hear are really doing bad imitations of other people," he says solemnly. "And they're afraid you're going to notice it. If Howlin' Wolf told you he was really trying to sound like Jimmie Rodgers, you'd say 'nice try, missed it by a mile.' Well, that mile is his work. . . . To me, what artists do is take in all this information and send back a picture of something that's moving. Recordings are like little postings, an ongoing conversation that's part of living culture. You're always sending feelers out, to find new protein or carbohydrates, and sometimes what you bring back is a Salvation Army relic. Sometimes the most pleasant thing is to go backwards."

Among the other throwback moments on *Real Gone* is a soldier's letter home entitled "Day After Tomorrow." It doesn't talk explicitly about Iraq; in fact, it could be the voice of a Civil War soldier singing a lonesome late-night dirge. But Waits says he wrote it as a way to engage the world he lives in, at least in a distant, elliptical way. "I hate to sound cynical, but it seems to me that protest songs are like throwing peanuts at a gorilla," he says. "It's hard to believe that a song like that is gonna make any difference in the course we're on. But at the same time, that Pete Seeger song about the 'Big Muddy' became more than a song. I don't want to contribute to the rhetoric, or even assume I have the ability to speak about these things on an intelligent level. I know my own limitations . . . I can sound like I know a lot about something for five minutes. Don't stay too long, or I slide into idiot. But I also know that everybody feels like we're going ninety miles an hour down a dead-end street, and we didn't make that feeling up."

There's a corollary to Waits's theory about dancing while nobody's looking, and it has to do with being selective about information, and remaining ignorant when necessary. At one point when we're talking about the process of making *Real Gone*, Waits complains that breaking it down into such parts takes something away. "It's like we're separating all the ingredients—I had a little mint, I had the onions chopped and ready—well, it's not really as simple as a recipe. . . . Some things are better left unknown."

This, he continues, is what's wrong with the world. "Everything is explained now. We live in an age when you say casually to somebody, 'What's the story on that?' and they can run to the computer and tell you within five seconds. That's fine, but sometimes I'd just as soon continue wondering. We have a deficit of wonder right now."

He laments that even the thing he likes to do more than anything else—making records—has become a more clinical enterprise, drained of its mysteries and its surprise collisions. "I made a tape once called *The House of Sound*. I took twenty-four tracks, and did something different, completely unrelated, on each adjacent track. There was screaming, there were rhythmic things. I'd bring the parts up and down one or two at a time, and it was always different, depending on which rooms you entered. And then we'd go into the common room with everything happening at once, and it was like an orchestra tuning up, which is my favorite part. Somebody's playing scales, somebody else is going over a passage they trip up on, and the mashup of all the sounds is amazing. Sometimes when the piece starts I'm disappointed. Because they had a good thing going and ruined it. Making music when they didn't think they were making music yet—essentially, dancing while they thought nobody was watching. And it was amazing. If you ask me, we need more of that."

"All Stripped Down"
Paste
December 2004
Tom Lanham

Tom Waits should be giddy at the moment. Last night—in his first performance in five years, at Vancouver's intimate 2,400-seat Orpheum Theatre—he strolled onstage in his regulation baggy black suit and skewed porkpie hat, all spider-limbed and spectral, and then tore through most of the primal-blues jackhammers from his new album, *Real Gone*. He employed a pedal-activated, digital-delay device to re-create the vast vocal percussions that drive the disc—woofing nonsensical syllables like *"Acka, poom-poom"* or *"Boom chicky-tatta"* and replaying them as looped backbeats. Waits was more than animated—his lithe frame twitched and shuddered to the jarring rhythms.

And he was generous, as well. Alongside stark new numbers like "Metropolitan Glide," "Top of the Hill" and the guttural "Hoist That Rag" (all cowritten/coproduced with his wife, Kathleen Brennan), he tossed in crowd-pleasing classics like "Tabletop Joe," "Heartattack and Vine," and "House Where Nobody Lives," a signature track from his stellar 1999 Grammy winner *Mule Variations* (his first for hip indie label, Anti-). The show—featuring Marc Ribot on guitar, someone called Brain on drums, Larry Taylor on bass and Waits's son Casey on percussion—heads to Europe next, before reportedly swinging back through America in early 2005.

Waits should be overjoyed about other things, too. Like the smash-hit, sold-out London and San Francisco runs of *The Black Rider*, with Marianne Faithfull trilling the Brecht/Weill-ish lieder he composed for playwright Robert Wilson. Or another Wilson-commissioned soundtrack, *Alice*, whose "Kommienezuspadt" closed the Vancouver set. Or his umpteenth feature-film appearance, jawing over java with Iggy Pop in Jim Jarmusch's *Coffee and Cigarettes*. Or even "A Little Drop of Poison," the delectable ditty he contributed to the *Shrek 2* soundtrack. After disappearing from the recording scene for most of the 1990s, this gravel-throated minstrel is experiencing a comeback, a renaissance rocketing the fifty-five-year-old right back to the singer-songwriter vanguard—turf he first staked out back in 1973 with his decadent Asylum Records debut, *Closing Time.*

But today, when Waits shuffles into King Fortune Seafood, a Chinese restaurant a few blocks from the Orpheum, he's simply smiling about last night's triumph. He's comfortable with it, as he is with all his other lauded coups of late, seemingly happy to be back, happy to be hitting the road again and flexing those stage muscles. Sure, he's also become the pet character actor of top-flight film directors like Jarmusch, Robert Altman, and Francis Ford Coppola. And during his thirty-year career, his songs have been covered by everyone from The Eagles and Rod Stewart to Johnny Cash and Bruce Springsteen (who ironically chose "Jersey Girl," Waits's note-perfect spoof of the Boss and his working-class-isms).

But Waits is remarkably humble about all this. So when he sits down at a secluded corner table, he thoughtfully sips several cups of jasmine tea and contemplates—in yarn-spinning raconteur style—much larger issues. Like what his good friend Fred "Herman Munster" Gwynne told him before he passed away, back when they were acting together in Coppola's *Cotton Club.* "He said that when he goes to heaven, and God says 'What did you do while you were down there?' he'll go, 'I got a little piece of film I'd like to show ya,'" chuckles Waits, whose steely, blue-eyed gaze is as hypnotic and unwavering as Rasputin's probably was. "'It's just a little clip from a Bertolucci thing I did called *Luna.*' Fred said, 'That's all I'm gonna show Him, not *The Munsters* stuff, just the *Luna* clip.' And that was it, just a great little moment for him." Waits immediately liked Gwynne, he recalls, because "he was a seeker—he was always on a quest."

The same tribute could be paid to Waits. His melancholy work—initially peopled with *Munster*-type misanthropes—has grown increasingly numinous and metaphysical over the years. When he warns on *Real Gone*, "Don't go into the barn," he feels no need to spell out why—you can hear in his Doberman snarl that something quite tragic, possibly bloody, took place there. And he's not interested in the incident itself—just the haunted funereal pall, the sense of threat left behind. But when Waits himself arrives at the pearly gates someday, what life moments would he show? After talking with him for over an hour, one feels that it might be his whirlwind romance with Brennan, whom he met while working on Coppola's *One from the Heart*. She taught him how to rethink himself—that he didn't need the headaches of a major label or the smarmy industry figures who went with it, that they could go it alone as a songwriting couple and find receptive outlets later, once the music was completed. That purity of vision—uncluttered by any accepted rules of rockdom—paved the path for *Real Gone* and its startling human-beatbox experiments. And for the new relaxation that's swept over the Northern California–based Waits, even on the eve of his demanding new tour.

So what kind of footage would the man choose to screen? It might not be *Luna*, but it's damned close. So sit back and dim the lights . . . 4, 3, 2, 1—roll clip.

Tom Lanham: Interesting menu here. . . . Like that old *National Lampoon* fake Chinese menu, with Twice Chewed Lobster in Hissing Sauce and Sweet 'n' Sour Land Shrimp . . .

Tom Waits: Nobody chews my lobster but me, I'll tell ya. But you've heard about regular people who've been in car accidents or suffered a stroke or something, or had some kind of injury at work, like a blow to the head. And as a result of the injury, they are now gourmands. They crave only the most exotic foods. And they're usually working-class people, so all of a sudden at the dinner table, you've got Fred Flintstone getting very effete, until his whole family doesn't know who in the hell he is. They're like, "What—did you have your brain replaced?"

TL: This first question is rather odd but bear with me. Have you ever seen the Joe Dante film *Gremlins*? Or met Dante at all? Because there's actually a *Nighthawks*-era Tom Waits gremlin in the film, murmuring to himself in the gremlin bar. Or at least it looks that way.

TW: No! Really? I dunno—I probably have seen it somewhere, 'cause I've got kids. But I've never sat down and watched it front to back.

TL: Well, that shoots down my whole theory.

TW: Backup! Do you have backup for this?

TL: I'm smarter than I look. I'm curious about how your persona—or early perception of it, at least—has become intertwined with pop culture.

TW: Gee, I dunno. . . . That's a tough one. My own personality intertwined with pop culture. . . . Oh, the character. Yeah. But I don't have a lotta contact with it—I'm on the road a lot. But you mean unshaven, cigarette, eggs and whiskey, sleeping till three in the afternoon? I don't know where that fits into pop culture, because I'm not really an expert on pop culture. But it's kinda like a Cantinflas character. But it's a ventriloquist act, ya know. There's me, and then there's that. And that's not me.

TL: I'm left with all these remarkable visuals of you, though. Like you working that chewing gum as the diner guy in *Rumble Fish* saying, "Think about it—thirty-five summers . . ." and trying to keep Rusty James in line.

TW: *Rumble Fish*—I love that picture. Yeah, that was a good moment, really cool. Francis just said, "Write your own dialogue." He says, "I'm not even gonna tell ya what to say—man, this is your diner, this is your apron, your spatula. I'm not gonna give you any lines. You just make it all up." So it was fun. And that's what I'd rather do in every picture, 'cause I can't remember lines. . . . But the "thirty-five summers" thing—it was because I was thirty-five, I'd had thirty-fve summers.

TL: And then there's the image of you as Renfield in *Dracula*, eating what appeared to be real bugs.

TW: Oh, yeah—I did eat bugs! They have a bug wrangler on every film, ya know. If there are bugs in the movie, there's a bug wrangler. And they were mealworms. Protein, ya know. But I've eaten earthworms as a child.

TL: But mealworms have huge pincing mandibles. They bite back.

TW: So you have to kill 'em with your jaws. You have to kill 'em first. And the wranglers don't like it, 'cause these are their little actors. "Floyd! He's been with me for thirty years! In the name of God, what have you done?" I didn't even know there was such a thing as a bug wrangler on a film, but I found out.

TL: When did you first start to realize that you'd formed your own stark visual identity?

TW: Gee, I dunno. But like any business, whether you're a fisherman or you repair refrigerators or you're an airline pilot or a lion tamer, at a certain point you realize you have to ask yourself a question—"Can I parlay this into a business? Can I make money off this?" And at a certain point you realize—yeah, I can take this somewhere. But it's always a gamble. What I was really pursuing was my dream of it all, about being in music. I was in music, ya know. The way it appears visually, or whatever perspective from other people's vantage point, is one thing. But mine's from the inside. I have all these heroes, and I love music and I wanna be a part of it. I've been inspired, and now hopefully someday I'll get an opportunity to inspire somebody else. And that's how it works, really. People who make songs don't go to school to learn how to do it. You sit down next to the record player, and you write down the words and try and figure out these changes, and that's how everybody does it. And as far as whether you think you can make it, well, there are levels of "making it." For me, I was happy to be making another record, going on the road, putting the band together, and doing it.

TL: But you've always understood the importance of other art besides music—books, films, paintings. And you have to seek them out. As a kid back in Indiana, I learned that early—we really had to fight for culture out there.

TW: That's why so many American presidents come from the Midwest—because it's so flat, they have to dream. Roy Orbison? I said, "Where'd you get that voice, man? What—did you listen to opera all your life?" And he goes "Nah, man—if there was a dance a hundred miles away on Saturday, I heard the sound of the dance coming across the plains, and by the time the voice reached me, it was all watery. So when I was a kid, that's the way I wanted to sound, like those dances sounded." I thought that was a fascinating little anecdote . . .

TL: But you understand, appreciate the thrill of discovering a good book or movie. I just saw *The Black Rider* for the first time, with Marianne Faithfull singing your songs, and I can't believe I've lived this long without discovering Robert Wilson's work. And it had such amazing detail, like one of the actors bending his middle fingers inward for every scene. I don't know why.

TW: You wanna know why? 'Cause Wilson choreographs every physical movement that you see onstage. He does it first. Every finger, every eyelash, every hair, every jaw—everything. And then he shows them how he wants 'em to do it, and when he wants 'em to do it, and then he winds it up like a clock. And lets it tick, tick, tick, tick. And there are marks all over the stage, for where you have to be for light. And if you're not where you need to be for light, well. . . . When it comes to choreography, Wilson's just amazing. And it's all timed to the pit, all the musicians in the pit. I mean, I'd seen *Einstein on the Beach* at BAM—it was like nine hours long, and you had to go out and get coffee and come back, take a nap for a while. It was the strangest experience—more like being on a long flight to Hong Kong. You wake up and people are in different positions, the light's different. Then you go back to sleep or read a little bit—very strange. But Wilson's more like an inventor, a real visionary, and he's meticulous about what he wants and doesn't want. It's not a democracy. That's why what you're seeing is a very specific vision from one man's mind—you're not seeing a collaboration.

TL: So how do you write music for such a perfectionist?

TW: You know, you kinda sit in the dark at a long table for several different workshop periods. It's almost like being at Cape Canaveral—that kinda feeling, ya know? And you're watching the stage with him, plus you're dealing with a lot of sleep deprivation, because you're working long hours with bad coffee and no food, no windows, in a strange country, with jet lag. And I think that goes into the work, as well. You're in a state. But everyone trusts him so much—he's like a professor, like the best professor. For me, in all my years in school—nothing like Wilson. Like you'll always remember a particular teacher? I'd say Wilson is my teacher. I mean, I didn't go to college. But there's nobody that's affected me that much, as an artist.

TL: What are some key lessons he taught you?

TW: I dunno. That's a good question. I never really boiled it down like that. I remember once, he had a huge explosion in the theater—he'd asked somebody to get rid of a particular piece of furniture onstage, and it was still there thirty minutes later. And he said, "Get that chair offstage or I'm gonna throw it in the ulster!" He was so irate. And if he wants to do music for a particular scene, he does the music, on a microphone. He just starts making sounds—he goes *"Bž-bksh, meeee-oowr! Whooo-eee, plow-plow-plow-plow, koo-tee-koo, bleerm, bleerm!"* Know what I mean? You make things right now. It's not a magical thing. You're at the edge of the cliff and it's time to jump. And you just have to trust that you won't hit the rocks.

TL: Did that give you the initial idea for your human beatbox sounds that finally materialized on *Real Gone*?

TW: It did, yeah.

TL: Which you put to good use last night onstage. You'd bark out something like *"Acka, poom-poom,"* hit a digital-delay pedal on the floor, and it'd repeat as tape-looped percussion.

TW: Yeah. And the device stopped working halfway through the show. It's called a Boomerang. I just go *"Acka, poom-poom,"* and it becomes something I can sing over.

TL: And *Real Gone* feels like a continuation of the wild percussive experiments of *Bone Machine*, one of your most important albums.

TW: Yeah, I think so. It picks up maybe where that one left off. A lot of people think it picks up where *Rain Dogs* left off, but I dunno. But hopefully, you get better as you go, get more refined. I write songs a lot quicker now.

TL: And you've also learned how to constantly reinvent yourself. Not for the audience's sake, of course, but to keep yourself interested, amused.

TW: Well, that's really the goal, isn't it? You have to keep yourself interested, and you have to be endlessly curious. And I may be a bit more eccentric, and I don't really care what people think. And to a large degree, I don't care what anybody thinks. Because I have my own kinda world I'm in. When you start worrying about intervals, that's when you know you're a composer. When you lay awake at night, worrying about a particular section of a song. Like last night, I was looking at the wall and the light was really low, and one eye was kinda cockeyed. And it looked like a skull with a big cloud coming out of its head, and a hand with a white glove. And I thought, "Well, that's pretty out there for this hotel, to do something like that!" And then I looked at it again in the morning, and it was a bouquet of white roses. But it was out of focus. So that's what I do when I'm making stuff up. I don't see what's there. I learned that when I was little. We had drapes, and the drapes had all these water stains on 'em. But there were also patterns, like leaves and camels and all that stuff. But there were all these really dramatic water stains, and I thought the water stains were part of the design of the fabric. And there were all these shapes, so I made my own shapes out of 'em. And I still do that. When I'm looking at any kind of pattern, I'll find, say, noses or something.

TL: There's a really sad adage that says the older we get, the less we look up in wonder at the world—the more beauty, or the appreciation of it, gets trampled underfoot.

TW: See, that's where we're at—we have a deficit of wonder. I think it's because of computers. When I ask people questions now, they get on their computer— "Gimme a few minutes and I'll let ya know. . . ." And I'm like, "Noooooo!" I want 'em to wonder about it, man! I don't wanna know the answer—I just want 'em to wonder about it.

TL: That's slowed down, while the rest of technology keeps speeding up. To the point where you can't just watch a CNN news broadcast—you have to multitask to read the endless bulletins at the bottom of the screen.

TW: First of all, I don't have a TV, so I am so out of it. Now the only show I've seen in the last fifteen years, I swear to God, is *Pimp My Ride*. And somebody sent me that on tape. And I thought, "Man, I hope this is #1, 'cause I just love it." But I don't have any TV. And there really is no such thing as multitasking. You can only do one thing correctly at a time. So if you're gonna do seven things, each one of those things is getting one-seventh of your time. Even though you're doing 'em at the same time. That's why my phone is a camera, my watch is a rifle—it's just insane. But they're selling us on this stuff, and it's affecting everything, even the election. Touch-screen voting? Forget about it—what's more corruptible than computers?

TL: Wait a minute! No TV? That means you're missing some great new shows this season, like *Lost* and *Desperate Housewives*!

TW: I heard they're good. But I'm afraid of incorporating all that into my diet— I'm afraid it'd just send me off. I dunno, it'd be like eating Styrofoam. You remember in the old days, when you'd send away for something from the back of a cereal box? And you had to wait for thirty days, and it was coming from Battle Creek, Michigan? Life is different now, because in the time that it took for it to arrive, a lot of wonder took place. I remember wondering about the town of Battle Creek—What's it look like? Is it like the North Pole? Who lives in it? Is there an actual creek?

TL: And finally, the postman arrives like on *The Simpsons* and goes "Here it is, kid—here's your stupid spy camera!"

TW: You know what I did when I was little? You could get a signet ring with your initials on the ring—a silver one. You send in the form and they'll send you a ring—it was unbelievable. So I wanted the ring, I sent it in, the ring comes. So I'm wearing the ring, but three weeks later, seventeen cases of salve show up, in shoe-polish-shaped cans. I was required to sell seventeen cases to friends, relatives, neighbors, but it was in small print. And I was like, six, and so scared to death—I thought I was gonna wind up in jail, ya know? It was my very first conflict.

TL: In our neighborhood, a kid sent away from a comic book for a "Scary, realistic-looking seven-foot-tall Frankenstein." But when it arrived, it was just a seven-foot-long sheet of plastic with a cheesy monster printed on it. He hung it from his upstairs window anyway and pretended to like it.

TW: Nobody really wants to know. . . . Well, do you really wanna know how magicians do their tricks? You think you wanna know, but you don't. And when you do, you wish you didn't. But you can't un-know it. You can't un-ring a bell. There are things I just don't wanna know. And I think that's probably true with regard to myself, as well—there are things people don't wanna know about me. They wanna continue to wonder about me, and I think that's fine. I promote that. So over the years, I've usually given untrue answers to things. Just because—well, why not? Truth. Truth is overrated, as well as intelligence is overrated. Don't ya think?

TL: I think it takes a certain degree of smarts to appreciate both the abyss and beauty, like you seem to do, album after album. To understand that the grotesque is just as important as the sublime.

TW: I think my wife probably opened me up to that. I used to tell my wife, "Baby, I'm just meat and potatoes," and she'd say, "Oh, the hell you are!" But she's the one who does deeply contemplate the mysteries of life and tries not to contribute to the troubles of the world. I used to think that if you talk about death, that it would come to visit you. Now I think it's the other way around. And it is all around us, all the time. Or maybe I'm just getting older and starting to embrace that . . .

TL: Bowie once said that the two key questions an artist is faced with once he hits fifty are: How much time do I have left? And what the hell am I supposed to be doing with it anyway?

TW: Bowie's right, he's right about that. What am I supposed to be doing? Those are the really big questions, and I haven't figured 'em out. And you can't live in show business—there's not enough protein there, ya know? Career, family— they're always in some ways somewhat symbiotic, and at the same time diametrically opposed. But I'm OK with those questions now. Or maybe I have a lot of answers that are looking for questions. Yeah—that's it, in a nutshell. All my answers are just answers looking for questions.

ORPHANS: BRAWLERS, BAWLERS & BASTARDS (2006)

On July 25, 2006, Waits announced, via his record label Anti-, plans for a small-scale tour.

> Iconoclast and reclusive touring artist Tom Waits is making an unprecedented move by taking his always unpredictably stunning live show on the road, mostly in cities (Atlanta, Memphis, Louisville, Nashville) where he hasn't been seen onstage since the mid- to late '70s. As for Asheville, North Carolina, Tom has never played a gig; he hasn't performed in Akron, Ohio, or Detroit since the '80s. The most recent stop on this extraordinary tour is Chicago, where Waits played the Chicago Theatre for three sold-out nights on his *Mule Variations* tour in '99. "We need to go to Tennessee to pick up some fireworks, and someone owes me money in Kentucky," says Waits about why he's chosen this particular time and route to tour.

The tour was to promote a new three-CD set of rarities he had accumulated over the years. Waits told the *Observer*, "It's all in there. . . . Crop failures, dad dying, train wrecks. It all gets handed down, and everything you absorb you're going to secrete. A lot of those old songs stick to you, and others blow right through you, and some of them get trapped in there. You keep hearing them every time you sit down at the piano." It was a lot of music, and it was meant to appease the die-hards as well as anchor Waits to the songwriting greats of the past thirty years.

"Tom Waits: Call and Response"
Stop Smiling
October 27, 2006
Katherine Turman

Tom Waits sums up the fierce fascination fans have for all things Waitsian: "If you spill something, they want it." That's probably because even Waits's detritus is cooler than other artists' best efforts. And it's part of the raison d'être for his three-CD assemblage, *Orphans: Brawlers, Bawlers & Bastards*, a career-spanning effort of sublime offal. A read-between-the-lines of a "Bastard" helps illuminate what makes Waits tick. In "Children's Story," he recites, in his world-weary rasp, "Once upon a time there was a poor child with no father and no mother, and everything was dead. And no one was left in the whole world. Everything was dead. . . . The moon was a piece of rotten wood. . . . The earth was an overturned piss-pot. And he was all alone. . . ." Waits ends the narration with a throaty chuckle. Deadpan, dark, but possessed of a wicked humor, Waits's arcane appeal incites in journalists a frenzy to invent new adjectives to capture and describe the nearly forty-year, multifaceted career and life of Thomas Alan Waits.

Even when Waits claims he's telling the truth, he may not be. As his lyrics attest, he's a master yarn-spinner, a teller of tales tall and small. And though much is made of his persona, it seems the persona and person are one. What seems to be reasonably accurately documented, however, are the facts that Waits was born on December 7, 1949, in Pomona, California, lived in San Diego, and in 1971, signed to Asylum Records. Nineteen records ensued from 1973 to 2004 on various labels, garnering, along the way, Grammy Awards, Academy Award nominations, film roles, a wife/collaborator in Kathleen Brennan, three children, and the rightful adoration of a large and very rabid cult of cultural dissidents who elevated Waits to living icon status. As a folk hero, Waits's name is part of the pantheon of boho coolness populated by such contemporaries and collaborators as William Burroughs, Robert Wilson, Charles Bukowski, Jim Jarmusch.

If Tom Waits is impossible to compartmentalize, he's easy to like. Sometimes, his voice is akin to Abraham Lincoln's visage: craggy, sepia-toned, unsmiling. When he's relating a story or singing—as opposed to merely answering a question—his voice, if possible, gets even more resonant, more dramatic, wrapping a deceptively quixotic cocoon around the bewitched listener. He uses music biz terms like "added value" with a deadpan irony and understated emphasis, waxes ecstatic on strange and unusual facts about insects, and, as records from *Swordfishtrombones* to *Franks Wild Years* attest, creates one-of-a-kind aural soundscapes that open a gargoyle-guarded gateway into the Waitsian alternate universe. For these reasons and many more, Tom Waits is rightfully revered—and sometimes feared.

Calling from his home in rural Sonoma County, California, Waits was by turns shy, thoughtful, uncomfortable, teasing, pithy, recalcitrant, amusing, endearing, and, for lack of a more descriptive adjective, just plain cool. He's the kind of guy you'd want to spend a late afternoon with in the gloomy half-light of a near-empty bar—with plenty of quarters for Waits to control the jukebox and conversation. But we happily settled for an early evening on the phone.

Katherine Turman: Thanks for calling.

Tom Waits: All right, OK.

KT: Sorry I couldn't make it to your recent shows.

TW: That's OK, we were in out-of-the-way places.

KT: What made you decide to do a tour like this, including one city you hadn't played in thirty years—and what was the highlight of any of the shows, in Asheville, Nashville . . . ?

TW: Yeah, we played a lot of "-villes." I worked with a guitar player, Duke Robillard, who started a group called Roomful of Blues and the Fabulous Thunderbirds, a great blues guitar player. My son [Casey Waits] played drums. Larry Taylor, who has been with me for years, who used to play with Canned Heat and Jerry Lee Lewis—he's played with everybody. Then on keyboards was Bent Clausen. So I don't know what made me go out. I really wanted to find out if I like doing this. I wasn't really going out to make money. You know. I've been doing it for a long time, and it's usually a lot of headaches, and the physics of most of the auditoriums is maddening from night to night. [It's] what everybody deals with. It kinda rattles me, and I usually end up kinda a nervous wreck by the end of it. So

I wanted to see if I could go out and actually enjoy playing. That was the whole objective of it. And I did.

KT: So, I don't know if you read the *New Yorker* . . .

TW: It comes out so often I can never keep up with it.

KT: Yeah, they pile up and you feel guilty. But there was an interesting article about stage fright, about how paralyzing it can be. Would your feelings about playing qualify as stage fright?

TW: I don't know if it's fright. I'm always afraid things will go wrong. Plus, you're taking this whole thing and you're moving it all around the country, it's always awkward. It's like, for me, moving somebody who has been in an accident, you know: "Don't move me, don't move me," that's the first thing the show says to me at the end of rehearsal. "Whatever you do, don't move me, I like it here."

KT: Maybe the country singers in Branson who have their own theaters have the right idea?

TW: I've thought of that Branson deal. I've discussed that with other artists. Just the idea that you don't go on the road, they go on the road and come to you. Perfect sense to me.

Getting out in front of all those people, after a while, if you're well prepared, it's fun. I'm not always well prepared. But this time I was, so I think that was a big part of it.

KT: Like you, I'm a native Californian. Do you draw inspiration from other places, or do you prefer home?

TW: I like going to guitar shops and pawnshops and salvage yards, and I really like to go to hardware stores to see what they got out there. I like to go to hardware stores in Europe. I bought a two-by-four guitar in Cleveland; a guitar made of a two-by-four. I thought, man, something like that could really go. Everybody has a two-by-four lying around their yard. Send me a two-by-four and I'll make a guitar out of it.

KT: You don't ever have to tour again, you could just make guitars.

TW: You don't see a lot when you're on the road, needless to say. You see the gig and the town on the way in and the town on the way out, but there's something sort of exciting about that at the same time; the stealth. You come in and sting 'em and go. That's what I call it. It sounds like a rockabilly title. [*Sings a la Elvis*] "Ya sting 'em and go."

KT: Wasn't Asheville the home of the inventor of the Moog synthesizer?

TW: You know, I don't know.

KT: He recently died.

TW: Bob Moog. He started making theremins toward the end. Interesting man. My first experience with a theremin was this gal Lydia, the granddaughter of Léon Theremin, who was living in Russia. We were in Hamburg doing *Alice*, this Robert Wilson thing. So we wanted a theremin player, and someone said, "I know Lydia," and she came in and she looked like a little Russian doll, a traditional Russian sweater, and her theremin looked like a hot plate. And inside, all the connections were held together with cut-up little pieces of beer cans that she twisted around the wires to hold the connections together. And the aerial was literally a car aerial from like a Volkswagen. And when she played, she sounded like [violinist] Jascha Heifetz.

KT: That brings us to these three CDs that I've been trying to absorb. . . . Even twenty years ago, all these fifty-four songs would have been on cassette tapes.

TW: Oh, yeah, it would have been a mess. It's kind of overwhelming. Mainly, I was afraid I was going to lose all this stuff, because I don't really keep good records. I don't have a big vault or a real organized room with all my stuff, I don't know, maybe like you, I imagine, when I want something, I can't find it. And when I don't need it anymore, I find it. So mainly I was concerned I'd lose all this stuff, so I wanted to get this out. A lot of the stuff I bought from a guy in Moscow who had this stuff on a CD that he'd collected.

KT: Really?!

TW: Black market stuff of my own, from a guy in Russia, it was weird. Some of it I never had the original or the DAT or the multitrack or even the half-inch. I just did it and then, you know, sing 'em and go. So I'm starting to get more archival as I get older. "Oh, we better hang on to this honey, we'll need this in our old age." I don't know. We'll use it as a coffee table.

KT: Were there any songs or bits of songs you didn't remember?

TW: No, I remember, but I had to have my memory jogged by listening to the stuff, like, "Oh yeah, I remember that." What happens, it's kinda like making dinner, and then someone tells you there are going to be a lot of people who are going to be coming, you're not just making dinner for yourself. And all of a sudden you're thinking about silverware and that type of thing. And you start getting a little more meticulous. Kathleen sequenced the whole thing. She is much better about all the details, and then when you get in there, and you start remixing stuff, and then you rerecord something and then say, "Oh, while we're in here, let's do this." You start spackling the spare room and before you know it, you have a window and a new door, and you've changed the color of the room; it's the natural evolution when you start to work. It's like turning on a saw—then the saw goes looking for wood. I'm the saw.

KT: Was it immediately apparent that it needed to be divided into the *Brawlers*, *Bawlers*, and *Bastards* categories?

TW: No, that kinda came later, because it was almost impossible to sequence. A lot of disparate sources, and it made for this weird skyline. I couldn't really listen to it without dozing, and then jolting.

KT: Like in school?

TW: Yeah. Air traffic control. So it was, slow songs over here, spoken things here, more blues stuff over here . . .

KT: I don't know if I'm supposed to laugh at "Children's Story," but I do. What's the origin?

TW: Oh right. We did this [playwright Robert] Wilson thing—"Woyzeck." That was part of the play, but it never became part of that *Blood Money* record; didn't know how to do it . . .

KT: When you were a kid, what kind of stories were told to you?

TW: Yeah, uh, geeze . . .

KT: Nothing about the world being an "upside-down piss-pot," was that the phrase?

TW: An "overturned piss-pot" . . . I added that line. [*recites*] "He is there to this day, all alone."

KT: I picture little kids sitting in a circle, looking at you, confused and horrified.

TW: I don't know, most children's stories have a dark element. You know, there's the three brothers, one was kinda slow in the head, not very ambitious, and the other one, left home early, you know, and got lost . . . they're always kinda sad or frightening . . . most of them are cautionary tales. In a way, it's a cautionary tale. When my kids were young, I would make stories up, and say, "OK, give me the elements, what do you want in there?" OK, tree, polar bear, and a typewriter. OK, all right. That's how we usually start. Stories kind of tell themselves, especially when you're searching for the next chapter. It's a kind of a real condensed version of what you do when you're really writing. You know, when you're writing for kids, you have to come up with stuff on the spot.

KT: Let me ask something specific: On *Real Gone*, you had "Day After Tomorrow," then on these CDs, there's "Road to Peace," with the underlying politicism. Where did "Road to Peace" come from?

TW: The *New York Times*. When you read the paper every day, it's hard to avoid that seeping into your consciousness and all that, you know. That was written not long ago. A lot of these were recorded within the last year. They're new stuff. I don't want to go into the origin of everything, but for me, they're from questionable sources, I didn't put any liner notes because I didn't want to overexplain it, I wanted to throw it out there and say "OK, hope it all hangs together." Like that. [*pause*] That one is a Bukowski poem, "Nirvana," and that "Pontiac," that's my father-in-law. If you go down to the market with him, you'll get that speech. Different every time, more cars, different cars, if he sees a Lincoln or a Hudson or an Impala, it gets him going.

KT: You mentioned Bukowski—have you seen the movie *Factotum*?

TW: No. Hey, I'm glad his stories are getting turned into movies. I'm a big Bukowski fan, so who knows, what you really want to do is be valid and vital in some way, here after you're gone, and to still remain a presence and influence and still be able to sprout and bloom and bear fruit, so I guess that's what everybody wants.

KT: I know Bukowski had a hand in *Barfly*, but once you're gone, people can do whatever they want with you and your work . . .

TW: That's a reason to stick around! Watch them, stay on the porch with a shotgun.

KT: You're very protective about not letting your songs be used in ads, so I'd think you'd want to protect your stuff for infinity.

TW: Well, within reason. With commercials and all that, see that my grave is kept clean and all that.

KT: With honoring people you like, for instance, including Bukowski, on these records, would you ever want to develop a film from one of his books, or is there someone lesser known whose memory you'd want to keep alive?

TW: I never really thought about that [*pause, thinking*].

KT: Like if there's some writer no one has heard about . . . for instance, you did the Daniel Johnston "King Kong" song, is that because you like the song, or him?

TW: Well, [Jim] Jarmusch played me that stuff years ago, and played me his version of "King Kong" and I tried to stay as true to that as I could, if you hear the original, you'll see what I mean. I got all his records . . . I thought I'd really discovered this . . . it's real outsider art. Interesting thing about outsider art is that it's such big business. These outsider artists are creating false biographies for themselves, saying they're victims of mental illness and child abuse, and they grew up poor in the South, and they're creating these false backgrounds, because you aren't really qualified as an outsider unless you've had no formal art education, so you have to prove that you have no art education at all, it's an interesting turn of the tables.

KT: It seems so ironic that you can buy "outsider art" from a gallery online. Are you an Internet person?

TW: I'm not. No. No, I'm really . . . pretty backward. You can spend $400,000 on a painting that was done on the back of a cereal box with a Bic pen, which is an interesting place to be at with the economy what it is now.

KT: You talk about being backwards Internet-wise, but with the technology of recording now—is there anything you need technology wise, or is a two-by-four guitar enough for you?

TW: It seems like you can create digitally—you can re-create everything that was once done in analog. As soon as vinyl left, someone put pops and cracks over a song, so I guess culturally we're always burying something and digging it up, and burying it in order to dig it up. They do the same thing with hairdos and shoes and furniture. It's what we do. As far as the sound stuff, most of the people I know are always looking for some very obscure apparatus that will give them some unusual sound source that they can use in the studio. Then someone says, "There's this thing called Amp Farm." It's a farm, and you hit the thing, and seven hundred thousand sounds come up and you can pick from there. There's no reason to have seven hundred thousand amplifiers anymore.

KT: But you'd rather?

TW: I'd rather have the devices, but you roll with it. I'm not an audiophile by any stretch of the imagination.

KT: So when CDs came about, did you think they were a passing phase?

TW: I figured it was like the bagel. They were designed to be carried in your pocket. And the outer surface was hard and leathery, so that the bread would be protected inside. It's just as big as your hand and fits right in your pocket. CD is the same way. More room on the shelf. I have pockets that CDs fit in, and I appreciate that sometimes.

KT: Even with fifty-something songs on these CDs, you have two hidden tracks.

TW: It's the little prize in the cereal box. If you dig to the bottom, you'll get the plastic rod and reel. It's an added value. I played the records for somebody and they said, "I never heard any of these things." I said, "Oh, good." Some people pay such careful attention to what you're doing. If you spill something, they want it. I'm the same way. If Maria Callas or Claudio Arrau or Salif Keïta or Studs Terkel or John Jacob Niles—I don't know all his stuff. I know the basic stuff, but I don't know the stuff he did when he was nine. Some people find it interesting that you have—that you've done all these things parallel to everything else that you've done. That's kind of what we did.

KT: One thing that struck me is it seems you don't have casual fans. No one says, "Oh, I like that one Tom Waits song."

TW: Damn! It's supply and demand. Stay away. They get hungry. When they're hungry, they eat more. They eat better. That's always been my theory.

KT: I don't believe that one.

TW: I'm being silly.

KT: I need to be across a table from you so I can see when your eyebrow is going up.

TW: I roll them.

KT: If you were a technology guy, we'd have videophones.

TW: Crime has them. Somewhere, someone is doing something with it that you can only imagine. Crime is way ahead of us. As a casual device, it doesn't have much of a future, but it's probably great for prostitution. What was I going to say . . .

KT: About supply and demand?

TW: Oh yeah, I sound like a real businessman. You asked about other people. There's a guy named Frank Stanford who I really like who is a writer, I'd like to see more. You should check him out. He's a poet, novelist, short-story writer. He died in the '70s.

KT: It makes me sad when you discover someone new, and want more from them, but they're gone and their work is done . . .

TW: You know what's worse? When somebody goes, "Isn't he dead?" And it turns out they're not dead. But you just haven't heard anything from them, so you just assume they are dead. If you don't put out a record for a couple years, people start circulating rumors that you have throat cancer. Or diabetes and you had one of your legs removed. Or you lost an eye in a fight. It's amazing what they manufacture. Part of the folk process. [*Pause*] Here's something interesting—you know the angle between a branch and trunk of a tree? If you look at a leaf from that tree, you'll see the exact same angle on the main pulmonary leaf vein that goes down the center of the leaf.

KT: Is there a word for that?

TW: Find a leaf, and you tell me if I'm right. We're out in the sticks. Out here in the country, I like to say we watch a lot of TV. But TV stands for "Turkey Vultures." Well, I guess they're the turkeys of the vulture world. The reason they circle as long as they do is that they weigh almost nothing, and what they're really trying to do, you think they're circling and trying to land, but a lot of them are unable to land, they weigh so little. It's like watching a leaf try to land in a windstorm. At the bird sanctuary and bird rescue, they say most of the vultures brought in were hit by cars while dining. When they eat, they eat so much that they can't take off. So if they have to leave hurriedly, they're frightened, there's caution, and they'll throw up everything they had to eat so they can get back up in the air . . .

KT: That's horrible imagery.

TW: To get that lift. We've got things that we do that they probably are shocked at as well. Humiliating things we all have to do. Trying on clothes.

KT: It must be sad to be a turkey vulture; they must be unloved.

TW: I don't know if sadness is really part of their world. They have a special hole in the top of their beaks so they can breathe when their head is inside the carcass of another animal. Just like us, you know. Their babies are white. I came across a nest of vultures in the wood, they're snowy white, look like little balls of fur. They're very sweet when they're young. Have you ever seen a baby pigeon?

KT: No.

TW: You never will. But they exist.

KT: I wonder why you never see birds falling out of the sky. Where do birds go when they die?

TW: Oh [*sadly*]. There's probably one particular tree that's owned by the insurance company where they go. It's probably in Madison, Wisconsin. The tallest tree in Madison, actually. The insurance tree.

KT: Owned by Mutual of Omaha.

TW: That's it. I find those things interesting. Birds, and . . . what did you think of the strange and unusual facts about insects, "Army Ants"? They say it's going to be a hit. If it could just get more strings on it. I get a kick out of that.

KT: [*laughing*] That's one of your "picks to click," as they say in the biz?

TW: I always wanted to do a voice-over for a nature program like [Richard] Attenborough does. So I put that together and sent it to the Discovery Channel, I wanted to see if I could get some extra work. I also sent "King Kong" to what's his name . . .

KT: Peter Jackson.

TW: Peter Jackson! I wrote him a long letter and sent "King Kong" to him. And I said "You probably have a spot at the beginning of the film or the end—or somewhere in the middle." I didn't hear back from him either. I'm starting to get nervous.

KT: I was just watching something on the History Channel on the bubonic plague—you might have done well on that?

TW: You know, they tried to get me involved in one of those things. This project that they're doing in England. . . . I don't know if it's ever going to happen, but they said, "pick a disease" and they had this long list of these terrible diseases, and they want you to write a song about this disease, then they're going to put it all on a record. It's just gotten out of hand.

KT: Do you have a favorite disease?

TW: I didn't want to get involved. I just said no, "I can't pick a disease."

KT: Is scurvy a disease? Then you can write a sea shanty sort of song.

TW: Scurvy is a disease. Finding rhymes is hard for diseases. Scurvy. What rhymes with scurvy?

KT: Well, curvy.

TW: I knew you were going to say that. That's about the extent of it. "She had scurvy, but she was so curvy. . . ." That's not going to fly.

KT: What about gout?

TW: There again. But no one wants to sing about disease in that way. It's almost like conjuring it. And inviting it over.

KT: Do you believe in self-fulfilling prophecies?

TW: Ummm. I don't know. Well, I think there are things that are waiting to happen, then there's the tipping point, and all they need is your enthusiasm. Or maybe *just* your enthusiasm, because it already had the enthusiasm of millions of others and it was waiting for one more. And you provided that. That's what the butterfly effect is—that just the wings of a butterfly can create a monsoon and all that. So, I believe in those things. . . . Here's something interesting. I have a recording of crickets that's slowed down. That's all; it's just slowed way down. But what you hear is what sounds very much like, in fact it sounds exactly like . . . if I didn't tell you you were listening to crickets, you'd say, "What is this, the Vienna Boys' Choir"?

KT: It's high sounding?

TW: It's four-part harmony: bass, cello, viola, violin. It's orchestral, and the melody that they're singing, it's the beginning of the melody for "Jesus Christ Superstar." You think I'm making that up, but I'm not.

KT: Well, I can't see your eyebrows.

TW: Only one has gone up. It's quite astonishing, really. Nothing has been done to the tape. Manipulated in any way. Other than the fact that it was slowed down.

KT: If you were to combine that with the song of the whales, what would you have?

TW: That's a good question.

KT: In the '80s, it was all about the song of the whales.

TW: A good friend of mine, Richard Waters, created an instrument called the waterphone, and he used to go out on the rocks and claims to have been able to communicate in some way with the whales.

KT: What did they tell him?

TW: He was just surprised that there was any call and response at all. It's an interesting instrument; you probably have heard it a lot in horror movies but didn't know what it was. It's, um . . . you bow it. If you can imagine putting two pizza pans together facing each other and creating a vessel, then coming up at a straight angle out of the pans, you'd have metal dowels. And all the way around the circumference of the pan, so it looks like a fence. And they're all varying lengths. In the center of the pan, there's a pipe, into the center of the pan, and there's a hole, and the first thing you do is fill that with water through that pipe. Then you hold on to the pipe, and you take a bow and you bow around the circumference of the pan, along the fence of dowels, and the sound is just amazing.

KT: It sounds as if it should be in a museum, maybe it qualifies as outsider art?

TW: Easily. It qualifies as an unusual sound source. Hang on a minute [*talks to Kathleen*].

KT: I guess it's your dinnertime; what are we having for dinner tonight?

TW: I don't know. It's up to me. Unfortunately.

KT: What are you in the mood for?

TW: I don't know. I guess it's dog again! Last night's dog. I guess we have to wrap this up.

KT: OK, I'll hurry. So . . . your filmic career, I saw that you have two films—*Texas Lullaby* and *The Good Heart*—coming up?

TW: I do not know what's happening with those. I hesitate to talk about things that may never. . . . You wait on these things.

KT: In your film career, you've been typecast, is that what you'd say?

TW: For a lot of people, it's "Go ahead, typecast me, just cast me." It's like some people say, "the only trouble with tainted money is there 'taint enough." I'm not actively trying to alter my image in such a way so that I can play presidents or terrorists. I'm just letting it kind of go along. Now and then I get a call from somebody that's an interesting project, and you do it. I guess the ideal way to do it is to come up with all your own ideas . . . movies are expensive and time-consuming as hell.

KT: Isn't music the same?

TW: Yeah, but it doesn't feel as overwhelming, because it's more in my domain. I'm like the director when I go into the studio, and I'm in it, so. But in a movie, you're really . . . you're either wallpaper or a chair, or . . .

KT: When you say president or terrorist, wouldn't you look forward to the challenge . . .

TW: Of being a president? I don't know. If somebody asked me to, I'd give it some thought. If I thought I could do it. You really want to be able to do it in such a way that you pull it off. I do some acting, but I'm not really an actor.

KT: What's next—do these three records allow you a clean slate for the future—or are you sitting on the porch relaxing?

TW: I'm not on the porch; there are a million things to do. I'll probably go on the road, do some shows, after Christmas sometime. I'll probably go to Australia, Sumatra, or someplace.

KT: Musically, what are you working on?

TW: Writing stuff, we're always making new tunes up, that doesn't ever stop.

KT: Do you wish it ever would?

TW: No, no, I love doing it, I love nothing better than being in a room and the door locked, and the piano and the tape recorder going. It's a great job, making up tunes.

KT: From the outside, it looks like you have the ideal career, you're not dependent on hit after hit, or public tastes—or is it a different view on the inside?

TW: It's different. Like everything. If you're a doctor, great for your kids if they're sick and you're home. It's not so great your dad's a doctor when he's at a hospital in Mexico for three weeks. There's something great about everything that a dad does, sometimes. It's great if you want tickets to the Chili Peppers, then it's cool if your dad is in music, otherwise, it's like "Awwww."

"Tom Waits: Haunted Songster's Revelatory Dispatch from the Twilight Zone"
Now
November 16, 2006
Tim Perlich

Way out in rural Northern California where Tom Waits and his accomplice, Kathleen Brennan, are holed up on a converted chicken ranch, counting constellations qualifies as exciting nightlife. The only roadhouse for miles stopped booking mariachi bands when it lost its license for live entertainment. Don't even ask.

Besides, Waits hasn't seen the bottom of a bourbon bottle in fourteen years. At least that's what he says. For the first time in our conversation about his amazing new three-disc *Orphans* set of oddities and outtakes—which frequently digresses into discussions about the reliability of the '49 Hudson's flathead six, the influence of Civil War tunes on contemporary hip-hop, the favorite cartoons of 1930s blues great Memphis Minnie, and the stage antics of Stompin' Tom Connors—it sounds like he's on the level.

His impressive output over the past few years makes for convincing evidence that Waits has been far too busy creating the most provocative music of his career to get shitfaced with his old runaround gang of hoodoo hustlers and deli delinquents. And the massive *Orphans* compendium (out November 21) of just the stuff he held back—the cut-ups, collabos, covers, and creative experiments in controlled chaos—should clear up any doubts.

"I'm just out here trying to build a better mousetrap," growls Waits over the phone. "If somebody doesn't like what I do, I really don't care. I'm not chained to public opinion, nor am I swayed by the waves of popular trends. I just keep on doing my own investigations.

"We started putting stuff together for this collection a while ago. Time is always a collaborator. I'd begin working on something and think, 'Oh, this one over here needs a little more pepper and that one over there could use some nitro, and I'd end up writing different parts and adding more and more pieces to it. Who knows? If I had more time I might've shot three of 'em in the head and written three new ones to take their place. I wouldn't say that this is just stuff that was lying around. Maybe only about twenty-five songs are from other collaborations; the rest is all fresh material."

Compiled on the beautifully packaged *Orphans* set are fifty-four rare and previously unheard tunes thematically split into three groups, separating Waits's more confrontational *Brawlers* from the heavy-hearted ballads of *Bawlers*, while his creepy revisions of Daniel Johnston's "King Kong" and the seven dwarves' work song "Heigh Ho," recast here as a prison work song, wind up on the *Bastards* disc along with other intriguing one-offs.

Waits is eager to share the credit (and blame) for the ambitious project with his constant companion, Brennan, who plays a much larger role in his whole music-making process than people may realize.

"Kathleen and I collaborate on everything. We wrote the songs together, and Kathleen picked the categories, only she wanted to call the *Bawlers* disc *Shut Up and Eat Your Ballads*—you know, for people who don't get enough slow songs in their diet. Any one of my songs probably could've fit into any of the three categories. Songs are either slower than your heart rate, at around the same tempo as the beating of your heart or faster, and you act accordingly.

"I didn't want to lose these songs. I don't have a big archive, I've just got some tapes I keep in a drawer along with my hair oil, some pizza, and bug spray. And like pictures in a family photo album, I'm not sure if these songs will mean anything to anybody else but me. There's one song I wrote with [*Ironweed* novelist] William Kennedy out in Albany. He came across this poem written on a bridge by some hobos, so he copied it down and saved it for years. He showed it to me and suggested we turn it into a song, so we did."

Another song on the *Bastards* disc, "Home I'll Never Be," was similarly born of a fragment from the past that serendipitously came his way. Despite the song's being credited to Beat poet Jack Kerouac, the forlorn hymn to the highway life turns out to be one of Waits's most personally revealing. When he poignantly sings the lines "Father, father, where you been? I've been in this world since I was only ten," it's not really Kerouac's life he's singing about. Waits is calling out to his own father, who left home never to be seen again after a divorce in 1960, when Waits would've been ten years old.

"Kerouac's nephew had this song of Jack's, or at least some of his words he wanted me to record. I guess Jack was at a party somewhere and snuck off into a closet and started singing into a reel-to-reel tape deck, like, 'I left New York in 1949, drove across the country. . . .' I wound up turning it into a song, and I performed it at a memorial for Allen Ginsberg.

"I found Kerouac and Ginsberg when I was a teenager, and it saved me. Growing up without a dad, I was always looking for a father figure, and those guys sorta became my father figures. Reading *On the Road* added some interesting mythology to the ordinary and sent me off on the road myself with an investigative curiosity about the minutiae of life."

Another important role model for Waits was *Twilight Zone* creator Rod Serling, whose authoritative tone and cadence can be heard in Waits's meditation on "Army Ants." Apparently, Waits was an avid *Twilight Zone* fan back in the early 1960s, and Serling's prime-time morality plays about the dark side of human behavior left a lasting impression.

"Rod Serling had these great eyebrows and that indelible voice. There was something about the humanity of his *Twilight Zone* stories that was very appealing. He'd never shy away from controversial subject matter—there were bombs going off all the time, right there on prime-time television for everyone to see.

"One of my favorites was this one called 'In Praise of Pip,' where Jack Klugman—who looked exactly like my father—plays an alcoholic bookie who gets shot in the gut during a holdup. As he's dying, he has a vision of his son Pip as a child asking him for help, 'cause he's now a soldier bleeding to death in a Vietnam field hospital. So he tries to make a deal with God to take him and let his son Pip live. That's a good one."

Apart from what Waits's off-the-cuff choice might suggest about his own troubled relationship with his father, the *Twilight Zone* fifth season opener from 1963 is also significant for another reason. When Klugman as Max Phillips says, "My kid is dying. In a place called South Vietnam. There isn't supposed to be a war going on there, but my son is dying," it was one of the very first instances in popular culture to call into question the US military presence in Vietnam.

In a similar way, Waits uses a factual account of a recent suicide bombing in the song "Road to Peace" to raise his own questions about the US government's role in the current Middle East crisis.

Although Waits maintains an even hand in dealing with the emotionally charged issues throughout his uncharacteristically political throwdown, the lines where he sings, "The fundamentalist killing on both sides / is standing in the path of peace / and tell me / why are we arming the Israeli army / with guns and tanks and bullets" could prove very controversial. But typical of Waits, he doesn't seem overly concerned about the potential fallout.

"I read an article in the *New York Times* about a young Palestinian suicide bomber who got on a bus in Jerusalem disguised as an Orthodox Jew. The story seemed to humanize what was going on in a significant way. It haunted me, and that's why I write many of my songs, because something's haunting me and I need to get it outta my head. What else could I do? Nobody in Washington is calling me up to discuss our foreign policy."

No less surprising than Waits recording such an overtly political song is hearing him getting busy with some nasty beatboxing on the *Bastards'* track "Spidey's Wild Ride." Waits has tried a bit of beatboxing before during the *Real Gone* sessions, but the beats he busts on "Spidey's Wild Ride" suggest he's been checking out some old school Biz Markie joints. Who knew Waits was a hip-hop fan?

"I had fun doing that song—just some singing and some beatboxing. It's very rudimentary yet, at the same time, very complete. What's interesting to me about hip-hop is that it doesn't have any conventional wisdom—the form is still being defined. You can put some hot sauce in the milkshake because it's still largely a lawless territory. If you want, you could record a mariachi calypso foxtrot with a Samoan singer in a bullring.

"The production can also be very cheap—all you need is three fingers, a drum machine, and a sampler and you can record a hit song in your closet. I've done some recording in the closet myself and the washroom, in the garage, and in the car too, whatever."

Although Waits assures me that he's about to start recording again right away, he's reluctant to discuss which direction he may head next, joking, "Who knows, maybe I'll do a Mexican rockabilly record." It's unlikely that Waits will be setting aside any writing time to compose new songs for the forthcoming Scarlett Johansson album, which is reportedly slated to be a Waits covers project.

"I read something about that in the newspaper," says Waits. "I guess that's cool, I dunno. I wasn't aware that she sang. Over the years a number of different people have done versions of my songs that I've enjoyed. I thought what Jeffrey Lee Pierce did with "Pasties and a G-String" was pretty cool and so was Johnny Cash's recording of "Down There by the Train." I saw Solomon Burke open for the Rolling Stones in Los Angeles not too long ago. He came out with his cape and scepter and sat on this big throne and did my song "Always Keep a Diamond in Your Mind"—that was pretty exciting.

"When you write songs, you do it with the idea that other people might want to sing them. That's part of the Tin Pan Alley tradition. What I do comes out of my fascination with that whole thing. You know, you sit at a piano with the window open and something blows in that goes through you and turns into a song.

"The problem with hip-hop is that artists aren't covering each other's songs. I mean there are some songs which influence other songs but they're not being reinterpreted in a variety of styles. So in a way, what you have are sorta like tomatoes without seeds."

It's through covers that the work of singer-songwriters is kept alive and relevant long after they're gone and Waits appears to be writing songs to last.

"Some songs you write and once they're recorded you never sing them again while others are like riddles—you keep going back to them to try figuring out what they mean because you don't always know when you write them. And you never can tell what's gonna stick and what's gonna fade. You know that "Chain Hang Low" tune by Jibbs? It goes [*mumbling*], 'Do your chain hang low, do it wobble to the flo', do it shine in the light? Is it platinum, is it gold?' That melody dates back to the Civil War!

"Some people talk and talk their whole lives and no one remembers one thing they've said. Other people say one thing and it gets repeated one hundred years later, which just shows you it's all about quality not quantity."

"Interview: Tom Waits"
Pitchfork
November 27, 2006
Amanda Petrusich

Tom Waits's latest endeavor, *Orphans: Brawlers, Bawlers & Bastards*, is a three-disc compendium of thirty new tracks and a mess of hard-to-find soundtrack pieces, all organized into three categories that manage to accurately encapsulate more than three decades of brutal noisemaking. Like most of America, I'm so convinced that Tom Waits exists in a world populated only by freight trains and barmaids, rodeo clowns and shortwave radios, that to hear him say "Chamillion-aire" is about as jarring as a car crash. Here, Waits opens up about his songwriting, Scarlett Johannson, and his own glorious artifice.

Amanda Petrusich: Have you ever thought about living anywhere besides California?

Tom Waits: I've been around. Chicago, New Orleans, New York, L.A., Portland [Oregon]. California has the public image, the land of milk and honey. It has one of those images that's completely and utterly removed from what it really is. Like all great fantasies. Where are you calling from?

AP: Brooklyn.

TW: Everybody's from Brooklyn! We lived in New York for a while. About four-teen different places in two years.

AP: Do you ever miss it?

TW: I don't know. Sometimes when I go back I go, Oh man, I remember this. The energy of it. It's like a big dragon. But I'm a hothead. I wasn't well suited for the temperament of that town. I need something that's a little more . . . not as volatile. I get in arguments with shop owners. And slowly, all the little businesses in our neighborhood, the lights started going out and I had to go further and further from home to get supplies. I'm better off here in the sticks where I can't hurt myself.

AP: You have a fine reputation for haunting California's salvage yards and pawnshops. What attracts you to certain objects?

TW: I'm interested in things when I don't know what they are. Like "Hey, Ray, what the hell is this?" Oh, that's lipstick from the 1700s, that's dog food from the turn of the century, that's a hat from World War II. I'm interested in the minutiae of things. Oddities.

AP: Do you collect anything?

TW: Like little ceramic dogs? I collect instruments. It's ongoing.

AP: There's a blues singer in Clarksdale, Mississippi, named Super Chikan who makes the most beautiful-looking guitars out of oilcans and other bits of hardware that he paints and strings. He has a guitar made out of a toilet seat that he calls the Shit-tar. Do you ever make your own instruments?

TW: I have friends who are builders who make instruments. "Alternative sound sources" is the technical way of saying it, which could really be anything—maybe something you found along the side of the road. I think hardware stores can be fascinating if you go in there with a mallet! I look for things that are left of center, something you've only seen your whole life, but never heard. Hit it! With a stick! I have a guitar made out of a two-by-four that I bought in Cleveland. You know, in Iraq, you can't have a guitar in the window of a music store because it's too sexy. You know, the curves. So I could go over there with these two-by-four guitars and really take the country by storm.

AP: Do you have a favorite instrument?

TW: I have a Chamberlin I bought from some surfers in Westwood many years ago. It's an early analog synthesizer; it operates on tape loops. It has sixty voices—everything from galloping horses to owls to rain to every instrument in the orchestra. Including the human voice [*sings a scale in "synthesizer voice"*]. Eleven-second samples! I like primitive things. I've used that a lot over the years on different recordings.

I have a Stroh violin. Stroh is the guy who created the violin with the horn attached to the bridge. This was around when orchestras played primarily in pits. In old theaters, the string players would complain that they couldn't be heard in the balcony. So this guy created the Stroh violin, which was a way of amplifying sound before electricity. It sounds almost like the violin is coming out of the horn of a 78 record player. He made Stroh basses, Stroh cellos. He even has a one-string Stroh violin. Those are interesting. I used one on a record called *Alice*.

AP: Do you have a favorite sound?

TW: Bacon. In a frying pan. If you record the sound of bacon in a frying pan and play it back it sounds like the pops and cracks on an old 33 1/3 recording. Almost exactly like that. You could substitute it for that sound.

AP: There is a long human history of seeking impure sounds. In his book *Deep Blues*, Robert Palmer talks about the influence of West African music on early American blues, and how so many African musicians aggressively eschewed clean sounds—by attaching pieces of tin to their drums, humming into flutes, things like that. Do you have a natural affinity for sloppier tones?

TW: I think it lets you incorporate your own voice into the voice of the instrument. By nature, I think we're all curious and looking for mutations all the time. It's not peculiar to me. I guess it's a question of taste. How do you like your eggs?

AP: You sing Jack Kerouac and Charles Bukowski on this record. To what extent has literature influenced your music?

TW: I'm usually more concerned with how things sound than how they look on the page. Some people write for the page and that's a whole other thing. I'm going for what it sounds like right away, so it may not even look good on the page. But I'm still a word guy. I'm drawn to people who use a certain vernacular and communicate with words. Words are music, really. I mean, people ask me, "Do you write music or do you write words?" But you don't really, it's all one thing at its best. Sometimes when you're making songs you just make sounds, and the sounds slowly mutate and evolve into actual words that have meaning. But to begin with, most people who make songs just start out with [*makes noises*].

AP: Sure, and the Beats were very musical writers.

TW: And the Beats were performing their work in clubs, shouting their work. That's another element of it.

AP: What sorts of movie roles are you attracted to?

TW: I do some acting. And there's a difference between "I do some acting" and "I'm an actor." People don't really trust people to do two things well. If they're going to spend money, they want to get the guy who's the best at what he does. Otherwise, it's like getting one of those business cards that says about eight things on it. I do aromatherapy, yard work, hauling, acupressure. With acting, I usually get people who want to put me in for a short time. Or they have a really odd part that only has two pages of dialogue, if that. The trouble is that it's really difficult to do a small part in a film, because you have to get up to speed—there are fewer scenes to show the full dimensions of your character, but you still need to accomplish the same thing that someone else has an hour and a half to do. In terms of making them anatomically correct. And you have to make sure that you're working with people who you really trust and admire and feel safe with. That's not always the case, and if you want to stay working, you have to take chances a lot of time.

AP: It seems like that's the same case with making records. How different do you think your music would be if you hadn't married Kathleen Brennan?

TW: It's so hard to say. Everything would be different. She's a remarkable col-laborator and we have a real rapport, and that's really what anybody who is working with anybody else is looking for. It clicks.

AP: I'm interested in the way songwriting works in your home. Less the artistic process, more the physical one—do you and Kathleen write in the same room, do you snack, do you bicker?

TW: Sometimes we go in the car, just take the tape recorder and go on a long trip. Sometimes we just sit around the piano—if we have a deadline, it tightens up the perimeters of the whole thing. We work independently and we work together. If both of you know the same stuff, one of you is unnecessary. Hopefully we're coming at it from different angles. But I don't really know how it works. It's one of those things where you can't really take it apart.

AP: What was it like touring with your son on drums?

TW: He's been playing drums since he was eight. He's a big strong guy, taller than me. He's a giant of a man. He has a lot of interest in music, he does beatboxing, and listens to music and it stays with him. He was playing with old-timers—he's only twenty-one. With families and music, you're usually looking for something that can make you unique. And it can be hard to find that. But he was excellent; it was terrific playing together, as you'd imagine it would be. You learn as much from your kids as they learn from you.

AP: The new record is such an interesting compendium of your work, giving equal weight to all sides of your sound. How did you decide to organize the songs into *Brawlers, Bawlers,* and *Bastards?*

TW: It was just a big pile of songs. It's like having a whole lot of footage for a film. It needs to be arranged in a meaningful way so it will be a balanced listening experience. You have this big box with all these things in it and it doesn't really have any meaning until it's sequenced. It took some doing. There's a thematic divide, and also pacing and all that. There are different sources to all these songs and they were written at different times. Making them work together is the trick.

AP: Was there a song where it wasn't immediately evident to you which disc it would fit best on?

TW: Yeah. But, you know, ballads went on one—we wanted to call it *Shut Up and Eat Your Ballads*. The blues and gospel stuff seemed to go together. And the more uncategorizable stuff wound up on *Bastards*. That's the stuff that's spoken word. After a while it made sense. "Form three lines. You're in the wrong line, buddy."

AP: You cover Leadbelly's "Goodnight Irene," which is one of my favorite songs. It's also, I think, one of your strongest vocal performances. Do you listen to a lot of early American folk and blues?

TW: Oh yeah, sure. Over the years, yeah I have, and I still do, sure. Most of the things you absorb you will ultimately secrete. You know that. You take something in and that's just what happens, whether it's Jack Teagarden or Bo Carter or Memphis Minnie or Barbecue Bob. It's all out there and available for you to enjoy, absorb, and be nourished by. Which is a pretty great thing—somebody did something a hundred years ago and it lasted three minutes and now they're gone and everyone who worked on it is gone, but *it's* not gone. It's still just as fresh as it was the day it was recorded. I always find that interesting. We don't really know of what we do, how it's going to still be around. But I try to keep that in mind when I record. I've recorded stuff I know I'll never sing again, and I've recorded stuff that I know I will keep singing, in order to try and solve the riddle. But I think it's good to listen to as much as you can, of the old and the new.

AP: Are there any new artists or people performing right now that you're excited about?

TW: Missy Elliott. I'm crazy about her. She did some video where she's on the beach doing the jerk in a wife beater. She's out of her mind. She's so natural. It's like she's always been around. Chamillionaire. I listen to a lot of stuff that my kids listen to. You know, Jay-Z, the Beastie Boys, all that. Most of the stuff that dominates the household is not stuff I'd necessarily listen to, but now I put on what the kids put on. My wife, when I met her, she had a remarkable record collection. And they were all still in their sleeves! I couldn't believe it. She took care of her records. Rachmaninov, Beefheart. For me, most of my records were out of their sleeves and in a drawer somewhere. I married a record collection.

AP: What moment in your career are you most proud of?

TW: Most of the time I just want to make another record. This stuff is always the best stuff, the fresh material. It's always what's up ahead. I don't really have one of those "Oh, that was my big moment" things.

AP: I'm sure you know Scarlett Johansson is recording an album of your songs?

TW: Well no, I read about it in the paper.

AP: No one consulted you beforehand?

TW: No, no. But, you know, more power to her.

AP: Are you excited to hear it?

TW: I don't know if I'm excited to hear it, but I'm curious. People make songs so that somebody else will hear them and want to do them. I guess it's an indication that the songs aren't so ultra-personal that they can't possibly be interpreted by anyone else. I've seen her in movies. I don't know what she's going to do with the tunes. When you get a hold of somebody else's song, you make it your own. That's all you can do. And that usually requires a certain amount of tailoring. Cut the sleeves off, lay some buttons. Everybody does something different to a song, that's the tradition.

AP: In your artist's statement for the new record, you say that your voice is really your instrument, which certainly seems true to anyone who has ever heard your records. Some of my favorite singers are the ones who sound a little out of control. Are you ever surprised or offended by what your voice can or cannot do?

TW: If you're still pushing the envelope and wanting to find out what this baby can do, or if you're still trying to imitate things—most people start out by imitating. Slowly you develop your own voice. I like vocal word stuff. But I don't always write with an instrument, I usually write a cappella. It's more like drawing in the air with your fingers. It's closest to the choreography of a bee. You're freer. You have no frets to constrict you, there are no frets on your voice, and that's a good feeling. So for composing melody, it's something you can do anywhere.

AP: Did you always know you wanted your voice to sound a certain way?

TW: I talked to Robert Siegel, the newscaster on NPR, and he said that most announcers and people in radio, they want their voices to sound older. Because a lot of the news you're delivering is very serious and very heavy, and you don't want to sound like a little kid talking about how thirty-three people were killed in a roadside bomb. You have to compose your voice and your whole demeanor so that it's situated to give weight, dignity, and gravity to all the things you're saying. You want the same thing for your voice when you're a singer. You want your voice and how you're approaching it to suit the material.

AP: There is a rich and wonderful American history of tough, scrappy songwriters—everyone from Ramblin' Jack Elliott to Bob Dylan—compulsively mythologizing themselves, inventing backstories, changing their names, developing personas to work alongside songs. Is there a Tom Waits mythology?

TW: I'm sure there is. The fact is most of the things that people know about me are made up. My own life is backstage. So what you "know" about me is only what I allowed you to know about me. So it's like a ventriloquist act. And it's also a way of safely keeping your personal life out of your business. Which is healthy and essential. I'm not one of those people the tabloids chase around. You have to put off that smell—it's like blood in the water for a shark. And they know it, and they know that you've also agreed. And I'm not one of those. I make stuff up. There's nothing that you can say that will mean the same thing once it's been repeated. We're all making leaner versions of stories. Before there was recording, everything was subject to the folk process. And we were all part of composing in the evolution and the migration of songs. We all reached out, and they all passed through our hands at some point. You dropped a verse or changed the gender or cleaned up a verse for your kids or added something more appropriate for your community. Anything that says "Traditional," it's "Hey, I wrote that, I'm part of that." Just like when a joke reaches you—how did it reach you? If you could go back and retrace it, that would be fascinating.

AP: So the second you write something down, it's fiction.

TW: There is no such thing as nonfiction. There is no such thing as truth. People who really know what happened aren't talking. And the people who don't have a clue, you can't shut them up. It's the same with your own stories, the ones that circulate around with your family and your friends. We're all part of the same hypocrisy.

AP: Do you keep a notebook?

TW: Oh yeah, everybody does! Life is too confusing. Monkey wrenches, pocketknives, dog food, instant coffee, lipstick. You gotta get it organized somehow.

AP: Thanks so much for talking with me.

TW: Oh! OK. All right. I'll leave you with a few little things out of my book here. In Los Angeles, it's illegal for a man to beat his wife unless he's on the courthouse steps. In Tulsa, it's against the law to open a soda bottle without the supervision of a licensed engineer. In Texas, the Encyclopedia Britannica is banned because it contains the formula for making home brew. In Clarendon, Texas, it's illegal to dust any public building with a feather duster. In Washington, it's illegal to paint polka dots on the American flag. There are only two things you can throw out the window of a moving car, legally. Do you know what they are?

AP: Um . . .

TW: Water. And feathers. Everything else you can get in trouble for.

"My Wild Years and the Woman That Saved My Life"
Word
December 2006
Mick Brown

"My career," Tom Waits once said, "is more like a dog. Sometimes it comes when you call. Sometimes it gets up in your lap. Sometimes it rolls over. Sometimes it just won't do anything. In recent years it has been walking on its hind legs, doing cartwheels, and even singing in tune."

A strange dog, indeed.

Waits was born in Pomona, California, in 1949, the son of a Spanish teacher. A recalcitrant student, he dropped out of high school at the age of fifteen, continuing his education as "a jack-off of all trades," including washer-up and short-order cook at a pizza parlor, and nightclub doorman. "Place must have been really hurting if they had me as their bouncer. Everybody got in. . . ."

His career can be neatly divided into two distinct parts. Between 1974 and 1979 he made a series of albums about that area of town marked out by the pawnbroker, the tattoo parlor, and the flophouse hotel—wonderful stories in which raindrops were diamonds, every hooker was an angel, and skid-row bums were "little boys." With his boho threads and graveyard pallor, Waits didn't just sing the life of the inebriated barfly, down in the gutter but looking up at the skies—he appeared to be living it, to the point where it became hard to tell if he was an actor playing a part, or whether the part was playing the actor. Either way, what was clear was that Waits, who was drinking heavily and living badly, was at risk of being annihilated by his creation.

In 1980 he married Kathleen Brennan, a script-editor whom he had met while working on the soundtrack for Francis Ford Coppola's film *One from the Heart*. A radical overhaul ensued. Waits fired his manager Herb Cohen and severed relations with his producer Bones Howe. He left his record company, Asylum, and signed with Island. His first record under the new arrangement, *Swordfish-trombones*, was also the first Waits had produced himself, and marked a radical shift in direction. The songs became more abstract—wheezing polkas, funeral marches, and drunken sea shanties; suites written for rattling bones and chains; country blues rewritten as a Tod Browning script. He enjoyed an extracurricular career as a film actor and collaborated on stage productions with the avant-garde theater director Robert Wilson. He stopped drinking, and all but gave up touring, preferring to spend the time with his growing family. The abiding curiosity about all this was that Waits's radical swerve toward the avant-garde, the idiosyncratic, and the willfully obscure has made him more successful, in commercial terms, than at anytime in his career. His album *Mule Variations*, released in 1999, brought him his first UK Top 10 entry in twenty-five years, and his highest ever position (#20) in the United States.

This month sees the release of a new three-album set called *Orphans*. It is the Waits aficionado's dream, every facet of his extraordinary canon rolled into one package: the plangent sentimentalist, the avant-gardist; the shamanistic bone-shaker and channeler; the barroom storyteller. One album, subtitled *Bawlers*, consists of lovelorn ballads, piano blues, and Irish airs. *Brawlers* stirs together rockabilly, Beefheartian yodels, and roughneck blues and roll. *Bastards* is a collection of off-kilter instrumentals, tall tales, yarns and poems, including tributes to two of Waits's great literary influences and idols, Jack Kerouac and Charles Bukowski, and the bleakest children's story you've ever heard ("Once upon a time there was a poor child / with no father and no mother / and everything was dead / and no one was left in the whole world"). Waits says his own children "can do it word for word. They get all choked up. . . ."

The origins of *Orphans* are complicated. A handful of the songs have already appeared elsewhere in various projects. "King Kong" is Waits's cover of a Daniel Johnston song, which was previously released on a tribute album, *The Late Great Daniel Johnston: Discovered Covered*, in 2004. "What Keeps Mankind Alive" first appeared on an anthology of the songs of Brecht and Weill in 1990; a scarifying version of "Heigh Ho," on a Hal Willner–produced compilation of Walt Disney songs originally released in 1988. "Little Drop of Poison" has already been heard on the soundtrack for Wim Wenders's film *The End of Violence* (and contains a vintage piece of Waits's wordplay: "I'm all alone, I've smoked my friends down to the filter").

Of the remainder, some are recordings from the sessions for *Mule Variations* and *Real Gone* that were not included on those albums, plus some songs from that period that have been recorded anew; some are completely new songs. As Waits puts it: "Kathleen and I wanted the record to be like emptying our pockets on the table after an evening of gambling, burglary, and cow-tipping." The treasures here are too numerous to count, but a few stand out. "Down There by the Train" is Waits's roof-raising, gospelized version of one of his own compositions that was first recorded by Johnny Cash on *American Recordings* in 1994. "Road to Peace," the most explicitly political song Waits has ever recorded, is an epic dissertation on the Israeli-Palestine conflict, which moves from the story of a young suicide bomber to a pitiless anatomy of the futility of war, invoking Henry Kissinger's infamous observation that "We have no friends / America only has interests," and concluding that "maybe God himself he is lost and needs all of our help / and he's lost upon the road to peace." Meanwhile, "Bend Down the Branches" and "World Keeps Turning" are Waits at his most unrepentantly romantic and heartfelt. But as much as this collection is a demonstration of Waits's extraordinary range as a composer and musician, it is also testament to his singular talents as a singer. Nobody sounds like Tom Waits—but here, nobody sounds like Tom Waits in quite as many different ways and guises. "At the center of this record is my voice," Waits says. "I try my best to chug, stomp, weep, whisper, moan, wheeze, scat, blurt, rage, whine, and seduce. With my voice, I can sound like a girl, the bogeyman, a theremin, a cherry bomb, a clown, a doctor, a murderer. I can be tribal, ironic, or disturbed. My voice is really my instrument."

Waits lives with his wife and three children in a large, rambling, wood-framed house in Sonoma County, Northern California. Wine country (an irony: he gave up drinking fourteen years ago). Large and rambling—or so I've been told. Waits guards his privacy fiercely, and never entertains journalists at home. His preferred meeting place on this occasion is the Little Amsterdam, a run-down roadhouse, a few miles from the town of Petaluma, on a quiet back road which appears to be seldom bothered by traffic. The restaurant is faced with foreclosure (only optimists need apply), dark, nicotine-stained and, at lunchtime, completely devoid of custom. Waits is well known here. One wall is devoted to framed photographs and news clippings about him.

Waits's affection for old cars—dilapidated Caddies, pickup trucks—is well known too, and it occasions a mild frisson of surprise to see him turn into the parking lot in a new, top-of-the-range 4WD Lexus, carrying a bulging black attaché case under his arm. He is dressed in a black suit. He looks fit and healthy. He has spoken in the past of how he spent most of his childhood wishing he were an old man—an ambition in which he was to prove remarkably successful. In his thirties, he looked like a man in his sixties. Now he seems to be reversing the process, and at the age of fifty-six he looks ten years younger. Only his familiar rough, tubercular growl suggests a punishing and misspent youth.

He is an arresting talker; conversation follows a rambling, circuitous path, replete with digressions and parenthetical thoughts, ruminative pauses, jokes, and tall stories. Occasionally, to illustrate a point—or simply for the sheer hell of it—he bursts into song, rocking back on his chair, his hands reaching out, as if for an invisible piano.

From his case he pulls a few scraps of paper—notes and aide-mémoires for the conversation, written in a spidery hand. Digging deeper, he produces a flattened and rusted tin can. "Here, this is for you. I found it on the way here." Noting my expression of bemusement (and gratitude, of course), he goes on. "Those are hard to find, because nowadays it's all aluminum. That's a real tin can. I don't think you'll get through the airport with that. Put it in your baggage. You still might get in trouble. . . ."

Mick Brown: It's very noticeable watching television here how America is being kept in a state of constant anxiety over "the war on terror." But here you are in a very quiet and beautiful part of the country—do you feel insulated from all of that?

Tom Waits: Well, first of all, I don't have a TV. That helps. I pick up the newspaper. 'Course you can't really get around it. They run us with fear. We're all dominated by it, but there's nothing new about that. It's just this is the current form of fear. In the '50s it was Communism, so this is just a new "-ism." And there'll be another "-ism" after this, I guess. I try to stay current with things. I have a lot of friends who keep me current. But I threw the television in the swimming pool about a year ago, and I haven't been able to get a picture on it. I'm still trying.

MB: You got rid of it because you were sick and tired of it, or you didn't want your children exposed to it?

TW: That was more it. When they were kids there was the danger of flipping around the dial, you know. Especially giving them the changer and then leaving the room. You come back and you don't know what they'll be watching. And the strange thing about it, with the ability to flip channels so quickly, it makes you wish that you could change the channels on other things when you're bored. Like your mother talking to you, or your teacher. Or even reading a book: "I want a picture now. I'm sick of these words." I think also what happens is that kids, without knowing it, are editing a very peculiar film for themselves. Because that's what editors do in films. They say, you know what? I'm bored. We need a new image. So when you sit down and do this for an hour and a half you've created a film—dental surgery to the Middle East conflict, to newborn baby, to a diaper commercial, to a swimming pool filled with dead bodies. You've edited your own film based on your inability to hold attention.

MB: And constructed a very distorted view of the world . . .

TW: Distorted or not. Maybe that's the only vision to have of it. I don't know. Because I don't even know if there's a real vision of the world. As soon as it reaches your eyes, your imagination takes hold. If you tell somebody seven words that have no relationship to each other the mind will go to work—refrigerator, heartbeat, dog crap, diving board, Dutch Masters, and broken watch. OK, I get it . . . we're all spies and now we've been given this puzzle. The mind never sleeps. Not till you're dead. And sometimes it works harder while you're asleep than while you're awake.

MB: Do you ever find yourself thinking too much?

TW: I don't know if I think too much. My wife would say I don't think enough. But she's not here, so I'll say, yes, I think much too much and I need a break. I'm like everybody. My life is like an air traffic controller. Moments of boredom broken up by moments of sheer terror. Some days I'm floating down the creek on a lily pad, then the next moment the wind is tearing my skin off. And you just deal with it.

MB: Do you like being the age you are? Does life become better, more interesting to you, as you get older?

TW: Do you mean I can go back to when I was nineteen?

MB: I can't offer you that deal, I'm afraid. But is fifty-six a good age to be?

TW: It's really the only age to be when you think about it. I'm on the home-stretch. None of us can go back, but you go back in your mind to your imagina-tion. Nobody lives in a linear fashion. Some days I'm about nine; other days I'm about ninety. We're all trying to move forward and backward. I think what hap-pens is your past goes from being like a little film to a photograph and from there it gets more like an abstract painting—the further I get from my past, the more it gets like an out-of-focus image or a Rauschenberg. I remember when I was a kid, being in a car with my folks, and we go on a long drive to visit my grandmother over maybe a hundred railroad tracks. We were always waiting for trains to pass. And the magic of that for a kid, hearing the bell—*ding, ding* and counting the cars as they go by. And then the other thing—I knew we were getting further out of town when I could smell horses. When I got that smell, then I was glued to the window, looking for my first horse. As soon as that smell hit, it was like perfume to me—it was like the smell of watermelon, or coffee, or popcorn. That was like a promise of all these great things. This was in Southern California. La Verne, Pomona. Let's see . . . Snoop Dogg lives out there now. Crazy. It was like a lot of orange groves and just the one road, Foothill Boulevard. It wasn't this grid, like the back of a radio, that it is now. It was much simpler then. I was eight or nine. That was a long time to go without a cigarette, stuck in the car with my family. I couldn't wait to get to my grandparents so I could smoke. I was smoking two packs a day by the time I was eleven.

MB: Do you miss it?

TW: Smoking? I don't. I laid that off and I laid off drinking. My wife said, "You drank enough."

MB: Wives are often better at knowing what's good for you than you know yourself.

TW: Well, it comes from love, you know? "I want you to stick around, goddamn it!" I saw a guy at a crap table in Las Vegas with his wife. I'd been playing craps next to him for an hour, and his face getting redder and redder, getting angrier and angrier. And finally he grabbed his chest and he went down on the carpet. His eyes rolled back. And his wife was pounding on his chest in the middle of the casino, screaming, "You can't die on me now, Ray!" She said that over and over again. And then I heard, "New shooter coming out, get him out of here." This is Las Vegas. And then there's a little ripple through the crowd while they bring the stretcher, and Ray's gone. It closed up like the ocean.

MB: Your parents separated when you were eleven; what effect did that have on you?

TW: Huge. But I didn't understand why at the time. It was an extreme loss of power, and totally unpredictable, as you can imagine. I was in turmoil over it for a long time. I stayed with my mother and two sisters. But when I think back on it, my dad was an alcoholic then. He really left—this is getting a little personal—to sit in a dark bar and drink whatever, Glenlivet. He was a binge drinker. So there was no real cognizance of his drinking problem from my point of view. So he kind of removed himself—he was the bad tooth in the smile, and he kind of pulled himself out. So in a sense I come from a family of runners. And if I had followed in my father's footsteps I'd be a runner myself, and so would my kids.

MB: So do you think that has a hereditary aspect that you've had to be alert to?

TW: Well, like anything, the genetic pull to following your father's footsteps, whether he teaches at Harvard or died on the Bowery . . . there's a path that he left for you. And you get to a crossroads eventually and you see his path, and there's a magnetic quality to it, so yeah I was pulled. But he was a great story-teller, so in a way what I've done was a way of honoring him.

MB: There have always been a lot of religious allusions in your records, both musical and lyrical, of a Salvation Army band, a revival tent variety, and on this record you've got a traditional gospel song, "Lord I've Been Changed," and a gospel song you've written yourself, "Down There by the Train." Is it the music you love or the sentiment?

TW: I don't know . . . I always thought religion should be more visceral and that you should get beat up a little by it, you know? I was hitchhiking through Arizona, it was New Year's Eve and I got stuck in a little town called Stanfield, Arizona. You think Arizona's hot—in January it's ten below zero—and I'm not getting any rides. I'm about seventeen. And an old woman named Mrs. Anderson comes out to the sidewalk and I'm with my good buddy Sam, and she says, "It's getting a little cold, it's getting a little dark, it's New Year's Eve, come in the church." And they sat us down in the back of the church, and it was all Pentecostal. They had a band up there: two Mexican guys and a black drummer and an old guy on the guitar—very weird—and a boy about seven playing piano. And they did this talking in tongues. I had never experienced anything like this before, so as far as I was concerned it was like scat singing; they were just going crazy. We were in the back, starting to laugh because it was unusual, and we were young and naive. And at the end of the service they took up an offering and they gave all of the money to us. They said, "We want to honor our wayfaring strangers, our travelers in the back who've come a long way to be with us tonight." They gave us a basket of money, and we bought a motel that night, warm with a TV, trucks out the back. And we got up next morning, and we hit a ride and went all the way to California. That was probably the most pivotal religious experience I've had. If I was going to join a church, I'd join that church.

MB: "Down There by the Train" pursues that theme of redemption. What's the history of that song?

TW: How many years ago, I don't know, Johnny Cash did a version of it, when he was doing the first of those *American Recordings* with Rick Rubin. I don't know who asked me; somebody said, "You got any songs for Johnny Cash?" I just about fell off my chair. I had a song and I hadn't recorded it. So I said, "Hey—it's got all the stuff that Johnny likes—trains and death, John Wilkes Booth, the cross . . . OK!"

MB: It's such a wonderful song, the idea that even the worst sinners will be saved. "Charlie Whitman is holding on to Dillinger's wings, down there by the train . . ."

TW: Yeah, yeah, available to all. Charles Whitman—he's the one that went up a tower in Texas and shot all those people. He was probably bipolar. [*Reaches in* *his bag and pulls out a promotional copy of the new album, the sleeve printed with strange and unusual facts]* We got the famous last words of dying men here, all that sort of stuff. Oscar Wilde: "Either that wallpaper goes or I do." Isn't that beautiful? That at that final moment he could still be witty. He'd leave you with his wit. I dug that. W. C. Fields: "On the whole I'd rather be in Philadelphia." You know, he was so paranoid because he grew up poor that he put money in hundreds of banks all over America. Every time he was on the road he'd put money in a bank, and he'd make up a name for the account. And when he died he was penniless. But he had millions of dollars, apparently, all spread out, and he'd forgotten the names. They're probably still there. What else we got here . . . Queen Elizabeth was annoyed by her red nose. Her attendants were accustomed to powdering it every few minutes to keep it presentable. Wow! That's something else. That's not a bad job to have. We all should have somebody to do that.

MB: What made you decide to structure the new record in this way, as three quite discrete albums?

TW: It was hard to sequence because the tempos were different, the subjects were so different. At first, to be honest with you, when we tried to sequence it in a normal fashion—like an up-tempo song, then a ballad, paced like you traditionally try to do, but it didn't make any sense. You didn't know why we went from this terrible thing to this light thing. It needed a faucet and a sink. It just didn't work. So Kathleen said, "Oh yeah—slow ones, rockers, spoken, in a general way. If you're a ballad, you go over there. Door Number Three." And it worked.

MB: You didn't sit down one day a couple of years back and say, "OK, I'm going to write forty-five new songs to go with these odds and ends"?

TW: No, no. They happened over time and then they were put in a drawer. Some were recorded, and then we didn't do anything with it. Or we made a record and the song didn't fit on the record. Or it was a song that fell behind the stove while we were making dinner, can't use it. Well, let's cannibalize it, cut it up, and use it for bait. No! It's a good song! OK, fuck it, let's just put it over here. And then I lose them. Then it's in a drawer with microphones and hair oil—"I knew it would be ruined if you didn't use it." Then I end up buying some of the songs from a guy in Russia, for big money [*laughs*]. This is a guy who's somehow got hold of these tapes. A plumber! In Russia! I'm talking to him on the phone in the middle of the night, negotiating a price for my own shit!

MB: You're kidding me.

TW: No! I'm not kidding. Poor Little Lamb . . . there's probably twelve, thirteen things on there that this Russian guy had.

MB: How did he come to have them?

TW: I don't know! That's the weird thing. It's the Internet now, you know? I had no DATs on these, I had no multitracks. I don't have a vault. He had recordings of these songs, good recordings. These were recordings that had come off the desk at one session or another, and then I didn't get the DAT of. I did the project, and then these got lost and there was only one copy and someone got hold of it and made two copies and he sold them to somebody and . . . who knows? When you don't keep track of things meticulously, which I try to but I'm not good at, and now I've got people collecting weird stuff of mine.

MB: So some of these are old songs that you've recorded anew, having bought them from a man in Russia?

TW: Right. Songs that might have been on *Mule Variations*, or outtakes from *Real Gone*. And then after we did *Real Gone* we just carried on and wrote a whole bunch of new songs. You say, you'd better keep going. We'd better get a holding tank. And then they say, "Hey, the project's over." But it doesn't really end until someone takes it from you and says, "We need this—we have to master it." So a lot of those we just kept writing. And then the cover versions are just affectionate tributes—the Kerouac, and the Bukowski.

MB: You do two versions of the same Jack Kerouac piece, one entitled "Home I'll Never Be" and the other, "On the Road."

TW: Yeah, one is a ballad and one is a blues. What happened is, I made the song first with Primus, the rocker version, "Home I'll Never Be," and then Hal Willner asked me to come down and play for an Allen Ginsberg memorial. There were a lot of people there talking about him. I didn't have a band. So I said, Well, this is an actual song written by Jack Kerouac—and an a cappella song they found on one of the tapes. [*sings*] "I left New York, 1949. To go across the country without a dad blamed dime! Montana in the cold, cold fall! Found my father in a gambling hall. . . ." Kerouac sang it alone on a microphone—it's on a collection of his work—and it's beautiful, very touching. So I tried to do my version like that. I ended up liking it. Somebody had the tape from that night, so we stuck it on there.

MB: It seems very much like an act of homage for you. And to precede that with the Charles Bukowski poem, "Nirvana," about a young man on the road, stopping in a café and being struck dumb with a sense of wonder: "The curious feeling swam through him that everything was beautiful there / and it would always stay beautiful there. . . ." What I love about that Bukowski poem is that it's completely unapologetic in its sense of wonder, completely innocent and openhearted.

TW: Yeah, and we've all been on that bus, where you wish you could just freeze everything right now. Like people say, "Shoot me! Things are good. Shoot me right now!" [*laughs*] The moment in the church in Arizona was like that for me. 'Course, in that community you wouldn't want to say "Shoot me," because they would.

MB: There's that wonderful entry in Jack Kerouac's letters where he describes a similar scene, that he later dramatized in *On the Road*, where he's in a diner in Wyoming having breakfast, and a cowboy walks in—the first cowboy Kerouac's seen—and he describes it as if the very essence of life itself was gusting in the door. You seem to be very alive to those kinds of moments, those epiphanies, in your songs.

TW: Well, I think once you've experienced some of those moments you try to influence them. You're always waiting for them to happen, the way cats wait for things to move around the house; you sit quietly and wait, you know. You never know when they're going to happen, and you want to be ready. I think that's what people look for in songs. I write down song titles usually, and usually something that you're going through emotionally will make a particular title leap out at you. This is what my wife says—there's something that you're already working on inside that this song will be the manifestation of, now you have a container. The first thing that anybody ever created was a container. Someone made a bowl to hold the water. And then they made a song about the bowl that held the water. You know, people only travel really with their seeds and with their songs. In Bosnia they interviewed a lot of the refugees—they'd left with nothing and they asked them what they had, and they had seeds, in their pockets, from their gardens. And their songs. That was it. Once you're nourished in that most fundamental way, everything else will follow.

MB: So do you feel writing songs, making music, is an honorable calling?

TW: Gee, I don't know. There are times when it seems very . . . trifling and trivial. Making these little songs up, I feel like I'm gluing macaroni onto a piece of cardboard and painting it gold. And then other times . . . when Johnny Cash wants to sing one of your songs, you think, "Oh man. . . ." Because there's a hierarchy in music, and there's certain indications that you're doing better, you're getting closer to the source.

MB: Who's at the top of that hierarchy for you?

TW: Gee . . . well, there's a lot of people. That's a big room. I'd say, the Gershwins and Bob Dylan and Louis Armstrong and Ray Charles. Howlin' Wolf, people like that. Giants among men. Judy Garland and Bessie Smith and Billie Holiday . . .

MB: It's invidious to ask, but I'll ask it anyway—do you have any sense of your own position in that hierarchy?

TW: I don't know. It would be presumptuous of me to say. It's better to have some things like that said about you rather than say it yourself. [*looking momentarily discomfited, rifles through his notes*] But I was going to say, I've just found some things here I wanted to mention . . . the thing about songs is that they're about so many things. Crop failure. My son died. Cautionary tales. There's a song about everything. And when you think about how songs were written and how they were kept alive before the recording industry, that to me is fascinating. 'Cause we were all part of writing those songs when it says "Traditional" or "Negro spiritual" or "public domain." Like all the songs that Alan Lomax collected. Those were songs that were written by all of us. Those were songs that if you learned it, you would change a verse or line. Just like a recipe. When you got a recipe from your neighbor, or if somebody asked for a recipe, the traditional thing to do was to change one thing about it. You never gave anybody your recipe. No, it's only a cup and a half of flour, honey instead of sugar, chopped quince instead of apples. And that's how songs moved along. You would add your verse. Or, it doesn't apply in this town, in this weather, with that gender. I have to change it to make it fit.

MB: And now things are recorded, enshrined, like a monument.

TW: Right. But it also keeps it from decomposing in the ground. Like being buried in a coffin.

MB: You said a song very often begins with a phrase or a title that becomes a container. Can you give me an example of that?

TW: Oh, all right. [*consults notes*] Here's some titles that aren't songs yet. "I'm in Love with the Girl on the Mud Flaps"—like the big semitrucks. "I'm in Love with the Girl on the Raisin Box." "Things Will Be Different in Chicago." You can almost hear the song. [*sings in a robust, Bierkeller baritone*] "Things will be different in Chicago. . . ." So I pick 'em according to cadence and rhythm and the value of the sentence. "They All Died Singing"—that's a title. I love all these circus freaks— you know, Turtle Boy, Mule-Faced Woman, Camel Girl. There was an act in the early 1900s, they were Siamese twins—two women and they both sang—and they billed themselves as The Two-Headed Nightingale. One was a soprano; one was a contralto. They used to break people's hearts. There's a song right there.

MB: You like places in songs, don't you? Minneapolis. Kentucky Avenue. On this album you've got Elkhart, Indiana, in "The First Kiss."

TW: My theory is that if you're going to make a song it's like packing somebody a lunch. You've got to give me weather, a name of a town, you've got to give me something to do and something to eat. It helps with the atmosphere. If you want to invite somebody into a song of yours it's kind of like inviting them into your home, and you have to give them some place to sit down. Because there's too many songs that are already written that are well furnished. "With a new song you've got to use some old tricks."

MB: A lot of the *Bawlers* are cowritten with Kathleen—more of the *Bawlers* than the *Brawlers*. Who's the more sentimental of the two of you? Is she bringing out your sentimentality, or are you bringing out hers?

TW: A little of both. The chemistry between two people you can never really go back in and pick out what bits are you and what bits are me. It's a melting pot. We've melted. But she will say to me things like, "If you write another song where you take somebody's finger off, I'm going to leave you. If you lop somebody's arm off, or if you make another guy blind in a song, I'm going to leave you."

MB: So she's the humanitarian in the partnership?

TW: Well, she's from the Midwest. Like the song "A Little Rain," which is on *Bone Machine*. [*Sings in a bleary manner*] "Well, the iceman's mule is parked / outside the bar / where a man with missing fingers / plays a strange guitar / and the German dwarf / dances with the butcher's son / and a little rain never hurt no one. . . ." She says, "Why do you have to take his fingers off? Why can't you just let him play the guitar like a normal guy in a bar? God! And why does the German guy have to be dwarf? And if he is, why do we have to know? It's not a film!" "But honey, sometimes you gotta shorten people, lop off a limb. It's just artistic license."

MB: If there's a picture hanging straight on the wall, you like to tilt it to one side.

TW: Yeah, yeah, I do. I get pleasure like that.

MB: And Kathleen comes along and straightens it.

TW: Sometimes. It's an ongoing battle. Wait for the bell and come out fighting. The only trouble is when the gloves come off. We're always arm wrestling over various things, and when you get into lines in a song, a line that you love . . . [*breaks into his voice, then his wife's*] "You know what? The weakest part about this song is that third line, scratch it." "Are you kidding me? I'm going to move it up front. It's the most important line in the song!" Somebody told me if you're stuck in a song and you can't move, take out the best lines. Get rid of them. Now finish it. That's good advice.

MB: I get the sense that marriage to Kathleen changed you enormously.

TW: Oh God, yeah, no question about it. In a good way. I'm alive because of her. I was a mess. I was addicted. I wouldn't have made it. I really was saved at the last minute, like deus ex machina. I'm like the Road Runner, you know, who ran off the cliff and looked around, and just before he dropped like a bullet, he ran back on the smoke from his feet, back to the cliff. That's me. I've been fortunate enough to be able to walk on smoke. I got sober about fourteen years ago; it was a big turning point. And then having kids, you know . . . once you've had kids you can't imagine not having kids. So my wife and kids really did save my life.

MB: It's a paradox, isn't it? Cyril Connolly said, "There is no more somber enemy of good art than the pram in the hall." But for you it seems to have been the opposite—the pram in the hall, domestic life, was the catalyst for a radical transformation in your music.

TW: You know, Nikola Tesla [the inventor of alternating current] said the reason he was celibate was . . . he said, "Name me one important invention that was created by a man who was married." 'Course he was also compulsive. He had to wash his hands a hundred times. He had a thing about threes—everything had to be divisible by three, the number of steps to the door, the number of times he'd go around the house before he entered the door—three, three, three, three. He worked with Edison and then quit. He's really the reason we got electricity. But Edison got the medicine. And Tesla got the receipt.

MB: But for you a stable, happy domestic life has been a boon to creativity, not a detriment.

TW: I guess so. In the old days my home was on the road, and that eventually got very scary for me. I felt I was looking for my home out there. It's like looking for food, or looking for money 'round a Coke machine.

MB: There's a lot of romantic idealism about that kind of life, which experience proves to be just that . . . romantic idealism. Charles Bukowski's life seems to exemplify that.

TW: Well, none of us really know what Bukowski's life was like. We know what we have read, and what we've gathered from the work and what we've imagined. Essentially, there's backstage and there's onstage, when you're a performer. You know what we allow you to know.

MB: Did you meet Bukowski?

TW: A couple of times. It's like when I met Keith Richards, you try to match them drink for drink. But you're a novice, you're a child. You're drinking with a roaring pirate. Whatever you know about holding your liquor you'd better let go of it right now. So I thought I could hang in there but I wasn't able to hang in there, with either one of them. They're made out of different stock. They're like dockworkers. But it was interesting. I met Bukowski at his house. Barbet Schroeder was a friend of mine, and they tried to get me to be in that movie, *Barfly*, playing Bukowski. They offered a lot of money, but I just couldn't do it, plus I didn't consider myself a good enough actor to do something like that. But Bukowski . . . I guess everybody when you're young and you enter the arts you find father figures. For me it was more profound because I had no father—no operating father—so I found other men that supplied all that for me. I was looking for those guys all the time.

MB: I understand after your father left home you'd go to your friends' homes and hang out with their fathers.

TW: [*laughs*] That's true. I was in the den, listening to Bing Crosby while my friends were out shooting hoops. "Tom! What are you doing, man? Talking to my Dad?" I'd say, "Yeah—what of it? You're not using him. I'm borrowing your father, for God's sake. You don't appreciate your father: he's been working for Aetna for twenty-nine years. . . ."

MB: So that's where you got your taste for double knits and Hoagy Carmichael.

TW: I probably did! It's kind of like you start imitating the things that are around you, whatever they are. I took note of Frank Sinatra. I liked the scar on the side of his face. He had this tremendous birthmark that he was always careful to obscure in photographs, but I saw one photo that showed this—it almost looked like a burn on the side of his face.

MB: You've recorded a song indelibly associated with Sinatra, "Young at Heart," on this new album. It's too corny to be true.

TW: [*dryly*] Yeah, that song always moved me. My wife just thinks it's hilarious because she says, "You sound so goddamned depressed singing it. When you say, 'And here's the best part / You have a head start / If you are among the very young at heart. . . .'" She says, "I don't believe that bullshit for a minute." [*laughs*] "Young at heart, my ass!"

Waits on living in Bush's America:
Excerpted from "Tom Waits: A Man of Many Words," *National*
December 1, 2009
Stephen Dalton

Living in Bush's America, Waits recalls, was hair-raising. "It felt like the person driving the truck has one eye and one arm, and his head is turned all the way around," he says with a dry laugh. "He's mashing down on the accelerator, getting closer and closer to the cliff, and we have tape over our mouths and our hands are tied. It was a scary time."

Warming to his theme, Waits insists the former president went astray after he missed his true calling in life. "I think the real problem was that Bush really wanted to be the commissioner of baseball, and the job was not available," he says. "Because we all have a thousand parallel lives that could have been our lives had we made different decisions along the way. We're at a crossroads every day. I could jump out of that window right now instead of just looking out of it."

Perhaps tired of the publicity machine, the rigmarole of another round of entertaining interviewers, dodging bullets aimed for the heart of his privacy, long-
distance phone calls from his house or just breaking free from his family for
extended periods, Waits decided to interview himself. To his credit, he did a com-
mendable job.

"True Confessions"
ANTI- Press Release
May 20, 2008
Tom Waits

I must admit, before meeting Tom, I had heard so many rumors and so much
gossip that I was afraid. Frankly, his gambling debts, his animal magnetism,
coupled with his disregard for the feelings of others. . . . His elaborate gun collection, his mad shopping sprees, the face-lifts, the ski trips, the drug busts, and
the hundreds of rooms in his home. The tax shelters, the public urination . . . I
was nervous to meet the real man himself. Baggage and all. But I found him to
be gentle, intelligent, open, bright, helpful, humorous, brave, audacious, loqua-
cious, clean, and reverent. A Boy Scout, really (and a giant of a man). Join me
now for a rare glimpse into the heart of Tom Waits. Remove your shoes and no
smoking, please.

Q: What's the most curious record in your collection?

A: In the seventies a record company in L.A. issued a record called *The Best of
Marcel Marceau*. It had forty minutes of silence followed by applause and it sold
really well. I like to put it on for company. It really bothers me, though, when
people talk through it.

Q: What are some unusual things that have been left behind in a cloakroom?

A: Well, Winston Churchill was born in a ladies cloakroom and was one-sixteenth
Iroquois.

Q: You've always enjoyed the connection between fashion and history . . . talk to us about that.

A: OK, let's take the two-piece bathing suit, produced in 1947 by a French fashion designer. The sight of the first woman in the minimal two-piece was as explosive as the detonation of the atomic bomb by the US at Bikini Island in the Marshall Isles, hence the naming of the bikini.

Q: List some artists who have shaped your creative life.

A: OK, here are a few that just come to me for now: Kerouac, Dylan, Bukowski, Rod Serling, Don Van Vliet, Cantinflas, James Brown, Harry Belafonte, Ma Rainey, Big Mama Thornton, Howlin' Wolf, Leadbelly, Lord Buckley, Mabel Mercer, Lee Marvin, Thelonious Monk, John Ford, Fellini, Weegee, Jagger, Richards, Willie Dixon, John McCormick, Johnny Cash, Hank Williams, Frank Sinatra, Louis Armstrong, Robert Johnson, Hoagy Carmichael, Enrico Caruso.

Q: List some songs that were beacons for you.

A: Again, for now . . . but if you ask me tomorrow the list would change, of course. Gershwin's second prelude, "Pathétique Sonata," "El Paso," "You've Really Got Me," "Soldier Boy," "Lean Back," "Night Train," "Come in My Kitchen," "Sad-Eyed Lady," "Rite of Spring," "Ode to Billy Joe," "Louie Louie," "Just a Fool," "Prisoner of Love," "Wang Dang Doodle (All Night Long)," "Ringo," "Ball and Chain," "Deportee," "Strange Fruit," "Sophisticated Lady," "Georgia on My Mind," "Can't Stop Loving You," "Just Like a Woman," "So Lonesome I Could Cry," "Who'll Stop the Rain?," "Moon River," "Autumn Leaves," "Danny Boy," "Dirty Ol' Town," "Waltzing Matilda," "Train Kept a Rollin'," "Boris the Spider," "You've Really Got a Hold on Me," "Red Right Hand," "All Shook Up," "The Cause of It All," "Shenandoah," "China Pig," "Summertime," "Without a Song," "Auld Lang Syne," "This Is a Man's World," "Crawlin' King Snake," "Nessun Dorma," "Bring It on Home to Me," "Hound Dog," "Hello Walls," "You Win Again," "Sunday Morning Coming Down," "Almost Blue," "Pump It Up," "Greensleeves," "Just Wanna See His Face," "Restless Farewell," "Fairytale of New York," "Bring Me a Little Water, Sylvie,"

"Raglan Road," "96 Tears," "In Dreams," "Substitute," "Good Time Charlie's Got the Blues," theme from *Rawhide*, "The Same Thing," "Walk Away Renée," "For What It's Worth," theme from *Once Upon a Time in America*, "Nowadays Clancy Can't Even Sing," "O Holy Night," "Mass in E Minor," "Harlem Shuffle," "Trouble Man," "Wade in the Water," "Empty Bed Blues," "Hava Nagila."

Q: What's heaven for you?

A: Me and my wife on Route 66 with a pot of coffee, a cheap guitar, pawnshop tape recorder in a Motel 6, and a car that runs good parked right by the door.

Q: What's hard for you?

A: Mostly I straddle reality and the imagination. My reality needs imagination like a bulb needs a socket. My imagination needs reality like a blind man needs a cane. Math is hard. Reading a map. Following orders. Carpentry. Electronics. Plumbing. Remembering things correctly. Straight lines. Sheetrock. Finding a safety pin. Patience with others. Ordering in Chinese. Stereo instructions in German.

Q: What's wrong with the world?

A: We are buried beneath the weight of information, which is being confused with knowledge; quantity is being confused with abundance and wealth with happiness. Leona Helmsley's dog made $12 million last year . . . and Dean McLaine, a farmer in Ohio, made $30,000. It's just a gigantic version of the madness that grows in every one of our brains. We are monkeys with money and guns.

Q: Favorite scenes in movies?

A: R. De Niro in the ring in *Raging Bull*. Julie Christie's face in *Heaven Can Wait* when he [Warren Beatty] said, "Would you like to get a cup of coffee?" James Dean in *East of Eden* telling the nurse to get out when his dad has had a stroke and he's sitting by his bed. Marlene Dietrich in *Touch of Evil* saying "He was some kind of man." Scout saying "Hey, Mr. Cunningham" in the scene in *To Kill a Mockingbird.* Nic Cage falling apart in the drugstore in *Matchstick Men* . . . and eating a cockroach in *Vampire's Kiss.* The last scene in *Chinatown.*

Q: Can you describe a few other scenes from movies that have always stayed with you?

A: Rod Steiger in *The Pawnbroker* explaining to the Puerto Rican all about gold. Brando in *The Godfather* dying in the tomatoes with scary orange teeth. Lee Marvin in *Emperor of the North* riding under the boxcar, Borgnine bouncing steel off his ass. Dennis Weaver at the motel saying "I am just the night man," holding on to a small tree in *Touch of Evil.* The hanging in *Ox-Bow Incident.* The speech by Rutger Hauer in *Blade Runner* as he's dying. Anthony Quinn dancing on the beach in *Zorba.* Nicholson in *The Witches of Eastwick* covered in feathers in the church as the ladies stick needles in the voodoo doll. When Mel Gibson's Blue Heeler gets shot with an arrow in *Road Warrior.* When Rachel in *The Exorcist* says "Could you help an old altar boy, Father?" The blind guy in the tavern in *Treasure Island.* Frankenstein after he strangles the young girl by the river.

Q: Can you tell me an odd thing that happened in an odd place? Any thoughts?

A: A Japanese freighter had been torpedoed during WWII and it's at the bottom of Tokyo Harbor with a large hole in her hull. A team of engineers was called together to solve the problem of raising the wounded vessel to the surface. One of the engineers tackling this puzzle said he remembered seeing a Donald Duck cartoon when he was a boy where there was a boat at the bottom of the ocean with a hole in its hull, and they injected it with ping-pong balls and it floated up. The skeptical group laughed, but one of the experts was willing to give it a try. Of course, where in the world would you find twenty million ping-pong balls but in Tokyo? It turned out to be the perfect solution. The balls were injected into the hull and it floated to the surface, the engineer was elated. Moral solutions to problems are always found at an entirely different level; also, believe in yourself in the face of impossible odds.

Q: Most interesting recording you own?

A: It's a mysteriously beautiful recording from, I am told, Robbie Robertson's label. It's of crickets. That's right, crickets, the first time I heard it . . . I swore I was listening to the Vienna Boys' Choir, or the Mormon Tabernacle Choir. It has a four-part harmony, it is a swaying choral panorama. Then a voice comes in on the tape and says, "What you are listening to is the sound of crickets. The only thing that has been manipulated is that they slowed down the tape." No effects have been added of any kind except that they changed the speed of the tape. The sound is so haunting. I played it for Charlie Musselwhite and he looked at me as if I pulled a leprechaun out of my pocket.

Q: You are fascinated with irony; what is irony?

A: Chevrolet was puzzled when they discovered that their sales for the Chevy Nova were off the charts everywhere but in Latin America. They finally realized that "Nova" in Spanish translates to "no go." Not the best name for a car . . . anywhere. "No va."

Q: Do you have words to live by?

A: Jim Jarmusch once told me "Fast, cheap, and good . . . pick two. If it's fast and cheap, it won't be good. If it's cheap and good, it won't be fast. If it's fast and good, it won't be cheap." Fast, cheap, and good . . . pick (two) words to live by.

Q: What is on Hemingway's gravestone?

A: "Pardon me for not getting up."

Q: How would you compare guitarists Marc Ribot and Smokey Hormel?

A: Octopus have eight and squid have ten tentacles, each with hundreds of suction cups and each have the power to burst a man's artery. They have small bird-like beaks used to inject venom into a victim. Some gigantic squid and octopus with one-hundred-foot tentacles have been reported. Squids have been known to pull down entire boats to feed on the disoriented sailors in the water. Many believe unexplained, sunken deep-sea vessels and entire boat disappearances are the handiwork of giant squid.

Q: What have you learned from parenthood?

A: "Never lend your car to anyone to whom you have given birth." —Erma Bombeck

Q: Now Tom, for the grand prize . . . who said, "He's the kind of man a woman would have to marry to get rid of"?

A: Mae West.

Q: Who said, "Half the people in America are just faking it"?

A: Robert Mitchum (who actually died in his sleep). I think he was being generous and kind when he said that.

Q: What remarkable things have you found in unexpected places?

A: 1. Real beauty: oil stains left by cars in a parking lot.

2. Shoe-shine stands that looked like thrones in Brazil made of scrap wood.

3. False teeth in pawnshop windows, Reno, Nevada.

4. Great acoustics: in jail.

5. Best food: airport in Tulsa, Oklahoma.

6. Most gift shops: Fátima, Portugal.

8. Most unlikely location for a Chicano crowd: a Morrissey concert.

9. Most poverty: Washington, DC.

10. A homeless man with a beautiful operatic voice singing the word "bacteria" in an empty dumpster in Chinatown.

11. A Chinese man with a Texan accent in Scotland.

12. Best night's sleep—in a dry riverbed in Arizona.

13. Most people who wear red pants—St. Louis.

14. Most beautiful horses—New York City.

15. A judge in Baltimore, Maryland, 1890, presided over a trial where a man who was accused of murder and was guilty, and convicted by a jury of his peers . . . and was let go—when the judge said to him at the end of the trial, "You are guilty, sir . . . but I cannot put in jail an innocent man." You see—the murderer was a Siamese twin.

16. Largest penis (in proportion to its body)—the barnacle.

Q: Tom, you love words and their origins. For $2,000 . . . what is the origin of the word bedlam?

A: It's a contraction of the word Bethlehem. It comes from the hospital of Saint Mary of Bethlehem outside London. The hospital began admitting mental patients in the late fourteenth century. In the sixteenth century it became a lunatic asylum. The word bedlam came to be used for any madhouse—and by extension, for any scene of noisy confusion.

Q: What is up with your ears?

A: I have an audio stigmatism whereby I hear things wrong—I have audio illusions. I guess now they say ADD. I have a scrambler in my brain and it takes what is said and turns it into pig latin and feeds it back to me.

Q: Most thrilling musical experience?

A: My most thrilling musical experience was in Times Square, over thirty years ago. There was a rehearsal hall around the Brill Building where all the rooms were divided into tiny spaces with just enough room to open the door. Inside was a spinet piano—cigarette burns, missing keys, old paint, and no pedals. You go in and close the door and it's so loud from other rehearsals you can't really work—so you stop and listen, and the goulash of music was thrilling. Scales on a clarinet, tango, light opera, sour string quartet, voice lessons, someone belting out "Everything's Coming Up Roses," garage bands, and piano lessons. The floor was pulsing; the walls were thin. As if ten radios were on at the same time, in the same room. It was a train station of music with all the sounds milling around . . . for me it was heavenly.

Q: What would you have liked to see but were born too late for?

A: Vaudeville. So much mashing of cultures and bizarre hybrids. Delta blues guitarists and Hawaiian artists thrown together resulting in the adoption of the slide guitar as a language we all take for granted as African American. But it was a cross-pollination, like most culture. Like all cultures. George Burns was a vaudeville performer I particularly loved. Dry and unflappable, curious, and funny—no matter what he said. He could dance too. He said, "Too bad the only people that know how to run the country are busy driving cabs and cutting hair."

Q: What is a gentleman?

A: A man who can play the accordion, but doesn't.

Q: Favorite Bucky Fuller quote?

A: "Fire is the sun unwinding itself from the wood."

Q: What do you wonder about?

A: 1. Do bullets know whom they are intended for?
2. Is there a plug in the bottom of the ocean?
3. What do jockeys say to their horses?
4. How does a newspaper feel about winding up papier-mâché?
5. How does it feel to be a tree by a freeway?
6. Sometimes a violin sounds like a Siamese cat; the first violin strings were made from catgut—any connection?
7. When is the world going to rear up and scrape us off its back?
8. Will we humans eventually intermarry with robots?
9. Is a diamond just a piece of coal with patience?
10. Did Ella Fitzgerald really break that wine glass with her voice?

Q: What are some sounds you like?

A: 1. An asymmetrical airline carousel created a high-pitched haunted voice brought on by the friction of rubbing and it sounded like a big wet finger circling the rim of a gigantic wine glass.
2. Street corner evangelists.

3. Pile drivers in Manhattan.

4. My wife's singing voice.

5. Horses coming/trains coming.

6. Children when school's out.

7. Hungry crows.

8. Orchestra tuning up.

9. Saloon pianos in old westerns.

10. Roller coaster.

11. Headlights hit by a shotgun.

12. Ice melting.

13. Printing presses.

14. Ball game on a transistor radio.

15. Piano lessons coming from an apartment window.

16. Old cash registers/"ca-ching."

17. Muscle cars.

18. Tap dancers.

19. Soccer crowds in Argentina.

20. Beatboxing.

21. Foghorns.

22. A busy restaurant kitchen.

23. Newsrooms in old movies.

24. Elephants stampeding.

25. Bacon frying.

26. Marching bands.

27. Clarinet lessons.

28. Victrola.

29. A fight bell.

30. Chinese arguments.

31. Pinball machines.

32. Children's orchestras.

33. Trolley bell.

34. Firecrackers.

35. A Zippo lighter.

36. Calliopes.

37. Bass steel drums.

38. Tractors.
39. Stroh violin.
40. Muted trumpet.
41. Tobacco auctioneers.
42. Musical saw.
43. Theremin.
44. Pigeons.
45. Seagulls.
46. Owls.
47. Mockingbirds.
48. Doves.
The world's making music all the time.

Q: What's scary to you?

A: 1. A dead man in the backseat of a car with a fly crawling on his eyeball.
2. Turbulence on any airline.
3. Sirens and searchlights combined.
4. Gunfire at night in bad neighborhoods.
5. Car motor turning over but not starting, it's getting dark, and starting to rain.
6. Jail door closing.
7. Going around a sharp curve on the Pacific Coast Highway and the driver of your car has had a heart attack and died, and you're in the backseat.
8. You are delivering mail and you are confronted with a Doberman with rabies growling low and showing teeth . . . you have no dog bones and he wants to bite your ass off.
9. In a movie . . . which wire do you cut to stop the time bomb, the green or the blue?
10. McCain will win.
11. Germans with submachine guns.
12. Officers, in offices, being official.
13. You fell through the ice in the creek and it carried you downstream, and now as you surface you realize there's a roof of ice.

Q: Tell me about working with Terry Gilliam.

A: I am the Devil in *The Imaginarium of Dr. Parnassus*—not a devil . . . The Devil. I don't know why he thought of me. I was raised in the church. Gilliam and I met on *Fisher King*. He is a giant among men and I am in awe of his films. *Munchausen* I've seen a hundred times. *Brazil* is a crowning achievement. *Brothers Grimm* was my favorite film last year. I had most of my scenes with Christopher Plummer (he's Dr. Parnassus). Plummer is one of the greatest actors on earth! Mostly I watch and learn. He's a real movie star and a gentleman. Gilliam is an impresario, captain, magician, a dictator (a nice one), a genius, and a man you'd want in the boat with you at the end of the world.

Q: Give me some fresh song titles you two are working on.

A: "Ghetto Buddha," "Waiting for My Good Luck to Come," "I'll Be an Oak Tree Some Day," "In the Cage," "Hell Broke Loose," "Spin the Bottle," "High and Lonesome."

Q: You're going on the road soon, right?

A: We're going to PEHDTSCKJMBA (Phoenix, El Paso, Houston, Dallas, Tulsa, St. Louis, Columbus, Knoxville, Jacksonville, Mobile, Birmingham, Atlanta). I have a stellar band: Larry Taylor (upright bass), Patrick Warren (keyboards), Omar Torrez (guitars), Vincent Henry (woodwinds), and Casey Waits (drums and percussion). They play with race-car precision and they are all true conjurers. I'm doing songs with them I've never attempted outside the studio. They are all multi-instrumentalists and they polka like real men. We are the Borman Six and as Putney says, "The Borman Six have got to have soul."

PERMISSIONS

INDEX

All song and album titles by Waits unless otherwise attributed.